Studies on Interdisciplinary Economics and Business

Özer Özçelik (Ed.)

Studies on Interdisciplinary Economics and Business – Volume I

PETER LANG

Bibliographic Information published by the Deutsche Nationalbibliothek
The Deutsche Nationalbibliothek lists this publication in the Deutsche Nationalbibliografie; detailed bibliographic data is available online at http://dnb.d-nb.de.

Library of Congress Cataloging-in-Publication Data
A CIP catalog record for this book has been applied for at the Library of Congress.

Cover image: fotolia, monsitj
Cover Design: © Olaf Glöckler, Atelier Platen, Friedberg

ISBN 978-3-631-77174-7 (Print)
E-ISBN 978-3-631-78227-9 (E-PDF)
E-ISBN 978-3-631-78228-6 (EPUB)
E-ISBN 978-3-631-78229-3 (MOBI)
DOI 10.3726/b15308

Peter Lang -Berlin · Bern · Bruxelles · New York · Oxford · Warszawa · Wien

This publication has been peer reviewed.

www.peterlang.com

Foreword

The book Studies on Interdisciplinary Economics and Business – Volume I is a collection of research papers on a wide range of social science issues written by researchers from several different universities and institutions.

Ozturk and Surun investigate the relationship between financial development and economic growth was investigated in the period of 1980–2014 in case of Turkey. Akıncı explores the relationship between special consumption tax policies and foreign trade deficits in Turkey during the period of 2006: Q1-2016: Q2. Aysu investigates the short and long-term effects of total expenditures spent on the programs as part of ALMPs (Active Labor Market Policies) on unemployment. Dogan reviews challenges for managers in the near future.

Erkan and Bozduman explore specify comparative advantages in Germany's export on the basis of technology and factor intensity between 2000 and 2016. Sigeze, Balli and Guresci examine the relationship between exports and R&D expenditures analyzed utilizing Probit and Tobit models for Turkey. Çetindere Filiz, Duran and Behdioğlu reviews just in time production system. Pelenk determines the effect of the innovation culture on employees' creative performance.

Bakirtaş investigates the effect of tax wedge on youth unemployment with panel VAR approach. Kutluk Bozkurt reviews digital marketing channels of businesses and digitalization in tourism sector. Bilge explores whistleblowing in terms of Turkish labor law. Yalcin reviews customer focused new product design process. Celik researches Basel IV and examines Basel IV reform or a new era. Gül, Okoth and Altinirmak conduct a comparative analysis of the web-based investor relations of companies in the telecommunication sector, and which are traded in BİST (Borsa İstanbul) and NYSE (New York Stock Exchange).

Dil Şahin tries to foresee the changes and expectations that are experienced in human resources in the digital transition phase. Ünsal finds the effects of macroeconomic factors on economic growth in Latin American countries. Ceyhan, Kamaci and Peçe explore the impact of military spending on economic growth in Turkey has been analyzed using the ARDL model for the period 1961–2016. Çelebi Boz reviews industry 4.0 and energy politics. Yıldırım Söylemez investigates approach of theory of constraints in production process of enterprises.

Akay explores empirically examine the effect of general competitive strategies (cost leadership, differentiation, focusing and being stuck in the middle) firm performance. Hirlak and Kara investigate and examine the effect of leadership in change, organizational change and change management and to interpret this in terms of the business world. Alsu and Apaydin investigate the closing price of gold per ounce was forecasted using artificial neural network (ANN) model. Karahan spots on the literature reviews that explain the basic concepts of auditing activities, the scope of their work, and when and how to audit events. Misirdali Yangil conceptualizes the social sustainability of the businesses and to establish its framework. Yaman investigates advertisement is to promote sales of the advertised product. Muhammet Atalay investigates industry 4.0 and its development and pioneers.

Contents

Salih Özturk[1] and Hatice Surun[2]

An Empirical Analysis on the Relationship between Financial Development and Economic Growth: The Case of Turkey (1980–2014)

1 Introduction

The technological, industrial and economic developments that have emerged with the industrial revolution have also led to progress and development in financial markets. Especially, together with technological improvements, countries have been focused to prosperous growth and development. In this context, it has begun to develop in financial markets and the increase in per capita income has been one of the most decisive factors in terms of the indicator of economic growth. If how advanced are financial markets in a country, it means that the country is also economically developed.

The relation between financial development and economic growth, first mentioned by British journalist Walter Bagehotin his "Lombard Street" article in 1873, examining the effects of banking sector to industrialization process. The Bank of England even accepted the "Bagehot Principle" in the sense that a middle way between "Currency Principle" and "Stand-by" theories (Serin, 1987, 55). In particular, along with industrialization from the 1960s on inflation increased in all countries, particularly mainly in the USA. Depending on the rise in inflation, changes in the financial markets also propelled to change and development of the financial system. On the other hand, the introduction from the fixed exchange rate to flexible exchange rate system (Bretton Woods) in international markets at the beginning of the 1970s brought changes into the financial system. Schumpeter stated that changes of the time and developments brought financial innovations along itself and development of technology contributed to the development of the financial system in this context.

Most economists have stated that there is a positive causality relationship between financial market development and economic growth. As the financial

1 Prof. Dr., Namık Kemal University, Faculty of Economics and Administrative Sciences, Department of Economics, Instructor, salihozturk@nku.edu.tr
2 Namık Kemal University, Faculty of Economics and Administrative Sciences, Department of Economics, PHd student, haticesurun@gmail.com

developments increase, they claim that the production of goods and services in that economy and the GNP would increase. Another opposite view is that, the relationship between the two variables is not clear. Defenders of the first view in this context defend the supply-side hypothesis. Economists who claim to have a negative impact on the economy also defend the demand-side hypothesis. It is widely accepted that financial development in economics literature drives economic growth.

The next sections of the study consist of four sections. In the first part, the theoretical and empirical literature on the relation between financial development and economic growth has been searched. In the second part the financial sector and economic growth relationship in the context of Turkey's economy is mentioned. In the thirdpart, information about econometric model and data set have been given. In the fourthpart, econometric tests (unit root, cointegration and causality tests) used in the study and the findings have been presented. Finally, with an assessment the study has ended.

2 Literature

2.1 Theoretical Literature

Financial markets and institutions form the basis of the financial system. Financial markets are financial instruments are the places where the purchase and sale of financial instruments are made, that is, they are the markets fund supply and demandare formed. Financial markets are the markets where there are transactions that provide and regulate the flow of funds. Financial institutions are the institutions that act on these processes. Financial markets are also wider than the money and capital markets, and these are the markets that include these markets. The financial market consists of savings owners, consumers, investors, investment and financing instruments.

Financial intermediation institutions, while the funds are transferred to those who need them from the savings owners, contribute to the economy (Parasız, 1997, 54). In this context, there are contributions such as reducing the risk in the market, directing savings more effectively and reducing the tendency to bury. Again financial markets also balance savings and demand.

Financial markets have three important roles: Providing liquidity, providing information and risk sharing (Erdoğan and Orhan, 2015, 29). The functions of the financial markets mentioned above also increase the efficiency of the markets same time. Thanks to its ability to provide liquidity saving owners try to maximize their profitability by choosing lower-cost, higher-return vehicles. Having information about the market they also get rid of the problem of reverse asymmetry.

Insurance companies, banks (lenders), companies engaged in securities transactions and social security institutions are the financial intermediation institutions. Financial institutions effectively activate the market as institutions regulating the purchase and sale of funds in the market. Financial intermediaries also play an active role in the money supply in the economy. The financial intermediation function allows individuals to invest their funds in confidence and to borrow these funds for the firm to process the borrowing and giving process smoothly in the economy (Arslan, 2009, 77). They help reduce risks. They provide economies of scale for saving owners. Financial intermediary institutions also provide funds and investment opportunities to the individuals or institutions they are intermediary with less cost. Fig. 1 summarizes the functions of financial intermediaries.

The financial system has functions such as reducing risks, generating resources, providing investment information, and directing savings. In this context, the financial system contributes to the effective allocation of funds, It also prevents asymmetric information problems that impede the transfer to investment of savings. As a result, it will also provide efficient distribution of resources which is the main aim of economics.

The role on economic growth of the financial sector have been studied and discussed in the literature for a long time. The concept of financial development can be described as follows: 1) Strengthening financial contracts, 2) The emergence of types certain specific financial contracts, 3) Increase of volume of financial contracts, 4) Increase in the number and size of financial intermediaries (Levine, 2004, 4).

Joseph Schumpeter (1912), who pioneered the issue, emphasized the impact of the financial sector on growth (Schumpeter, 1932). Where Robinson (1952), argued that financial development is an output or a secondary product of economic growth only in the real sense of the economy, and that there is only one-way causality between variables. If economic growth is provided, the financial sector will also grow at the same rate.

According to Hugh T. Patrick (1966), there is a bi-directional relationship between financial development and economic growth (Patrick, 1966, 174–189). The first is the demand-side hypothesis, the other is the supply-side hypothesis. The demand-side hypothesis is towards economic growth from financial development. The supply-side hypothesis defends the effectiveness of financial markets by stating that the financial sector is an engine for economic growth.

In the 1970s the literature emphasized the importance of mobilization of domestic resources in particular. Especially, McKinnon (1973) and Shaw (1973)

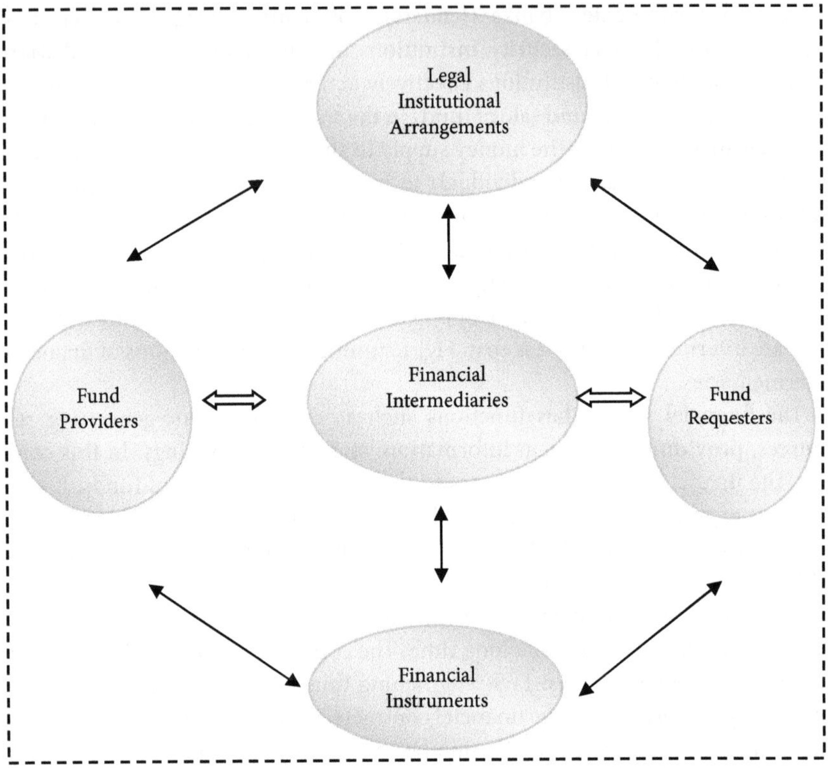

Fig. 1: Structure of Financial System

suggested that liberalization in the financial sector should be abolished all kinds of constraints in the financial sector.

Towards the end of the 1980s, Paul Romer, Robert Lucas and Robert Barro talked about the internal growth factor in their work. Lucas (1988) stated that financial developments are not exactly a decisive criterion of economic growth in the long run. With it, Stern (1989) argues that there can be no causal relationship between financial development and economic growth in the long run (Çeştepe, 2016, 16).

Robert G. King and Ross Levine (1993) determined the relationship between financial development and economic growth in their study made in 80 countries between 1960–1989 by analyzing with per capita GDP and economic growth data together with various variables years. (King, Levine, 1993). They have come to the conclusion that financial services are positively influencing economic growth by increasing capital efficiency.

2.2 Empirical Literature

In the literature investigating the relationship between financial development and economic growth, together with financial development and economic growth, has been made in the analysis about the concept of trade openness. Findings in the analyses are separated from each other with different results. The studies that support the supply-side hypothesis that Schumpeter advocates are as follows: According to the work done by Aslan and Küçüksoy (2006), Soultanaev (2010), Altıntaş and Ayrıçay (2010), Karaca (2012) and Mercan and Peker (2013), Tsaurai (2013), Al-Jafari (2014) and Murthy, Patra and Samantaraya (2017) the financial developmentsupports economic growth.

There also were carried out studies supporting the demand-side hypothesis that Robinson defends. Examples of these studies: They are studies of Kar (2010), Menyah, Nazlıoğlu and Rufael's (2013). Altaee and Al-Jafari (2015) examined the relationship between financial development, outward openness and economic growth in Bahrain. As a result, Causality relationship from financial development and trade openness to economic growth were determined.

According to Altunç (2008), Yücel (2009), there is a two-way causality relation between financial development and economic growth. Similarly to Turkoglu (2016), he determined a two-way causality relationship between economic growth and financial development in his work. Soultanaev (2010) has analyzed that the developments in the banking sector leading to economic growth. Results related to similar studies have been explained as detailed in Tab. 1.

3 Financial System and Economic Growth in Turkey

When examining the financial system in Turkey it has been in the same period with developments in the world financial system and development. Turkey has been implementing a trade-oriented development strategy since 1980. And living through the process of financial liberalization since 1989. Our country in this context, despite the fact that it faced serious economic problems from 1994 until 2000 had an impressive growth performance until 2010. This growth momentum of Turkey's economy, brought along the need for examination of a causal link between financial development and economic growth.

Financial institutions in the functioning of the financial system are divided into two as financial and loaning institutions. If we define financial institutions,

Tab. 1: Some Empirical Studies on the Relationship between Financial Development and Economic Growth*

Writers	Period	Country	Methodology	Results
Ergeç (2004)	1988–2001	Turkey	Causality Test	Causality in the indicators of financial development in the short term have been observed. There is a long-term causality relationship between variables.
Aslan and Küçükaksoy (2006)	1970–2004	Turkey	Unit root and Causality tests	There is an interaction from financial development to economic growth. Supply-side hypothesis has been define.
Yücel (2009)	1989–2007	Turkey	Granger Causality and Cointegration	Between variables bidirectional relationship have been detected.
Altunç (2008)	1970–2016	Turkey	Granger Causality and Cointegration Test	The supply pioneer and the demand-pushing hypothesis have been identified.
Soultanaev (2010)	1995–2008	Latvia, Estonia, Lithuanian	VAR (Vector Autoregressive Model)	Developments in the banking sector cause economic growth.
Karaca (2012)	1990–2011	India	Causality Test	There is a one-way and positive causality relationship between financial development and economic growth.
Murthy, Patra ve Samantaraya (2017)	1971–2012	Turkey	Unit root, Cointegration Causality tests	There is positive causality from financial development to economic growth.
Tsaurai (2013)	1994–2014	Argenrina	Unit root and causality tests	There are positive meaningful and one-way causality among the variables.
Menyah, Nazlıoğlu, Rufael (2013)	1965–2008	African Countries	Panel Data Panel Causality	The demand-side hypothesis does not apply in 21 countries. In all three countries, the supply-side hypothesis does not apply.
Mercan, Paker (2013)	1992–2010	Turkey	Causality Test	Deviations between the variables are close to the long-term equilibrium level. The supply-side hypothesis has been reached.
Kar, Nazlıoğlu, Ağır (2014)	1989–2007	Turkey	Causality	There is a bi-directional causality relationship. The results also support the demand-side hypothesis.

Asghar, Hussain (2014)	1978–2012	Developed Countries	Panel Causality Panel Cointegration	There is a causal relationship between variables.
İnançlı, Altıntaş, İnal (2014)	1997–2014	D-8 Countries	Unit Root, Panel, Cointegration Test	Financial development has a positive impact on economic growth.
Oruç, Turgut (2014)	1990–2010	Turkey	VAR (Vector Autoregressive Model), ECM (Error Correction Model)	In the long term negative correlation has been determined. In the short term, has been found consistency in the economy.
Altaee, Al-Jafari (2015)	1980–2012	Bahrain	Phillips-Perron test, VECM (Vector Error Correction Model)	The one-way causality relationship is supported by the supply-premise hypothesis
Saaed, Hussain (2015)	1966–2010	Kuwait	Granger Causality	There is a causality relationship between variables.
Ak, Aydın, Altıntaş (2015)	1980–2010	Turkey	Dynamic Ordinary Least Square (DOLS), Modified Ordinary Least Squares (FMOLS), Johansen Cointegration	Financial development has an impact on growth. Impact is negative and limited.
Türkoğlu (2016)	1960–2013	Turkey	Unit Root Test Causality Test	There is a bi-directional causality relationship between variables.
Lawal, Nwanji, Asaleye and Ahmed (2016)	1981–2013	Nigeria	Johansen Cointegration Test, Granger Causality	There is equilibrium in long-term in between variables.
Çeştepe, Yıldırım (2016)	1986–2015	Turkey	Cointegration Test, VECM model and Granger Causality	There is equilibrium in long-term in between variables. There is causality short-term and long term.
Sönmez, Sağlam (2017)	1990–2015	Turkey	Johansen Cointegration Test, Causality	The causality relation couldn't be found.

Note: ➢ *The table was created by the author.*

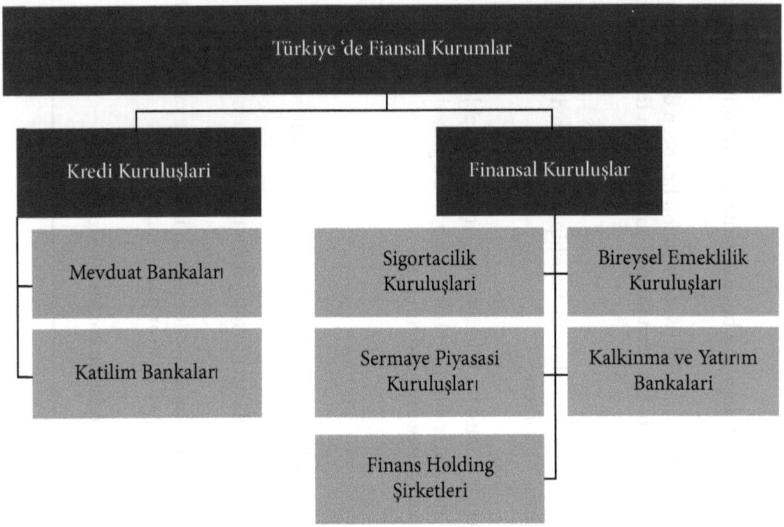

Fig. 2: Financial Institutions in Turkey. Source: Central Bank Publications, 2015, 5

according to the legislation lender institutions are deposits and participation banks. Financial institutions consist of financial holding companies, development & investment banks and institutions' activating in insurance, private pension and capital market that are out credit institutions (Developments in Financial Stability in Turkey, 2015, 2) (Fig. 2).

4 Model and Data Set

In this part of our study, relationship between financial development criterion and economic growth by considering data of Turkey economy is examined. In this context, firstly, appropriate variables are included in the model to relate the financial development variable to economic growth. And the cointegration and the causality relation between the variables has been analyzed through econometric estimation methods.

In our study, data based on the period between 1980 and 2014 has been used. In many of the studies examined, economic growth variable has been taken as level values to per capita gross domestic product. For this reason, in order to express economic growth, firstly the per person real GDP (Y1) level values was tried to be analyzed by taking the primary difference of the data. Per capita GDP has been taken as a dependent variable in the study. Other variables used in the study are domestic credit provided by financial sector (X1), domestic credit to private sector (X2), domestic credit to private sector by banks (X3). All data used in the study were compiled from the World Bank data sheet. Our model is as follows:

$$Y_1 = \alpha_0 + \beta_0 X_1 + e_0 \tag{1}$$

$$Y_1 = \alpha_0 + \beta_0 X_2 + e_1 \tag{2}$$

$$Y_1 = \alpha_0 + \beta_0 X3 + e_2 \tag{3}$$

Y1: Gross Domestic Product (GDP per capita)
X1: Domestic Credit Provided By Financial Sector
X2: Domestic Credit To Private Sector
X3: Domestic Credit To Private Sector By Banks

Hypotheses have been developed to analyze the relationship between financial development and economic growth in the study. The purpose of the hypothesis test is to arrive at a conclusion as to whether the proposed hypothesis is valid. The hypotheses determined move from here are as follows.

H0: Financial development is not the reason for economic growth.
H1: Financial development is the cause of economic growth.

The first phase for to be examined of the relationship between financial development and economic growth is the determination of whether the stationary of series in data set. The stationary of the economic growth variable, which is the dependent variable, will be analyzed by the unit root test. In the same way The Augmented Dickey Fuller (ADF) unit root test will be carried for stationary the independent variables.

5 Econometric Methodology and Findings

5.1 Unit Root Analysis

The Augmented Dickey Fuller (ADF) unit root test is a commonly used test that investigates the presence of unit root in time series. In order for a time series to be stationary, the mean and variance must not change over time, and the covariance between the two periods must depend on the distance between only two periods, not the return calculated by this covariance (Gujarati, 1999: 713). The data we used in Tab. 2 are the unit root test results.

The stationary of variable domestic credit provided by the financial sector in our study was examined by the ADF test. As can be seen from Tab. 2, according

Tab. 2: Unit Root Test Findings (ADF) for Variable Domestic Credit Provided By Financial Sector (X1)

Level of Significance	Critical Values (level))	Critical Values (1st difference)
0,01	-3.639407	-3.646342
0,05	-2.951125	-2.954021
0,10	-2.614300	-2.615817
DF statistic	0.413715	-5.436133*

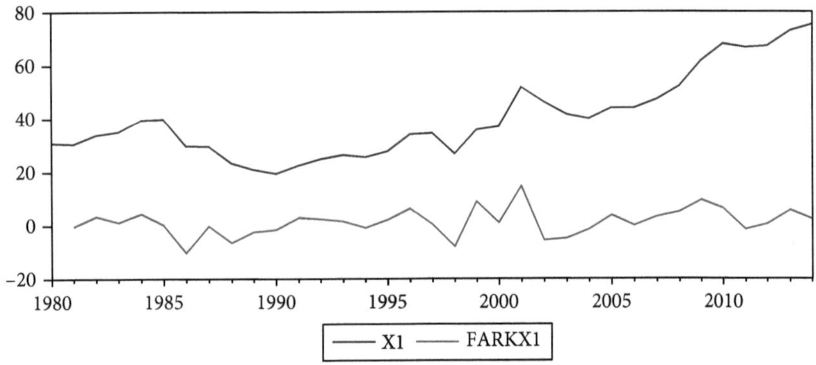

Graph 1: X1 Series Level and First Difference Line Graph

to the findings obtained, it was determined that the variable was not stationary in the level stage. The first difference of variable has been taken for the stationary of the variable. Critical values determined at significance levels of 0.01, 0.05 and 0.10 are also shown in Tab. 2. The line graph of the level and first difference series for the X1 variable has been given in Graph 1. In the first difference of the series appears to be stationary.

In Tab. 3, the analysis was continued with the Domestic Credit To Private Sector variable. Unit root test results are as follows.

Stationarity test has been applied to Domestic Credit To Private Sector (X2) variable from independent variables. It has been observed that at the level phase of the sequence according to the analysis is not stationary. The sequence was stationarized by taking the first difference of the sequence (Tab. 3).

When the line graph in Graph 2 is examined, it appears that the series has got stationary at first difference. Stationary of the independent variable in domestic credit to private sector by banks variable (X3) was tested. It has been observed that the level is not stationary at the level value of the sequence according to the

Tab. 3: Unit Root Test (ADF) Findings for Domestic Credit To Private Sector (X2) Variable

Level of Significance	Critical Values (level)	Critical Values (1st difference)
0,01	-3.639407	-3.646342
0,05	-2.951125	-2.954021
0,10	-2.614300	-2.615817
DF statistic	2.574459	-5.819844*

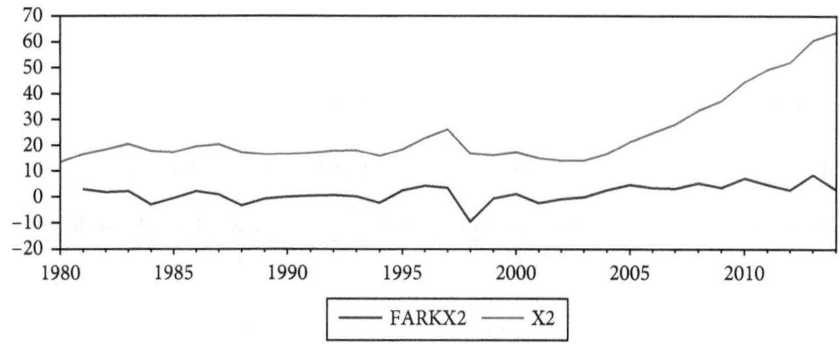

Graph 2: X2 Series Level and First Difference Line Graph

Tab. 4: Unit Root Test Findings (ADF) For Variable Domestic Credit To Private Sector By Banks (X3)

Level of Significance	Critical Values (level)	Critical Values (1st difference)
0,01	-3.639407	-3.646342
0,05	-2.951125	-2.954021
0,10	-2.614300	-2.615817
DF statistic	2.314834	-3.955523*

analysis. The sequence were stationarized by taking the first difference of the sequence (Tab. 4). This result is showed in the line graph in Graph 3.

For the X3 variable, line graph of the level value and first difference sequence are given in Graph 3.

In Tab. 5, for the Gross National Domestic Product (Y1) variable shows the results obtained from the ADF unit root test at the level and the first difference. According to these results, the variable became stationary in the first difference.

Graph 4 graphically demonstrates the sequence of Gross National Domestic Product (Y1) in both the level and the stationary state.

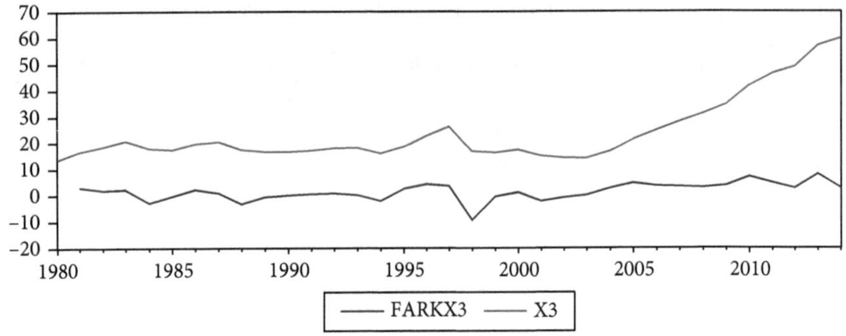

Graph 3: X3 Series Level and First Difference Line Graph

Tab. 5: Unit Root Test (ADF)Findings for the Per Capita GDP Variable (Y1)

Level of Significance	Critical Values (level)	Critical Values (1st difference)
0,01	-3.639407	1.423973
0,05	-2.951125	1.423973
0,10	-2.614300	1.423973
DF statistic	1.423973	-5.134841*

The ADF Unit root test has been applied to all variables in our model. And all the variables are seen to get stationared in first differences. It will be determined whether there is a cointegration relationship between the stationary sequences at this stage of our work.

5.2 Cointegration Analysis

Most of time series has a deterministic or stochastic trend. Series is stationarized to remove trends. This may cause the series to lose their long-term properties. Cointegration analysis is an improved method for determining whether there is a long-term relationship between time series. Tab. 6 examines the cointegration relationship between the Y1 dependent variable and the X1 independent variable. There is one cointegration vector according to the results of the trace test on the table. In this case there is a cointegration relationship between economic growth and domestic credit provided by financial sector. On the other hand, there is no cointegration vector according to the maximum eigenvalue statistic.

The same analysis has been made between Domestic Credit To Private Sector (X2) and economic growth (Y1). Tab. 7 shows both trace statistics and maximum

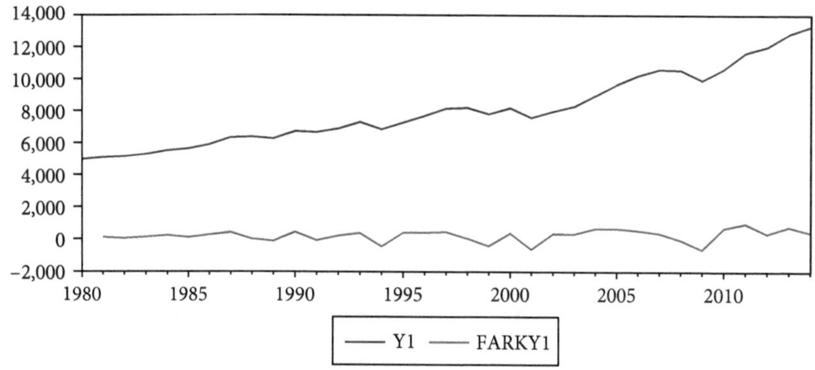

Graph 4: Y1 Series Level and First Difference Line Graph

Tab. 6: For Dependent Variable: Y1, Independent Variable: X1Co-integration Results

	r = 0	**Critic Value (%5)**	**r = 1**	**Critic Value (%5)**
L-trace	23.26401*	15.49471	11.37145	3.841466
L-max. eigenvalue statistic	11.89256	14.26460	11.37145	3.841466

Tab. 7: For Dependent Variable: Y1, Independent Variables:X2 Co-integration Results

	r = 0	**Critic Value (%5)**	**r = 1**	**Critic Value (%5)**
L-trace	20.20281*	15.49471	13.53523	3.841466
L-max. eigenvalue statistic	6.667587*	3.841466	11.37145	3.841466

eigenvalue statistical results. According to the results, there is a co-integration relationship between the loans given to the private sector and economic growth.

A cointegration test was also conducted between domestic credit to private sector by banks (X3) and the economic growth (Y1) variable. The analyzed test results are given in Tab. 8. According to these results, the trace and maximum eigenvalue test statistics are larger than the critical value. This indicates that there is a cointegration relationship between the two variables. Cointegration between variables indicates a long term relationship. In this context, when we examine our economic growth and financial development data, there is a significant relationship between them.

Tab. 8: For Dependent Variable: Y1, Independent Variable: X3Co-integration Results

	r = 0	Critic Value (%5)	r = 1	Critic Value (%5)
L-trace	20.91934*	15.49471	13.31489	14.26460
L-max. eigenvalue statistic	7.604453*	3.841466	11.37145	3.841466

In our study, variables of financial development and economic growth data were analyzed separately. When the relevant results are considered as a whole, the existence of cointegration relationship between financial development data and economic growth has been determined.

5.3 Granger Causality Test

Determination of whether any causality relationship between the two variables exists is analyzed by the Granger causality test. In our study, Granger causality test was performed between economic growth and financial development variables. In Tabs. 9, 10 and 11, results of the Granger causality relationship between the variables X1, X2 and X3 and economic growth (Y1) are given.

According to the results in Tab. 9, there is no causality relationship between the domestic credit provided by financial sector (X1) and economic growth (Y1).

When we examine the results in Tab. 10, it is seen that there is no causality relation between the domestic credit to private sector (X2) and economic growth (Y1).

In Tab. 11 the probability value at the 5 % significance level is "0.037". According to the result of the test, there is a causality relation from the variable domestic credit to private sector by banks(X3) to the economic growth (Y1).

According to the Granger causality test results, it is determined that there is a causality between domestic credit to private sector by banks and the economic growth variable. Based on data what we use in our work, we can say that at least one of the financial developments is the economic growth reason. The other two variables (X1 and X2) are not the Granger cause.

6 Conclusion and Assessment

In our study where the relationship between financial development and economic growth in Turkey is examined a contribution to the literature is intended. Financial developments have an important share in the functioning of the economic structure. Especially, the development of financial markets is an indication that the economy of that country is also in a strong structure.

Tab. 9: Granger Causality Test Results for Y1-X1 Variables

Hypothesis	Observation Number	F-statistic	Probability
DX1 is not the Granger cause of DY1	32	0.771	0.472
DY1 is not the Granger cause of DX1	32	0.008	0.991

Tab. 10: Granger Causality Test Results for Y1-X2 Variables

Hypothesis	Observation Number	F-statistic	Probability
DX2 is not the Granger cause of Y1	32	2.367	0.112
DY1 is not the Granger cause of DX2	32	0.852	0.437

Tab. 11: Granger Causality Test Results for Y1-X3 Variables

Hypothesis	Observation Number	F-statistic	Probability
DX3 is not the Granger cause of DY1	32	3.732	0.037 *
DY1 is not the Granger cause of DX3	32	0.852	0.437

In the financial markets, fund flow to from savings owners to the financial intermediaries institutions take place. In this context they play a decisive and effective role in the economic structure.

In this study, made by examining the example of Turkey, the relationship between financial development and economic growth in the between 1980 and 2014 the years has been analyzed. So, it is examined whether there is a meaningful relation between the variables. In the first step, it has been found to be non-stationary the sequences. And with the ADF unit root test, the sequences are stabilized. In the second step, the effect between variables with the Johansen cointegration test was determined. In the last phase, applying Granger causality to the variables the relationship between the related variables was tested. Causality relationship between X1 (Domestic Credit Provided By Financial Sector) and X2 variable (Domestic Credit To Private Sector) and economic growth could not be found. In our analysis, one-way causality relationship was identified from domestic credit to private sector by banking (X3) to economic growth.

As a result, in our study the relationship between financial development and economic growth in Turkey has been analyzed. And causality between domestic credit to private sector by banking and economic growth has been determined. Banks are the main actors of the financial system. For the development of the financial sector, it is important policy steps to facilitate the use of credit must be taken by the government and the Central Bank. Thus, with the development of the financial sector, the infrastructure of the economy will be strengthened. The robust structure in the economy will positively contribute to economic growth by affecting also financial markets.

References

Abdulkadhim, Hatem, Al-Jafari, Mohamed Khaled, December (2014), "Financial Development, Trade Openness and Economic Growth: A Trilateral Analysis of Bahrain", https://www.researchgate.net/publication/287695988.

Afşar, Muharrem (2006), Financial System and Operation, Eskişehir, Turkey. Afşar, Asst. Assoc. Dr. Aslı, "The Relationship between Financial Development and Economic Growth", Anadolu University, Eskişehir Vocational School, p. 189.

Ak, Mehmet Zeki, Aydin, M. Kemal, Nurullah, Altıntaş, December (2015), "Affect to Growth of Financial Development and Trade Liberalization in Turkey", Eskisehir Osmangazi University, Journal of Economics and Administrative Sciences, Volume: 10, Issue: 3, pp. 29–45, Eskişehir, Turkey.

Altunç, Ömer Faruk (2008), "An Empirical Analysis of Causality between Financial Development and Economic Growth in Turkey", Eskişehir Osmangazi University, İİBF Journal, October 2008, Volume: 3, Issue: 2, pp. 113–127, Eskişehir, Turkey.

Arslan, Hanifi, Monetary (2009), Theory and Policy, Bursa, Turkey, Alfa Publications, p. 77.

Asghar, Nabila, Hussain, Zakir Fınancıal Development, Winter (2014), "Trade Openness and Economic Growth in Developing Countries Recent Evidence From Panel Data", Pakistan Economic and Social Review, Volume: 52, Issue: 2, pp. 99–126.

Aslan, Özgür, Küçükaksoy, Ismail (2006), "Financial Development and Economic Growth Relation: An Econometric Applications on Turkey Economy", Istanbul University Economics Faculty – Econometrics and Statistics Journal, Econometrics and Statistics, Issue: 4, pp.12–28.

Aslan, Özgür, Korap, Levent (2006), "Financial Development and Economic Growth Relationship in Turkey", Muğla University Social Sciences Institute Journal, Issue: 17, pp. 1–20.

Çeştepe, Prof. Dr. Hamza, Yildirim, Assoc. Dr. Ertugrul (2016) "Financial Development and Economic Growth Relationship in Turkey", International Management, Journal of Economics and Business Administration, ICAFR 16, Special Issue, pp. 2–16.

Erdogan, Seyfettin, Orhan Osman Z, October (2015), Monetary Policy, İstanbul, Turkey, Umuttepe Publications, p. 29.

Ergeç, Etem, H. (2004), "Causality Relationship between Financial Development and Economic Growth-Turkey Example: 1988–2001", Osmangazi University, Journal of Social Sciences, Volume: 5, Issue: 2, pp. 51–66.

Gujarati, D.N. (1999), Basic Econometrics (Trans. by U. Şenesen, G.G. Şenesen), Istanbul, Literature Publications.

Hepsag, Aycan (2009), "Testing in Framework the McKinnon Complementarity Hypothesis of the Validity of the Financial Liberalization Policies – The Case of Turkey", BDDK Banking and Financial Markets, Volume: 3, Issue: 1.

İnançlı, Selim, Altintas, Nurullah, İnal, Veysel, September (2016), "Financial Development and Economic Growth Relationship: D-8 Example", Kastamonu University, Journal of Faculty of Economics and Administrative Sciences, Issue: 14.

Kar, Muhsin, Nazlıoğlu, Şaban, Ağır, Hüseyin (2014), "Trade Openness, Financial Development and Economic Growth in Turkey: Linear and Nonlinear Causality Analysis", BDDK Banking and Financial Markets, Volume: 8, Issue: 1.

Karaca, Orhan (2012), "Economic Growth and Financial Development: A Causality Analysis for Turkey", BDDK Banking and Financial Markets, Volume: 6, Issue: 2, pp. 85–111.

King, Robert G., Levine, Ross, 1 August (1993), "Finance and Growth: Schumpeter Might Be Right", The Quarterly Journal of Economics, Volume: 108, Issue: 3, pp. 717–737.

Levine, Ross (2014), "Finance and Growth: Theory and Evidence", Working Paper, 10766, http://www.nber.org/papers/W10766.

Menyah, Kojo, Nazlioglu, Shaban, Yemane, Wolde-Rufael (2013), "Financial Development, Trade Openness and Economic Growth in African Countries, New Insights from a Panel Causality Approach, Economic Modelling", Volume: 37, pp. 386–394, journal homepage: elsevier.com/locate/ecmod.

Mercan, Mehmet, Peker, Osman, April (2013), "The Impact to Economic Growth of Financial Development: An Econometric Analysis", Eskişehir Osmangazi University Journal of Economics and Business Administration, Volume: 8, Issue: 1, pp. 93–120.

Murthy, Dogga, Patra, Satyanarayana, Kumar, Suresh, Samantaraya, Amaresh (2017), "Trade Openness, Financial Development and Index and Economic Growth Evidence from India (1971–2012)", he current issue and full text archive of this journal is available at, www.emeraldinsight.com/1757-6385.htm.

Oruç, Semiye, Turgut, Ahmet (2014), "Financial Deepening, Economic Growth and Turkish Finance System: 1990–2012", Selçuk University, Journal of Social Sciences Institute, Dr. Mehmet Yildiz Private Issue, pp. 109–118.

Patrick, T. Hugh (1966), "Financial Development and Economic Growth in Underdeveloped Countries", Economic Development and Cultural Change, Volume: 14, Issue: 2, pp. 174–189.

Parasiz, İlker, October (1997), Money-Banking and Financial Markets, Bursa, Turkey, Ezgi Bookstore, p. 54.

Saaed, afaf Abdull, Hussain, J. Majeed Ali (2015), "The Casual Relationship among Trade Openness, Financial Development and Economic Growth Evidence from Kuwait", Journal of Emerging Issues in Economics, Finance and Banking, (JEIEFB) An Online International Research Journal (ISSN:2306-367X), Volume: 4, Issue: 1.

Schumpeter, Joseph (1932), The Theory of Economic Development, Harvard University Press.

Serin, Vildan (1987), Monetary Policy, Marmara, Istanbul, Turkey, University Publications, p. 55.

Sönmez, Filiz Erataş, Sağlam, Yağmur (2017), "Effects on Economic Growth of Financial Development and Trade Openness: European Transition Economies Example", Anadolu International Conference in Economics, April 11–13, Eskisehir, Turkey.

Tsaurai, Kunofiwa (2013), "Investigating the Relationship between Financial Development Trade Openness and Economic Growth in Argentina: A Multivariate Causality Framework", Aude, Volume: 13, Issue: 3, pp. 39–55.

Developments in Financial Stability in Turkey (2015), Ankara, Turkey, Central Bank Publications, p. 5.

Türkoğlu, Asst. Associate Professor. Musa (2016), "Effects to Economic Growth of Financial Development and in Turkey: Causality Analysis", Nevsehir Haci Bektas Veli University, Journal of the Institute of Social Sciences, Volume: 6, Issue: 1, s. 84–93, Nevsehir, Turkey.

Yücel, Fatih (2009), "Causal Relationship between Financial Development Trade Openness and Economic Growth: The Case of Turkey", Journal of Social Sciences, Volume: 5, Issue: 1, pp. 33–42, ISSN 1549-3652.

Adil Akinci[1]

The Relationship between Special Consumption Tax and Current Account Deficit in Turkey[2]

1 Introduction

The reduction of current account deficit has a significant effect in ensuring macroeconomic stability of developing countries. Significant increases occurred in the current account deficits of developing countries, especially along with the commercial liberalization process experienced after 1980. The increase in the number of countries with current account deficit, the fact that current account deficits became permanent, the fact that current account deficit increased the vulnerability of the country's economy to external shocks and became the leading indicator that countries might have economic problems took the current account deficit issue to a significant position in the economics literature. Countries resort to a number of financial measures in fighting against current account deficit to ensure macroeconomic stability. One of the tools used in the reduction of current account deficit is special consumption tax.

The special consumption tax, which was enacted by a law regulated in 2002, is a tax type that is taken over certain product or product groups and is included in the taxation on expenditures within the Turkish Tax System. The special consumption tax is subject to taxation in order to achieve some financial objectives rather than being a source of revenue for the public administrations in order to finance the public expenditures in the general quality. At the beginning of these financial objectives is to reduce the consumption of some products or product groups in particular. In this context, special consumption tax is applied in order to reduce the consumption of some imported products or product groups in Turkey, which has a problem of foreign trade deficit.

In this study, whether special consumption tax was an effective political tool in fighting against current account deficit during 2006:Q1-2016:Q2 period in

---

1 Assistant Professor, Kırklareli University, School of Applied Sciences, adil.akinci@klu.edu.tr.

2 This paper was presented at the International Congress on Turkish World Social Sciences Research conference held at Tirana, Albania, September 11–15, 2017.

Turkey was tested using the econometric analysis. In this context, Autoregressive Distributed Lag (ARDL) cointegration test of time series models and then Toda Yamamoto Causality analysis were used as an econometric analysis method.

2 Effects of Special Consumption Tax on Current Account Deficit

Special consumption tax is an expenditure tax collected through private goods or goods groups, and its most important difference from general expenditure taxes is that it is a tax type applied to certain goods or wholly related goods groups usually at different rates. Special consumption tax aims to reduce the consumption of the goods selected to be taxed rather than ensuring the financing of public expenditures in general quality (Edizdoğan and Çelikkaya, 2012: 237–239).

The concept of current account deficit is expressed as foreign exchange deficits in the balance of foreign payments as a result of the international trades of countries within the scope of imports and exports with other countries (Özker, 2012: 52). When current account deficit becomes constant, the debt of the country increases and it has negative effects on the economic stability of the country in the long term (Pehlivanoğlu and Beşel, 2013, 63). Therefore, states need to take some financial measures to be able to remove the current account deficit problem. In this context, states also use the special consumption tax to regulate the economy. By reducing the consumption of imported goods by special consumption tax, it is intended to reduce the current account deficit and to remove the current account deficit problem in the long term by developing domestic industry (Edizdoğan and Çelikkaya, 2012: 242).

3 Literature Review

It is seen that the literature has been formed recently when empirical studies that examine the relationship between current account deficit and special consumption tax are examined. In their study, Uğur et al. (2012) examined the relationship between current account deficit and special consumption tax during 2005:01-2011:12 period in Turkey using the Granger Causality test and the Dolado – Lütkepohl Causality tests. As a result of the test results obtained, while causality from current account deficit to special consumption tax was determined, no causality was determined from special consumption tax to current account deficit. In their study, Pehlivanoğlu and Beşel (2013) examined the relationship between current account deficit and special consumption tax during 2006:01-2013:05 period in Turkey using the Gregory-Hansen cointegration test and Toda-Yamamoto Causality test, and as a result of the analysis results, no relationship was determined between the two variables. In their study, Yaraşır Tülümce and Özpençe (2014) examined the relationship between current account deficit and special consumption tax during 2005:01-2013-09 period in Turkey using the Granger Causality test, and as a result of the findings obtained, they found a bi-directional causality relationship from current account deficit to special consumption tax and from special consumption tax to current account deficit.

4 Econometric Application

4.1 Data and Method

The data set of the study consists of the 2006:Q1-2016:Q2 period. In the study, the net amount of current account deficit to gross domestic product ratio (ca) was used as a dependent variable, and the special consumption tax revenues to gross domestic product ratio (otv) was used as an independent variable. The seasonally and calendar adjusted form of the series belonging to the variables were used, and their logarithms were taken to stabilize. The data on the variables were obtained via the Central Bank of the Republic of Turkey Electronic Data Distribution System (EDDS).

To be able to apply the cointegration tests developed by Engel-Granger (1987), Johansen (1988), Johansen and Juselius (1990) which are used extensively in investigating long-term relationships between the variables, the series need to be non-stationary from the level and become stable when their differences are taken equally. In other words, the degree of integration of variables must be the same. Pesaran, Shin and Smith (2001) developed the bound testing approach to remove these restrictions. This test can investigate long-term relationships between variables without considering the degree of integration of variables. In this study, the bound testing approach developed by Pesaran, Shin and Smith (2001) was used because the series were stationary at different levels. Then, the causality test developed by Toda-Yamamoto (1995) was used to reveal the causality relationship between the variables.

4.2 Empirical Findings

4.2.1 Unit Root Test

Whether there was a unit root in the series was analyzed using the Augmented Dickey-Fuller (ADF) test and Phillips-Peron (PP) test. According to the results

Tab. 1: Unit Root Test Results

Variable		ADF		PP	
		Fixed-Trend	**Fixed**	**Fixed-Trend**	**Fixed**
ca		−2.2788	−2.1748	−2.2712	−2.1592
Δca		−7.1299	−7.2187	−7.1198	−7.2066
otv		−3.6150	−3.6702	−2.9164	−3.0413
Δotv		−3.7548	−3.757803	−7.0498	−7.0709
Critical Values	**%1**	−4.2050	−3.6055	−4.1985	−3.6009
	%5	−3.5266	−2.9369	−3.5236	−2.9350
	%10	−3.1946	−2.6068	−3.1929	−2.6058

Note: The * sign indicates that the variable is stable by %1, the ** sign indicates that the variable is stable by %5. The "Δ" sign refers to differencing operator, in other words, the first difference values.

of the ADF and PP unit root tests in Tab. 1, it is seen from the test results that the "ca" variable includes unit root in fixed-trend and fixed level values, and when the first difference is received, it does not include unit root in fixed-trend and fixed values, in other words, it is stationary I(1). It is seen from the test results that the "otv" variable does not include unit root in fixed-trend and fixed level values, in other words, it is I(0).

4.2.2 ARDL Model

The study will be continued with ARDL since the variables have different degrees of stationarity. The most important step in the implementation of the ARDL test is to determine the appropriate the length of the delay. For this purpose, the models up to 4 delays were estimated due to the use of quarterly data, and the calculated information criteria and the existence of autocorrelation were examined. According to the results in Tab. 2, it was determined according to AIC, SC and HQ criteria that the delay length was minimum, there was no autocorrelation and the 1st delay length was the most appropriate delay length.

After determining the appropriate delay length, the long term cointegration relation was examined. F statistic is calculated by bound testing to be able to determine the long term cointegration relation. It is decided on the presence of the long-term relationship by comparing the F statistic found with critical values.

According to the results in Tab. 3, since F-statistic result "4.45" is greater than the upper value "3.87" critical value, it shows that the presence of a long term cointegration relationship between the variables.

Long-term and short-term coefficients are determined by establishing the ARDL model for examining the long-term relationship between the variables.

Tab. 2: Determination of Delay Length

Number of Delays	AIC	SC	HQ	LM (1)	LM(4)
1	***-3.1901***	***-3.0263***	***-3.1297***	***0.6203***	***0.8335***
2	-3.1113	-2.8631	-3.0203	0.3771	0.6793
3	-3.0163	-2.6820	-2.8946	0.4895	0.6999
4	-2.9611	-2.5389	-2.808508	0.4945	0.6299

Tab. 3: Bounding Test Results

dependent variable:	"ca"	
F statistic:	4.4555	
Critical Values (k=2)		
	Lower Value	***Upper Value***
%5	3.10	3.87

Tab. 4: Results of the ARDL (1,1) Model

Variables	Coefficient	t-statistic	Prob
ca(-1)	0.564378	5.229518	0.0000
otv	-0.246273	-1.076218	0.2884
otv(-1)	-0.441779	-1.803524	0.0790
c	-3.068836	-3.993345	0.0003

The model to be used to investigate the long-term relationships is the ARDL (1,1) equation. The results obtained from the model are presented in Tab. 4.

Long term coefficients were calculated by taking into account the ARDL (1,1) model. Long term coefficients are presented in Tab. 5.

When the ARDL long-term results are examined, there is a statistically significant relationship at a significance level of 5 % between "ca" and "otv" in the long term. After the long-term relationship was revealed, short-term relationships were examined by establishing the error correction model [ect(-1)] based on the ARDL (1,1) model. Error correction model results are presented in Tab. 6.

According to the error correction model results, the fact that the short-term error term coefficient (-0.4356) is between -1 and 0 and is statistically significant (Prob:0.0000) shows that the error correction model works. This parameter forces variables to converge to long term equilibrium value. There is a causality relationship between the variables since the error term parameter is significant.

Tab. 5: ARDL (1,1) Model Long Term Coefficients

Variables	Coefficient	t-statistic	Prob
otv	−1.5794	−4.0090	0.0003
c	−7.0447	−4.2717	0.0001

Tab. 6: Error Correction Model Based on ARDL (1,1) Model

Variables	Coefficient	t-statistic	Prob
d(otv)	−0.2462	−1.2196	0.2299
ect (-1)	−0.4356	−4.6913	0.0000

Tab. 7: Toda-Yamamoto Causality Test Results

Dependent Variable: ca	Chi-sq	Df	Prob
"otv"	0.312295	1	0.0101
Dependent Variable: otv	**Chi-sq**	**Df**	**Prob**
"ca"	0.439098	1	0.5076

4.2.3 Toda Yamamoto Causality Analysis

In order to determine the relationship between the variables, the causality relationship between the "ca" and "otv" variables was examined by the Toda-Yamamoto causality test proposed by Toda-Yamamoto (1995) which does not consider the degrees of stationarity of variables, and they are presented in Tab. 7.

When the results in Tab. 7 are examined, it is seen that there is a causality relationship from "otv" variable to "ca" variable and that there is no causality relationship from "ca" variable to "otv" variable.

4.3 Evaluation of Empirical Findings

The presence of a long-term relationship between the variables was determined by the fact that the F-statistic calculated as the result of econometric analysis, in which the relationship between current account deficit and special consumption tax was examined by the ARDL model, one of time series analysis, was greater than the upper critical value. The presence of a long term relationship between the variables shows that there is a significant relationship between current account deficit and special consumption tax, in other words, the changes in special consumption tax affect the current account deficit.

The findings obtained from the econometric analysis reveal that special consumption tax affects the current account deficit differently in the short and long term. When the long term results in Tab. 5 are examined, it is seen that 1 % increase in special consumption tax will lead to -1.57 % decrease in current account deficit in the long term. The short-term relationship between the special consumption tax and current account deficit was examined by the error correction model established after determining the long-term relationship. When error correction model results in Table 6 are examined, the fact that the error correction term is between 0 and -1 and statistically significant at a significance level of 5 % shows the validity of the model established, and the error correction term coefficient shows that 43 % of deviations due to long-term equilibrium are corrected quarterly. When short term coefficients were examined, it is seen that 1 % increase in special consumption tax will lead to -0.24 % decrease in the current account deficit in the short term; however, it was determined from the test results that it is statistically insignificant at a significance level of 5 %.

According to the Toda-Yamamoto causality analysis performed after revealing the short and long-term relationships, it was concluded that there was a unidirectional causality relationship from special consumption tax to current account deficit.

5 Conclusion

As a result of the findings obtained from the econometric analysis, a long-term relationship was determined between current account deficit and special consumption taxes during 2006: Q1-2016: Q2 period in Turkey. The facts that 1 % increase to be made in special consumption tax in the long term leads to -1.57 % decrease on current account deficit, and that 1 % increase to be made in special consumption tax in the short term leads to -0.24 % decrease on current account deficit show that special consumption tax is an economically effective policy tool on current account deficit.

To be able to close the current account deficit balance which has a great importance in ensuring the macroeconomic equilibrium of the countries, it is necessary that the goods and services that increase the current account deficit since they are imported are encouraged to be produced with domestic opportunities within the country. In this context, attention should be paid to invest in human capital power that will increase production and to use resources more efficiently. Since natural resources, such as energy, which lead to current account deficit cannot be produced within the country, wastage should be avoided on their consumption and it is necessary to raise the awareness of public on conscious consumption of them.

References

Dickey, David A. and Fuller,Wayne A. (1981), "Likelihood Ratio Statistics for Autoregressive Time Series with a Unit Root", Econometrica, 49(4): 1057–1072.

Edizdoğan, Nihat and Çelikkaya, Ali (2012), *Vergilerin Ekonomik Analizi*, Dora Yayıncılık, Bursa.

Özker, A. Niyazi (2012), Kamu Açıkları Yapısal Dinamikler ve Süreçte Çözümlemeler, Dora Yayıncılık, Bursa.

Pehlivanoğlu, Ferhat and Beşel, Furkan (2013), "Relationship between Foreign Trade Deficit and Special Consumption Tax Revenues with Structural Breaks in Turkey", Journal of Economics and Sustainable Development, 4(17): 63–72.

Pesaran, M.H., Shin, Y. and Smith, R.J. (2001), "Bounds Testing Approaches to the Analysis of Level Relationships", Journal of Applied Econometrics, 16: 289–326.

Phillips, P.C.B. and Perron, P. (1988), "Testing for a Unit Root in Time Series Regression", Biometrika, 75(2): ss. 335–346.

Toda, H. Y. and Yamamoto, T. (1995), "Statistical Inference in Vector Autoregressions with Possibly Integrated Processes", Journal of Econometrics, 66: 225–250.

Uğur, Ahmet, Akbaş, Yusuf Ekrem and Şentürk, Metin (2012), "Özel Tüketim Vergisi Oranlarındaki Artış Cari Açığa Çözüm Olabilir Mi?" Journal of Yasar University, 26(7): 4572–4588.

Yaraşır Tülümce, Sevinç and Özpençe, Özay (2014), "Türkiye'de Özel Tüketim Vergisi ve Cari Açık Arasındaki İlişkinin Analizi", Elektronik Sosyal Bilimler Dergisi, 13(49): 280–291.

Ahmet Aysu[1]

Active Labor Market Policies and Unemployment: Evidence from Panel Cointegration

1 Introduction

The struggle with unemployment is one of the primary goals of economic policies due to the fact that it causes economic and social problems. In developed and developing countries, various policies on the labor market are implemented in order to reduce unemployment. Labor market policies are categorized in two ways. Policy implementations such as unemployment insurance that do not directly help the individuals, who want to work, find a job are called passive labor market policies. On the other hand, direct approaches to increase the possibility of finding a job for the labor that is not employed such as training activities aimed at unemployed individuals, help for job search, incentives given to employers to increase employment are called active labor market policies (ALMPs). These policies are put into practice especially for fighting against structural unemployment (Nie & Struby, 2011: pp. 35–36).

ALMPs have been implemented in many countries for many years. In the early 20th century, employment offices were set up, economic programs to combat unemployment in the Great Depression era were applied, and vocational trainings began to be implemented in the later years (Boeri & Van Ours, 2008: p. 255). ALMPs are often accepted as a key factor in the success that Sweden attained in the rate of unemployment from the mid-1940s to early 1990s (Forslund & Kruger, 2010: p. 159). Currently, ALMPs are regarded as necessary for policy mix applied in fighting against inflation and ensuring full employment. Especially in the fight against inflation, it has been recommended to implement labor mobility enhancing programs such as vocational training to prevent increasing unemployment in low-productivity sectors due to contractionary policies (Calmfors et al. 2004: p. 3). In the early 1990s, the problem of high and persistent unemployment appeared in many OECD member countries. In the Job Strategy report published by OECD in 1994, policy recommendations to increase employment

1 PhD, Erciyes University, Faculty of Economics and Administrative Sciences, Department of Public Finance, ahmetaysu@erciyes.edu.tr

were presented. Among these, there are also some recommendations regarding strengthening and expanding ALMPs (OECD, 1994).

OECD member countries have labor market policies and a classification for the action type regarding these policies. According to this, the following stand out as ALMPs among the labor market policies: *Public employment service and administration* which includes services and activities that will help jobseekers to be employed both in public and private sectors and reduce unemployment; *Training* financed by the public and aiming to improve the skills of the target groups; *employment incentives* in which the jobs to be supported are often in private sector, and that help job seekers and other target groups to be recruited or help those who are likely to lose their jobs continue employment; *supported employment and rehabilitation,* which supports the integration of persons with lower work capacity in the labor market through employment support and rehabilitation; *direct job creation* aiming to create additional jobs for those who are unemployed for a long time or who face some difficulties in the labor market; and finally, *Start-up incentives* that involves various measures such as financial assistance, providing loan, business advice in order to encourage the unemployed and other target groups to start up their own business and become entrepreneurs (EC, 2006).

The aim of this study is to investigate the short and long-term effects of total expenditures spent on the programs as part of ALMPs on unemployment. The rest of the paper is organized as follows. Section 1 presents the theoretical framework and empirical literature review on the relation between ALMPs and unemployment. Section 2 introduces the data and model. Section 3 discusses the methodology and empirical findings. Last section presents concluding remarks.

2 Theoretical Perspective and Related Literature

ALMPs can affect employment from different channels. First, the fact that thanks to the training programs job seekers' capabilities are developed and that activities for job seeking are more effective with active employment agencies can contribute to a more efficient match between vacant jobs and job seekers. Second, in the case of training programs or subsidies provided to new entrepreneurs, labor productivity may increase through on-the-job learning. Third, ALMPs ensure that unemployed individuals keep in touch with the labor market even though they haven't been working actively for a long period of time. That the competition among jobseekers is strong can cause the wages to decrease and increase labor demand. Fourth, subsidies provided for employment as part of new job creation programs can reduce labor costs, creating an income effect, and thus an effect increasing labor demand can emerge. Fifth, active policies can reduce the disutility of being unemployed. By contributing to the protection of labor capabilities, they can lead to higher wage demands for unemployed individuals in the wage bargaining process (Estevão, 2003: pp. 4–6).

The main objective of ALMPs is to facilitate the adaptation of the labor to structural changes by contributing to the development of human capital. The development of human capital, in turn, will provide positive contributions to economic growth. It also serves different purposes, such as increasing the probability for individual to be employed, contributing to social equity by increasing the employment opportunities of disadvantaged groups in the society and stabilizing employment in the face of cyclical fluctuations (Biçerli, 2005). The objectives of ALMPs differ in the economic crisis, recovery and normal periods. In the times of economic crisis, for instance, maintaining the existing level of employment in the economy is the main objective (Brown & Koettl, 2015: p. 2).

ALMPs have been criticized from various aspects. The most criticized aspects are deadweight loss associated with wage subsidies and job creation schemes and substitution effects. Deadweight loss refers to those employed from the target group even in a situation where there is no job creation program. The substitution effect, on the other hand, means that subsidized employment changes relative wages and rearrange employment opportunities among different groups seeking a job (Calmfors, 1994). There are some opinions stating that job matching services provided by employment services reduce the efforts of individuals to search for jobs, programs developed for specific groups in the society reduce individuals' fear of being out of a job and decrease their motivation to seek work and the reflection of this situation on the employment is negative (Escudero, 2015: pp. 33–35).

In the analysis they conducted with the data of 20 OECD member countries belonging to the years between 1998 and 2008, Nie and Struby (2011) found that ALMPs have an effect decreasing unemployment. In this context, it is suggested that the effect of training and job search assistance reducing unemployment is bigger compared to other active policy implementations. In the study conducted by Boone and Van Ours (2004) with 20 OECD countries including their time period between 1985 and 1999, it was revealed that labor market training was the most effective program to reduce unemployment.

As a result of the analysis of the data belonging to 15 industrialized countries, Estevão (2003) found that ALMPs made a positive contribution to the level of employment in the private sector. In a detailed study including the data of 21 OECD member countries covering the years between 1982 and 2003, Bassanini

Tab. 1: Variables and Sources

Variable	Unit	Data Source
Total public expenditures for active labor market policies (active)	% of GDP	OECDstat online database
Unemployment, total (unemp)	% of total labor force	World Development Indicator online database
GDP per capita (percad)	constant 2010 US$	World Development Indicator online database
Openness	Sum of exports and imports-% of GDP	World Development Indicator online database

and Duval (2006) stated that expenditures made for ALMPs had a negative effect on unemployment.

In his study, Nickell (1997) also showed that ALMPs has a negative effect on both long-term and short-term unemployment. In the study he conducted with the data of 31 developed countries, Escudero (2015) presented empirical evidence that ALMPs reduced unemployment and increased employment. However, in their study, Baker et al. (2003) found that there was no significant relationship between ALMPs and unemployment.

Programs within the context of ALMPs such as public employment services, training, employment incentives, start-up incentives, direct job are also examined specific to various countries (Sahnoun & Abdennadher, 2018; Kluve, 2010). The impact of these practices on employment differs according to the country and the method chosen, depending on the characteristics of the labor market in the country. There is no full consensus on the effects in the applied literature.

3 Data and Econometric Methodology

In the analysis, annual data of 17 OECD member countries from 1991 to 2015 were used, based on the availability. The countries whose data were used include Australia, Austria, Belgium, Canada, Denmark, Finland, France, Germany, Ireland, Japan, the Netherlands, Norway, Portugal, Spain, Sweden, Switzerland, and the USA.

The impact of active employment policies on unemployment will be tried to be estimated within the framework of the following model.

$$unemp = \beta_{0i} + \beta_{1i} percad + \beta_{2i} Openness + \beta_{3i} active + \varepsilon_{it}$$

As in the time series, it is important to determine the stationarity characteristics of the series in the panel data. Stationarity analysis provides a priori information about the choice of the model estimation method. The correct choice of the estimation method ensures reliable results. Stationarity properties of the series were investigated by LLC panel unit root test developed by Levin et al. (2002) and IPS panel unit root test developed by Im et al. (2003). Both methods test the null hypothesis which suggests that the series are non-stationary. However, while LLC test assumes that the autoregressive parameters are homogenous for all the cross sections, they can change in the IPS test.

The long-term relationship between the series was examined by panel cointegration tests developed by Pedroni (1999) and Westerlund (2006). In the Pedroni (1999) test, seven different tests' statistics developed from the error terms obtained from the panel regression model are used to test the null hypothesis that suggests no cointegration. The cointegration test developed by Westerlund (2006) allows structural breaks and can be used in situations where cross-sectional dependence is existent and non-existent. In this test, the null hypothesis indicates a cointegration.

Estimators of FMOLS developed by Pedroni (2000) and DOLS developed by Kao and Chiang (2000) were used to predict the long term cointegration coefficients between the variables. PMG *(Pooled Mean Group)* estimators developed by Peseran et.al. (1999) were preferred in order to separate long and short-term effects. In the PMG estimator, the assumption is that the long-term coefficients are homogeneous across the cross sections, but that the short-term parameters differ between the cross-sections.

4 Analysis Results

The results of the panel unit root test conducted to investigate the stationarity characteristics of the series are shown in the table below.

The results of the panel root test indicated that the series of the Unemp and Active variables had a unit root. According to the LLC and IPS test statistics, the null hypothesis which expressed the existence of a unit root could not be rejected. At the first difference of these series, the null hypothesis was rejected at a significance of 1 %, and the result was that the series were stationary. The openness variable was found to be stationary based on the results of the LLC test. The results of IPS test indicated that it was stationary in model II, but not in model I. At the first difference, it was seen that the series of the Openness variable were stationary in all test results. The Percad variable was stationary in its level according to the constant model in the LLC test. According to other test results, the null hypothesis could not be rejected. Series were stationary in all test results in the first difference. Based on the results of the unit root test, it was found that the series were stationary and integrated at first order (I).

Tab. 2: Panel Unit Root Tests

Variables	**LLC Model I**	**LLC Model II**	**IPS Model I**	**IPS Model II**
Unemp	-0.018	1.312	-0.530	1.658
Percad	-3.585**	2.446	1.291	4.131
Openness	-1.832*	-3.445**	0.824	-2.999**
Active	-1.179	0.838	0.296	0.648
Δunemp	-6.622**	-6.661**	-6.882**	-5.860**
Δpercad	-7.306**	-9.337**	-6.000**	-6.909**
Δ Openness	-17.058**	-15.132**	-14.423**	-11.963**
Δactive	-12.782**	-10.897**	-12.730**	-10.206**

Note: *Lag lenght selected by Modified Schwarz info criterion. Δ is the difference operator. Model I results based on model with intercetp and Model II results based on model with intercept and trend. ** and * indicates level of significance at 1 % and 5 % respectively.*

The cointegration relationship between the series was examined by the panel cointegration tests of Pedroni (1999) and Westerlund (2006).

According to the results of Pedroni cointegration test, the null hypothesis indicating no cointegration could not be rejected based on the group adf statistic, panel adf statistic and panel pp statistic results. According to these test results, there seems to be a long-term relationship between the variables in the model. Other test statistics (panel v, panel rho, grouprho, grouppp) indicate that there was no long-term cointegration relationship between the variables.

The Westerlund (2006) test results, in which structural breaks were taken into account in the investigation of the cointegration relationship between the series, are displayed in the table below.

According to the test results of Model I and Model II, the null hypothesis that suggested a cointegration could not be rejected. These results indicate a long-term relationship between the series. According to the results of Model 3 and Model 4 which took structural breaks into consideration, no cointegration relationship was detected. However, according to the bootstrapped-p values, which are used when the cross-sectional dependence is taken into consideration, the null hypothesis that suggested a cointegration in all four models could not be rejected even at a significance level of 10 %. Thus, it can be stated that the variables are cointegrated.

The Panel DOLS and Panel FMOLS results, used in estimating the coefficients of the cointegration vector, are shown in Tab. 5. Accordingly, active employment

Tab. 3: Panel Cointegration Tests

Pedroni (1999)	Statistic	P-value
Panel v Statistic	−0.370	0.64
Panel rho statistic	0.608	0.72
Panel PP statistic	−1.340	0.09
Panel ADF statistic	−2.007	0.02
Group rho statistic	2.531	0.99
Group PP statistic	−0.402	0.34
Group ADF statistic	−2.502	0.00
Included Observations	425	

Note: *Pedroni test results based on the model with no intercept and trend. Lag length selected by Akaike information criterion.*

Tab. 4: Westerlund (2006) Panel Cointegration Tests

Model	Description	Statistic	Asym p-value	Boost. p-value
Model 1	No break in constant	0.359	0.360	0.987
Model 2	no break in const & trend	-1.410	0.921	0.753
Model 3	break in const	282.64	0.000	0.162
Model 4	break in const & trend	118.346	0.000	0.491

Note: *Bootstrap p-values were obtained from 1000 replications. Maximum break number is taken 4.*

Tab. 5: Panel DOLS and Panel FMOLS Estimation Results

	DOLS	FMOLS
Percad	−0.0007*	−0.0007*
Openness	0.0141	0.0024
Active	−1.2802*	−2.6450*
R-Squared	0.913	0.829

Note: *The number of differenced lags/leads determined by Akaike information criterion in DOLS estimation. * indicates the level of significance at 1 % level.*

policies have a negative impact on unemployment. According to the estimation results of both DOLS and FMOLS, the coefficient of the active variable was negative and significant at 1 %. Therefore, active employment policies had a positive contribution to the fight against unemployment.

Both estimators indicate a statistically significant and negative relationship between GDP per capita and unemployment rate. This result supports the phenomenon known as the Okun Law (Okun, 1962) in the literature, which indicates that the increases in economic growth reduce unemployment. However, the value of the growth coefficients obtained from both estimates was quite low. Although there was a significant negative relationship, the impact of economic growth on decreasing unemployment was very weak, since the coefficient was very low. In fact, this situation suggests a jobless growth phenomenon. Economic growth may not always lead to an increase in employment for various reasons, such as problems related to the labor market, increase in productivity brought by technological development, structural changes in the economy (Çaşkurlu, 2014).

A positive relationship was found between the openness variable and unemployment. However, this relationship was not statistically significant. There have been different views in both theoretical and empirical studies conducted on the effect of openness on unemployment. While there are studies which have revealed that the impact of openness on unemployment is negative, there are also studies indicating positive results (Yanikkaya, 2013; Gozgor, 2014; Felbermayr et al. 2011).

The PMG estimation results for the decomposition of short term and long-term dynamics are given in Tab. 6. The assumption of the PMG estimator that the long-term coefficients were homogeneous between the units was tested with

Tab. 6: PMG Estimation Results (Peseran et al. 1999)

Variable	Coefficient	Std. Error
Long-Run		
Percad	−0.0054***	0.0000
Openness	−0.1808***	0.0433
Active	−5.6825***	2.1536
Short-Run		
EC	−0.0836***	0.0226
Δpercad	−0.0080***	0.0226
Δ Openness	0.0240*	0.0002
Δactive	−0.0541	0.7874
Constant	4.3572***	1.1748
Hausman test	3.41 (p value =0.18)	

Note: *Δ is the difference operator, EC corresponds to the error correction term. The null hypothesis in the Hausman test is homogeneity of the long-run coefficient in the PMG estimation. *** and * indicates the level of significance at 1 % and 10 % respectively.*

the Hausman test. It was seen that the long-term coefficients were homogeneous according to the result of the Hausman test performed after the model established was estimated with PMG and MG method. According to the PMG estimation results, as in the FMOLS and DOLS estimations, economic growth and active employment policies had an effect decreasing unemployment. A one point increase in openness rate leads to a 0.18 point decrease in unemployment.

When the short term dynamics were examined, the error correction coefficient was found to be negative and significant, which supported the long-run relationship between the variables. This coefficient also shows the convergence rate of the deviations in the equilibrium in the short-run to the next long-run equilibrium (8 %). In the short-run, it was seen that economic growth had a negative impact on unemployment with a significance at 1 % and openness had a positive effect with significance at 10 %. The impact of openness on unemployment differed in the short and long-run. In the short-run, active employment policies had no significant effect on unemployment.

5 Concluding Remarks

Regardless of their development level, countries face the problem of unemployment. Economic conditions that have changed under the influence of globalization have also brought up the productive capacity of the countries and hence the imbalances in the labor market. Countries are implementing ALMPs to increase the productivity and mobility of the labor, especially in order to fight against structural unemployment. The effectiveness of ALMPs, which are among the policy recommendations of international organizations such as the OECD, is controversial. There is no complete consensus on the effectiveness of these policies in studies that handle the subject from the macro and micro-economic perspectives in the literature.

The impact of ALMP on unemployment was considered in terms of public expenditure spent on these policies in the study. In the analysis of the data of 17 OECD countries between 1991 and 2015, it was found out that the expenditures on ALMPs had an effect decreasing unemployment in the long-run, but did not have a significant impact in the short-run. Another consequence of the analysis is that economic growth had a little effect on reducing unemployment in the long and short-run. Based on these results, ALMPs had a stronger effect on reducing unemployment compared to economic growth.

These results were obtained from the data of developed countries. Undoubtedly, many factors such as the development level of the country, characteristics of the labor market, education level, institutional structure and quality affect the employment level. It is also important to consider the ALMPs in a comprehensive evaluation framework by performing their benefit-cost analysis.

References

Baker, D., Glyn, A., Howell, D., and Schmitt, J. (2003). "Labor Market Institutions and Unemployment: A Critical Assessment of the Cross-country Evidence". Center for European Studies Working Paper Series No. 98.

Bassanini, A., and Duval, R. (2006). "Employment Patterns in OECD Countries: Reassessing the Role of Policies and Institutions". OECD Economics Department Working Papers No. 486. OECD Publishing (NJ1).

Biçerli, M. K. (2005). "Aktif İstihdam Politikaları İşsizliği Azaltır Mı?" Çimento İşveren Dergisi, 6(19): 4–15.

Boeri, T., and Van Ours, J. (2008). The Economics of Imperfect Labor Markets. Princeton: Princeton University Press.

Boone, J., and Van Ours, J. C. (2004). "Effective Active Labor Market Policies". IZA Discussion Paper Series. IZA DP No 1335.

Brown, A. J., and Koettl, J. (2015). "Active Labor Market Programs-Employment Gain or Fiscal Drain?" IZA Journal of Labor Economics, 4(1): 12.

Calmfors, L. (1994). Active Labour Market Policy and Unemployment: A Framework for the Analysis of Crucial Design Features. OECD Economic Studies No. 22.

Calmfors, L., Forslund, A., and Hemström, M. (2004). The Effects of Active Labor-Market Policies in Sweden: What Is the Evidence?, in J. Agell, M. J. Keen, & A. J. Weichenreider (Eds.) Labor Market Institutions and Public Regulation (pp. 1–62). Cambridge, MA: MIT Press.

Çaşkurlu, E. (2014). "İstihdamsız Büyüme (İstihdamsız İyileşme) Sorununa Karşı Kamusal Politikalar ve Önemi: Türkiye Açısından Bir Değerlendirme". Amme İdaresi Dergisi, 47(2): 43–76.

EC (2006). Labour Market Policy Database Methodology. European Commission 2006, http://ec.europa.eu/eurostat/documents/3859598/5896441/KS-BF-06-003EN.PDF/51701111-3a9e-4aca-99e7-44c4cfe2f93d?version=1.0 (Accessed on 19.07.2018).

Escudero, V. (2015). "Are Active Labour Market Policies Effective in Activating and Integrating Low-Skilled Individuals?" An International Comparison. PSE Working Papers No 2015-01.

Estevão, M. (2003). "Do Active Labor Market Policies Increase Employment?" IMF Working Paper No: WP/03/234. International Monetary Fund.

Felbermayr, G., Prat, J., and Schmerer, H. J. (2011). "Trade and Unemployment: What Do the Data Say?" European Economic Review, 55(6): 741–758.

Forslund, A., and Krueger, A. (2010). "Did Active Labor Market Policies Help Sweden Rebound from the Depression of the Early 1990s?" in Reforming the Welfare State: Recovery and Beyond in Sweden. University of Chicago Press.

Gozgor, G. (2014). "The Impact of Trade Openness on the Unemployment Rate in G7 Countries". The Journal of International Trade & Economic Development, 23(7): 1018–1037.

Im, K. S., Pesaran, M. H., and Shin, Y. (2003). "Testing for Unit Roots in Heterogeneous Panels". Journal of Econometrics, 115: 53–63.

Kao, C., and Chiang, M-H. (2000). "On the Estimation and Inference of a Cointegrated Regression in Panel Data", in Baltagi, B. H. et al. eds., Nonstationary Panels, Panel Cointegration and Dynamic Panels, 15, Amsterdam: Elsevier, 179–222.

Kluve, J. (2010). "The Effectiveness of European Active Labor Market Programs". Labour Economics, 17(6): 904–918.

Levin, A.; Lin, C., and Shin, C. J. (2002). "Unit Root Tests in Panel Data: Asymptotic and Finite-Sample Properties". Journal of Econometrics, 108: 1–24.

Nickell, S. (1997). "Unemployment and Labor Market Rigidities: Europe versus North America". Journal of Economic Perspectives, 11(3): 55–74.

Nie, J., and Struby, E. (2011). Would Active Labor Market Policies Help Combat High Us Unemployment? Economic Review-Federal Reserve Bank of Kansas City, Third Quarter, 35–69.

OECD (1994). The OECD Jobs Study: Facts, Analysis and Strategies. OECD Publishing https://www.oecd.org/els/emp/1941679.pdf, (Accessed on 19.07.2018).

Okun, A. (1962)."Potential Gnp: Its Measurement and Significance", in Proceedings of the Business and Economic Statistics Section of the American Statistical Association, 7: 89–104.

Pedroni, P. (1999). "Critical Values for Cointegration Tests in Heterogeneous Panels with Multiple Regressors". Oxford Bulletin of Economics and Statistics, 61(S1): 653–670.

Pedroni, P. (2000). "Fully Modified OLS for Heterogeneous Cointegrated Panels," in Baltagi, B. H. ed., Nonstationary Panels, Panel Cointegration and Dynamic Panels, 15, Amsterdam: Elsevier, 93–130.

Pesaran, M. H., Shin, Y., and Smith, R. P. (1999). "Pooled Mean Group Estimation of Dynamic Heterogeneous Panels". Journal of the American Statistical Association, 94(446): 621–634.

Sahnoun, M., and Abdennadher, C. (2018). "The Assessment of Active Labor Market Policies: Evidence from OECD Countries". Economia Politica, 1–27.

Westerlund, J. (2006). "Testing for Panel Cointegration with Multiple Structural Breaks". Oxford Bulletin of Economics and Statistics, 68(1): 101–132.

Yanikkaya, H. (2013). "Is Trade Liberalization a Solution to the Unemployment Problem?" Portuguese Economic Journal, 12(1): 57–85.

Basak Dogan[1]

Challenges for Managers in the Near Future

1 Introduction

Management is one of the few cases that are considered to be the same age as the history of humanity. Along with the development of humanity, management assumed the task of establishing a balance and order in every field it was applied in a character that could keep up with the emerging changes. At this point, important tasks fall to individuals who are defined as managers and apply the management work.

Manager can be defined as a person who works with others and tries to achieve the goals of the organizations, using his/her accumulation of knowledge and individual skills and abilities in the field of management (Koçel, 2015, p. 85). The success of a manager is measured by how much the organization can achieve its goals. A manager who wants to be successful should adapt himself/herself and his/her organization to the changing environmental conditions.

The changes occurring in organizations' environmental conditions may create pressure on organizational structures and force organizations to become faster and more flexible working mechanisms. Therefore, to review the factors like employees, organizational culture interacting with the organizational structure, and the decisions taken and practices implemented to make the organizational structure functional may come into question. Even in some cases, environmental changes may have effects that will completely change the organizations' reasons for existence, their goals and the organizational strategies that will take them wherever they want to reach in the future.

The environmental changes that have taken place recently and are taking place nowadays lead to a number of difficulties that need to be coped with for managers in the near future, within the scope of a system approach and by influencing each other and organizations with successive effects. Among these changes, it is foreseen that the fact that the employees of Industry 4.0 and generation Z get into business life will have significant effects on organizations. What can managers do in the face of these effects? Which steps can they take to continue the existence of the organizations they manage and to be successful? It is first necessary to explain these two concepts to be able to give answers to these questions.

---

1 Asist.Prof.Dr., Kırklareli University, School of Applied Sciences.

2 Industry 4.0

Industry 4.0, which came to the fore for the first time at the Hanover Fair in 2011, is defined as the smart production period during which all living and non-living objects with a certain economic value can communicate and interact with other objects through internet connections along with the developments in the fields of artificial intelligence, 3D (three-dimensional) printers, robotics and bio, nano and space technology (Aksoy, 2017, p. 37).

This period, which has begun to be discussed very recently, is also referred to as the Fourth Industrial Revolution since it shares similarities identical to some developments that have changed the course of the world and can be regarded as a revolution. It is stated that the basic dynamic that distinguishes Industry 4.0 from three other industrial revolutions that occurred prior to it is that this revolution has been triggered not by economic, political or social events but by technological developments and progresses (Görçün, 2017) and that these technological developments and progresses are based on Internet technology that allows people to communicate with machines (Brettel, Friederichsen, Keller and Rosenberg, 2014, p. 37).

It is necessary to understand the bases of Industry 4.0 to understand its effects it can create on organizations. For this reason, let's review the industrial revolutions experienced priorly (they are also expressed visually in Fig. 1) though briefly:

- Industry 1.0 (First Industrial Revolution) refers to the period that started in England in the 18th century and during which steam powered machines were invented and began to be used in the industrialization process. Industry 1.0 is a period that influenced all existing industrial relations (Görçün, 2017, p. 5), as well as social, economic, political and cultural factors, and thus the organizations. While there was a low volume and relatively slow production in the workshop-type production centers where labor-intensive manufacturing was more at the forefront in the previous period, steam powered machines led to a significant increase in production amount and production rate. Organizational structures, that are the basis of modern businesses, emerged. Within the new order brought by mechanization, capital intensity came into question and the implementation of new organizational practices became a necessity. Workers, managers and entrepreneurial classes (Küçükkalay, 1997) also appeared during the Industry 1.0 period.
- Industry 2.0 (Second Industrial Revolution): The fact that the electrical energy was included in the industrialization process and began to be used in production is regarded as the main development that pave the way for transition to

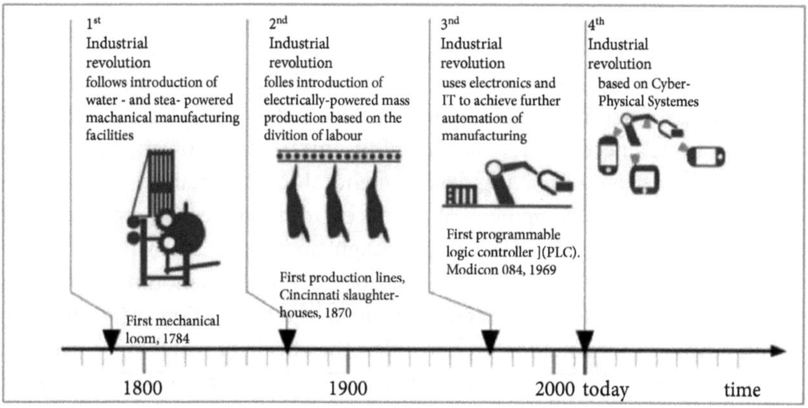

Fig. 1: Historical development of industries. Source: http://ecipe.org/blog/manufacturing-the-future/

Industry 2.0. In this period, a development process was initiated in the sense of general functioning and management practices in organizations along with the fact that scientific methods for management began to be discussed. The fact that the applications such as the division of labor and specialization, determination of managerial functions indicated in Frederick Taylor's work entitled Principles of Scientific Management dated 1911 and in Henri Fayol's work entitled General and Industrial Management dated 1916 were actually used by entrepreneurs like Henry Ford took the efficiency of the production processes to quite different dimensions.

The developments such as the simultaneous inclusion of petroleum energy in the industrialization process, then the development of the plastic industry, and the discovery of simple engines and their use in production (Görçün, 2017) took place during Industry 2.0 and opened the door of the next industrial revolution.

- Industry 3.0 (Third Industrial Revolution) is an automation period that started from the 1970s and during which electricity began to be used in serial production (Davutoğlu, Akgül and Yıldız, 2017) and programable machines were seen in production for the first time along with the combination use of electronics and information technologies (Görçün, 2017). Thus, mechanical and electronic technologies began to be replaced by digital technologies. So, the changes taking place in production systems led to transformations in the structures of the organizations, and more flexible organizations (matrix, network, virtual organizations, etc.) began to be formed with the effect of the System Approach and Contingency Approach. Along with the fact that strategic thinking thoroughly gained a place in organizational practices, the occurrence of significant paradigm shifts revealed that adaptation to the environment was a necessity for sustainability. This period also paved the way for a number of groundbreaking developments since it contained the advances that enabled the development of advanced technologies (microelectronics, internet, computers, etc.) (Davutoğlu, Akgül and Yıldız, 2017)).

- Industry 4.0 (Fourth Industrial Revolution) is a phenomenon resulting from the combination of ideas aimed at ensuring the integration of the industry with advanced information technologies, the effects of which have begun to be seen over the past decade. In this process, which is based on the production based on cyber-physical systems, it is aimed to maximize efficiency in production by means of the robotic technologies.

Industry 4.0 focuses on production systems that do not need a human factor (Görçün, 2017, p. 141). In the factories that are described as "smart", it is aimed to construct a production system based on self-operated (autonomous) machines and based on perfected industrial processes (Görçün, 2017, p. 142). Therefore, the exclusion of human, who is one of the basic production factors (labor, labor force, man power), from production system will come to the fore.

The removal of human-induced mistake, and ensuring a full standardization in production processes by excluding human factor from production processes are regarded as the practices that will increase the organizational efficiency in the Industry 4.0 process. However, how much it is possible to take the human factor out of production processes completely is also a disputed issue.

Schwab (2017, p. 45) indicated that there are roughly two opposing views regarding the effect of Industry 4.0 on labor markets:

- Those who argue that the workers who are made unemployed by technology will find new jobs and that technology will initiate a new welfare period.
- Those believe that this process will lead to an increasing social and political armageddon by creating massive technological unemployment.

The view that the human factor, which has been considered as one of the basic factors of production since classical economists, cannot be completely abstracted from the production processes and that the human factor has to be used not in the functioning of these systems but in the design and implementation stages is an accepted view for the present. However, it is highly probable that there will be a differentiation in the nature of human factor. Employees who will follow the developments in technology and have the qualifications to adapt to them will be positioned at a different point from the current employee profile.

With respect to the qualifications of workers, as a result of adaptation to technology, there are predictions that the mass of people who are now described as white-collar and who represent the educated/senior or mid-level manager will continue their existence in business life and that the mass of people who are described as blue-collar and who represent the uneducated/worker class will stay out of the business life. These predictions were mentioned in the report entitled Mastering the Fourth Industrial Revolution on the World Economic Forum website, that gathered with the theme of Industry 4.0 in 2016. Then, worrying predictions that it could lead to a global unemployment problem along with a successive effect, especially countries with advanced industrialized countries, were put forward. It is also necessary to take into consideration that unemployment is a triggering factor for some social problems. Therefore, although Industry 4.0 has been triggered not by economic, political or social events but by technological developments and progresses, it may lead to the emergence of situations that will trigger economic, political or social events when some developments that may occur during this process are taken into account.

Görçün (2017, p. 159) states that automation and robots can be used instead of labor force during Industry 4.0 process for the works that do not create an added value or cause non-productiveness when used. Since such works can be performed by any worker and do not require expertise, it will be possible to utilize the specialized labor force in the works requiring higher added value and expertise. Therefore, when we consider from this point of view, it is possible to say that the importance of applications that will create added value and increase efficiency for organizations will increase gradually.

It is admitted that the Industry 4.0 process will change the nature of working in all sectors and professions. But here, there is an uncertainty on to what extent automation will replace the labor force, how much time it will take, and how much it will go further (Schwab, 2017, p. 44–45). It is stated that employment will increase in high income-generating, cognitive and creative works and in paradoxically low income-generating handicrafts but will largely decrease in middle income-generating routine and repetitive works in the near future (Schwab, 2017, p. 47).

In an article on the internet page of the International Robotic Federation (cited by: Özdoğan, 2017, p. 67), it is stated that 1 million industrial robots are used today and that these robots are responsible for the formation of about 3 million new jobs. It is predicted that employment ratios will increase in THE sectors such as consumer electronics, food, solar and wind energy and advanced battery production, along with the continued use and spread of industrial robots. According to a research conducted by Metra Martech market research company (cited by: Özdoğan, 2017, p. 68), it has been revealed that the amount of industrial robots is inversely proportional to unemployment in Brazil, Japan, China, South Korea, Germany and the United States.

Ultimately, the goal in the Industry 4.0 process is not to cease the use of human factor in production processes but to increase the importance of the human factor in organizations and to increase employment opportunities by developing appropriate skills in technology.

3 Generation Z

The time intervals formed by economic and social movements around the world are expressed by the concept of generation. The individuals who are indicated to be in the same generation are born in the years close to each other, have similar characteristics due to shared social and historical events and show similar reactions to events (Çetin Aydın and Başol, 2014).

Some studies concerning how organizations can be better managed have divided the changes in characteristics which can be observed in humans into generations and attempted to understand the characteristics of people the managers will work with by examining the characteristics of each generation (Koçel, 2015, p. 572). To know the characteristics of people on the basis of generations may help managers to put better managerial practices into practice.

When the period from the end of the World War II up to the present is examined, the generations that are involved or are likely to involved in business life can be classified as shown in Tab. 1:

The Traditionalists and Baby Population Explosion Period generations are not involved in business life as of today. Generation Z get a start in a new business life. Therefore, nowadays, although Generation Z is mainly involved in business life, we also see the presence of the employees of both Generation X and Generation Y.

Another challenge that managers are likely to face in the near future will be the uncertainty about the employees of Generation Z who have just begun to make their presence felt in business life. Many regulations and practices in business life, in which Generation X and Generation Y are mainly involved, have been developed or adapted according to the employees of Generation X and Generation Y. How much will Generation Z who have just begun to be involved in business life be able to adopt these regulations and practices? How positively or negatively will the diversity resulting from the coexistence of the Generations X, Y and Z affect the organizations?

Tab. 1: Generations in business life. Source: Koçel, T. (2015) İşletme Yöneticiliği, p. 572

		Age range as of 2018*	General description
Those born before 1945	Traditionalists	73 and above	Acquiescence
Those born between 1946–1964	Baby Population Explosion Period	between 54–72	Normativeness
Those born between 1965–1976	GenerationX	between 42–53	Competitiveness
Those born between 1977–1997	GenerationY	between 21–41	Creativeness
Those born after 1998	GenerationZ	20 and below	Affectivity

* *The age ranges are expressed as of 2014 in the original form of the table.*

There will be a number of points that require the harmonization of the Generations X, Y and Z for a more efficient and effective use of human factor, which is considered as the most important strategic source of businesses, and the most important responsibility for this harmonization will be on the shoulders of managers.

It is accepted that the Generation X emerged in the period during which the revolutionary changes in information and communication technologies began to appear (transition period between Industry 2.0 and Industry 3.0). They were also adapted to these changes by gradually learning during their lives. They are generally sensitive to social problems and are satisfied. The fact that they have high motivation, are respectful to authority and have competitive characteristics in business life (Koçel, 2015) is also the basic characteristics of this generation.

Generation Z is highly dependent on Internet technology and social media tools that develop accordingly since they were born and grown in a period during which revolutionary changes in information and communication technologies were quite advanced. The facts that they have low faithfulness, prefer having fun to working, that they want to live the moment they are in are their typical characteristics. Generation Y with a quite dominant entrepreneurship characteristic in business life seeks for a meaning in the works and prefer their guiding managerial qualities like coaching and mentorship to authoritarian managerial qualities (Koçel, 2015). The encouragement of them to produce innovative ideas and the appreciation of them for the contributions they make to the functioning appear a need in business life for Generation Y (Çetin Aydın and Başol, 2014). Therefore, spiritual factors can be easily used to motivate this generation.

Generation Z refers to a generation that is predicted to differ from previous generations since they were born and grown up in a digital age. It is accepted that Generation Z has digital knowledge and skills without needing for any extra education and that internet technologies and digital equipments are parts of their daily life (Somyürek, 2014). Therefore, it is quite reasonable idea that this generation can be very easily adapted to the digitalization that is expected to be experienced in business life along with the Industry 4.0.

Although strengths and weaknesses associated with business life of the individuals of Generation Z have not been clearly determined since they are not yet in business life, it is predicted that those in this generation may be unfaithful to the brands and the organizations they work with, may not be determined and ambitious, and can give up easily because they are bored quickly (Çetin Aydın and Başol, 2014) due to their low sense of belonging (Taş, Demirdöğmez and Küçükoğlu, 2017). Since Generation Z is accepted as a generation who mainly likes acting individually instead of team work and who can create the areas where they can express themselves (Taş et al., 2017), they will have positive attributes such as creativity, seeking rights, being more successful than other generations with respect to different sociological groups, as well as compelling requests to personalize everything and unwillingness to do standard works (Çetin Aydın and Başol, 2014). The fact that Generation Z has creative, multiple attention and multiple decision-making skills (Altuntuğ, 2012, s. 206) will also increase the contribution they will make to their organizations.

4 Conclusion and Suggestions

When all resources in an organization are used effectively and efficiently and the goals of the organization are achieved, it is obvious that important tasks fall to managers. Managers may sometimes face some difficulties with respect to ensuring that all components that make up the organization work in harmony and the harmonization of environmental changes with the organization.

In today's rapidly changing world, managers are constantly facing environmental changes each passing day, and these changes, resulting from almost multiplier effect of globalization, bring out unpredictable uncertainties for organizations. Industry 4.0 and the Generation Z who have just begun to be involved in business life can be mentioned as two important uncertainties that may lead managers to face some difficulties in the near future.

Industry 4.0 is a phenomenon that has the principle of increasing productivity using self-managing cyber-physical systems and therefore anticipates excluding the human factor, which is one of the important strategic resources of organizations, from production. This phenomenon, which is characterized as the Fourth Industrial Revolution, will inevitably affect the labor force all over the world. At this point, managers should structure their organizations in such a way that cyber-physical systems work together with the human factor in order not to face a dilemma like "machine against man" (Schwab, 2017, p. 49). The applications such as designing organizational structures with a flexibility to adapt to possible changes, and making organizational cultures education-oriented with the aim of understanding constantly evolving knowledge and technology and increasing the qualifications of employees can be suggested in this context.

The harmonization of Generation Z, which is considered to very easily adapt to the Industry 4.0 process, with the organizations designed for the employees of Generations X and Y is necessary for organizations to be successful in the future. It is anticipated that the works that generation Z-work will work will be quite different from the works described today. For this reason, managers can get more efficient results by supporting this generation on how they can improve their qualifications to adapt to the works that may emerge instead of teaching them what to do. The applications such as flexible working hours, creating an organizational culture that supports creativity, acting in a communication-oriented manner, and trying to create a collective contribution by creating an individual working area in technology-supported offices will be useful to achieve the maximum efficiency from the employees of Generation Z.

References

Aksoy, S. (2017). "Değişen Teknolojiler ve Endüstri 4.0: Endüstri 4.0'ı Anlamaya Dair Bir Giriş", *SAV (Sosyal Araştırmalar Vakfı) Katkı*, Nisan (4): 34–44.

Altuntuğ, N. (2012). "Kuşaktan Kuşağa Tüketim Olgusu ve Geleceğin Tüketici Profili", *Organizasyon ve Yönetim Bilimleri Dergisi*, 4(1): 203–212.

Brettel, M., Friederichsen, N., Keller, M. and Rosenberg, M. (2014). "How Virtualization, Decentralization and Network Building Change the Manufacturing Landscape: An Industry 4.0 Perspective", *International Scholarly and Scientific Research & Innovation*, 8(1): 37–44.

Çetin Aydın, G. and Başol, O. (2014). "X ve Y Kuşağı: Çalışmanın Anlamında Bir Değişme Var mı?" *Electronic Journal of Vocational Collages*, 4(4): 1–15.

Çetin, C. and Karalar, S. (2016). "X, Y ve Z Kuşağı Öğrencilerin Çok Yönlü ve Sınırsız Kariyer Algılamaları Üzerine Bir Araştırma", *Yönetim Bilimleri Dergisi*, 14(28): 157–197.

Davutoğlu, N. A., Akgül, B., Yıldız, E. (2017). "İşletme Yönetiminde Sanayi 4.0 Kavramı ile Farkındalık Oluşturarak Etkin Bir Şekilde Değişimi Sağlamak", *Akademik Sosyal Araştırmalar Dergisi*, Eylül (52): 544–567.

Dünya Ekonomik Forumu (Şubat 2016). Mastering the Fourth Industrial Revolution. Accessed: 05.07.2018, http://www3.weforum.org/docs/WEF_AM16_Report.pdf

European Centre for International Political Economy. Manufacturing the Future: Industry 4.0. Accessed: 13.07.2018, http://ecipe.org/blog/manufacturing-the-future/

Görçün, Ö. F. (2017). *Dördüncü Endüstri Devrimi: Endüstri 4.0.* İstanbul: Beta.

Koçel, T. (2015). *İşletme Yöneticiliği.* İstanbul: Beta.

Küçükkalay, M. (1997). "Endüstri Devrimi ve Ekonomik Sonuçlarının Analizi", *Süleyman Demirel Üniversitesi İktisadi ve İdari Bilimler Fakültesi Dergisi*, Güz (2): 51–68.

Özdoğan, O. (2017). *Endüstri 4.0: Dördüncü Sanayi Devrimi ve Endüstriyel Dönüşümün Anahtarları.* İstanbul: Pusula.

Schwab, K. (2017). *Dördüncü Sanayi Devrimi.* İstanbul: Optimist.

Somyürek, S. (2014). "Öğrenme Sürecinde Z Kuşağının Dikkatini Çekme: Artırılmış Gerçeklik", *Eğitim Teknolojisi - Kuram ve Uygulama*, 4(1): 63–80.

Taş, H. Y., Demirdöğmez, M. and Küçükoğlu, M. (2017). "Geleceğimiz Olan Z Kuşağının Çalışma Hayatına Muhtemel Etkileri", OPUS - Uluslararası Toplum Araştırmaları Dergisi, 7(13): 1031–1048.

Birol Erkan[1] and Elif Tugce Bozduman[2]

A Research on Comparative Advantages in Germany's Technology-Intensive Exports

1 Introduction

Germany is one of the few advanced countries in the world economy with a share of manufacturing industry in gross value added of around 20 %. In many technology-based product groups, it is not wrong to say that the first country that comes to mind in the world is Germany. As most indicators show, Germany's manufacturing sector is particularly strong in the field of middle-range technologies and earned the country important market shares in world trade.

Nevertheless, the global advantages of developed countries such as Germany have declined relatively in recent years. The most important reason for this is the technological developments in developing countries, particularly China and e Republic of Korea which are less affected by the global economic crisis. Due to the recent technological investments of countries such as China and a number of relative cost advantages, the share of global added value of developed countries such as Germany has gradually decreased.

When the Gross Domestic Product (GDP) of the countries is analyzed, it is observed that there are significant changes in the ranking of the top countries after the year 2000. While China's position in the GDP rankings was 7 at the beginning of the 2000s, it has started to increase since 2005 (Tab. 1).

Germany, which followed the US and Japan in the world GDP rankings between 2000 and 2006, lost its place to China and Japan in the following years. However, there is a similar issue in the export order of the world. Until 2008, Germany, the leader of world exports, could not protect its place and left it to China. (Tab. 2).

According to standard macroeconomic indicators (Tab. 3), the German economy has been outperforming other member countries of the European Union during the recent Great Recession and the still ongoing European financial crisis (Federico Foders, 2014). Germany's economic growth rate was negative in 2009 due to the global economic crisis and the euro crisis. Nevertheless, Germany's

1 Assoc. Prof. Dr., Uşak University, birol.erkan@usak.edu.tr.
2 PhD Student, Uşak University, tugcebozduman@gmail.com.

Tab. 1: World GDP Ranking (Top 5, 2000–2016). Source: (https://datacatalog.worldbank.org/dataset/gdp-ranking)

Rank	**2000**	**2001**	**2002**	**2003**	**2004**	**2005**	**2006**	**2007**	**2008**
1	US	US	US	EU	EU	EU	EU	EU	EU
2	EU	EU	EU	US	US	US	US	US	US
3	Japan	Japan	Japan	Japan	Japan	Japan	Japan	Japan	Japan
4	***Germany***	***Germany***	***Germany***	***Germany***	***Germany***	***Germany***	***Germany***	China	China
5	UK	UK	UK	UK	UK	UK	China	***Germany***	***Germany***
Rank	**2009**	**2010**	**2011**	**2012**	**2013**	**2014**	**2015**	**2016**	
1	EU	EU	EU	EU	EU	EU	US	US	
2	US	US	US	US	US	US	EU	EU	
3	Japan	China	China	China	China	China	China	China	
4	China	Japan	Japan	Japan	Japan	Japan	Japan	Japan	
5	***Germany***	***Germany***	***Germany***	***Germany***	***Germany***	***Germany***	***Germany***	***Germany***	

Tab. 2: World Export Ranking (Top 5, 2000–2016). Source: (https://data.worldbank.org/country/china?view=chart)

Rank	**2000**	**2001**	**2002**	**2003**	**2004**	**2005**	**2006**	**2007**	**2008**
1	US	US	US	***Germany***	***Germany***	***Germany***	***Germany***	***Germany***	***Germany***
2	***Germany***	***Germany***	***Germany***	US	US	US	China	China	China
3	Japan	Japan	Japan	Japan	China	China	US	US	US
4	France	France	China	China	Japan	Japan	Japan	Japan	Japan
5	UK	UK	France	France	France	France	France	France	France
Rank	**2009**	**2010**	**2011**	**2012**	**2013**	**2014**	**2015**	**2016**	
1	China	China	China	China	China	China	China	China	
2	***Germany***	***Germany***	***Germany***	***Germany***	***Germany***	***Germany***	***Germany***	***Germany***	
3	US	US	US	US	US	US	US	US	
4	Japan	Japan	Japan	Japan	Japan	Japan	Japan	Japan	
5	France	France	France	France	Holland	Korea	Korea	Korea	

Tab. 3: Various Macro-Economic Indicators of German. Source: The World Bank Data (https://data.worldbank.org/)

Years	GDP (billion $)	GDP growth (%)	GDP per capita ($)	Unemployment (%)	Inflation (%)	Current Balance (%GDP)	Import (billion $)	Export (billion $)	Openness to Trade (%)
2000	1.950	2,96	23.817	7,92	–0,45	–1,73	595	601	61,33
2001	1.951	1,69	23.678	7,77	1,27	–0,36	587	621	61,92
2002	2.079	0,00	25.205	8,48	1,35	1,91	586	677	60,75
2003	2.506	–0,71	30.359	9,78	1,20	1,43	724	816	61,45
2004	2.819	1,17	34.165	10,73	1,09	4,47	857	999	65,84
2005	2.861	0,70	34.696	11,17	0,62	4,60	935	1.080	70,43
2006	3.002	3,70	36.447	10,25	0,30	5,70	1.078	1.237	77,12
2007	3.440	3,26	41.814	8,66	1,69	6,78	1.251	1.480	79,39
2008	3.752	1,08	45.699	7,52	0,83	5,62	1.407	1.631	80,97
2009	3.418	–5,61	41.732	7,74	1,75	5,81	1.123	1.292	70,66
2010	3.417	4,08	41.785	6,97	0,75	5,64	1.266	1.444	79,31
2011	3.758	3,66	46.810	5,82	1,07	6,08	1.500	1.684	84,73
2012	3.544	0,49	44.065	5,38	1,54	7,02	1.414	1.630	85,89
2013	3.753	0,49	46.530	5,23	1,96	6,74	1.480	1.704	84,84
2014	3.891	1,93	48.042	4,98	1,79	7,43	1.509	1.778	84,48
2015	3.376	1,74	41.323	4,62	2,01	8,91	1.312	1.582	85,72
2016	3.478	1,94	42.232	4,12	1,32	8,54	1.327	1.604	84,27
2017	3.677	2,22	44.469	3,73	1,53	8,07	1.459	1.737	86,92

economic growth rate has been around 2 percent in recent years. Germany's per capita income has doubled in the last 17 years. Germany has suffered the least damage from the effects of the economic crisis and has succeeded in bringing the unemployment rate to the ideal levels (about 4 percent). At the same time, the country has reached the optimal level of inflation (average 2 percent). Germany's foreign trade is surplus and the ratio of current surplus to GDP is very high (8 percent). In addition, In addition, openness to trade in Germany has been steadily rising. In other words, Germany opens out more every year.

2 Methodology

In the study, it is aimed to find out comparative advantages in Germany's export according to technology level (factor intensities). In this context, at the outset, revealed comparative advantages (RCA) are calculated for the purpose of measuring the comparative advantages of Germany's export between 2000–2016 by using Balassa Index (RCA) and Vollrath Index (RXA). However, symmetric states of RCA (RSCA) is calculated as well. Then, with regard to the data of the year 2016 and the SITC Rev.3 classification, the comparative advantages of Germany were tried to be determined in the 10 product groups with the highest exports in the world.

RCA indices are calculated using UN Statistics Office, International Standard Industrial Classification (ISIC Rev.3) and Standard International Trade Classification (SITC). Germany's technological RCA indices are calculated using "appropriate average" values. The appropriate average refers to taking the arithmetic average of the remaining series by eliminating the highest and lowest values in a series (http://www.statistics.com/resources/glossary/t/trimmean.php). If an arithmetic mean is used, the export figures of some sectors (and thus the revealed comparative advantage coefficients calculated by us) may be periodically very low or too high. For this reason, "appropriate average" values of the series are calculated so that the assessment can be healthier.

3 Literature Review

The Theory of Absolute Advantages which is the first theory of international trade was put forth by Adam Smith (1766) (Smith, 1991). According to Smith, countries should export goods they can produce at a lower price, and import what they produce at a higher cost. Ricardo's first theoretical contribution is not related to the prices of countries' own manufactured goods. According to Ricardo, a country must trade foreign goods on the basis of price differences in relative terms relative to the product in the other country (Ricardo, 1817). According to Ricardo's theory of comparative advantage, a country must export goods that it can produce relatively cheaply (at lower labor cost) than its trading partners, vice versa. In this case, the gains from foreign trade will both maximize the country's prosperity and increase the world economic prosperity with the free trade channel (Sharma, 2004).

Comparative advantages are one of the basic concepts used in international trade. However, empirical measurement of the concept is difficult. Because the concept of comparative advantage is defined in terms of relative autosurvey prices that cannot be observed in the post-trade balance. For this reason, if the concept of comparative advantages should be measured empirically, then post-trade data should be used (Veeramani, 2006).

There are many indices that are used to measure competitiveness. The most important of these is, of course, Balassa's Revealed Comparative Advantages (RCA) Index. According to Balassa, RCA measures changes in relative price differences of production factors by measuring the relative trading performance of the country in certain commodities (William A. Messina, 2001). It has been possible to identify which sectors have potential competitive advantage and disadvantage through the use of comparative advantage coefficients, such as the Balassa Index (Ramirez, 2004).

Balassa Index (RCA) is formulated as $(X_{ij}/X_j)/(X_{iw}/X_w)$ (Balassa, 1965):

In this formula, 'j' represents the country, 'i' product group, and 'w' represents the world. While the fractional share represents the domestic specialization in the mentioned form, the denominator also shows the world's specialization (Erkan, 2012). The fact that the index value is greater than 1 shows the comparative advantage of the country's exports of that product, vice versa. If the RCA coefficient is between 1 and 2, it has a weak comparative advantage, between 2 and 4 it has a comparative advantage at medium level, and at 4 and above it has a strong comparative advantage (Jeroen Hinloopen, 2001).

Vollrath Index, unlike Balassa Index, prevents double counting of countries and sectors (Erkan, 2016). Thus, competitive power values can be calculated more realistically. If a sector (product) in a country has a significant share in world total exports, Vollrath Index is higher than Balassa Index (Erkan, Erdoğan, & Kara, 2018).

Vollrath Index (RXA) is formulated as $(X_{ij}/X_{-ij})/(X_{i-jw}/X_{-i-jw})$(Vollrath, 1991):

$X_{i,j}$ → country j's export for the good "i"
$X_{-i,j}$ → country j's total export except the good "i"
$X_{i,-j}$ → world export for the good "i" except $X_{i,j}$
$X_{-i,-j}$ → total world export except $X_{-i,j}$ and $X_{i,-j}$

Vollrath Index is interpreted in the same way as Balassa Index. If the RXA > 1, there is a comparative advantage; whereas the RXA < 1, there is a comparative disadvantage. If the logarithmic value of the RCA and RXA indices (lnRCA and ln RXA) is positive, it has comparative advantage, vice versa.

Because the RCA coefficients are between zero and infinite and are asymmetric, a monotone transformation process is applied to the corresponding index. The RCA coefficient found by this process can be formulated as (RCA-1)/(RCA+1) (Erkan, 2012). This index is called the "symmetrically explained comparative advantage (RSCA)" index (Nalini Ranjan Kumar, 2008). In this case, the extreme values in this conversion result will be less weighted, the index will become symmetrical and the result will be between -1 and +1 (Filiztekin, 2006).

In the literature, there are studies measuring the comparative advantages of Germany's exports using the revealed comparative advantage coefficients. However, many of these studies are product based. For example, in the study done by Hacer Simay Karaalp and Nazire Deniz Yilmaz, Germany's comparative advantages in textile and garment industry were compared with Bangladesh, Turkey and China for the period 2000–2010. The results of the analyses made reveal the relative weakness of Germany relative to other countries (Hacer Simay Karaalp, 2013). The analysis made by Elżbıeta Czarny and Małgorzata Żmuda confirmed that the German economy specializes in exports of technologyintensive difficulttoimitate goods. In this case, it can be said that Germany is comparatively superior in export of R & D-based products (Elżbıeta Czarny, 2018). The study made by Federico Foders and Manuel Molina Vogelsang by using RCA and RXA set out to empirically analyze the trade and technology specialization and the price/cost performance of the German economy over the period 1990–2011 (Federico Foders, 2014). The results confirmed that Germany specialized in medium-range technology products.

3.1 Analysis by SITC Technology Classification

In the study, levels of specialization and comparative advantage in Germany's export on the basis of technology and factor intensity is calculated for the period 2000–2016. Balassa Index and Vollrath Index which are the revealed comparative advantage (RCA) indices are calculated according to SITC Technology Classification and ISIC Rev.3.

The results of Germany's comparative advantages analyzed according to SITC Technology Classification are shown in Graph 1. Since lnRCA values in the export of hard to imitiate science-based and capital-intensive goods has been positive a stable manner, Germany has a comparative advantage in exporting such products. As a matter of fact, Germany is mainly exporting these products.

Tab. 4: SITC Trade Classification and ISIC Rev. 3 Technology Intensity Definition. Source: OECD, Directorate for Science, Technology and Industry, Economic Analysis and Statistics Division, 2011, HUFBAUER, Garry and Chilas, John; (1974), "Specialization by Industrial Countries: Extent and Consequences", The International Division of Labour: Problems and Perspectives-International Symposium, Germany, pp. 3–38

Technological Based Standart International Trade Classification (SITC)		**International Standard Industrial Classification (ISIC Rev.3)**	
Raw material-intensive goods (RMIG)	Live animals and food items Agricultural raw materials Mineral fuels and mineral oils Animal and vegetable oils fertilizers	***High-technology industries (HTI)***	Aircraft and spacecraft Pharmaceuticals Office, accounting and computing machinery Radio, TV and communications equipment Medical, precision and optical instruments
Labour-intensive goods (LIG)	Textile fibers (fibers) Manufacturing goods Other production goods	***Medium-high-technology industries (MHTI)***	Electrical machinery and apparatus, n.e.c. Motor vehicles, trailers and semi-trailers Chemicals excluding pharmaceuticals Railroad equipment and transport equipment, n.e.c. Machinery and equipment, n.e.c.
Capital-intensive goods (CIG)	Beverages, tobacco and products Electric energy Products used in painting Essential oils, resinoids, perfumery, cosmetics Rubber articles Iron and steel Non-ferrous metals Land vehicles	***Medium-low-technology industries (MLTI)***	Building and repairing of ships and boats Rubber and plastics products Coke, refined petroleum products and nuclear fuel Other non-metallic mineral products Basic metals and fabricated metal products
Easy to imitate science-based goods (EISBG)	Organic chemical products Inorganic chemical products Medicine and pharmacy products Non-original plastics Chemical substances and products Office machines, automatic data processing machines Communication, voice recording and voice recorder	***Low-technology industries (LTI)***	Manufacturing, n.e.c.; Recycling Wood, pulp, paper, paper products, printing and publishing Food products, beverages and tobacco Textiles, textile products, leather and footwear
Hard to imitate science-based goods (HISBG)	Plastics in the original state Tools and transport Professional and scientific measuring and control devices Photographic equipment, optical equipment, watches		

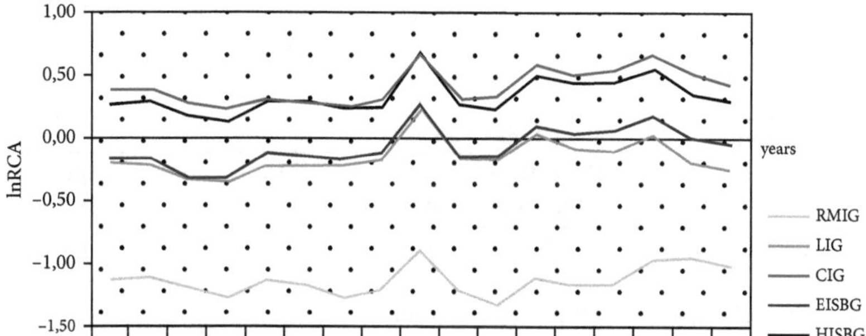

	2000	2001	2002	2003	2004	2005	2006	2007	2008	2009	2010	2011	2012	2013	2014	2015	2016
RMIG	-1,1	-1,1	-1,1	-1,2	-1,1	-1,1	-1,2	-1,1	-0,8	-1,1	-1,3	-1,1	-1,1	-1,1	-0,9	-0,9	-1,0
LIG	-0,1	-0,2	-0,3	-0,3	-0,2	-0,2	-0,2	-0,1	0,25	-0,1	-0,1	0,05	-0,0	-0,0	0,03	-0,1	-0,2
CIG	0,40	0,38	0,27	0,24	0,31	0,29	0,25	0,29	0,68	0,33	0,34	0,58	0,52	0,53	0,67	0,52	0,43
EISBG	-0,1	-0,1	-0,3	-0,3	-0,1	-0,1	-0,1	-0,1	0,29	-0,1	-0,1	0,10	0,05	0,06	0,20	0,02	0,0
HISBG	0,28	0,29	0,17	0,13	0,29	0,29	0,24	0,24	0,66	0,27	0,25	0,51	0,45	0,45	0,56	0,36	0,29

Graph 1: Comparative Advantages of Germany's Export by Factor Density (According to SITC Technology Classification). Source: It is calculated by using data from the UN Comtrade database

Nevertheless, Germany's easy to imitiate science-based product exports have a slight advantage over the past few years.

Considering Germany's excellence in the export of technological equipment and scientific products, it can be expected that the export of labor intensive products will be significantly disadvantageous. However, the comparative disadvantage of Germany's labor-intensive product exports is insignificant. In fact, Germany has even gained comparative advantage over the years in the export of this product group. It can be said that Germany's labor quality and productivity are high in this case.

As can be seen in the Graph 1, Germany has an obvious comparative disadvantage in exports of raw materials intensive products. Germany is a net importer of these product groups. The common detail on the Graph 1 is that Germany's values of lnRCA peaked in all product groups in 2008, and declined after 2009.

When compared periodically (2000–2008, 2009–2016), comparative advantages in the exports of high value added products in Germany have been increasing steadily. Compared with the 2000–2008 period, the RCA coefficients of the capital intensive, easy to imitiate and hard to imitiate science-based goods increased in the period of 2009–2016. In other words, Germany has become more competitive in the exports of technological and innovative products.

Tab. 5: Comparative Advantages of Germany's Export by Factor Density (According to SITC Technology Classification). Source: It is calculated by using data from the UN Comtrade database

Product Groups	RCA Index Values				
	Periodic Average		Min	Max	Appropriate Average
	2000–2008	2009–2016			
Raw material-intensive goods	−1,14	−1,11	−1,31	−0,89	−1,13
Labour-intensive goods	−0,18	−0,10	−0,35	0,25	−0,16
Capital-intensive goods	0,35	0,49	0,24	0,68	0,41
Easy to imitate science-based goods	−0,13	0,02	−0,32	0,29	−0,07
Hard to imitate science-based goods	1,35	1,49	1,14	1,94	1,40

When evaluated as the appropriate average, as can be seen from the Tab. 5, there is a comparative advantage in Germany's capital-intensive and hard to imitiate science-based good exports.

3.2 Analysis by ISIC Rev. 3

The results of Germany's comparative advantages analyzed according to ISIC Rev.3 are shown in Graph 2. Accordingly, in the period 2000–2016, Germany has a stable comparative advantage in the export of medium-high-technology industries.

Nevertheless, although Almanya has been a comparative disadvantage in the export of high-technology industries generally, the disadvantage has been diminishing gradually in recent times. In fact, in recent years, Germany has managed to achieve comparative advantage in the export of this product group.

The disadvantage in the export of medium-low-technology industries of Germany has been increasing steadily in recent times. This shows that the comparative advantages of Germany's exports are transforming from low-technology industries to medium-high and high-technology industries.

When compared periodically (2000–2008, 2009–2016), comparative advantages in the exports of medium-high and high technology industries in Germany have been increasing (Tab. 6). Compared with the 2000–2008 period, the RCA coefficients of low-technology industries, medium-high-technology industries and high-technology industries increased in the period of 2009–2016. Germany has become more competitive in the exports of high value added products.

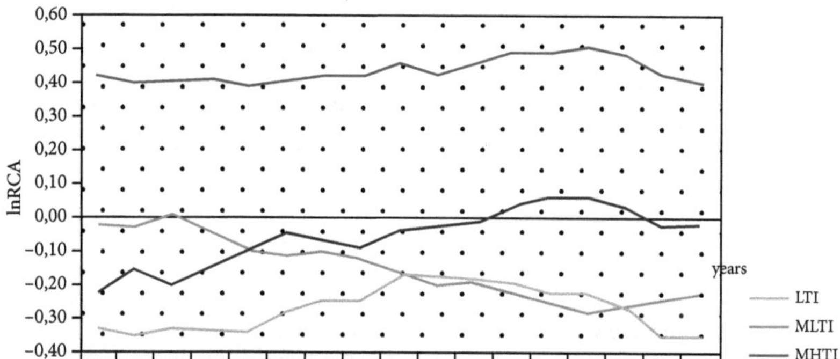

	2000	2001	2002	2003	2004	2005	2006	2007	2008	2009	2010	2011	2012	2013	2014	2015	2016
LTI	−0,3	−0,3	−0,3	−0,3	−0,3	−0,2	−0,2	−0,2	−0,1	−0,1	−0,1	−0,1	−0,2	−0,2	−0,2	−0,3	−0,3
MLTI	−0,0	−0,0	−0,01	−0,0	−0,0	−0,1	−0,1	−0,1	−0,1	−0,1	−0,1	−0,2	−0,2	−0,2	−0,2	−0,2	−0,2
MHTI	0,42	0,40	0,41	0,41	0,40	0,42	0,43	0,42	0,47	0,43	0,46	0,49	0,50	0,51	0,49	0,43	0,41
HTI	−0,2	−0,1	−0,1	−0,1	−0,1	−0,0	−0,0	−0,0	−0,0	−0,0	−0,0	−0,04	−0,06	−0,06	−0,03	−0,0	−0,0

Graph 2: Comparative Advantages of Germany's Export by Factor Density (According to ISIC Rev.3). Source: It is calculated by using data from the UN Comtrade database

Tab. 6: Comparative Advantages of Germany's Export by Factor Density (According to ISIC Rev.3). Source: It is calculated by using data from the UN Comtrade database

Product Groups	**RCA Index Values**				
	Periodic Average		**min**	**max**	**Appropriate Average**
	2000–2008	**2009–2016**			
Low-Technology Industries	0,75	0,78	0,70	0,84	0,76
Medium-Low-Technology Industries	0,93	0,79	0,76	1,01	0,86
Medium-High-Technology Industries	1,52	1,59	1,49	1,67	1,55
High-Technology Industries	0,89	1,02	0,80	1,07	0,95

When the comparative advantages of Germany are analyzed according to the 10 products with the highest exports in the World by using SITC Rev.3, 3 digit classification, it appears that exports of 5 products are advantageous (Tab. 7). As it can be seen in the Tab. 7, Germany has comparative advantages in the exports of high value added (R&D or capital based) products such as "medicament include vet., electric circuit equipment, electrical equipment, passenger cars etc.,

Tab. 7: Product-Based Comparative Advantages of Germany (According to the 10 Products with the Highest Exports in the World, SITC Rev.3, 3 Digit).

Product Code (SITC)	Product Name	RCA	RXA	Comparative Degree	RSCA	Factor Intensity
333	petrol,oil, crude	0,00	0,00	disadvantage	−1,00	row material
334	heavy petrol, oil	0,25	0,22	disadvantage	−0,60	row material
542	medicament include vet	1,67	1,82	weak advantage	0,25	R&D based
752	computer equipment	0,51	0,49	disadvantage	−0,32	R&D based
764	telecomes equipment	0,44	0,41	disadvantage	−0,39	R&D based
772	electric circuit equipment	1,60	1,72	weak advantage	0,23	R&D based
776	valvis, transistors	0,41	0,38	disadvantage	−0,42	R&D based
778	electrical equipment	1,02	1,02	weak advantage	0,01	R&D based
781	passenger cars etc.	2,44	3,12	medium advantage	0,42	capital
784	motor vec. parts/access	1,73	1,92	weak advantage	0,27	capital

motor vec. parts/access). When it comes to attention, the Vollrath Index (RXA) value of such product groups, where Germany has a comparative advantage, is greater than the Balassa Index (RCA) value. As stated in the literature section of the study, the reason for this is that exports of the mentioned product groups of Germany have significant weight in world exports.

4 Conclusion

In the study, the comparative advantages of Germany's technology-intensive products was addressed and analyzed within the ISIC and SITC Technology Classification. ISIC Rev. 3 technology classification analysis shows that Germany has a comparative advantage only in high-medium technology products.

According to the SITC Rev.3 technology classification, the competitiveness of Germany has been measured and analyzed in the 10 most product-exported product groups in the world. Considering the results of the analysis, it is seen that

5 out of 10 have competitive power. According to Balassa, Symmetrical Balassa and Vollrath Index results, Germany has moderate comparative advantages the products such as "542 medicament include and", "772 electric circuit equipment", "778 electrical equipment", and "784 motor vec. parts/access products", and weak comparative advantages the product "781 passenger cars etc."

When analyzed on the basis of factor intensity (SITC Rev.3 Technology Classification), it is seen that 3 of the mentioned products (542 medicament include, 772 electric circuit equipment, 778 electrical equipment) are based on R&D, and 2 of these products (781 passenger cars etc, 784 motor parts/access) are capital intensive.

The findings in the study show that Germany has specialized in exports of popular product groups on a global basis, resulting in analyzes using exploited comparative advantages. In addition, Germany's global comparative advantages are predominantly based on technology. However, Germany, which has taken its place in categories such as world value added and exports to developing countries such as China, has to increase its comparative advantages in exports of high-tech products (competitive power) in order to be a bigger global power.

References

Ağır, H., & Yıldırım, S. (2015). Türkiye ile BRICS Ekonomilerinin Makroekonomik Performans Karşılaştırması: Betimsel Bir Analiz. KSÜ Sosyal Bilimler Dergisi, 39–65.

Altay, B., & Gürpınar, K. (2008). Açıklanmış Karşılaştırmalı Üstünlükler ve Bazı Rekabet Gücü Endeksleri: Türk Mobilya Sektörü Üzerine Bir Uygulama. Afyon Kocatepe Üniversitesi İ.İ.B.F Dergisi, 257–275.

Amighini, A. (2005). China in the International Fragmentation of Production: Evidence from the ICT Industry. European Journal of Comparative Economics, 2(2), 203–219.

Balassa, B. (1965). Trade Liberalisation and "Revealed" Comparative Advantage. The Manchester School of Economic and Social Studies, 99–123.

Balassa, B. (1977). Revealed Comparative Advantage Revisited: An Analysis of Relative Export Shares of the Industrial Countries 1953–1971. The Manchester School, 327–344.

Balassa, B., & Noland, M. (1989). Revealed Comparative Advantage in Japan and the United States. Journal of International Economic Integration, 4(2), 8–22.

Bosworth, B., Collins, S. M., & Virmani, A. (2007). Sources of Growth in the İndian Economy. NBER Working Paper Series, 1–49.

Çeştepe, H. (2012). Türkiye'nin Seçilmiş Ortadoğu Ülkeleriyle Ticaretinin Analizi. Ekonomik ve Sosyal Araştırmalar Dergisi, 23–43.

Elżbıeta Czarny, M. Ż. (2018). Competitiveness as the Ability to Adjust: The EU-10 Exports Structure and Its Convergence to the German Pattern. Comparative Economic Research, 21(1), 119–133.

Engin, E. (2013). Açıklanmış Karşılaştırmalı Üstünlükler Yaklaşımına Göre Türkiye Oluklu Mukavva Ambalaj Sektörünün Rekabet Gücü. İstanbul: İstanbul Kültür Üniversitesi Sosyal Bilimler Enstitüsü Yayınlanmamış Yüksek Lisans Tezi.

Erkan, B. (2009). Ülkelerin İhracat Performanslarının Belirlenmesinde Açıklanmış Karşılaştırmalı Üstünlüklerin Kullanılması: Yükselen Ekonomiler Örneği. Manisa: Manisa Celal Bayar Üniversitesi Sosyal Bilimler Enstitüsü Yayınlanmamış Doktora Tezi.

Erkan, B. (2011). STIC Teknoloji Sınıflandırmasına İlişkin Açıklanmış Karşılaştırmalı Üstünlüklerin Belirlenmesi Türkiye ve Diğer N-11 Ülkelerinin Karşılaştırılması. Finans Politik ve Ekonomik Yorumlar, 35–48.

Erkan, B. (2012). BRIC Ülkeleri ve Türkiye'nin İhracat Uzmanlaşma ve Rekabet Düzeylerinin Karşılaştırmalı Analizi. Ekonomik ve Sosyal Araştırmalar Dergisi, 101–131.

Erkan, B. (2012). Türkiye ile Sınır Komşuları Arasındaki Dış Ticaretin Karşılaştırmalı Üstünklükler Perspektifinde Analizi. Pamukkale Üniversitesi Sosyal Bilimler Enstitüsü Dergisi (11), 3.

Erkan, B. (2016). Türkiye'nin Canlı Hayvan, Et ve Deniz Ürünleri İhracatındaki Rekabet Gücünün Analizi. İnsan ve Toplum Bilimleri Araştırmaları Dergisi, 1843–1864.

Erkan, B. (2017). Türkiye'nin İhracatında Uzmanlaşma ve Rekabet Edebilirlik Düzeyi: Avrupa Birliği Piyasası-Küresel Piyasalar Karşılaştırmalı Analizi. İnsan ve Toplum Bilimleri Araştırmaları Dergisi, 68–88.

Erkan, B., & Batbaylı, Ş. (2017). Karadeniz Ekonomik İşbirliği Örgütü (KEİ) Üyesi Ülkelerin Küresel Rekabet Pazarlarındaki Karşılaştırmalı Üstünlükleri. Marmara Üniversitesi Siyasal Bilimler Dergisi, 31–49.

Erkan, B., Erdoğan, N., & Kara, O. (2018). The Power of Competitiveness of the Toy Sector in Turkey and the Necessity of Specialized Toy Organized Industrial Zones. O. Kara (Dü.) içinde, Global and Regional Studies in terms of Economical and Social Issues. Almatı/Kazakistan: Al-Farabi Kazakh National University, s. 10–30.

Erkan, B., & Sarıçoban, K. (2014). International Journal of Business and Social Science. 5(8(1)), 117–130.

Erkekoğlu, H., Kılıçarslan, Z., & Göknar, H. (2014). Kayseri İlinin Mobilya Sektörü Rekabet Gücü: Açıklanmış Karşılaştırmalı Üstünlük Endeksi. Erciyes Üniversitesi İktisadi ve İdari Bilimler Fakültesi Dergisi, 1–22.

Federico Foders, M. M. (2014). Why Is Germany's Manufacturing Industry so Competitive? 69. Kiel Institute for the World Economy: IFW.

Filiztekin, A. (2006). Türkiye'de Açıklanmış Karşılaştırmalı Üstünlüklerin Evrimi. Uluslararası Ekonomi ve Dış Ticaret Politikaları, 1(1), 107.

Gürpınar, K., & Barca, M. (2007). Türk Mobilya Sektörünün Uluslararası Rekabet Gücü Düzeyi ve Nedenleri. Eskişehir Osmangazi Üniversitesi İİBF Dergisi, 41–61.

Hacer Simay Karaalp, N. D. (2013). Comparative Advantage of Textiles and Clothing: Evidence for Bangladesh. Fibres & Textiles in Eastern Europe, 1(97), 14–17.

Hufbauer, G., & Chilas, J. (1974). Specialization by Industrial Countries: Extent and Consequences. The International Division of Labour: Problems and Perspectives–International Symposium, Germany.

Jeroen Hinloopen, C. V. (2001). On the Empirical Distribution of the Balassa Index. Review of World Economics, 137(1), 13.

Kösekahyaoğlu, L., & Sarıçoban, K. (2017). Ticaret Sonrası Verilerle Rekabet Gücünün Ölçülmesinde Kullanılan İndeksler Üzerine Bir Literatür Taraması. Akademik Sosyal Araştırmalar Dergisi, 424–444.

Messina, William A. Jr. (2001). Cuba: A View of Revealed Export Advantage. ASCE.

Nalini Ranjan Kumar, A. R. (2008). Export of Cucumber and Gherkin from India: Performance. Agricultural Economics Research, 21(1), 131.

Özekicioğlu, H., & Kılıç, C. (2017). Küresel Ekonomi Çağında Çin ve Hindistan. İktisat Politikası Araştırmaları Dergisi, 19–34.

Ramirez, J. (2004). Impact of Free Trade Agreements (FTA) on Competitiveness: Identifying and Preparing for. International Business Strategies in Latin America–Sumaq Summit 04, Colombia.

Ricardo, D. (1817). https://www.econlib.org/library/Ricardo/ricP.html. On the Principles of Political Economy and Taxation.

Saboniene, A. (2009). Lithuanian Export Competitiveness: Comparison with Other Baltic States. Inzinerine Ekonomika–Engineering Economics, 2, 49–57.

Sachs, J. D., Bajpai, N., & Ramiah, A. (2002). Understanding Regional Economic Growth in İndia. Asian Economic Papers, 1–49.

Şahinli, M. A. (2011). Açıklanmış Karşılaştırmalı Üstünlükler Endcksi: Türkiye Pamuk Endüstrisi Üzerine Bir Uygulama. SÜ İİBF Sosyal ve Ekonomik Araştırmalar Dergisi, 227–239.

Sharma, A. (2004). The Indian Economy since Liberalisation: The Structure and Composition of Exports and Industrial Transformation (1980–2000). Industrial Dynamics, Innovation and Development, 3.

Şimşek, N., & Sadat, S. A. (2009). ECO Pazarında Türkiye: 1997–2005 Dönemi Rekabet Gücü Analizi. Sosyo Ekonomi Dergisi, 135–158.

Smith, A. (1991). Wealth of Nations. London: Prometheus Books.

Turan, S. (2008). Değişen Dengeler Işığında Orta Asya'daki Küresel ve Bölgesel Güç Odakları Üzerine Bir İnceleme. ISSA 2. Uluslararası Sosyal Bilimciler Kongresi (s. 858–873). Bişkek and Kırgızistan: Kocaeli Üniversitesi.

UNCTAD. (2017). Handbook of Statics. New York and Geneva: United Nations.

UNIDO. (2017). Industrial Development Report 2018. Viyana: United Nations Industrial Development Organization.

UNİDO. (2017). İndustrial Development Report 2018. Viyana: United Nations İndustrial Development Organization.

Uyanık, T. (2011). Hindistan Ülke Raporu. Ankara: T.C. Başbakanlık Dış Ticaret Müsteşarlığı İhracatı Geliştirme Etüt Merkezi.

Veeramani, C. (2006). India and China: Changing Patterns of Comparative Advantage? http://www.globelicsindia2006.org/Veeramani.pdf.

Vollrath, T. L. (1991). A Theoretical Evaluation of Alternative Trade Intensity Measures of Revealed Comparative Advantage. Weltwirtschaftliches Archiv, 265–280.

WTO. (2017). World Trade Organization. 04 09, 2018 tarihinde WTO Statics: stat.wto.org/CountryProfiles/adresinden alındı

Yalçınkaya, H., Çılbant, C., Erataş, F., & Hartoğlu, D. (2014). Açıklanmış Karşılaştırmalı Üstünlükler Ekseninde Rekabet Gücünün Analizi: Türk–Çin Dış Ticareti Üzerine Bir Uygulama. Yönetim ve Ekonomi Araştırmaları Dergisi, 41–57.

Yavuz, M. Y. (2006). Çin'de Piyasa Ekonomisi Uygulamaları ve Toplumsal Sonuçları. İzmir: Ege Üniversitesi Sosyal Bilimler Enstitüsü Yayınlanmamış Yüksek Lisans Tezi.

http://www.statistics.com/resources/glossary/t/trimmean.php. (16.12.2014).

Ciler Sigeze[1], Esra Balli[2], and Gulcin Guresci[3]

Factors behind R&D Expenditures and Export Decision: Evidence from Turkish Firms

1 Introduction

Most of the studies that are related with export-oriented growth agree that export is an important dynamic of sustainable growth. Regarding this, the successful growth performance of the export-oriented strategies of the Taiwanese and South Korean economies since the end of 1960s is often documented in the literature. For this reason, examining the effect of exports on growth, productivity and employment is of great importance (Aldan and Gunay, 2008). Considering Turkey's economy, it is seen that since the beginning of the 1980s the import substitution policies have been replaced by the export-oriented growth policies. To encourage exports, Turkey has taken steps towards creating strategies that tempt exports. Tab. 1 shows the share of exports, the share of R&D expenditures and the share of high-tech exports in Turkey's GDP between the years 2000 and 2016. Accordingly, it is seen that Turkey's exports fluctuated in the period studied. Although high technology exports tend to increase, this rate is at very low levels. Besides, Tab. 1 shows that Turkey remains below the OECD average in terms of the share of R&D expenditures in GDP.

Turkey's export and import structure is shown in Fig. 1. Sectors concerned in the classification according to SITC Rev3 are categorized as follows: (0) live animals and foodstuffs; (1) drinks and tobacco; (2) non-renewable raw materials except fuel; (3) mineral fuels, oils and alkaline products; (4) animal and vegetable fats, oils and waxes; (5) chemical, industrial and related industrial products not elsewhere specified; (6) processed goods divided into major classes; (7) machinery and transport vehicles; (8) various manufactured goods and (9) goods not classified in SITC.

1 Research Assistant Dr., Çukurova University, Faculty of Economic and Administrative Sciences, csigeze@cu.edu.tr.

2 Asst.Prof. Dr., Erzincan Binali Yıldırım University, Faculty of Economic and Administrative Sciences,esra.balli@erzincan.edu.tr

3 Asst.Prof. Dr. Dokuz Eylül University, Faculty of Economic and Administrative Sciences, gulcin.guresci@deu.edu.tr.

Tab. 1: Exports of Turkey, the Export of High Technology, R&D Expenditures (2000–2016)

Year	Exports (%GDP)	High-Tech Export (%GDP)	R&D (%GDP)
2000	19.45	4.83	0,48
2001	26.58	3.87	0,54
2002	24.46	1.79	0,53
2003	22.24	1.93	0,48
2004	22.75	1.90	0,52
2005	21.02	1.47	0,59
2006	21.65	1.85	0,58
2007	21.22	1.89	0,72
2008	22.83	1.62	0,73
2009	22.57	1.74	0,85
2010	20.45	1.93	0,84
2011	22.26	1.84	0,86
2012	23.67	1.83	0,92
2013	22.27	1.88	0,94
2014	23.76	1.94	–
2015	23.35	2.16	–
2016	21.97	2.03	–

Fig. 1 shows that Turkey's export rate in groups like live animals and foodstuffs (0), processed goods divided into major classes (6) and various manufactured goods (8) takes place higher than its import rate. On the contrary, Turkey's import dependency is at high level in groups like oils and alkaline products (3) and the equipment and transport (7). The second part gives the literature, the third part summarizes the data, models and methodology, the fourth one reports the results, and the last part is conclusion.

2 Literature Review

According to Cohen and Levinthal (1989), R&D expenditures have two consequences: First one is the direct increases in the innovation channel and productivity, and the second one is the learning by exporting. Firms cannot easily make decisions about R&D expenditures and exports related to this. Wakelin's study (1998) can be considered as an example for this. According to Wakelin (1998), the most important reasons of the small firms for not allocating their resources into R&D expenditures are the initial costs and finding new markets.

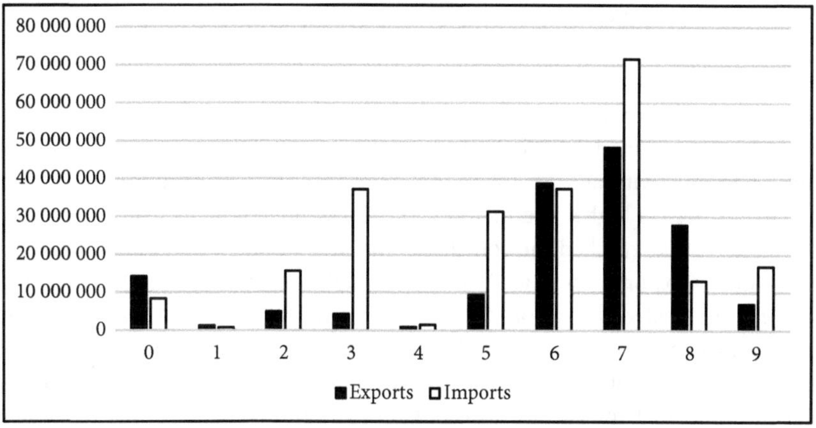

Fig. 1: Turkey's export and import structure. Source: TURKSTAT

According to Aldan and Günay (2008), large and more efficient firms mainly prefer to enter into export markets, and as a result of these decisions, the labor productivity and employment of those firms have been increasing. Griffith, et al. (2006) studied the effect of innovation by examining four European countries and reached the conclusion that innovation activities affect the level of productivity. Crépon, et al. (1998) found an evidence supporting Hall and Mairesse (1995) argued that the repetitive R&D expenditures lead to an increase in productivity. Griffith (2003) showed that R&D expenditures affect innovation and firms' ability to adapt new technologies. Roper and Love (2002) found that effect of export performance of the firms at manufacturing sector have different in the UK and Germany. Besides, in these two countries, they found that product innovation is important in terms of profitability and exports level. In addition to all these, many scholars agree that export-oriented growth strategies increase the technological efficiency of firms and countries as exporters would have the opportunity to learn more advanced technologies through exports. Aw and Hwang (1995) compared the output differences of the exporting and non-exporting Taiwanese electronics producers and observed differences in productivity levels between these firms. On the other hand, Bernard and Jensen (1999) showed the firms with high productivity are more inclinable for the exporters. Aw et al. (2011) observed positive effects of Taiwanese firms' decision to R&D activities and exports. Braymen et al. (2011) found positive relationship between R&D decision and the export decision in four years-time since the establishment of new firms in the USA. Esteve-Pérez and Rodríguez (2013) showed that there is a dependency relationship between exports and R&D activities in the study of exports and R&D in Spain. Yang and Chen (2012) found that R&D is of significance on both exports and productivity in Indonesia. In their study that Lööf et al. (2015) examined the effects of exports, innovation and exogenous information on productivity, authors found that firms that make continuous innovation and export have a higher productivity rate through learning by exporting. Yang and Chen (2012) reached the conclusion that R&D is effective both on productivity and on exports. Aw et al. (2007) reached the conclusion that the efficiency of the firm affected the export decisions. Sjöholm (1999) found that exporting firms achieved high efficiency levels. Neves et al. (2016) found that in Portugal, export activities cause to increase in R&D investments. Cetin and Cincera (2015) found that the export decisions of firms and companies that carry out R&D activities. Lechevalier and Ito (2010) showed that companies that invest in R&D and exports can pursue these activities.

3 Data, Model, and Methodology

This study uses data obtained from the World Bank's Turkey-Enterprise Survey carried out 2002, 2005, 2008 and 2013 (face-to-face interviews with the manufacturing companies), and 2118 observations used in the model. The companies involved in the study are included in the sample each year independently from other years, so the data set is based on a pooled structure. The main motivation of the World Bank to form this data set is to provide a comprehensive set of information that can be used by researchers to understand the behavior of Turkish firms. At the same time, this dataset is very important in terms of showing the important factors such as the constraints on firm growth, obstacles on creating employment and increasing productivity, the company's competitiveness in international markets, and the reactions of firms to structural reforms made in Turkey. Although the scope of the data set is quite wide, many variables used in the study are not available for use. Therefore, parallel to the discussions in the literature, the variables used in the models are calculated by the authors. This study examines the determinants of R&D expenditures at firm level. Firstly, the decision of the firms whether make R&D expenditures are considered. For this purpose, the Probit model is used. This model is a widely used one for estimating the conditional probability of an event. On the other hand, the dependent variable is the binary variable. This variable gets the value 1 if the firm is making R&D expenditures and 0 if it does not. Following the terminology of Greene (2002) y^*, which is a latent variable that affect the firms' status of R&D expenditures the model is represented by equation (1).

$$y^* = x'\beta + \varepsilon, \varepsilon \sim N(0,\sigma^2) \quad (1)$$

$$y = r \; if \; y^* > 0$$

$$y = 0 \; if \; y^* \geq 0$$

$$P(y=1|x) = \int_{-\infty}^{x'\beta} \phi(t)dt = \Phi(x'\beta) \quad (2)$$

Where, x, β and $\Phi(.)$ express the set of independent variables, the parameter vector, and the cumulative normal distribution function, respectively (Greene, 2003: 666). Secondly, we used the Tobit model proposed by Tobin (1958) to estimate the determinants of R&D expenditures. Tobin (1958) estimated the model by considering that dependent variables are censored on the left at zero on a basis of expenditure on durable consumer goods of individuals. Similarly, as y^*-the latent variable that affects the firms' R&D expenditures- is restricted to values equal to or greater than 0, the dependent variable for the Tobit model defined as follows (Greene, 2003: 764):

$$y = y^* \; if \; y^* > 0$$

$$y = 0 \; if \; y^* \leq 0$$

So as to examine the determinants of R&D intensity, following Yang and Chen (2012) the model is written as follows:

$$RD = \beta_0 + \beta_1 SIZE + \beta_2 SKILL + \beta_3 DEXP + \beta_4 MNC + \beta_5 \ln LPR + \beta_6 Gov.Support + \beta_7 D2002 + \beta_8 D2005 + \beta_9 D2008 \quad (3)$$

In the Probit and Tobit models, dummy variables indicating Size, Skill, DEXP, MNC, lnLPR, 2002, 2005, 2008 used as independent variables. Tab. 2 gives the definition and statistics of these variables.

4 Empirical Results

Tab. 3 shows the results of the determinants of the R&D expenditures for manufacturing firms in Turkey. Accordingly, Probit and Tobit models results are similar. The lnLPR, SIZE, SKILL, DEXP, and GovSupport variables in this study affect R&D participation decision positively as expected. Compared to the reference year, the firms' R&D participation decisions were positive in 2002, 2005, and 2008, however, in 2008 the firms' R&D expenditure level was negative.

Tab. 2: Variables and Summary Statistics

Variable	Definition	Average	Std. Dev.
lnLPR	Labor productivity: ratio of total sales to total labor hours	10.268	2.205
SIZE	Total sales	140.719	496.424
SKILL	Ratio of university graduates to total employees	14.537	20.026
RD	Dummy, 1 if R&D expenditures is positive or 0 if there is not.	0.122	0.328
DEXP	Dummy, 1 if firm performs export	0.465	0.498
MNC	Foreign ownership: Share of foreigners in the firm (%)	3.559	15.323
GovSupport	Supports from the governments or European Union sources within last three years	0.076	0.265
2002	if the firm was interviewed with in 2002 the dummy variable is 1, or 0 if it was not.	0.196	0.397
2005	if the firm was interviewed with in 2005 the dummy variable is 1, or 0 if it was not.	0.150	0.357
2008	if the firm was interviewed with in 2008 the dummy variable is 1, or 0 if it was not.	0.318	0.465
2013	if the firm was interviewed with in 2013 (reference year) the dummy variable is 1, or 0 if it was not.	0.334	0.472

5 Conclusion

This study tries to show Turkey's manufacturing firms' probability of R&D expenditures and the determinants of R&D expenditures utilizing Probit and Tobit models by using the face-to-face data obtained from the World Bank in 2002, 2005, 2008 and 2013. As the firms involved in the study are included in the sample, each year independently from other years, the data is based on a pooled structure. According to results; among the manufacturing firms in Turkey, in comparison with the non-exporting ones, the exporting firms more tend to make R&D activities. In parallel, labor productivity positively affects the tendency to make R&D and the level of R&D expenditures. Similarly, the firms taking government support and having more qualified workers are statistically found to have more probability in making R&D activities, in comparison to those with no government support and fewer qualified workers. The results also reveal that while firms were take part in R&D in the previous years than they were in 2013, R&D expenditure levels dropped significantly in 2008. R&D expenditures

Tab. 3: The Determinants of R&D of the Manufacturing Firms in Turkey

	Probit Model	Tobit Model
Constant	-2.783***	-38.958***
	-0.235	-4.809
lnLPR	0.087***	1.563***
	-0.022	-0.386
SIZE	-0.00003	-0.002
	-0.00007	-0.001
SKILL	0.003**	0.049
	-0.001	-0.03
DEXP	0.394***	2.717*
	-0.081	-1.421
MNC	-0.001	0.329***
	-0.002	-0.031
GovSupport	0.322***	3.250
	-0.124	-2.209
2002	0.659***	-1.442
	-0.114	-1.904
2005	0.265*	0.683
	-0.134	-1.862
2008	0.561***	-9.742***
	(0.097)	-1.989
Sigma		13.713***
		-1.038

The parentheses are the standard error of the contents; and ***, **, and * indicate the coefficient, and significance level at 1 %, 5 %, and 10 % levels, respectively.

cause to increase in a direct proportion to the increase in foreign share in firms. However, another factor that can be explained by the domestic dynamics is that while the government support has a positive effect on making R&D, it does not reflect on expenditure level.

References

Aldan, A., & Gunay, M. (2008). Entry to export markets and productivity: analysis of matched firms in Turkey, TCMB, Working Paper No: 0805.

Aw, B. Y., & Hwang, A. R. M. (1995). Productivity and the export market: a firm-level analysis. *Journal of Development Economics*, *47*(2), 313–332.

Aw, B. Y., Roberts, M. J., & Winston, T. (2007). Export market participation, investments in R&D and worker training, and the evolution of firm productivity. *The World Economy*, *30*(1), 83–104.

Aw, B. Y., Roberts, M. J., & Xu, D. Y. (2011). R&D investment, exporting, and productivity dynamics. *American Economic Review*, *101*(4), 1312–44.

Bernard, A. B., & Jensen, J. B. (1999). Exceptional exporter performance: cause, effect, or both? *Journal of International Economics*, *47*(1), 1–25.

Braymen, C., Briggs, K., & Boulware, J. (2011). R&D and the export decision of new firms. *Southern Economic Journal*, *78*(1), 191–210.

Cohen, W. M., & Levinthal, D. A. (1989). Innovation and learning: the two faces of R & D. The Economic Journal, 99(397), 569–596.

Crépon, B., Duguet, E., & Mairessec, J. (1998). Research, innovation and productivity: an econometric analysis at the firm level. *Economics of Innovation and New Technology*, *7*(2), 115–158.

Çetin, D., & Cincera, M. (2015). Circular Causality of R&D and Export in EU countries. *World Journal of Applied Economics*, *1*(1), 82–105.

Esteve-Pérez, S., & Rodríguez, D. (2013). The dynamics of exports and R&D in SMEs. *Small Business Economics*, *41*(1), 219–240.

Greene, W. H. (2003). *Econometric analysis*. Pearson Education, Indias.

Griffith, R., Huergo, E., Mairesse, J., & Peters, B. (2006). Innovation and productivity across four European countries. *Oxford Review of Economic Policy*, *22*(4), 483–498.

Griffith, R., Redding, S., & Van Reenen, J. (2003). R&D and absorptive capacity: theory and empirical evidence. *The Scandinavian Journal of Economics*, *105*(1), 99–118.

Hall, B. H., & Mairesse, J. (1995). Exploring the relationship between R&D and productivity in French manufacturing firms. *Journal of Econometrics*, *65*(1), 263–293.

Ito, K., & Lechevalier, S. (2010). Why some firms persistently out-perform others: Investigating the interactions between innovation and exporting strategies. *Industrial and Corporate Change*, *19*(6), 1997–2039.

Lööf, H., Larijani, P. N., Cook, G., & Johansson, B. (2015). Learning-by-exporting and innovation strategies. *Economics of Innovation and New Technology*, *24*(1–2), 52–64.

Neves, A., Teixeira, A. A., & Silva, S. T. (2016). Exports-R&D investment complementarity and economic performance of firms located in Portugal. *Investigación económica*, *75*(295), 125–156.

Roper, S., & Love, J. H. (2002). Innovation and export performance: evidence from the UK and German manufacturing plants. *Research Policy, 31*(7), 1087–1102.

Sjöholm, F. (1999). Exports, imports and productivity: results from Indonesian establishment data. *World Development, 27*(4), 705–715.

Tobin, J. (1958). Estimation of relationships for limited dependent variables. Econometrica: Journal of the Econometric Society, 26(1), 24–36.

Wakelin, K. (1998). Innovation and export behaviour at the firm level. *Research Policy, 26*(7), 829–841.

Yang, C. H., & Chen, Y. H. (2012). R&D, productivity, and exports: Plant-level evidence from Indonesia. *Economic Modelling, 29*(2), 208–216.

Aysel Cetindere Filiz[1], Cengiz Duran[2], and Sema Behdioglu[3]

Just in Time (JIT) Production System

1 Introduction

The manufacturing industries in the world have undergone a tremendous change in the last three decades. Due to this there are drastic changes in management approach, techniques used in production and process, expectations of customer, attitudes of supplier, as well as competitive behavior. In the highly dynamic and rapidly changing modern era, the global competition among organizations has led to higher expectations from the manufacturing organizations. The global marketplace has witnessed an increased pressure from customers and competitors in manufacturing as well as service sector (Singh & Ahuja, 2012, p. 58). Rapid developments in transportation and information technologies have also led to changes in market conditions, and this has supported the formation of a dynamic competitive environment. In a dynamic competitive environment, businesses have begun to tend to gain competitive advantage by quickly meeting customer demands. Rapid changes in technology over time have increased the diversity of customer needs and new approaches have become a current issue to be used in production processes due to the swift increase in population.

The impact of the 1973–74 recession was acutely felt in the automobile-manufacturing sector. Just as the North American automotive industry began to recover from that economic slowdown, the 1980s brought increased globalization of markets and exerted fierce worldwide pressure on firms to compete more effectively in order to protect profit margins. Throughout the decade, manufacturing management teams were vigorously searching for methods to enhance production quality, productivity and efficiency. It was during this period that a Japanese management technology called just-in-time (JIT) was introduced to North American manufacturers. Through the late 1980s and early 1990s JIT gained widespread acceptance as an effective management strategy. It

1 Assit.Prof.Dr., Ondokuz Mayıs University, Faculty of Economics and Administrative Sciences, aysel.cetindere@omu.edu.tr.
2 Assoc.Prof.Dr., Dumlupınar University, Faculty of Economics and Administrative Sciences, cengiz.duran@dpu.edu.tr.
3 Prof. Dr., Dumlupınar University, Faculty of Economics and Administrative Sciences, sema.behdioglu@dpu.edu.tr.

was a technology that permitted many firms to compete successfully in the face of growing competition (Brox & Fader, 2010, p. 2705). Economic conditions, which Japanese were in after WWII, have played the role in emergence of Just In Time (JIT) system. The inadequate labor and capital resources, as well as limited natural resources in this period, led the Japanese to seek ways to use limited resources at the lowest possible cost so that their economic assets could survive. As a result of this trend, JIT system was originally developed and applied by Taiichi Ohno in Toyota motor factory in Japan. Hence, the JIT system is also known as the Toyota Production System (TPS). At the base of this system, there is a structure in which the satisfaction of the customer is intended and the unnecessary expenditures are removed by providing continuous improvement. In this system, the input sources to be used in production come to enterprise as needed, thus the enterprise works with zero or very low inventory levels.

JIT is a manufacturing approach initially used in Japan that is emphasized on excellence through continuous improvement in productivity and quality indexes in all the phases of the production cycle. Some JIT's definitions and concepts have been proposed. These concepts range from the strict sense of just-in-time production applied to material flow to the concept of a management philosophy focused on increasing customer satisfaction and obtaining competitive advantage in the market. Hence it can be stated that the initial concept related to material flow has now been transformed into another concept which considers JIT as a tool which impels the competitive advantages of companies (Alcaraz et al., 2014, p. 761).

2 Just In Time (JIT) Production System

JIT, known by names like stockless production and zero inventory, aims to put an end to improper resource utilization with optimal use of production resources. For this purpose, the system is tried to be developed with the lowest production cost by optimizing the physical resources to meet the customer's quality and delivery requirements. For this, a system that requires new concepts and behaviors at every stage of production, from sub-industry relations to deliveries, to realize zero inventory, zero defect and zero supply period is introduced (Demir & Gümüşoğlu, 2009, p. 566). The principles of management in the JIT system are summarized with 4P model (Philosophy, Process, People and Partners, Problem Solving) as shown in Fig. 1.

The philosophy of the JIT system can be described as *an approach that aims to improve work, process and methods by removing all unnecessary things*. Shigeo Shingo, who works in Toyota as an engineer and has made himself known with

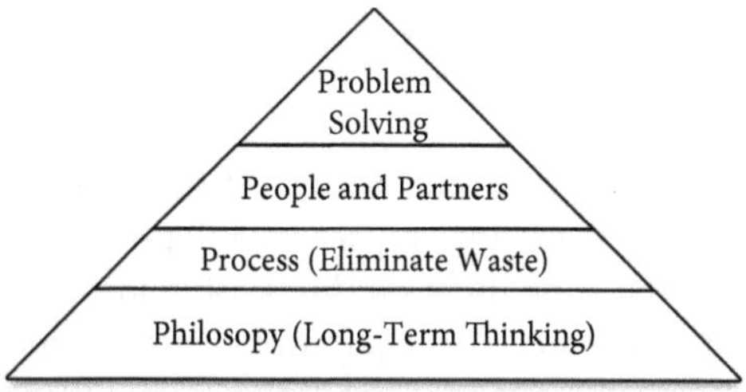

Fig. 1: 4P Model of the Toyota Way. Source: Liker & Hoseus, 2008, p. 21

his works in the production field, stated that there are seven types of waste that arise during the production process. These are (Üreten, 1998, p. 216–217):

1. ***Overproduction*:** Extra-manufactured products show that funds for organizations are wasted. Overproduction waste usually occurs when the business is fast. When this happens, more raw material is consumed and a fee is paid for the unnecessary work, so unnecessary stock is created. Under these circumstances, more raw material is consumed and more money is paid for the unnecessary work, so unnecessary stock is created. This means additional material management, additional space for holding stock, and paying additional interest to the bank for the money used to carry the stocks. You may also need extra people to check stocks, extra paperwork, extra computers, more forklifts or warehouses and so on (Suzaki, 2015, p. 31).
2. ***Waiting*:** It is idle time for workers or machines due to bottlenecks or inefficient production flow on the factory floor. It includes small delays between processing of units. When time is being used ineffectively, then the waste of waiting occurs. This waste occurs whenever goods are not moving or being worked on. This waste affects both goods and workers, each spending time waiting. Waiting time for workers may be used for training or maintenance activities and should not result in overproduction (Shah & Patel, 2018, p. 3795). The waiting process is not a process that adds value to the product. For this reason, it is necessary to minimize waiting in processes.
3. ***Transportation*:** Moving products from one place to another is not a process that adds value to the product. This process is costing for organizations. Poorly planned settlements may require long haulage. This can also lead to handle products two or three times; so that the products that are thrown in an irregular manner are then held in the temporary warehouse and shifted to the stock warehouse. In order to remove this waste, it is necessary to

consider improvement in settlement, coordinates of processes, transportation methods, building maintenance, workplace organization (Suzaki, 2015, p. 33).

4. ***Over-processing:*** Over-processing waste relates to spending more time, efforts, and resources to produce higher quality product than is required by the customer, or producing these products using inappropriate tools. Many organizations use high precision equipment where simpler tools would be sufficient. Over-processing is considered the most difficult type of waste to identify and eliminate (Al-Baik & Miller, 2014, p. 2023).
5. ***Inventory*:** This means to waste the organization's funds to products-raw materials or stocks that are unnecessarily manufactured. In order to reduce stock levels; it is necessary to remove unused materials (building maintenance/workplace organization), not to manufacture parts that are not desired from the next process (line balance), not to buy or bring materials in big lots (saving obtained by reducing the volume may benefit more than ending stock waste), to manufacture products in small batches (shortened preparation time/more frequent changing of model) (Suzaki, 2015, p. 35).
6. ***Excess Motion:*** All the motions agents do other than manufacturing. An operator can be very "busy" searching for a tool through the whole plant for three hours, but does not add any value to the product. On the contrary, a three hour fee and three hour late manufactured product -rather than delivering the product to the customer- increases the product's cost (Suzaki, 2015, p. 36). This waste is related to workplace ergonomics and includes all instances of bending, stretching, walking, lifting, twisting, and searching for parts or tools. Jobs that need excessive human movement should be analyzed and redesigned to reduce the required amount of motion (Al-Baik & Miller, 2014, p. 2023).
7. ***Defects or Rework Waste*:** In addition to physical defects which directly add to the costs of goods sold, this may include errors in paperwork, late delivery, production according to incorrect specifications, use of too much raw materials or generation of unnecessary scrap. When defect occurs, rework may be required; otherwise the product will be scrapped. Generation of defects will not only waste material and labor resources, but it will also create material shortages, hinder meeting schedules, create idle time at subsequent workstations and extend the manufacturing lead time (Shah & Patel, 2018, p. 3794). As a result of manufacturing faulty product, these products will be reprocessed and errors will be eliminated or these products will be discarded. If the right production is done for the first time, these costs will not be encountered.

In the JIT system, it is aimed to produce outputs with lowest possible supply time and lowest cost by continuously identifying all types of waste and variance and eliminating them. Waste in the JIT system is seen as a symptom of problems rather than being seen as a problem (Yüksel, 2013, p. 196). At the core of the JIT system is rapid processing time and reduced inventory levels. By reducing inventory levels, storage costs and location-related costs are avoided when product demand is subsided. In the JIT system, resources are brought to place to be used only when needed, and there are no waiting times to disrupt production. Thus, the cost increases that will be caused by resource waste, the delays in meeting customer needs and the complexity of the production environment will be avoided. The complexity of the production environment is both costly and time consuming, such as the transfer of resources to be used in production to the production environment and the extra processing that does not add value to the product. This production system, in which a production based on quality is carried out and targeted for "continuous improvement", which means "kaizen" in Japanese, is widely used in automobile and computer industries. Honda, General Electric, Ford, Boeing, Hewlett-Packard, IBM and Zara have benefited from the JIT system in their operations.

In the JIT system, it is asked from the agents to determine the quality problems and, after determining, to fix those problems by finding their sources. In this way, the rate of the faulty products will decrease, efficiency will increase and poor quality costs will diminish. In the JIT system, there must be an integrated effort, which everyone in the organization included, to meet and exceed the customer's expectations. To ensure this, an effort to improve quality at all levels in the organization is required. The Japanese have cultivated a continuous improvement culture by spreading quality improvements throughout the organization and combining them with leadership of top management. This culture is known as "*Kaizen*" or "*Continuous Improvement*" (Ersoy & Ersoy, 2015, p. 447–448). Toyota, the organization that best practices the JIT system, has the ability called "*Shojinka*"; the ability to quickly change the number of employees working at the workshop to adapt to changes in demand. It is very important for Shojinka to train the agent to be "functional". Rotation is being applied to Toyota agents for them to be very functional. A worker learns all the work in a work station by going around at certain times, and over time, specializes in the whole of the work. As implemented in Toyota, this rotation should involve chiefs, foremen, chiefs of production and all the agents in a factory (Sevindirici, 2009, p. 95). In a research on the JIT system, it has been observed that most organizations use decision-making mechanisms that are not centralized. In this system, subjects such as more participation of agents to management and job rotation are prominent

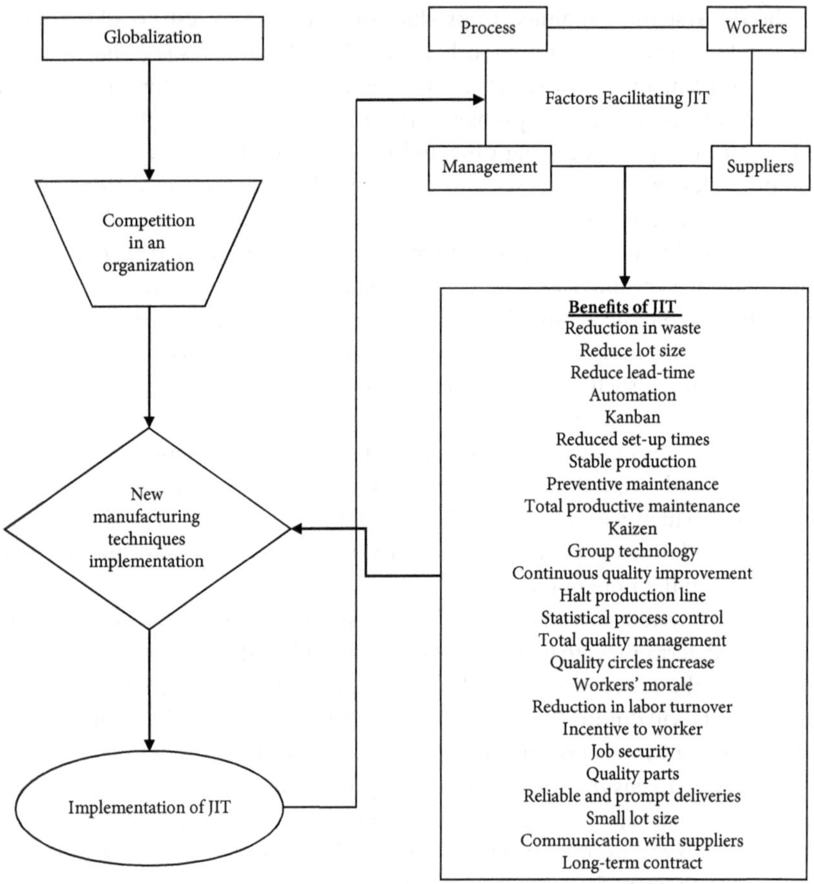

Fig. 2: Need of JIT. Source: Singh &Ahuja, 2012, p. 66

(Akgeyik, 1998, p. 81). For this, agents participate the teams that will be formed in order to solve problems at organizational level (Hay, 2000, p. 42). The need for JIT in an organization is highlighted in Fig. 2.

From the Fig. 2, it is clear that globalization leads to competition in an organization. To meet this competition organizations use modern techniques of manufacturing.

The JIT system is not new to the present scenario of industrialization. This technique is not limited to any particular country but due to its large potential of benefit it has a widespread application throughout the world. Many industries have adopted it and others are going to implement it for their survival in the fast competition at each stage in each area. Implementing JIT requires organizational changes as well as physical plant changes. Cultural transition barriers such as performance measures, organization structure and pay systems, often make organizational changes a tougher and longer process than the physical changes necessary for JIT. While solution to physical problems exists, JIT implementation often waits for organizational changes to catch up. Sustaining the continuous improvement philosophy of JIT is critically dependent on this organization transition. Implementing JIT requires a plan along with commitment. This plan should be an integral element in the company's total business plan (Singh & Garg, 2011, p. 28).

A smooth and stable demand is required for the implementation of the JIT system. To be able to achieve the superiority of the JIT system in the context of the stockless production, demand must not be variable (Yüksel, 2013, p. 196). There are six *intra-organizational* elements and one *non-organizational* element required for the implementation of the JIT system outside of Japan. The first among the intra-organizational elements is *the philosophy of just in time production*. Second is *related to the creation of quality in the source*. The other three are *related to production engineering*. These are, respectively, *improving production, cellular production or group technology*, the minimum machine preparation time when manufacturing one product after another. The sixth intra-organizational element is *the pull system and the control system called kanban*. As a non-organizational element, *relations with suppliers* in JIT system can be expressed (Hay, 2000, p. 4).

2.1 Quality at the Source

According to JIT, quality at source constitutes of two main principles: Total Quality Management (TQM) and Total Productive Maintenance (TPM). TQM and TPM are considered to be the key operational activities of quality management system. TPM increases the productivity of plant and equipment with an uncertain investment in maintenance. TPM includes the techniques of preventive maintenance (scheduled maintenance to avoid breakdowns), predictive maintenance (prediction of pending machine breakdowns and appropriate intervention to prevent them) and improvement maintenance (prediction of pending machine break downs and appropriate intervention to prevent them). TQM comprises of organization wide efforts to establish and install a setup where an organization continuously improves its ability to deliver high quality products and services to customers. Implementation of quality at source techniques aim to reduce manufacturing costs (e.g. costs occurring by the shorter life cycle of the machines, major equipment repairs etc.) while at the same time upgrading the quality of the products (Nisar et al., 2014, p. 69).

"Poka-Yoke" is one of the methods used to provide the quality at the source. Agents who work during production can make mistakes due to physical, psychological or physiological reasons. With Poka-Yoke method, it is aimed to minimize errors, which affect other processes when the errors occurred during production as a result of minor inattention are not noticed. With Poka Yoke, it is aimed to prevent errors before happening. By this way, waste rates reduce by minimizing errors in the system and efficiency increases (Paksoy & Bay, 2006, p. 2; Sevindirici, 2009, p. 83). Devices that automatically detect any faulty operation at the moment and automatically stop the machine/process in this case are placed for this purpose. Workers and engineers should work together to determine the cause of the error and make the necessary corrections immediately (Yüksel, 2013, p. 261–262).

In JIT system, one of the tools used to perform these corrections is *"Andon lights"*. Andon is the light that flashes when a worker pulls the rope to stop the line, the moment he noticed any error (Liker & Hoseus, 2008, p. 32). Although the lights vary depending on the application, generally, green light indicates normal conditions, yellow light indicates a problem and red light indicates the stoppage. Besides the lights are default in applications, the sound also can be used in warning systems (Yüksel, 2013, p. 201).

In the JIT system, it is an ordinary subject to stop machines in case any problem occurs. This subject is known as *"Jidoka"*. When an error occurs in this system, it is aimed to solve the error in real time or in active time. Active or real time refers to the time at which the fault occurred within the business process. Thus, feedback can be given to agents instantly. Agents see what goes wrong or abnormal in the process and try to solve it as soon as the problem occurs. At the same time problems caused by overproduction are also eliminated in this system and faulty production is prevented (Sevindirici, 2009, p. 84; Hay, 2000, p. 154). The reasons for "Jidoka" being so important are as follows (Sugimori et al., 1977, p. 557).

- To prevent making too much. If the equipment is made to stop when the required amount is produced, making too much cannot arise. Consequently, the just-in-time production can be accurately carried out.
- Control of abnormality becomes easy. It will only' be necessary to make improvements by directing attention to the stopped equipment and the worker who did the stopping. This is an important requirement when making up the system of full utilization of workers' capabilities' related next.

Although the Poka-Yoke or error prevention mechanisms can remove imperfections, the process capability of the machines must be taken into account; because at this point several factors can affect the quality of the product. For example, how can we guarantee that outer diameter of critical parts or the ability to solder a printed circuit board are always within specification limits? In practical terms, we can define the process capability as "the ability determined by the degree of diffusion or dispersion of product quality parameters". If we want to guarantee quality at the source to customer, we need to develop a reliable process capability (Suzaki, 2015, p. 127).

2.2 Levelling of Production

Provided that all processes perform small lot production and conveyance, if the quantity to be withdrawn by the subsequent process varies considerably, the processes within the company as well as the subcontractors will maintain peak capacity or holding excessive inventory at all times. Therefore, in order to make a just-in-time production possible, the prerequisite will be to level the production at the final assembly line (the most important line that gives out the production instructions to all processes) (Sugimori et al., 1977, p. 556). The organization should produce as much products as it can sell. In this way, the product stocks will no longer be needed. However, production needs to be programmed or smoothed in order to meet the changing demand. If the levelled production, which is using by Toyota, is divided into phases: In the first stage, the annual demand should be adjusted according to the monthly demand, and in the second stage the monthly demand should be adjusted according to the daily demand. Monthly adjustment is done by arranging the monthly production plan. The main production schedule is prepared according to the average daily production level for each process in the plant. This main production schedule is based on quarterly and monthly demand estimates. Daily coordination is based on daily production information. Kanban and sequential scheduling are used to set up this system (Çelikçapa, 1998, p. 182).

2.3 Cellular Production (Group Technology)

Production cells consist of machines with different specifications that come together to process the part families comprising of parts with similar shapes or process requirements. In a production cell, the workplace layout of the machines resembles a small assembly line and is generally U-shaped (Yüksel, 2013, p. 41). With the preference of U shaped lines in the JIT system, the investment and space requirement to be made for material movements and material transport vehicles is reduced, the production time is shortened in the system and coordination and communication are facilitated among the agents (Soyuer, 1999, p. 159). Taiichi Ohno is the organizer of the manufacturing system in a cellular fashion so that the workforce can be used more effectively. With this placement, the unnecessary movements or waste originating from the agents will be removed. The proximity and ease of access between the machines that is provided with the cellular placement increases productivity and efficiency. Cells must have the machinery and tools necessary for the production of certain product families. In this production process, machine preparation times have been reduced to minimum level. Agents must be capable of producing similar parts. With this placement, small lot production and part stock has decreased and the productivity of the agents has increased. Cellular placement allows for more variety and less costly production (Ersoy & Ersoy, 2012, p. 436). Group technology differs from a traditional facility layout in that a cross-trained worker may be required to run several machines within a cell. This technique is intended to eliminate operators' idle time resulting from producing smaller lot sizes and to increase operators' responsibility for quality of products being produced (Zhu et al., 1994, p. 5).

2.4 Pull System, Kanban and Machine Preparation Times

Pull systems are systems in which the next processes only demand parts from the previous processes in the amount that they will use, and they pull these parts or receive them from the previous system. The production schedule in the pull systems is regulated according to the final production process. By knowing what product and how much it will be produced during the last production process, it is ensured that only the parts needed for the process are pulled from the previous processes. At the same time, those in the other stages will not be able to produce without completing the work of the previous stage. Thus, each stage will produce to meet the demands of the subsequent stage. Pulling of the necessary amount of parts at the necessary time from the previous stage by the subsequent stages will minimize buffer stocks that will occur between these stages and fluctuations that will occur due to these buffer stocks. In this system, the cards showing how much to produce from which parts are called "kanban" (Acar, 2003, p. 16). The kanban system has some hypotheses. The *first* one is that if a part that needs to be produced at 5 pm has been produced at 5 am, that is a loss. What is correct and needed is that the piece is to be produced a few minutes before the required time. *Second*, the size of the batch in production must be adjusted to the smallest batch. To perform this, machine preparation times should be very little. Thus, the formation of semi-finished stocks will be prevented (Tekin, 2012, p. 38). Kanban as a main tool for production control in a JIT system. There are two types of Kanbans, which are used as a tool in the JIT production system. The 'withdrawal Kanban' is used to indicate the type and amount of product which the next process should withdraw from the preceding process. The 'production ordering Kanban' specifies the type and quantity of product which the current process must produce. Kanban is a pull based system. Parts/components are supplied when there is demand. Number of parts/components that are manufactured depends on customer's demand, in other words number of cards received by manufacturer. In Kanban system, parts/components are not produced until the manufacturer receives card. Kanban is a control mechanism that links production activities and transmitted demand information from final product buffers to the preceding workstation by using Kanban cards (Singh & Ahuja, 2012, p. 80).

To set up an effective JIT system, machine preparation times must be reduced to less than ten minutes. For this, it is aimed for production machines to process a product after another one less than ten minutes by the help of the Single Minute Exchange of Dies (SMED) technique improved by Shigeo Shingo (Yüksel, 2013, p. 196). In today's competitive world it is essential to speed up the die exchanging process. By reducing the time for exchanging the die, both the batch size and the stock level will be reduced and the production time will be shortened so that the factory will become flexible enough to respond to the changing market demand. The downsizing of the batch size also makes it easier to manage changing business priorities. These are the main reasons why shortening the die exchanging time is so important. The first reason to shorten the die exchanging time is not the increased capacity. Instead, we need to understand the total relations to the work (Suzaki, 2015, p. 54).

2.5 Relations with Supplier

A JIT production requires high quality, small lot sizes, and frequent delivery of raw materials. A good relationship with suppliers is crucial to achieve these requirements. For example, the Japanese make their vendors seem like the next level below the start of production (Zhu et al., 1994, p. 6). Production organizations using the JIT system often prefer to buy goods from their suppliers. Because they often buy goods from suppliers, suppliers give quality assurance to their products. If quality assurance is assured from the supplier, the parts are taken to the production process without the need for quality control when the parts come to the manufacturer. This saves time required for quality control of incoming parts. For this, the supplier must be integrated with the manufacturing plant. This will also reduce the stock the supplier has (Çelikçapa, 2000, p. 252). In order to reduce time losses due to inputs at the manufacturer, there is a time needed to work closely with the supplier organization to solve the problem, and mutual trust with the suppliers. Such a situation cannot be achieved with hundreds of suppliers. At the same time, this cannot be achieved when suppliers often change prices. The relations to be established with suppliers and the quality of the goods provided should be good. The profit both sides get should increase in the long term (Hay, 2000, p. 126). In the JIT system, the relationship between suppliers and manufacturers can be likened to a marriage. In order to establish such a relationship, there is necessity for a long-term, comprehensive and rigorous work which both sides will be pleased with. Just as the relationship between the supplier and the manufacturer, the relationship between the various departments must be good (Akgeyik, 1998, p. 80). Some important issues related to the relations with suppliers are as follows (Suzaki, 2015, p. 226):

- From a supplier point of view, the manufacturers are customers. Suppliers should provide *delivery, quality and cost* assurance to manufacturers. They should cooperate closely with manufacturers to understand their needs and to reflect these into their services.
- In terms of delivery, timely delivery in small batches with short intervals should be targeted to tighten the manufacturer-supplier relationship. In order to achieve this, a kanban system mixed loading and the delivery in short intervals can be applied between the manufacturer and the supplier.
- The idea of "quality at the source" should be applied as much as possible about quality. Poka-Yoke application and statistical process control should encouraged at the plant.
- In terms of cost, improvements similar to those made in the manufacturer's factory should be made. Sharing ideas to improve cost helps companies maintain their competitive position.

Organizations that implement the JIT system have abandoned many work related to manufacturing and transferred those to suppliers or subsidiary companies. They ask to subsidiary companies "*how good am I, how pleased you are from me*" instead of saying "*you are that good or bad*". In the first inference there is only the evaluation of the other side whereas in the second estimation the manufacturer tries to measure the satisfaction of the other side with an evaluation based on his own system. At the same time, the manufacturer organization is transparent in the accounts and relations with the subsidiary companies or suppliers (Yamak, 2015, p. 242).

3 Conclusion

JIT has become a new management practice in all types of organizations. In recent years, many organizations have showed significant improvements in business through JIT implementation. JIT strategies and philosophy can be effectively employed to realize fundamental improvements of manufacturing performance in the organization, thereby leading the organization to compete with others successfully in this highly competitive environment. JIT can prove to be an effective global strategy by which firms can enhance their performance and achieve competencies. Thus, in this highly competitive scenario, by using JIT the organizations could scale new levels of achievements (Singh & Ahuja, 2012, p. 91). In the JIT system, short-lived products can respond more quickly and easily to sudden changes in demand. Generally, the strategy of enterprises adopting the JIT system; to increase the speed of the processing times, to reduce the inventory levels, to eliminate waste, to ensure that every source needed in the system is kept at the desired level, time and place. In order for enterprises to use the JIT system, the demand for their products must have a proper and deterministic structure. Because adapting the production speed to be fast and to have no stock according to the changing demand requires this. In order to increase the speed of production in the JIT system, similar parts to be produced with the same equipment are produced in certain cells. Collecting and producing similar jobs in these production cells will reduce the machine setting times. It is very important that the production in the JIT system is carried out without interruption and realized at a certain quality level. Therefore, the maintenance of the machines using is provided with preventive maintenance, and the quality level of the products is ensured through collaborations and standards that will be improved in order to improve the resources provided by the suppliers. At the same time, for businesses, it is preferable situation for the suppliers to be close to production facilities, so that the needs of the customers can be met immediately.

References

Acar, N. (2003). Tam zamanında üretim. Ankara: Milli Prodüktivite Merkezi Yayınları.

Akgeyik, T. (1998). Stratejik üretim yönetimi. İstanbul: Sistem Yayıncılık.

Al-Baik, O. & Miller, J. (2014). Waste identification and elimination in information technology organizations. Empirical Software Engineering, 19(6), 2019–2061.

Alcaraz J. L. G., Maldonado, A. A., Iniesta, A. A, Robles, G. C. & Hernández, G. A. (2014). A systematic review/survey for JIT implementation: Mexican maquiladoras as case study. Computers in Industry, 65(4), 761–773.

Brox, J. A. & Fader, C. (2010). The set of just-in-time management strategies: an assessment of their impact on plant-level productivity and input-factor substitutability using variable cost function estimates. International Journal of Production Research, 40(12), 2705–2720.

Çelikçapa Odman, F. (1998). Endüstri işletmelerinde üretim yönetimi ve teknikleri. Bursa: Vipaş Yayınları.

Çelikçapa Odman, F. (2000). Üretim yönetimi ve teknikleri. İstanbul: Alfa Yayınları.

Demir, G. & Gümüşoğlu, Ş. (2009). Üretim Yönetimi (İşlemler yönetimi). İstanbul: Beta Basım Yayım Dağıtım.

Ersoy Saat, M. & Ersoy, A. (2012). Üretim/işlemler yönetimi. Ankara: İmaj Yayınları.

Ersoy Saat, M. & Ersoy, A. (2015). Üretim/işlemler yönetimi. Ankara: İmaj Yayınları.

Hay, E. J. (2000). Tam zamanında yönetim: Yeni üretim temellerinin uygulanması (Just-in-time breakthrough). (Çev: Oygur Yamak). İstanbul: Türkmen Kitapevi, 1988.

Liker, J. K. & Hoseus, M. (2008). Toyota kültürü. (Çev: Kıvanç Tanrıyar). İstanbul: Optimist Yayınevi.

Nisar, Q. A., Shakeel, H. K., Ahmad, S., Niazi, K. & Ashraf, S. (2014). Application of just-in-time principles to financial services. International Journal of Scientific & Engineering Research, 5(8), 6–78.

Paksoy, T. & Bay, M. (2006). Tam zamanında üretim sistemlerinde hata önleyiciler: Poka-yokeler. Akademik Bakış: Uluslararası Hakemli Sosyal Bilimler E-Dergisi, 10, 1–4.

Shah, D. & Patel, P. (2018). Productivity improvement by implementing lean manufacturing tools in manufacturing industry. International Research Journal of Engineering and Technology, 5(3), 3794–3798.

Singh, S. & Garg, D. (2011). JIT system: concepts, benefits and motivation in Indian industries. International Journal of Migration and Border Studies, 1(1), 26–30.

Singh, G. & Ahuja, I. S. (2012). Just-in-time manufacturing: literature review and directions. International Journal Business Continuity and Risk Management, 3(1), 57–98.

Sevindirici, İ. (2009). Üretim teknikleri. İstanbul: Kum Saati Yayınları.

Soyuer, H. (1999), Tam zamanında üretim sistemlerinin küçük ve orta ölçekli işletmelerde uygulanma koşulları. Gazi Üniversitesi İktisadi ve İdari Bilimler Fakültesi Dergisi, 1(2), 155–166.

Sugimori, Y., Kusunoki, K., Cho, F. & Uchikawa, S. (1977). Toyota production system and kanban system materialization of just-in-time and respect-for-human system. The International Journal of Production Research, 15(6), 553–564.

Suzaki, K. (2015). İmalatta mükemmellik yolu.(Çev: Saadet Özkal). İstanbul: Optimist Yayıncılık, 1987.

Üreten, S. (1998). Üretim işlemler yönetimi: Planlama-denetim kararları, karar modelleri ve iyileştirme yaklaşımları. Ankara: THK Matbaası.

Tekin, M. (2012). Üretim yönetimi. Konya: Güney Ofset Yayıncılık.

Yamak, O. (2015). Kalite odaklı mükemmellik: Değer yaratan kurumların sıçrama stratejisi. Ankara: Nobel Akademik Yayıncılık.

Yüksel, H. (2013). Üretim/işlemler yönetimi temel kavramlar. Ankara: Nobel Yayıncılık.

Zhu, Z., Meredith, P. H., & Makboonprasith, S. (1994). Defining critical elements in jit implementation: a survey. Industrial Management & Data Systems, 94(5), 3–10.

Saadet Ela Pelenk[1]

The Effect of Innovation Culture on Creative Performance: A Research in the Chemical Sector

1 Introduction

An innovative enterprise, while at least one innovation (Oslo Report, 2005), has not actually made innovation, but the innovation enterprise in the review period is also considered to be innovative. All activities related to the development or realization of innovations, including those planned for the future in this respect, are innovations. On the other hand, culture is the sum of the material and spiritual heritage of the communities and everything that a person teaches to convey to future generations (Yılmaz and Eroğlu, 2008, Kongar, 1972).

The cultural product of an innovative business should have the features that require this purpose and mission. So specific features of innovation culture; "questioning, rewarding, participant, cross-communication channels, mistakes, risk taking, project teams, etc."

Therefore, while the innovation culture provides a culture of innovation for the enterprise, the wage system is fair and the individual-organizational values are compatible. For the employee, joint decision making, discussion of ideas and different levels of disclosure will increase the employee's performance (Robbins, 1998). The aim of the research is the effect of innovative culture on creative performance. Chemistry businesses that respond to many basic needs from hygienic materials to basic needs for life are becoming more selective in their products and services as conscious consumers increase. The research emphasizes the contribution of Hannan and Freeman (1978) to the innovativeness of employees in competitive businesses, which is required by "organizational ecology theory".

2 Conceptual Framework

Culture, in terms of social sciences, is a hereditary phenomenon which includes religion, language, customs, education and knowledge. In this direction, human

1 Recep Tayyip Erdoğan University, Fındıklı Applied Sciences High School, Bank and Finance Department, Fındıklı/RİZE, saadetela.pelenk@erdogan.edu.tr.

is based on society, content and learning (Sökmen, 2013: 57). When we look at the general characteristics of the culture that it puts the human at the center of life, it is shared by the society (Kozlu, 1986).

Hannerz (1992), who believes in the dynamic nature of the culture, sees the world as an area of transnational cultural connection that allows for new cultural exchanges and diversity through the process of cultural interaction. Culture has been used as a universal name for all the products and the societies have tried to achieve a useful purpose for them (Özlem, 2000: 146). At this point, culture is a dynamic phenomenon (Hatch, 1993; Schein, 2010). Organizational culture as a sub-item of culture, is norm and value that influences employees' attitudes and behaviors (Dinçer, 1992: 271).

According to Martin and Siehl (1983), subculture facilitates acceptance of new ideas by staying within non-appropriate boundaries against the dominant culture; thus promoting the development of innovation (Dougherty, 1992). In this context, the ability of enterprises to innovate depends on the innovativeness of organizational culture (Ürper, 2008). At this point, an innovative enterprise should carry the characteristics of innovation culture (Özgenç, 2007: 78), and that creativity, continuous learning and information sharing are common (Brettel and Cleven, 2011: 255).Innovative culture should be addressed within community and organizational culture, should be placed between these two cultures (Ürper, 2008). For this aim, it is important how employees believe in innovation; links to the existing culture, feed the culture of innovation (Tzafirir et al., 2003).

An innovative cultural feature is as follows (Barker, 2002):

- Stocked information,
- Employee information,
- To meet environmental requirements,
- Creativity.

In the model of innovation culture, creativity and innovativeness (Martins and Terblanche, 2003), a number of cultural premises, such as strategy, structure, support mechanisms, and behaviors that support open communication, have been found to influence creativity and innovativeness.

Innovation features such as operating awards, ownership of innovation, efficient use of resources and open communication. At this point, Mc Lean (2005) has published several important studies, including cultural factors that support innovation; collect cultural factors that support innovation in six groups:

1. Organizational incentives should be given.
2. Management support.

3. Business groups should be supported.
4. Individuals, freedom and autonomy should be created.
5. Time and money are required.
6. Innovative obstacles must be removed.

Rewarding the employees involved in innovation ensures that the innovation is successful (Kanter, 1983, Ahmed, 1988, Martins and Terblanche, 2003). Rewards are awarded for the idea that reflects innovative values or the risk that employees take (Martins and Terblanche, 2003); internal rewards are more preferred than external rewards. Thus, employees produce more creative ideas (Kanter, 1983). At this point, there is a variety of work in innovative cultures that increase their creative performance (Ahmed, 1988, Martins and Terblanche, 2003).

Analysis of business values and employee qualifications are important, as innovation comes into play as a product of an internal and external environment that supports and motivates it (Luecke, 2011: 142–144; Cantin and Thom, 1996). In this respect, there are individual effects of ınnovative culture; for example, a change in organizational culture with less resistance (Hornsby et al., 2002), influencing innovation in the positive direction (Judge, 1997). Therefore, the behavior of employees are related to cultural influences in such matters as participation in decisions, openness, knowledge management, stability, control and continuity (Denison and Spreitzer, 1991).

The performance of an employee is influenced by the management structure and the application of the leadership (Kayalar et al., 2007: 46). Performance is the degree to which a specific purpose or task is performed (Borman and Motowidlo, 1993). The performance of the employee also forms the behavior (Bingöl, 2003: 273; Jucevicius, 2007) and provide job satisfaction (Erdoğan, 1991: 376), while professional development is the most effective way of learning. (Chen et al., 2003: 424–425). It has been shown that employees who increase their creative performances with autonomy, collectivism, participation and learning opportunities (Bakker and Demerouti, 2001), awards (Chandler, Keller and Lyon, 2000), career development and targeted achievement (Demerouti, Bakker, Nachreiner and Schaufeli (2001); Mc Lean, 2005), job satisfaction is expected to be positively affected (Bakker and Demerouti, 2001).

3 Method

In the study, the relational scanning method was used. Describe the purpose of the scanning models in the way they are; the aim of the relational (comparative) screening model is to examine whether more than one variable differs according to each other and groups (Karasar, 2015: 77).

4 Data Collection Tool

In practice, survey method was used with the respondents participating in the survey. The selection of the research sample was performed by easy sampling easily method. A questionnaire consisting of three parts, was used as data collection tool in the research. In the first part of the data collection tool, there is an information form consisting of participants' gender, marital status, age, education level and working time in business.

The second part of the questionnaire contains the "Creative Performance Scale" developed by Rice (2006) and adapted to Turkish by Akturan (2015) and reliability and validity studies were conducted. Scale consists of 9 items and one dimension in likert type of 5 (1-absolutely not, 5-strictly agree). In this study, the Cronbach Alpha coefficient was found to be 0.62. In the third part of the questionnaire," Innovation Culture Scale" developed by Hurley and Hult (1998) is included. The scale consists of 7 items and one dimension. In this study, the Cronbach Alpha coefficient of the scale was 0.61.

In the study, the relational scanning method was used. Describe the purpose of the scanning models in the way they are; the purpose of the relational (comparative) screening model is to examine whether more than one variable differs according to each other and groups (Karasar, 2015: 77).

5 Data Collection Method

In practice, survey method was used with the respondents participating in the survey. Questionnaires obtained from the research application were evaluated and data from 95 available questionnaires were evaluated after missing questionnaires and unsuitable surveys.

6 Sample of Research

Of the 95 employees who participated in the survey, 26.3 % were female and 73.7 % were male. The average age of participants was 34,36 ± 3,49, 11,6 % were below 30 years, 57,9 % between 31–35 years, 30,5 % 36 years and over. 57.9 % of participants were married and 42.1 % were married. 62.1 % of the participants were undergraduates and 37.9 % were trained at the graduate level. The average duration of work of the participants in the operation (year) is 5,08 ± 1,47, 32,6 % of the working time during the operation is less than 5 years, 67,4 % is 5 years and over.

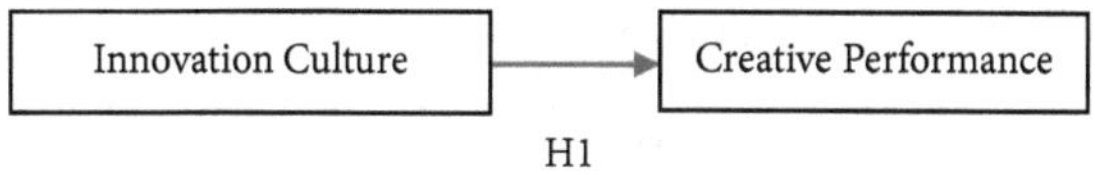

Fig. 1: Model of the study

7 Models and Hypotheses of Research

The model of the study was established as follows (Fig. 1). The independent variable in the research model is the "innovation culture" and dependent variable is the "creative performance"; so the model shows that the influence of innovative culture on the creative performance.

The hypothesis of the research was formed within the framework of the model of the research in Fig. 1. Accordingly, the hypothesis of the research;

H1: The culture of innovation has a positive and significant effect on creative performance.

8 Analysis of Data

SPSS 21.0 statistical software program was used to evaluate the data obtained in relation to the research. Cronbach Alpha test was performed to test the reliability of the research scales. Then, the averages, standard deviations and normality distributions of the research variables were determined (Çokluk, Şekercioğlu and Büyüköztürk, 2010: 17). Correlation and regression analyses were conducted to verify research hypotheses. The level of significance in the analyses was taken as 0.05.

9 Findings

Descriptive statistics for variables are given in Tab. 1.

The participants' creative performance score (4,08 ± 0,38) and innovation culture perception score (4,07 ± 0,42) were "high" according to Tab. 1. Correlation analyses showing the relationship between the variables are given in Tab. 2.

According to the results of correlation analysis in Tab. 2, there was a positive and significant relationship between innovation culture and creative performance ($r = 0,35$, $p < 0,05$).

The model showing the relationship between innovation culture perception and creative performance seems appropriate ($F_{(1; 93)} = 13,27$; $p < 0,05$). The

Tab. 1: Descriptive Statistics of Variables

Variables	Matter Number	$\bar{X}$	SS	Skewness
Creative Performance	9	4,08	0,38	−0,39
Innovation Culture	7	4,07	0,42	0,21

Tab. 2: Results of Correlation Analysis Between Variables

Variables	Creative Performance
Innovative Culture	0,353**

*p<0,05
**p<0,01

Tab. 3: Results of Regression Analysis on the Effect of Innovation Culture Algorithm on Creative Performance

Independent Variables	B	SH_B	β	t	p
Constant	2,788	0,358		7,794	0,000
Innovation Culture	0,318	0,087	0,353	3,643	**0,000**

$F_{(1;93)} = 13{,}274$; $p = 0{,}000$; $R^2 = 0{,}125$; $\Delta R^2 = 0{,}116$

perception of innovation culture accounts for about 12 % of the change in creative performance ($R^2 = 0{,}116$) (Tab. 3). According to the results of t test on regression coefficients and meaningfulness, “innovation culture has positive and significant positive effect on creative performance ($\beta = 0{,}35$; $t = 3{,}64$; $p < 0{,}05$)”. According to the results obtained, as the sense of innovation culture of businessmen increases, their creative performances also increase. According to the results of regression analysis, the mathematical model of the effect of novelty culture perception on creative performance is as follows:

Creative Performance = 2,79 + 0,35 * Perception of Innovation Culture

H1 Acceptance: The culture of innovation has a positive and significant effect on creative performance.

10 Result

21st Century businesses must be innovative to adapt to increased technology and environmental change. Innovation takes its place as a “cultural development and change" activity rather than a one-time activity. Achieved success in innovative culture enhances individual and business performance. Whether product-service, process or organizational innovation, an innovative environment brings confidence to employees and allowing the employee to improve himself /herself, thereby enable him/her to reach profitability opportunities.

The business acquiring this character is concerned with the adoption of innovative practices, approaches and norms in knitting. This is in fact a culture that emphasizes innovative values is ossified and made part of everyday life. At this point, the employee who does not see his/her job as a task and ideally adopts, will be more motivated to achieve. The creativity and productivity of the employee who catches a high motivational environment will increase and the contribution to the performance will increase as well.

According to the results of the research; "a positive and significant relationship was found between innovation culture and creative performance ($r = 0.35$, $p < 0.05$)". This result is supported by various researches (Kanter, 1983; Luecke, 2011; Jucevicius, 2007). Innovation culture can be defined as continuous learning, openness to change, adaptation, tolerance of risks, promotion of individual creativity, sharing of ideas, implementation, freedom of movement unrestricted by hierarchical authority, it has many features (Pelenk, 2016). At this point, the satisfaction and performance of employees who internalize such culture can also increase at the same time. In this context, managerial support, autonomy, performance feedback, participation and learning opportunities (Bakker et al., 2001), award (Chandler, Keller and Lyon, 2000), job satisfaction of employees whose career performance and goal achievement increase their creative performances (Mc Lean, 2005) are positively affected (Bakker et al., 2001; Günsel and Pelenk, 2017).

Innovative business alters and alerts every employee in their field of communication, their performances, their career development, their empowerment from their proposal system, their creativity, their job rotation and their continuous learning and their social projects. Turkey's higher level of sophistication and innovation by business executives, exhibiting a more participatory attitude, they believe in the continuity of the successful outcome of this process and in this case, the performance of employees is hoped will reflect more positive. From this point of view, the research can be examined in different sectors by expanding cultural variables or adding personality elements.

References

Ahmed, P. K. (1998). "Culture and Climate for Innovation". European Journal of Innovation Management, Cilt.1, Sayı.1, ss. 30–43.

Amabile, T. (1988). "A Model of Creativity and Innovation in Organizations". Reseaarch in Organizational Behavior, Vol.10, ss.123–167.

Brettel, M. and Cleven, N. J. (2011). "Innovation Culture, Collaboration with External Partners and Npd Performance", Creativity And Innovation Management, Cilt.20, Sayı.4.

Demerouti, E., Bakker, A. B., Nachreiner, F. and Schaufeli, W. B. (2001). "The Job Demands-Resources Model of Burnout", Journal of Applied Psychology, Vol.86, ss.499–512.

Denison, D. R. and Spreitzer, G. M. (1991). Organizational Culture and Organizational Development: A Competing Values Approach. Research in Organizational Change and Development, Vol.5, ss.1–21.

Günsel, A. and Pelenk, S. A. (2017). "Yenilikçi İnsan Kaynakları Yönetimi Uygulamalarının Yenilik Odaklı Bir Kültür Oluşturmadaki Rolü", Uluslararası Turizm, Ekonomi ve İşletme Bilimleri Dergisi, Cilt:1, Sayı:2, ss.57–68.

Hornsby, J. S., Kuratko, D. F. and Zahra, S. A. (2002). "Middle Managers Perception of the Internal Environment for Corporate Entrepreneurship: Assessing a Measurement Scale". Journal of Business Venturing, Sayı:17, ss. 253–273.

Kanter, R. M. (1983). The Change Matters: Innovation for Productivity in the American Corporation. New York: Simon & Schuster.

Luecke, Richard (2011). İş Dünyasında Yenilik Ve Yaratıcılık (Çev.Turan Parlak). Harvard Business Press, 2. Baskı, İstanbul: İş Bankası Kültür Yayınları.

Martıns, E. C. and Terblanche, F. (2003). "Building Organizational Culture That Stimulates Creativity and Innovation". European Journal of Innovation Management, Cilt.6, Sayı. 1, ss. 66–74.

Mclean, L. D. (2005). "Organizational Culture's Influence on Creativity and Innovation: A Review of the Literature and Implications for Human Resource Development". Advances in Developing Human Resources, Cilt. 7, Sayı. 2, ss. 226–246.

Oslo Report (2005). http://www.tubitak.gov.tr/tubitak_content_files/btypd/kilavuzlar/oslo_3_tr.pdf. (04.05.2018).

Pelenk, S. E. (2016). "Yenilikçi İnsan Kaynakları Yönetimi Uygulamalarının Yenilik Odaklı Bir Kültür Oluşturmadaki Rolü Bağlamında İş Tatmini Ve İş Performansı Üzerindeki Etkileri", Doktora Tezi, Kocaeli: Kocaeli Üniversitesi S.B.E.

Robbins, Stephan P. (1998). Organizational Behaviour. New Jersey: Prentice Hall.

Sniukas, Marc (2007). "Reshaping Strategy the Content, Process, and Context of Strategic Innovation". http://www.sniukas.com/wp-content/upload s/reshaping_sniukas.pdf/.(10.10. 2018).

Steele, J. and Murray, M. (2004). "Creating, Supporting and Sustaining a Culture of Innovation". Engineering, Construction and Architectural Management, Cilt.11, Sayı. 5, s. 320.

Tzafrir, S. and Gur, A. B. A. (2007). "H.R.M. Practices and Perceived Service Quality: The Role of Trust as a Mediator". Research and Practice in Human Resource Management, Cilt. 15, Sayı. 2, ss. 1–20.

Doğan Bakirtas[1]

The Effect of Tax Wedge on Youth Unemployment: A Panel VAR Approach

1 Introduction

Today, unemployment is the foremost economic problem faced by countries worldwide. The first group to be affected negatively as a result of the factors that cause a decrease in the production such as structural problems, lack of demand or crisis experienced in the economies of both developed and developing countries is employees. A decline in the production capacity and the existence of negative market factors decrease employment rates while increasing unemployment rates. Also, these kinds of problems lead to a drop in the level of economic growth that contributes positively to employment especially in the developing countries where the potential level of the young labour force is high (Ghose et al. 2008: p. 17). Although it is stated that young populations possessed by countries having the qualities of being dynamic, creative and open-minded make a positive contribution to the economic growth process (Günaydın & Çetin, 2015: p. 18), this contribution will come true with the expansion of employment opportunities for the young population.

It can be said that the youth unemployment rate is higher than the pre-crisis levels around the world, although it has declined significantly since the global crisis in 2009. It is observed in Arab counties that while the young unemployment rate was 26.4 in 2008, the same rate increased to 29.7 in 2018. Considering the same time periods, the rate in North Africa rise from 24.4 to 28.6. On the other hand, in North, South and Eastern Europe, youth unemployment rate which was 16 in 2008 went up to 17.8 in 2018. As for the world average, it is seen that the level of youth unemployment rate that was 12.3 in 2008 increased to 13.1 in 2018 (ILO, 2018).

Another factor that affects employment of the youth whose involvement in the labour market is declining due to many factors such as inadequate aggregate demand, demographic factors, insufficient labour and education policies, economic stagnation and crisis, is tax wedge (Murat & Şahin, 2011: pp. 19–27).

1 PhD, Manisa Celal Bayar University, Faculty of Economics and Administrative Sciences, Department of Public Finance, dogan.bakirtas@cbu.edu.tr.

The tax wedge can be defined as the difference between the gross labour income and the net take-home pay of the employee (Festa, 2015; OECD, 2018) or, in other words, the sum of taxes paid to the state per labour and social security contributions (Radu et al. 2018). Even though the definitions of tax wedge differ partly, the common point in these definitions is the employee's tax and financial obligations on the income. These obligations increase the cost caused by the labour to the employer. Business owners, who try to minimize their costs in order to make profit tend to employ unrecorded workers, participate in the underground economy and eventually reduce the labour capacity. In the process of reducing the labour capacity, the young labour force is the first to be chosen. The reasons may arise from the fact that the employers want to retain the key members of the business, young labour is inexperienced, investments in job shadowing are low, redundancy payments becomes higher as the service length increases (Casson, 1979: p. 58) and it is easy to relocate young workers as they are generally single and childless (Pastore, 2018: p. 3).

The rest of the paper is organized as follows: Section 1 presents the theoretical framework and empirical literature review on the relationship between the tax wedge and unemployment. Section 2 introduces the data and methodology. Section 3 discusses the empirical results. Last section presents concluding remarks.

2 Theoretical Framework and Literature Review

Economic activities are mainly determined by tax wedge on employment. Tax wedge has been regarded as a reason for rapidly increasing the unemployment rate in Europe since the 1960s and a reason behind the difficulty of reducing the unemployment rates (Morawski & Myck, 2010: p. 556).

While taxes on the labour *(personal income tax and social security contributions)* directly reduce labour demand since they increase labour costs and by lowering after-tax wages, they also reduce labour supply. The same effect is also observed with the final consumption tax, which leads to a decrease in real wages. Corporate taxes, on the other hand, can have an influence on the level of employment as they reduce investment and production. Meanwhile, companies deal with these tax and financial obligations by lowering the wages of employees (Cottarelli, 2012: p. 10). Because of an increase in tax wedge, labour costs to employers get higher and net wages to employees and employment decrease. In this case, the reflection of the increase in the tax is on employers and labour. If there is an increase in payroll taxes, labour demand decreases and this reduces equilibrium net wages for employees. In such a case, employment gives some of the tax burdens on labour in order to adapt to the new equilibrium (Carey, 2003: p. 39).

In terms of demand, tax wedge theoretically can have a positive or negative effect on participation in labour depending on income and substitution effect. The effect of tax wedge on the level of employment or wages depends on the tax incidence, which is dependent on supply flexibility. Tax wedges will have a greater negative employment impact on the condition that labour supply is flexible. This is more probable when the income effect is small and the substitution effect is large (Behar, 2009: p. 82).

There are many empirical studies in the literature which reveal the effects of tax wedge on unemployment and employment. According to the findings of an analysis performed by Nickell and Layard (1999) using the data of 20 OECD member countries between 1983 and 1994, a 5 % reduction in tax wedge results in a 13 % reduction in the level of unemployment. In another study conducted by Nickell (2003), it was pointed out that a 10-point increase in the tax wedge caused a decrease in the employment participation of 1 % to 3 % of working age population. Daveri and Tabellini (2000), who investigated the relationship between tax wedge and unemployment in a comprehensive way, analysed the relationship by using five-year data of 14 countries that they divided into three groups (ANGLO, EUCON and NORDIC) between 1965 and 1995. According to the findings of the analysis, it was found out that in the case that labour cost is high, the firms tend to reduce labour demand. They also stated that a 10 % increase in the tax wedge can increase the unemployment rate up to 4 %. In addition, they argued that the capital will come into prominence rather than the labour factor and this can reduce the marginal productivity of the capital in the long run.

Another comprehensive research was carried out by Gora et al. (2006) by including different country groups. In the analysis in which the data of eight new members of EU between 1996 and 2003 are used, a 1 % increase in tax wedge resulted in a decrease in the employment rate by about 0.5 %. In the same period, however, in the analysis performed for 14 OECD member countries, no finding was obtained regarding the effect of tax wedge on employment. In the analysis conducted by Dolenc and Laporsek (2010) using the data of 27 EU member countries between 1999 and 2008, it was found out that a 1 % increase in the tax wedge caused a 0.04 point decrease in the employment growth of the countries included in the analysis. Bassanini and Duval (2006) analysed the data of 21 OECD member countries between 1983 and 2003 with the aim of revealing the effect of tax wedge on employment and unemployment. According to the findings of the analysis, they suggested that a 10-point decrease in the tax wedge would lead to a 2.8 decrease in the unemployment rate and increase the employment rate 3.7 times. Radu et al. (2018), who investigated the relationship between labour costs and unemployment by cluster analysis, indicated that in the countries where the difference between labour costs and net wages is high and which have a high level of unemployment, some financial measures have to be taken in order to reduce labour costs. Another cluster analysis was conducted by Trpeski and Tashevska (2012), and it was found out that especially in the developed countries, the high tax wedge leads to a lower employment rate.

Besides all these above-mentioned studies, there are many other studies analysing the effects of tax wedge and/or labour costs on unemployment and/or employment in the literature (Elmeskov et al. 1998; Ederveen & Thissen, 2004; Gnip & Tomic, 2010; Morawski & Myck, 2010; Lehmann et al. 2013; Deskar-Skrbic et al. 2018). The common point of these studies is that an increase in the rate of tax wedge will lead to a decrease/increase in the employment/unemployment rate.

3 Data and Methodology

In the study, the data of 35 OECD member countries between 2000 and 2016 were used. Especially the availability of data on tax wedge has been the basic determinant of the selection of time period and cross-section.

Descriptions of the variables used in the analysis are shown in the table below (Tab. 1).

The OECD statistical database has several indicators of average tax wedge. Considering these indicators, it is seen that the tax burden differs among the individuals due to factors such as marital status, number of the children and income obtained (Aydın, 2013: p. 90). Since the scope of this study includes youth unemployment, the average tax wedge (as the percentage of labour cost) indicator calculated for those whose marital status is single and who earns 67 % of average income was used in the analysis. In their study, Dolenc and Laporšek (2010) suggested that the average wages do not reflect wage distribution in real life and the median value of income should be used in the studies to be carried out. In the analysis that they performed in their own study, they used the indicator represented by 67 % of average income.

The data used in the analysis on the youth unemployment rate, per capita growth rate and inflation were obtained from the World Bank's online database.

Since the time dimension is short, panel data analysis method is preferred in the study. Stationarity properties of the data was analysed through LLC test

Tab. 1: Variables Used in the Analysis

Variable	Unit	Data Source
Average tax wedge (taxwedge) Single person at 67 % of average earnings, no child	% of labour cost	OECD stat
GDP per capita growth (percagrwth)	Annual %	World Development Indicator
Inflation, consumer prices (cpi)	Annual %	World Development Indicator
Unemployment, total (unemp)	% of total labour force	World Development Indicator
Unemployment, youth total (yunemp)	% of total labour force ages 15–24	World Development Indicator

developed by Levin et al. (2002), IPS test developed by Im et al. (2003) and panel unit root tests developed by Breitung and Das (2005).

The relationship between the tax wedge rate and the youth unemployment rate is estimated by the PVAR (Panel Vector Auto-Regressive) model. This model incorporates the traditional VAR approach, which considers all the variables in the system internally, with a panel data approach that allows for individual unobserved heterogeneity. The first order panel VAR model can be formulated as follows (Love & Zicchino, 2006: p. 193):

$$z_{it} = \Gamma_0 + \Gamma_1 z_{it-1} + f_i + d_{c,t} + e_t$$

In this formula, zit represents the vector of endogenous variables (youth unemployment rate, tax wedge rate, inflation rate, GSYH per capita growth rate); fi symbolizes the fixed effects representing individual heterogeneity, dc,t represents dummy variable specific to the country, Γ_0 represents vectors of constant terms, Γ_1 shows matrix polynomial and et symbolizes error term. The panel VAR model established for the analysis was estimated by the Generalized Method of Moments (GMM).

In the evaluation of the dynamics of the VAR model, impulse-response functions and variance decomposition are used. After calculating the standard errors of the impulse-response functions, confidence intervals were obtained by Monte Carlo simulation. A period of 10 terms was used for the variance decomposition, which indicates how much change in one variable is explained by the change in the other variable. Panel VAR estimations were made by using Stata Code developed by Abrigo and Love (2015).

Tab. 2: Panel Unit Root Test Results

Variables	LLC	IPS	Breitung and Das (2005)
yunemp	-2.89***	-2.64***	-1.71**
percagrwth	-11.84***	-6.83***	-8.08***
cpi	-11.07***	-7.16***	-5.86***
taxwedge	-1.13	0.04	-0.36
Δtaxwedge	-14.70***	-9.55***	-5.42***

***Note:** The test statistics are based on the model with constant and trend. The lag lengths for the LLC and IPS tests are determined by the Schwarz information criterion. *** and ** indicates the level of significance at 1 % and 5 % respectively.*

Tab. 3: Lag Length Test Results for PVAR model

Lag Length	MBIC	MAIC	MQIC
1	-199,84	-10,08	-85,346
2	-145,27	-18,77	-68,94
3	-72,58	-9,33	-34,42

4 Empirical Results

The unit root test results of the variables used in the analysis are shown in the table below (Tab. 2).

According to LLC, IPS and Breitund and Das (2005) panel unit root test results, the null hypothesis that there is unit root was rejected for the variables of youth unemployment rate (yunemp), inflation rate (cpi) and per capita growth rate (percagrwth), and they are found stationary in level. Tax wedge variable, on the other hand, was found to be stationary in the first difference. In the analysis, the tax wedge variable was used by taking the first difference.

The results of the tests for determining the appropriate lag length in PVAR analysis are shown in the table below (Tab. 3).

Based on the statistical values of the Bayesian Information Criterion (MBIC) and the Hannan and Quinn Information Criterion (MQIC) tests, the PVAR model was estimated with one lag (Tab. 4).

In the stability test for PVAR (1) model estimated by Generalized Method of Moments (GMM) method, it is determined that all eigenvalues appeared in the unit circle. Therefore, the established models fulfil the condition of stability. Considering the estimation results obtained, it is seen that there is a positive relationship between youth unemployment and tax wedge. The increase in the

Tab. 4: PVAR (1) Estimation Results

	yunemp	percagrwth	cpi	taxwedge
yunemp(-1)	0,389***	0,498***	0,027	0,065***
	[0,05]	[0,05]	[0,03]	[0,02]
percagrwth (-1)	−0,393***	−0,017	0,067**	−0,011
	[0,04]	[0,051]	[0,02]	[0,01]
cpi(-1)	0,569***	−0,156	0,30***	0,023
	[0,09]	[0,13]	[0,09]	[0,02]
taxwedge(-1)	1,221***	−0,366***	0,818***	−0,221***
	[0,12]	[0,09]	[0,10]	[0,04]

***Note:** Values in square brackets indicate standard errors. ***, **, * indicate significance coefficients of 1 %, 5 % and 10 %, respectively.*

tax burden on those who earn the wage income increases the youth unemployment rate. Youth unemployment rate is affected by its own lagged value in the positive direction. The fact that the rate of youth unemployment is high in the previous period has an effect increasing the youth unemployment rate in the current period.

The effect of economic growth on youth unemployment is in the negative direction. In other words, the increase in the rate of economic growth reduces the youth unemployment rate. However, there is a positive relationship between inflation and youth unemployment. The tax wedge, on the other hand, has a negative effect on economic growth. The increase in tax responsibilities on wage income has an effect decreasing economic growth. It is also seen that the tax wedge has an influence increasing the inflation rate. The findings obtained as a result of the analysis are consistent with the other studies in the literature (Bassanini & Duval, 2006; Nickell & Layard, 1999; Deskar-Skrbic et al. 2018; Gnip & Tomic, 2010).

The results of the prediction error variance decomposition are shown in Tab. 5. The main descriptor of the prediction error variance of all the variables examined is primarily their shocks. Most of the changes in the youth unemployment rate are determined by their own shocks. It was observed that the tax wedge explains youth unemployment by around 12 %, while inflation explains it by around 8 % and growth rate explains it by around 4 %. The tax wedge has a higher share in explaining changes in youth unemployment compared to growth rate and inflation. The sensitivity of the youth unemployment rate to changes in the tax wedge is more than its sensitivity to changes in inflation and economic growth. While explaining the changes in youth unemployment, as the length of

Tab. 5: Variance Decomposition

Indicators	Period	yunemp	percagrwth	cpi	taxwedge
yunemp	1	1	0	0	0
	2	0.8318365	0.0396526	0.0448836	0.0836273
	3	0.7765124	0.0375244	0.0734365	0.1125267
	4	0.7669612	0.0378138	0.0787172	0.1165078
	5	0.7655035	0.0378234	0.0795295	0.1171435
	6	0.7650096	0.0377819	0.0797906	0.1174178
	7	0.7647671	0.0377674	0.0799166	0.1175489
	8	0.7646866	0.037763	0.0799601	0.1175902
	9	0.7646649	0.0377619	0.0799721	0.1176011
	10	0.7646586	0.0377615	0.0799755	0.1176044
percagrwth	1	0.4476282	0.5523717	0	0
	2	0.5428804	0.4466136	0.0032328	0.0072733
	3	0.5419992	0.4255704	0.0094097	0.0230207
	4	0.5361001	0.4209953	0.0147344	0.0281702
	5	0.535236	0.4204238	0.015537	0.0288032
	6	0.5351525	0.4203351	0.0156337	0.0288786
	7	0.5351341	0.4202665	0.015673	0.0289263
	8	0.5351137	0.4202419	0.0156944	0.0289502
	9	0.5351061	0.4202351	0.0157014	0.0289572
	10	0.5351044	0.4202335	0.0157032	0.028959
cpi	1	0.0104053	0.0723523	0.9172424	0
	2	0.0335283	0.0808695	0.7347519	0.1508504
	3	0.054385	0.078931	0.7194914	0.1471927
	4	0.0604586	0.0777559	0.7086362	0.1531492
	5	0.0608598	0.07733	0.7071577	0.1546525
	6	0.0608286	0.0772269	0.7067863	0.1551582
	7	0.0608575	0.0772006	0.7066825	0.1552594
	8	0.060878	0.0771898	0.7066361	0.1552962
	9	0.0608835	0.077186	0.7066212	0.1553092
	10	0.0608845	0.0771849	0.7066171	0.1553136
taxwedge	1	0.0555573	0.0000212	0.0062281	0.9381934
	2	0.122717	0.0003972	0.0084542	0.8684315
	3	0.1205717	0.0017442	0.0110975	0.8665866
	4	0.1204077	0.0017995	0.0122943	0.8654985
	5	0.1203498	0.0018214	0.0124504	0.8653785
	6	0.1203807	0.0018217	0.0124907	0.8653069
	7	0.1203877	0.0018219	0.0125079	0.8652825
	8	0.1203879	0.0018219	0.0125149	0.8652754
	9	0.1203877	0.0018219	0.0125169	0.8652735
	10	0.1203878	0.0018219	0.0125174	0.8652729

the term increases, the role of the tax wedge, economic growth and inflation does not change much.

Finally, the impulse response functions of the PVAR (1) model with its coefficients estimated are shown in the graph below (Graph 1).

The impulse response functions show how 1 % standard deviation shock in the model affects the other variables. The graphs in the last column of Graph 1 display the reactions that youth unemployment gave to a shock in the variables. According to this, youth unemployment responds positively to one standard error shock in the tax wedge. This reaction reaches its maximum point in the 2nd term and then disappears rapidly. Therefore, it can be seen that the reaction does not persist. Similarly, it was found that youth unemployment gives a positive response to one standard error shock and the response that increased until the 2nd term started to decrease rapidly. Youth unemployment increasingly gives a negative reaction to one standard error shock in economic growth till the 2nd term and starting from the 2nd term this reaction was shown to be decreasing. Youth unemployment has a decreasing positive response to its own shocks.

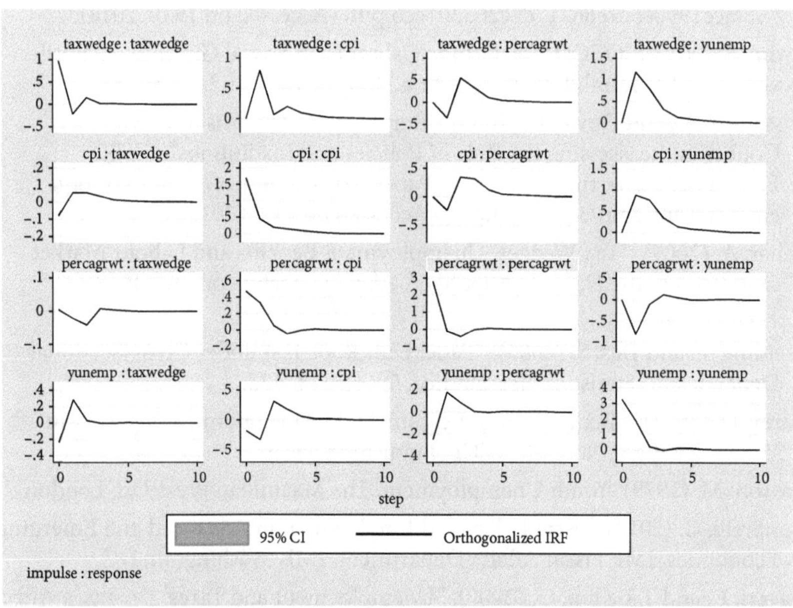

Graph 1: Impulse-Response Functions

5 Conclusion

Employment is a key factor affecting the economies of all countries. For this reason, many countries are looking for ways to struggle with unemployment, which is the leading economic problem. Another important factor that raises unemployment rates, although it emerges for various reasons, is the tax wedge, which can be briefly defined as the financial obligations both on employer or employees. While high labour costs reduce the level of employment in terms of employers, the high level of stoppage leads to a decrease in wages in terms of labour force. As a result, the labour market is negatively affected on both sides. In the case that employment rates are reduced, the first group that is considered to be dismissed is young employees. In this study, the effects of the tax wedge especially on youth unemployment were investigated, and according to the analysis results, it was found the tax wedge affects youth unemployment negatively.

References

Abrigo, M. R., and Love, I. (2015). "Estimation of Panel Vector Autoregression in Stata: A Package of Programs", https://pdfs.semanticscholar.org/09ad/677755facc1990e5c7e66217c2c265201ec6.pdf, (Accessed on 19.07.2018).

Aydın, S. (2013). "OECD Ülkelerinde Çalışanların Sosyal Güvenlik Kesintileri ve Vergisel Yükümlülükleri". Calisma Dünyasi Dergisi, 1(1): 80–93.

Bassanini, A., and Duval, R. (2006). "Employment Patterns in OECD Countries: Reassessing the Role of Policies and Institutions". OECD Economics Department Working Paper No. 486, https://www.oecd.org/employment/emp/36888714.pdf, (Accessed on 11.08.2018).

Behar, A. (2009). "Tax Wedges, Unemployment Benefits and Labour Market Outcomes in the New EU Members". AUCO Czech Economic Review, 3(1): 69–93.

Breitung, J., and Das, S. (2005). "Panel Unit Root Test under Cross-Sectional Dependence". Statistica Neerlandica, 59(4): 414–433.

Carey, D. (2003). "Tax Reform in Belgium", OECD Economics Department Working Papers, No. 354, OECD Publishing, Paris.

Casson, M. (1979). Youth Unemployment. The Macmillan Press Ltd, London.

Cottarelli, C. (2012). Fiscal Policy and Employment in Advanced and Emerging Economies. IMF Fiscal Affairs Department, IMF, Washington, DC.

Daveri, F., and Tabellini, G. (2000). "Unemployment and Taxes: Do Taxes Affect the Rate of Unemployment?" Economic Policy, 15(30): 48–104.

Deskar-Škrbić, M., Drezgić, S., and Šimović, H. (2018). "Tax Policy and Labour Market in Croatia: Effects of Tax Wedge on Employment". Economic Research-Ekonomska Istraživanja, 31 (1): 1218–1227.

Dolenc, P., and Laporšek, S. (2010). "Tax Wedge on Labour and Its Effect on Employment Growth in the European Union". Prague Economic Papers, 4: 344–358.

Ederveen, S., and Thissen, L. (2004). Can Labour Market Institutions Explain Unemployment Rates in New EU Member States? European Network of Economic Policy Research Institutes Working Paper, No. 27. http://aei.pitt.edu/6734/1/1130_27.pdf, (Accessed on 15.08.2018).

Elmeskov, J., Martin, J. P., and Scargetta, S. (1998). 'Key Lessons for Labour Market Reforms: Evidence from OECD Countries' Experiences", Swedish Economic Policy Review, 5(2): 205–252.

Festa, A. (2015). "Employment and Productivity. The Role of the Tax Wedge". EuroEconomica, 34(2): 193–150

Ghose, A. K., Majid, N., and Ernst, C. (2008). The Global Employment Challenge. ILO (International Labor Office) Publications, ISBN: 978-92-2-120305-6, Geneva.

Gnip, A. G., and Tomić, I. (2010). "How Hard Does the Tax Bite Hurt? Croatian vs. European Worker". Financial Theory and Practice, 34(2): 109–142.

Góra, M., Radziwiłł, A., Sowa, A., and Walewski, M. (2006). Tax Wedge and Skills: Case of Poland in International Perspective. CASE Report No. 64. http://www.case-research.eu/upload/publikacja_plik/10223856_rc64.pdf, (Accessed on 19.07.2018).

Günaydın, D., and Çetin, M. (2015). "Genç İşsizliğin Temel Makroekonomik Belirleyicileri: Ampirik Bir Analiz". Pamukkale Üniversitesi SBE Dergisi, 22: 17–34.

ILO (2018). "Youth Employment Trends", http://www.ilo.org/global/about-the-ilo/multimedia/maps-and-charts/enhanced/WCMS_600072/lang--en/index.htm, (Accessed on 19.07.2018).

Im, K. S., Pesaran, M. H., and Shin Y. (2003). "Testing for Unit Roots in Heterogeneous Panels. Journal of Econometrics", 115: 53–63.

Lehmann, E., Lucifora, C., Moriconi, S., and Van der Linden, B. (2013). Beyond the Labour Income Tax Wedge: The Unemployment-Reducing Effect of Tax Progressivity. TEPP Working Paper, No 2013-5. https://halshs.archives-ouvertes.fr/halshs-00870050/document, (Accessed on 19.07.2018).

Levin, A., Lin, C., and Shin, C. J. (2002). "Unit Root Tests in Panel Data: Asymptotic and Finite-Sample Properties". Journal of Econometrics, 108: 1–24.

Love, I., and Zicchino, L. (2006). Financial Development and Dynamic Investment Behaviour: Evidence from Panel VAR. The Quarterly Review of Economics and Finance, 46: 190–210.

Morawski, L., and Myck, M. (2010). "Klin'-ing up: Effects of Polish Tax Reforms on Those in and on Those out". Labour Economics, 17(3): 556–566.

Murat, S., and Şahin, L. (2011). "Nedenleri ve Sonuçları Bakımından Gençler Arasında Yaygınlaşan İşsizlik". Sosyoloji Konferansları Dergisi, 44: 1–48.

Nickell, S. (2003). "Employment and Taxes". CESifo Working Paper No. 1109, December 2003.

Nickell, S. (2003). "Employment and Taxes". CESifo Working Paper No. 1109, December 2003. https://papers.ssrn.com/sol3/papers.cfm?abstract_id=489443, (Accessed on 16.06.2018).

OECD (2018). Taxing Wages, OECD Publishing, Paris.

Pastore, F. (2018). "Why Is Youth Unemployment so High and Different Across Countries?" IZA World of Labor, ISSN 2054-9571, Institute for the Study of Labor (IZA), Bonn, Iss. 420. https://wol.iza.org/uploads/articles/420/pdfs/why-is-youth-unemployment-so-high-and-different-across-countries.one-pager.pdf?v=1, (Accessed on 01.08.2018).

Radu, C. F., Fenişer, C., Schebesch, K. B., Fenişer, F., and Dobrea, F. M. (2018). "Study of the Tax Wedge in EU and other OECD Countries, Using Cluster Analysis". Procedia-Social and Behavioral Sciences, 238: 687–696.

Trpeski, P., and Tashevska, B. (2012). "Labour Tax Wedge in the Republic Of Macedonia Trends and International Comparison". Annales Universitatis Apulensis-Series Oeconomica, 14(2): 571–585.

Aysegul Kutluk Bozkurt[1]

Digital Marketing Channels of Businesses and Digitalization in Tourism Sector

1 Introduction

The purchasing behaviors of consumer have been moved to digital environment with the development of technology, the increase of mobile devices and the improvement of life standards. The digital development is now challenging most industries. A significant share of marketing activities began to take digital activities since the early 2000s. Because now everyone has a phone in hand and many of the work is done by computer. At this point, capital owners and institutions do not want to miss this digital world where they are intensely interested. Research shows that internet users are getting bigger and bigger. Managers who realize that the internet is in every moment of our lives, have placed digital marketing exercises on their budget. It is some of the information that "We Are Social" identifies that the survey covers the year 2017 (digitalajanslar.com);

- "More than half of the world now uses at least one smartphone."
- "Nearly two-thirds of the world's population owns at least one mobile phone."
- "More than half of the web traffic worldwide now comes from a mobile phone."
- "Most of the mobile connections around the world are now "broadband""
- "More than one fifth of the world population shopped in the last 30 days".

It is not enough that businesses only exist on the Internet to capture successful. All digital media tools play an important role on consumer behavior. For this reason, digital marketing channels need to attract visitors and turn them into consumer positions. (Auger, 2005). The rapid development of social media channels such as Facebook, Twitter, Google Plus, Instagram, YouTube, and Foursquare, as well as recommendation sites like TripAdvisor, HolidayCheck, Zoover, and the fact that these developments can be tracked with different digital programs have changed. An also, using of social media rate has passed the general internet usage rate. That's why, sales marketing works can being done easily from social media tools. Now, tourism professionals have added social media,

1 Research Asst. Dr. Kirklareli University, aysegulkutluk@gmail.com.

internet advertising and digital sales channels to their promotional, branding and marketing efforts too. As a matter of fact, it is almost impossible for tourism sector to stay out of this area anymore. Because digital works has already become more profitable for businesses

2 Digital Marketing

The internet, the interactive dimension of the world, has become one of the most important communication fields. Lots of new concept and horizon like web pages, e-mails, online sales channels, virtual diaries, online social media, such as virtual game worlds came into our lives. Virtual world of the internet completely changed our understanding of time and space and generally expand the horizons of marketing and a new form of digital advertising was created (Dahan and Levi, 2012).

In a simple sense, digital marketing is the sale of products and services through one or more channels in an electronic environment (graphicmail.com.tr, 2018). In general meaning, digital marketing means "preferring the internet, mobile, and other interactive platforms to support and promote brands and businesses except using traditional media such as TV, radio, magazine". Digital marketing is part of every basic business decision taken from product development and pricing to public relations and even staff recruitment (Kingsnorth, 2017: 6). Digital marketing is also known as interactive marketing, online marketing, e-marketing and web marketing (dijitalmarketing.net). Digital marketing, allows interaction with the target market such as internet, mobile platforms and social media channels. An effective management process carried out in marketing field initiates with measuring and monitoring the effects of practices and work. (Bulunmaz, 2016).

We can understand from the following table that digitalization is increasing year by year. The following results have been found in the research of "Wearesocial": "*More than 200 million people got their first mobile device in 2017, and two-thirds of the world's 7.6 billion inhabitants now have a mobile phone. The number of internet users in 2018 is 4.021 billion, up 7 percent year-on-year. The number of social media users in 2018 is 3.196 billion, up 13 percent year-on-year. The number of mobile phone users in 2018 is 5.135 billion, up 4 percent year-on-year*".

Companies and brands who want to get the most accurate results in the search engines using the internet channel have to choose the correct digital marketing titles completely. These titles are; web site optimization, search engine marketing (SEM), video search engine optimization (VSEO), social media optimization (SMO), online screen advertising, QR codes. According to Ozdipciner, e-mail,

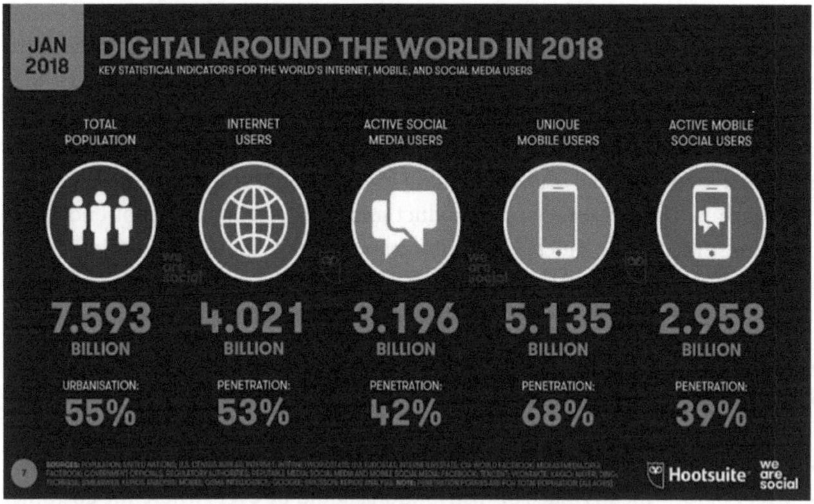

Fig. 1: Digital around the World in 2018. Source: wearesocial.com

blogs, podcasts and forums are also effective digital marketing strategies. Blogs, microblogs and forums are digital domains that help organizations interact with their potential customers. Moreover, e-mail marketing offers effective marketing services to a large consumer market. Sometimes there are competitions and campaigns held on Web sites. They are one of the effective ways of digital marketing. Online press releases and articles about new products and services are digital ads too that promote businesses themselves (Ozdipciner, 2010). Weinberg and Pehlivan (2011) say that, a company has not a standard formula for determining how much to invest in digital social media. Weinberg and Pehlivan reveal that various firm-specific features such as internal digital infrastructure, media selection and customer preferences affect investment decisions. Creating value within digital technologies is important for both the customers and the institutions. The more the digital world can interact with the customer, the stronger the association. That is, the service processes provided by digital technology create value through new customer experiences and interactions among customers (Bughin 2015).

2.1 The 4E's of Digital Marketing

A marketing mix is a collection of items that are brought together to capture and promote unique sales points of a brand or product. 4 elements called "The Four

Ps" proposed classification has been used by marketing companies, branding agencies and web design companies throughout the world. Unfortunately, in the early stages of marketing, consumers have bought products and services with lots of monies that they do not deserve to pay because of the reasons such as the lack of diversity and the inability to easily reach products and services. Now they are looking beyond that and are looking for more consumption experience and relationship. The advantage of a product and the price alone is not enough to buy. Consumers have much more information about almost everything thanks to digitalization (Alci, 2015). And of course the traditional marketing of 4P has left its place to 4E. Subsequently, Rothery (2008) developed the 4Es framework.

- *Experience* – means a product is an experience (including online experience)
- *Exchange* – means price (as money or credit is exchanged for product or services)
- *Evangelism* – promotion becomes evangelism.
- *Every place* – means place or distribution should be everywhere the customer wants it

From Product to Experience: Experience refers to the whole journey a customer can benefit from a product. It goes through an analysis of customers' habits and all his experience with a particular product what influences them and what follows after they bought the product (Rupin, 2013: 16). Tourism sector is no longer just selling rooms. They are selling entertainment, experience and notional things like human reactions. According to Epuran, tourists should be satisfied in all departments within a tourism resort. Because satisfied tourists take photos and videos happily with their smartphones. This is the success of the business. A happy and satisfied tourist is not afraid to share his happiness. He leaves positive comments on Tripadvisor and shares his unique vacation on social platforms. Another good aspect of these exchanges is that hoteliers have gained a new information channel to develop and customize their services to the new consumer (Epuran etc., 2015: 80).

From Place to Everyplace: There's many place for conveying business message: IM, SMS, countless social media websites, blogs, video games, product placement in places like TV, Movies, internet video clips...etc. İn digital marketing, place has become everyplace. The simplest model of digital marketing is Quick Read (QR) codes can also enhance two of the 'Ps': promotion and place. According to Chaffey and Smith (2013: 65) "These codes let users easily use a smartphone camera to scan a type of barcode to get digital information (web site, video clip, article, photo deal or a shop). They add these layers of information and can be used in many creative ways to enhance a product experience, add

Tab. 1: Directions to Tourism Business Managers. Source: Epuran, G., Ivascıuc, I.S. and Mıcu, Mıcu, A. (2015). From 4P's to 4 E's – How to Avoid the Risk of Unbalancing the Marketing Mix in Today Hotel Businesses, pp. 82

Experience	-Customise your product. Give client the possibility to choose the features of his touristic programme -Focus on selling entertainment and human interaction rather the product/ service features
Everyplace	-Create a space of communication between your customers -Be creative. Find new distribution channels on the internet
Exchange	-Calculate the value of your customers -Find out what it takes for a consumer to give attention, and engagement for your product
Evangelism	-Bring passion to your brand through engagement -Captures the company's or brand's point of view on the world, or on life, or on the country in which it operates

extra information or even bring a supermarket to you". Tourism business can use this code implementation their touristic product, or booking or promotion.

From Price to Exchange: It's about knowing the value of the visitors, leads, and customers. What is their engagement worth to companies? That is the question businesses have to ask themself. It is very easy to compare prices on the Internet. Thanks to companies like Booking and Expedia, more payment periods have been closed for products and services of the same quality. The purchase request to capture opportunities for affordable prices and opportunities has uncovered opportunity sites such as "yakala.co", "grupanya", "groupon" which provide the cheapest access to content such as restaurants, hotels and holiday packages. Consumers who frequently shop at any site are offered personalized prices or applications such as sending gifts to the consumer. Even consumers have the possibility to create their own payment plan (Penpece, 2013: 31–32).

From Promotion to Evangelism: Evangelism is the evolution of promotion that aims to create an entire brand experience that will convince a customer to engage with brand (Rupin, 2015: 17). Evangelism "is an improvised form of word of mouth marketing, where companies depend on existing customers" feedback as a marketing tool. An experience shared by a customer is influential than thousand advertisements. Small and limited budget may often depend upon evangelism marketing" (Saravanan and Saraswathy, 2017: 4). Promotion effort isn't enough any longer to gain customers. Companies have to figure out how to get consumers to allow them into their attention spans again. With so many more message channels, they can just confused people with messages and hope they'll pick them up. This is an old and imperfect method now. Growing power of the consumer, and weakening power of traditional media pave way for new marketing methods.

2.2 The Most Popular Digital Marketing Tools

There are numerous types of digital marketing that many companies follow, in this paper some major types are discussed as follows:

Web Sites: Nushair and friends described it as; web sites interact with customers, with diverse products and services, with comprehensive information, flexibility and simpler operations (Nusair et al., 2011) One of the most important factors of digital marketing is to have a user and sales-oriented website. Especially the home pages are one of the first things that reflect the first impressions of the website and the services provided. A fast-opening website, user-friendly design, responsive site structure and content must be properly organized to be careful to enhance the user experience and to convert visitors to customers. Therefore, it is necessary to fully understand the needs and requirements of the target group while the website is being created. It is necessary to create a website that is tailored to the customer profile created by the product and service spectrum. In this, a site should be built according to the answers of the questions such as what the target wants to do without operating the site, how to enjoy the sites, what are the factors that can attract the visitors back to the site. An also campaigns and promotions are always the focal point of in marketing. This is a very important criterion in digital marketing. Campaigns and promotions that encourage and motivate consumers to shop are a good digital marketing strategy (stratejikseo.com, 2018). Google, Adobe, Webtrends, Kissmetrics, GoSquared, ComScore and many other sites can meet business web analytics needs.

Social Media Management: When it comes to digital communication tools, it comes to social networks like Facebook, Twitter, Instagram and so on, which use online and virtual platforms such as web sites, microblogs and search engines. With the emergence of new means of communication, existing means of communication are now called "traditional means of communication". Traditional means of communication are categorized as written (magazines, newspapers, etc.), visual (television, cinema, etc.) and audio (radio). There is no such difference in digital marketing (Cizmeci and Ercan, 2015: 150).

"Corporate webpages are the most frequently used digital communication channel (90 % of respondents), followed by social networking sites like Facebook (73 %), LinkedIn (46 %), and Twitter (42 %)" (Tiago and Verissimo, 2014: 706). Social media, the most popular tool of digital marketing, has become a natural part of everyday life. It is easy to reach the internet almost everywhere. The use of different devices such as laptop computers, tablets and smartphones has become very common. On this count, it became much easier to communicate with friends, family and companies (Terttunen, 2017: 3). Kaplan and Haenlain

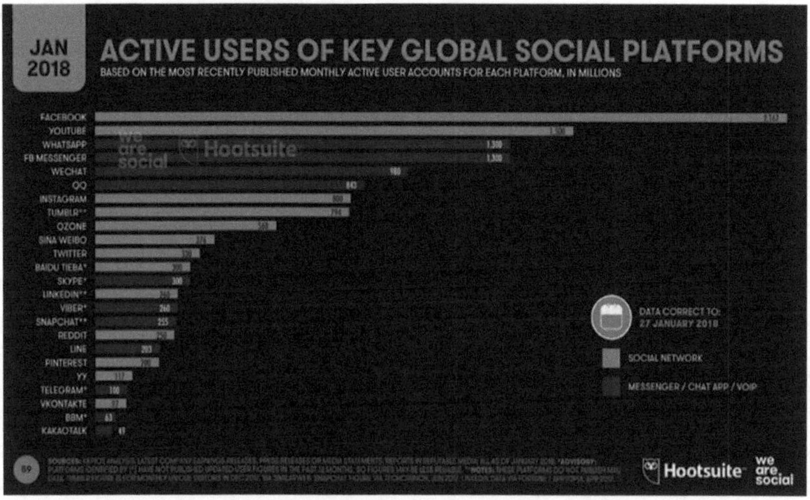

Fig. 2: Active Users of Global Social Platforms. Source: wearesocial.com

(2010, 61) define social media as "a group of internet-based applications that build on the ideological and technological foundations of web 2.0, and that allow the creation and exchange of User Generated Content". A strong digital marketing strategy includes all social media forums suitable for organization, including Facebook, YouTube, Twitter, LinkedIn, Google, Pinterest and Instagram. These tools have different goals: Twitter turned into a virtual phone used by customers to submit complaints or ask questions, whereas video-on-demand social media-such as Instagram and Pinterest- are very common for visual storytelling. Linkedin's latest release; it is also crucial to stay in touch with new trends such as the Impactor Program, a forum where industry leaders and wise leaders can share their wisdom (useinbox.com).

Search Engine Optimization (SEO): SEO, or search engine optimization, is a work that makes it easier for web sites to be found in search engines and to reach more users. In accordance with the theme of the site, the keywords are arranged and appropriate criteria are set up for the search engines. It is also divided into in-site SEO and off-site SEO. The works that is done not only on the site but also on the site from outside will make it easier for the site to be found in customer searches. (Öcal, 2018) Businesses must take advantage of their SEO work to maintain business presence and to make a difference between their competitors in a competitive market. SEO practices that offer more cost advantages over digital advertising work are also a technique that has been showing its effects for a long time. Because there are many factors that influence SEO works, companies have to have comprehensive knowledge of SEO and have to do their work in a complete and error-free way (stratejikseo.com, 2018).

E-mail Marketing: Sending e-mail is one of the easiest and fastest way to send your products and services to your customers collectively. By sending mass e-mails, more return rates can be provided to the advertised products and services by submitting them according to their interests (inboxmailmarketing.com, 2018). 75 % of digital marketers see that e-mail as the primary method of reaching high-quality potential customers. E-mail can be seen as a communication tool that gives more options for converting the audience to action (Chaffey, 2003).

Inbound Marketing: Inbound marketing is the latest popular digital marketing techniques. Because inbound marketing that can reach the target group that is clearly and correctly determined to achieve and contribute to the target audience by creating rich, quality and original content, is a way to turn related content into profit (stratejikseo.com, 2018). According to CMI founder Joe Pulizzi; inbound marketing is a marketing process that involves the creation and distribution of appropriate and valuable content to draw attention to the unidentified and unidentified target kit, putting them into action and to get them (in order to create a profitable client impulse) (Penpece, 2013: 47).

Inbound marketing is clearly different from traditional marketing tools with resilience to explicit call or purely product or service based advertising. "Contents" can be almost anything with a clear message, such as remarkable pictures, videos, blog posts, or news. For a good story, contents should be original, dynamic and shareable (useinbox.com, 2018).

C2B-C2C and B2B-B2C Marketing: The options are for digital communications between a businesses. Traditionally, the bulk of Internet transactions are between business and business or industrial and commercial markets, known as "B2B (business-to-business); and between business and consumer markets (like cars and cola), known as business-to-consumer (B2C). Customer-to-business models may play a significant role in some B2B or B2C sectors. In this model, a potential buyer approaches a marketplace of sellers who then compete for the sale. C2C models and the social media to support them have proved one of the most disruptive examples of online business technology. An early indication of the popularity of C2C is the growth of online consumer auctions at eBay and in niche communities focusing on interests such as sport, films or pastimes. More recently, a dramatic growth in C2C interactions has been fuelled by the growth of social networks: the 'Big 4' – that's Facebook, Google+,

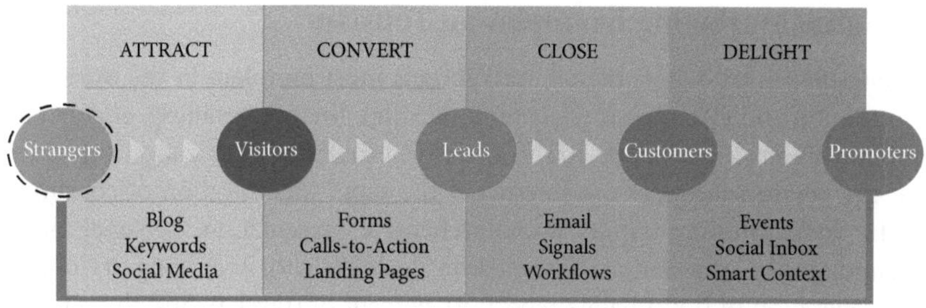

Fig. 3: Step by Step İnbound Marketing. Source: webrazzi.com, 2018

LinkedIn and Twitter – are now key to reaching many customers through 'social outposts' and key influencers on these platforms. C2B also involves customers developing their own content online, which is known as user-generated content (UGC), with businesses facilitating it" (Chaffey and Smith, 2013: 9-10-11).

Growth Hacking: Growth Hacking is the identification of the problems in front of the growth of initiatives and the finding of innovative solutions to these problems (leanmarketing.co). According to Carfi and Hermann, "Growth hacking is about the creative use of scalable and repeatable methods with the goal to optimize every digital touchpoint in order to get prospective customers to take action" (Carfi and Hermann, 2018; 5). A growth hacker is a rare combination: someone with the right marketing and technical skills who can come up with clever marketing hacks and also track their results (Griffel and Wadowski, 2014).

With digital marketing channels, it is possible to see how many people are on an operator's website instantly, how many people visited the pages, which devices they reached on the site, and which campaigns or channels they came from. This data, which can be accessed using Google Analytics and similar measurement tools, plays a crucial role in determining future strategies. When an effective digital marketing strategy meets the right tools and technologies, it becomes a tremendous structure. With this method, the user can set trends by determining how an individual searches for his products and how he/she purchases them, and ultimately, which digital marketing strategy should be emphasized in the future (Akgun, 2017).

"It is obviously that all the types of digital marketing that mentioned above are just some of the online marketing strategies, and more digital marketing strategies are being invented all the time."

3 Digital Marketing Examples on Tourism

Among the sectors where digital marketing is most prevalent in the world are; information and electronics, telecommunication, finance, retailing, energy and tourism (Olcer & Ozyılmaz, 2007). The world tourism organization explained that the key to success of the Internet is the rapid identification of consumer needs, direct communication, a comprehensive presentation, personalization and updating of information (Castaneda et al., 2009: 549). According to Google's new generation of travel habits report; 91 percent of travelers find the services and services they need through search engines on the internet. They explore the map view of where they will go, location information, weather, how to reach the hotel, and places to explore, via the internet (Coban, 2018).

In Spain, they established the Technological Tourism Development Organization in the name of SEDETTUR. This organization works on information technologies on the one hand, energy saving, design, security, health and quality on the other hand (Ozdipciner, 2010:11). "Hg2" is a phone application that creates an independent sophisticated travel guide for different points of the world. Within two weeks, 17 % of iPhone users lowered the app.16.239 times clicked (Ryan, 2017: 87). TripAdvisor has reached a level of 100 million downloads known as the free app and mobile landmark for iPhone and Android phones (turizm&yatırım, 2014: 12).

İn spite of the popularity of sites such as Expedia, Booking, Tripadvisor and the sites that give user reviews and recommendations, new and different alternative sites for tourists are emerging with digitalization. For example; Airbnb is a social network where people can rent their own apartments and rooms. "Airbnb is one of the earliest successful growth hacking method recorded in tourism sector. Airbnb was the result of two designers unable to afford their rent and decided to offer their space to people who needed accommodation to the upcoming design conference in 2007. The response from the people was positive and the Airbnb founders, Brian Chesky and Joe Gebbia saw an opportunity to solve the problem in the existing market. In 2008 Airbnb was launched and now the company is valued at 25 billion USA dollars with 2 million listings in 57,000 cities and 192 countries" (Lee, 2016: 9).

Travel agencies, tour operators, airline companies, accommodation operators and other tourism operators in the tourism industry have started to operate on the internet in order to benefit from the benefits provided by the internet. For example; 93 % of Ryanair ticket bookings and 90 % of Easyjet tickets are on their web sites. Investigations of the American Travel Sector Association on travel over the internet have shown that a large proportion of US travelers make airline tickets and accommodation reservations online (Boz, 2006: 39–40). KLM (Royal Dutch Airlines) states that the average response time for social media questions is 22 minutes and 13 different language channels. These announcements and sales from social media have resulted in € 25 million a year (Kingsnorth, 2017:153). Many airline companies also active in Turkey, which is available online sales. (It is the most famous Turkish airways is Turkish Airlines). The East Coast train operator has increased organic search earnings by 20 % between 2012 and 2013 thanks to SEO studis (Ryan, 2017: 405). When you look at Travel Trends and many other reports and researches; 8 out of 10 people have a meaningful significance to the feedbacks on Facebook, twitter, Instagram, wiki and blogs, and most of the bookings are made using social or mobile networks (Kutluk, 2013). Many travel agencies in Turkey (Mng, Anitur, ETS, Jolly ... etc.), Facebook, Twitter, Pinterest, YouTube, Vimeo, Tumblr, share the latest offers and travel-related news in all popular social networks like Google Plus. Like the travel agencies, most of the hotel companies have a blog page, and some places like restaurants, hotels and destinations are recommended. There is also a digital department that operates social media accounts for businesses.

A total of 6 million 730,000 followers are on Facebook, Twitter, Instagram, YouTube, Google+, LinkedIn and Pinterest for the "Turkey Home" campaign run by the Ministry of Culture and Tourism. Turkey as a destination with more than 5 million followers on Facebook, tourism promotion between platforms has the most followers in the world has entered the first among the five countries (Boztepe, 2018). In addition, tourists in Turkey in 96 percent of the hotel can benefit from the free internet connection between European countries, Romania, Poland, Slovakia, the Czech Republic, Montenegro, and then prefer to sixth place. Also, acts as digital travel agent, "Hotelrunner" took the "Odamax" within operating in Turkey (turizmdosyasi.com, 2018). Turkey can reach more tourist base from a more global environment.

4 Conclusion

Daily social relations have moved to the virtual world, and there it continues. There are online communities that bring people together from all over the world. This movement at the digital dimension allows individuals to share knowledge, to entertain each other and to encourage dialogue between different cultures (Budden et al., 2011). Significantly, "the number of touchpoints is increasing by over 20 % annually as more offline customers shift to digital technologies and younger, digitally oriented consumers enter the ranks of buyers" (Bughin, 2015).

Saatci states that the active use of digital marketing channels by hotel operators is an economical and effective way for tourism enterprises that do not have a huge marketing budget (Saatci, 2016: 79). Therefore, in a world where information is consumed rapidly and in a world where almost everything is digitized, managers in the hospitality sector have to constantly ask themselves "how digital are we?" (Ozkara, 2018). According to Gencer, tourism businesses need to be able to manage data management (because many important data can be collected from accommodation, eg wedding anniversary, allergy, social media birthdays), website management (along with SEO application to be visible on search engines), social media management, online reputation management and 360 ° virtual reality management (videos of 360 ° virtual images in Facebook ads generate less cost than 2-dimensional photos), very well (Gencer, 2017). Social media channels can drive traffic to hotels' websites and increase direct sales. Verbal and visual contents enable an effective marketing to the target community. It will be easier for Tourism Enterprises to adapt to the digital world with the help of digital agencies.

Experts realize that some digital guests spend about 30 percent more on their travel than average guests. Touristic facilities and online agencies must also be active in social media to capture these "The Digital Influencer " that use the internet over at least a few channels like smartphones, tablets, laptop computers. Cloud Arena Founding Partner "Arden Agopyan" says 84 percent of "Digital Influencer" are a positive website experience. Agropyan points out that: at least 22 web sites have been visited by these travelers while they are planning their travels. At least 4 social media channels including Facebook, Twitter and Instagram have been reviewed (tourism & investment, 2014: 11). Hence, tourism businesses can make their own ads to "Digital Influencer" and the effect will be great.

The Wizard Istanbul project, which was carried out as an example study using digital marketing in the introduction of destinations, responded to the questions of tourists via Twitter, Facebook and Wizardistanbul.com within minutes of questions about Istanbul, and informed more than 6000 tourists in just 1.5 months and answering more than 1,100 tourist questions were answered directly (Kutluk, 2012). After such projects, tourism operators started to use online chatbots widely in their web sites but sometimes it is noticed that they are inadequate in mutual communication. Therefore, the creation of online communities that can actually communicate can be more effective. Today, many destinations, hotels and museums around the world can be visited thanks to the latest digital applications-virtual reality. With this application, tourists can experience these places in a virtual way (Ozdipciner, 2010: 15). The attention of potential tourists should be gained by opening a blog, creating an account in social circles or being a member of recommended sites and loading content, information videos, photos about the company/touristic place. But more can be done. It is an effective digital marketing method is showing virtual reality applications that prepared with the latest technology for hotels or destinations in promotional fairs or in touristic congresses which are the areas where tourists can come to pass. An also, inbound marketing needs to be used more. More effective content can be created based on the likes of content. It is also important to answer incoming comments and to compare the performance of the company with its own performance.

Whichever digital channel the tourism business uses, it is absolutely necessary to monitor the traffic on these channels. It is important to record user numbers, visitor numbers, referrals, personal information and hobbies on behalf of defining the target groups for future digital marketing strategies. In this way, they will skip costly research such as target audience identification and market segmentation. The majority of tourism businesses have a digital identity. But they cannot manage it by themselves. It is necessary to get support from a better service-digital agency. Getting support from digital agents is a competitive advantage. Administrators or future managers need to devote time to topics such as web design, graphic design, SEO, growth hacking, digital advertising to take the right steps in the digital world. Digital strategies in tourism and hospitality education should be transferred to the students depending on the use of digital applications in the tourism sector. So when they graduate they will not be alien to digital developments. In addition, digital developments can be supported and encouraged by ministries and local authorities. For example; smart hotels, smart cities or smart destinations can be acted on.

References

Auger, P. (2005). The Impact of Interactivity and Design Sophistication on The Performance of Commercial Websites for Small Businesses, Journal of Small Business Management, 43 (2), 119–137.

Akgun, O. (2017). Dijital Pazarlama Nedir? http://www.omerakgun.com.tr/dijital-pazarlama-nedir.html (Accessed:10.07.2018).

Alci, B. (2015). Pazarlamanın 4P'sine veda, https://mediacat.com/pazarlamanin-4psine-veda/.(Accessed: 06.04.2018).

Boz, C. 2006. *Dünya'da Turizm Endüstrisinde İstihdam ve Çalışma Şartları*, Yayınlanmış Yüksek Lisans Tezi, Marmara Üniversitesi Sosyal Bilimler Enstitüsü, İstanbul.

Boztepe, M. (2018). Türkiye turizm tanıtım platformları arasında dünyada ilk beşte, https://www.aa.com.tr/tr/turkiye/turkiye-turizm-tanitim-platformlari-arasinda-dunyada-ilk-beste-/1098000, (Accessed: 12.07.2018).

Budden, C. B., Anthony, J. F., Budden, M. C., & Jones, M. A. (2011). Managing the Evolution of a Revolution: Marketing Implications of Internet Media Usage among College Students. *College Teaching Methods and Styles Journal*, 3(3):5–10

Bughin, J. (2015). Brand Success in an Era of Digital Darwinism. *Mckinsey Quarterly*, February.

Bulunmaz, B. (2016). Gelişen Teknolojiyle Birlikte Değişen Pazarlama Yöntemleri ve Dijital Pazarlama. *TRT Akademi*, 1(2), 348–365.

Carfi, C. & Hermann, F. (2018). The Beginner's Guide to Growth Hacking, https://www.frederikhermann.com/uploads/beginners_guide_to_growth_hacking.pdf (Accessed: 22.06.2018).

Castañeda, J. A., Dolores M. Frías, Miguel A. Rodríguez, (2009) "Antecedents of internet acceptance and use as an information source by tourists", Online Information Review, Vol. 33 Issue: 3, pp. 548–567.

Chaffey, D. (2003). Total E-mail Marketing. Great Britain: Marketing Insights Ltd.

Chaffey, D. & Smith, P. (2013). *Emarketing Excellence Planning and Optimizing Your Digital Marketing* (4th ed.). New York. NY: Routledge.

Cizmeci, F. & Ercan, T. (2015). The Effect of Digital Marketing Communication Tools in the Creation Brand Awareness by Housing Companies, *MEGARON*, 10(2):149–161.

Coban, S. (2018). Progo'dan, Turizm Taşımacılığına Dijital Çözümler, http://turizmgazetesi.com/news.aspx?id=85564, (Accessed: 22.07.2018).

Dahan Sanje, Gresi & Levi, Eser, 2012. "Reklam Ajanslarının Gerilla Pazarlama Uygulamaları: Türkiye Örneklemi Üzerinden Bir İnceleme". *İletişim Fakültesi Dergisi*, S(42), 37–47.

Epuran, G., Ivascıuc, I. S. & Mıcu, A. (2015). From 4P's to 4 E's – How to Avoid the Risk of Unbalancing the Marketing Mix in Today Hotel Businesses, Annals of "Dunarea de Jos" University of Galati Fascicle I. *Economics and Applied Informatics*, (2):77–85.

Gencer, M. (2017). İşte otelcilikteki 5 dijital pazarlama trendi, http://www.turizmguncel.com/haber/iste-otelcilikteki-5-dijital-pazarlama-trendi-h33572.html, (Accessed:13.05.2018).

Griffel, M. & Wadowski, C. (2014). Growth Hacking: Lean Marketing for Start-Ups, https://www.udemy.com/growth-hackinglean-marketing-for-startups/,(Accessed: 22.06.2018).

Kaplan, A. & Haenlain, M. (2010). Users of the World, Unite! The Challenges and Opportunities of Social Media. *Business Horizons*, 53(1): 59–68.

Kingsnorth, S. (2017). *Digital Marketing Strategy-An Integrated Approach to Online Marketing. (çev: Laden İldeniz).* Nobel Akademik Yayıncılık, Ankara.

Kutluk, A. (2012*). Hizmet Sektöründe Ağızdan Ağıza Pazarlamanın Müşterilerin Satın Alma Karar Sürecine Etkisi: Seyahat Acentesi Müşterileri Üzerinde Bir Uygulama (İstanbul Örneği).* Yayımlanmış Yüksek Lisans Tezi. Balıkesir Üniversitesi Sosyal Bilimler Enstitüsü, Balıkesir.

Kutluk, A. (2013). Guerilla Marketing on the Internet and an Evaluation on the Tourism Industry. *International Conference on Eurasian Economies* (17–18 September 2013), pp. 673–682, St. Petersburg, Russia.

Lee, J. (2016). *Growth Hacking for Start-Ups, How Growth Hacking Can Utilised for Growing Start-Ups.* Thesis, Business and Information Technology Oulu University of Applied Sciences, Finland.

Nusair, K. Khal, Parsa, H. G., Cobanoglu, C. (2011). Building a Model of Commitment for Generation Y: An Empirical Study on e-Travel Retailers. *Tourism Management*, 32(4): 833–843.

Oçal, A. (2018). Dijital Pazarlama Nedir? Dijital Pazarlama Teknikleri Nelerdir? https://pazarlamaturkiye.com/pazarlama/dijital-pazarlama-nedir-dijital-pazarlama-teknikleri-nelerdir/ (Accessed: 29.04.2018).

Olcer, F. & Özyılmaz, A. (2007). Elektronik Ticaret ve Sanal Organizasyonlarda Uygulanması. Süleyman Demirel Ün. *İİBF Dergisi*, 12(2):67–94.

Ozdipciner, N. S. (2010). Turizmde Elektronik Pazarlama, *IUYD*, 1:5–22.

Ozkara, T. (2018). Otelciler Dijital Pazarlamayı Ne Kadar Doğru Yönetiyor? https://www.turizmblog.com/2018/03/13/otelciler-dijital-pazarlamayi-ne-kadar-dogru-yonetiyor/,(Accessed: 03.06.2018).

Penpece, D. (2013). *Dijital İçerik Pazarlaması.* Karahan Kitapevi, Adana.

Rothery, G. (2008). The Matchmaker. *Marketing Age*, November/December.

Rupin, C. (2015). *Social Media as a New Engaging Channel in Brands' Relationship Marketing.* Thesis Helsinki Metropolia University of Applied Sciences European Business Administration, Finland.

Ryan, D. (2017). *Digital Marketing*, (çev: M. Murat Kemaloğlu). Türkiye İş Bankası Yayınları, İstanbul.

Saatci, G. (2016). *Sosyal Medya ve Gastronomi* içinde Bir İletişim Biçimi Olarak Gastronomi (Edt. Hakan Yılmaz). Detay Yayıncılık, Ankara.

Sarawanan, M. & Saraswathy, T. R. (2017). Evangelısm as a Marketıng Strategy-in the Challengıng and Innovatıve Busıness Scenarıo. *Intercontınental Journal of Marketıng Management* (4):6, 1–5.

Tiago, M. T. P. M. B. & Verı´ssimo, J. M. C. (2014). Digital Marketing and Social Media: Why Bother? *Business Horizons*, 57:703–708.

Weinberg, B. D. & Pehlivan, E. (2011). Social Spending: Managing the Social Media Mix. *Business Horizons*, 54(3):275–282.

http://graphicmail.com.tr/bilgi/dijital-pazarlama/, (Accessed: 25.06.2017).

https://wearesocial.com/blog/2018/01/global-digital-report-2018, (Accessed: 11.06.2018).

http://www.dijitalmarketing.net/2011/03/31/dijital-pazarlama-nedir-teknikleri-nelerdir/, (Accessed: 03.04.2018).

http://www.dijitalajanslar.com/2018in-ilk-ceyregine-ait-global-dijital-raporu/, (Accessed: 23.06.2018).

https://www.stratejikseo.com/dijital-pazarlama-teknikleri/, (Accessed: 18.03.2018).

https://useinbox.com/tr/en-iyi-5-yeni-dijital-pazarlama-araclari-ve-teknikleri/, (Accessed: 18.03.2018).

http://www.inboxmailmarketing.com/dijital-pazarlama-nedir, (Accessed: 19.03.2018).

https://leanmarketing.co/growth-hacking-nedir/, (Accessed: 02.03.2018).

https://www.marketingturkiye.com.tr/haberler/pazarlamanin-4psi-gitti-4esi-geldi/, (Accessed: 07.06.2018)

http://www.turizmdunyasi.com.tr/arsiv/yazi/172-hotelrunner-ve-odamaxcomdan-kuresel-buyume-icin-guc-birligi, (Accessed: 08.06.2018).

http://www.turizmdosyasi.com/ucretsiz-internette-turk-otelleri-dunya-devlerinin-onunde-h9782.html, (Accessed: 03.03.2018).

Erkan Bilge[1]

Whistleblowing in Terms of Turkish Labor Law[2]

1 Introduction

As a result of the fact that the communication network is highly developed, it seems that all kinds of information can be easily transmitted to anyone, relevant or irrelevant ones, in the shortest time. Accordingly, in daily life, or in the business life, people can easily share the information they have obtained or behavior they have met with others.

The fact that the employees share every situation they encounter in the workplace or any information they acquire arises, undoubtedly, some legal consequences. The fact that employees disclose any information or behavior related to the business, especially outside the workplace, leads to significant consequences for themselves, their workplace and the public. Furthermore, the employee who discloses may encounter consequences such as intimidation, harassment by other employees or superiors, dismissal or exposure to violence.

This is a matter of discussion that whether this behavior of employees is contrary to "duty of loyalty" or whether it is considered as "breach of confidence of employer, a behavior that does not conform to integrity and loyalty such as exposing the employer's professional secrets". It is very important, for both employee and employer/workplace, to determine whether the fact that employees act in that way causes any problem in terms of labor law.

2 Concept

The concept of Whistleblowing, which has no perfect translation in Turkish and means whistling, blowing a whistle, was first appeared in a law text published in 1963 by the United States of America. In this text, it was defined as "disclosure

1 Instructor, Kırklareli University LMYO Human Resources Management Program, e mail: erkanbilge@klu.edu.tr.

2 This study is the improved version of the presentation titled "Whistleblowing and its Evaluation in Terms of Labor Law" which was presented in the "1. Dmitri Yavoronitski International Social Sciences Congress" which was conducted between 10 and 13 August 2017.

of activities believed to be unethical or illegal, usually by existing or former employees", derived from the concept that British policemen blows a whistle to warn the public and other policemen in case of danger (Hersh, 2002: 243).

The concept, which is used in the sense of espionage, mole in terms of political science, is used, in working life, in sense of revealing and disclosing negative situations by employees that they faced in organizations.

There is no common term in the literature for the Turkish equivalent of the concept. The concept is worded with different terms such as information flight (Aydın, 2002: 81), disclosure of negative situations (Demirtaş and Biçkes, 2014: 99; Başol and Karatuna, 2015; 155), moral reaction to misconducts (Aktan, 2015; 19), announcement of unethical behaviors in organizations (Esen and Kaplan, 2012; 33), denouncing or disclosure of immoral practices in the organizations (Danışman, 2012; 227).

We will use the concept of disclosure in our study. Because the concept of disclosure, which means "to reveal, to exposure, to spread, to announce, to display publicly, to advertise something which is secret" (TDK, 2018), expresses whistleblowing, from our point of view, more accurately. Because the term disclosure expresses the existence of a situation which should not be revealed. Illegal or unethical situations encountered in working life are also the situations that are not desired to be revealed and spread by those exhibiting these behaviors.

It is seen that employees disclose negative situations both within the workplace/organization and outside the workplace/organization. Therefore, in the literature, the way of disclosing negative situations in organizations are examined within two basic structures as internal and external disclosure.

Internal disclosure of negative situations is the disclosure of illegal or unethical situations that an employee has encountered within the organization, or reporting to relevant persons within the organization. The fact that the employee discloses illegal or unethical situations that he/she has encountered within the organization to the outside authorities is defined as external disclosure (Eren and Orhan, 2013, 461). At this point, the outside authority means police, written or visual media, or the judicial authorities (Aktan, op. cit.: 26).

However, it is argued that it is not ethical to make an external disclosure without resorting to internal disclosure.

While whistleblowing is defined as disclosing negative situations in workplaces/organizations, it is also an important issue to determine which behaviors would be identified as "negative" at this stage. In order for any negative behavior to be considered a negative behavior that needs to be "disclosed":

- the behavior that is subject to disclosure should be contrary to the generally accepted ethical principles and the law,

- the person who discloses should have strong evidences, should not act depending on merely suspect and uncertain information,
- the behavior that will be disclosed by a discloser should be seriously harmful for workplace/organization, employees or society,
- the disclosing person, should not take any benefit, in any way, to himself/herself, to his/her friends, to his/her relatives or to the department where he/she works by means of this disclosure,
- the disclosing person, in the case that he/she encounters with a negative situation, should disclose internally, if the authorities do not take any action, resort to external disclosure method,
- the disclosing person should fulfill this disclosure voluntarily, not because of any obligation or pressure (Özler et al., 2010; 187)

3 Whistleblowing in Terms of Labor Law

Whistleblowing is undoubtedly an important concept in terms of work life. Because, in the working life, it is obvious that there are many behaviors or practices which are contrary to the laws and ethical values.

The fact that the legal boundaries of this situation are set for both public employees and those employed in the private sector will may force employees to take a stand against negative situations in an easier way. For public officials, since it should be evaluated in terms of public law, they are excluded from our study coverage.

In terms of labor law, the issue is handled in connection with the responsibility of loyalty and the obligation of confidentiality on an employee.

3.1 Responsibility of Loyalty of an Employee

Employees have some secondary obligations beside the obligation of performing the job which is the main obligation. The obligation of loyalty and responsibility for keeping secret are among them. Some of the behavioral obligations of the employee, apart from the performing work, in order to protect the interests of the employer and avoid harmful behaviors in the framework of honesty constitute the obligation of loyalty.

Loyalty is a comprehensive obligation and there are no concrete boundaries (Alper and Kılkış, 2016; 57). As a matter of fact, the Labor Law does not mention the obligation of loyalty directly. While the Labor Law No. 4857, in its Article 8/1, is describing the employment contract, it is stating that, "... an agreement whereby one party (the employee) undertakes to perform work in subordination to the other party (the employer) who undertakes to pay him remuneration." In addition, the situations in the 2nd Paragraph which is entitled with "For immoral, dishonorable or malicious conduct or other similar behaviors" of the Article 25 regulating the "Right to immediate termination of contract for justifiable reasons" constitute the frame of responsibility of loyalty. For example, the Article 25/II-b states that "the employee is guilty of any speech or action constituting an offence against the honor or dignity of the employer or a member of his family, or levels groundless accusations against the employer in matters affecting the latter's honor or dignity".

In addition, in part 396 of the "Debt of Workers" section of the Turkish Code of Obligations 6098, which regulates the "debt of care and loyalty", loyalty has been widely expressed.

In addition, in the Article 396 regulating the "Duty of care and loyalty" which is of the Part entitled with "Obligations of Employee" of the Turkish Code of Obligations Numbered 6098 states widely the obligation of loyalty. Accordingly, an employee has to perform the work diligently that he/she undertake and act loyal in protecting the rightful benefits of the employer. As long as the service relationship continues, the worker cannot serve in the third person for a fee contrary to the obligation of loyalty, and cannot be competition with his/her employer.

3.2 Confidentiality Obligation of Employee

In the Article 396/4 of the Turkish Code of Obligations Numbered 6098, it is stated that "An employee cannot use for his/her benefit or disclose information to others, such as production and business secrets, which he has learned at the time of his employment, during his/her continuing service relationship. The employee is obliged to keep the secret after the end of the service relationship to the extent necessary for the protection of the employee's rightful interests". In addition, the parties may set additional liabilities when establishing the employment contract. Additional liabilities may be set with collective labor contract provisions, workplace internal regulations or workplace practices (Alper and Kılkış, age; 53).

In the relevant paragraph (25/II-e) of the Article 25 of the Labor Law, there is a provision that "the employee commits a dishonest act against the employer, such as a breach of trust, theft or disclosure of the employer's trade secrets."

Although the worker's loyalty obligation and the obligation to keep secrets are emphasized, on the other side, it is stated in which circumstances these obligations will be raised. It is stated in the literature that the scope of the loyalty obligation is to be determined in the framework of honesty and goodwill rules, and the fact that employee protects the employer's interests during the business relationship, avoids from behaviors may be harmful to employer and workplace constitutes a general framework (Alper and Kılkış, op. cit.; 57) In this respect, it is also necessary for the employer to inform the employer in time of any unlawful situation that he/she has encountered in the workplace (Çelik, 2011; 139). Therefore, in the case that a part of information that the employer has acquired, in other words, the secrets he/she has learned includes unlawfulness and illegality, it is controversial whether he/she has contradicted to the obligation of loyalty.

The cases, in which a disclosure is considered whistleblowing are actually included in the definition. Any negativity, unlawful and unethical behavior in the workplace/organizations may be disclosed by the employee. We can list the subject of the disclosure as following (Aydın, op. cit.: 85–86):

- Health information
- Safety information
- Offenses committed in the workplace and tried to be kept confidential (financial crimes, bribery, etc.)
- Behaviors contrary to the law (employment without social security, etc.)
- Behaviors violating occupational health and safety
- Implementations damaging the environment

Therefore, on the above-mentioned topics, any behavior that would be harmful for employee, workplace, society, will not be considered in the context of obligation of loyalty or the responsibility of keeping secret.

4 Conclusion

Today, we encounter very often with the concept of whistleblowing, which is defined as disclosure of unethical or unlawful behaviors, negative situations in workplaces/organizations. In particular, the fact that communication tools have become more widespread with the development of technology has brought easiness of disclosure.

Undoubtedly, for employees, the obligation of loyalty and the responsibility of keeping secret are general rules. There are regulations related to this in both the Labor Law Numbered 4857 and Turkish Code of Obligations. Although these regulations have a broad framework, ultimately, unlawful and unethical behaviors are clearly stated. Therefore, the fact that employees disclose a negative situation in the workplace/organizations does not imply that they violated the mentioned laws.

In addition, although employees on disclosure are protected, it is expected that the situation that the discloser (whistleblower) confronts is firstly solved by disclosing it within the workplace/organization. If the internal disclosure does not result in any consequences, it is stated that performing the external disclosure indicates that the disclosing person is acting in good faith. In such a case, it would not require a legal sanction for the disclosing person of any negative situation to the public in various ways.

References

Aktan, Coşkun C. (2015). "Organizasyonlarda Yanlış Uygulamalara Karşı Bir Sivil Erdem, Ahlaki Tepki ve Vicdani Red Davranışı: Whistleblowing", Organizasyon ve Yönetim Bilimleri Dergisi, Cilt: 7, Sayı:2, s. 19–36.

Alper, Yusuf, Kılkış, İlknur (2016). İş ve Sosyal Güvenlik Hukuku, 2. Baskı, Bursa: Dora.

Aydın, Ufuk (2002). "İş Hukuku Açısından İşçinin Bilgi Uçurması (Whistleblowing)", Anadolu Üniversitesi Sosyal Bilimler Dergisi, Cilt: 2, Sayı: 2, s. 79–100.

Başol, Oğuz, Karatuna, Işıl (2015). "Örgütlerde Olumsuz Durumların İfşa Edilmesi ve Örgütsel İletişim İlişkisi", Marmara Üniversitesi İ.İ.B. Dergisi, Cilt XXXVII, Sayı: II, s. 153–170.

Çelik, N. (2011). İş Hukuku Dersleri, 24. Baskı. İstanbul: Beta.

Danışman, Sümeyra A. (2012). "Sosyal Bir Sorumluluk Olarak İhbarcılık", İş Ahlakı Dergisi, Cilt: 5, Sayı: 2, ss. 227–233.

Demirtaş, Özgür, Biçkes, Mehmet (Nisan/April 2014). "Makyavelizm'in Olumsuz Durumları İfşa Etme Niyeti Üzerindeki Etkisi: Bir Alan Çalışması", "İş,Güç" Industrial Relations and Human Resources Journal, Cilt/ Volume: 16, Sayı/Number: 2, pp. 98–112.

Eren, Veysel, Orhan, Ufuk (2013). "Kurumsal Sosyal Sorumluluğun Çalışanların Kötü Yönetimi İfşa Düzeylerine Etkisi Üzerine Bir Araştırma", International Journal of Social Science, Volume: 6, Issue: 2, ss. 455–468.

Esen, Emel, Kaplan, Hasan A. (2012). "İşletmelerde Ahlaki Olmayan Davranışların Duyurulması (Whistleblowing)", Dokuz Eylül Üniversitesi Sosyal Bilimler Enstitüsü Dergisi, Cilt: 14, Sayı: 2, ss. 33–52.

Hersh, Marion A. (2002). "Whistleblowers-Heroes or Traitors?: Individual and Collective Responsibility for Ethical Behaviour", Annual Reviews in Control, Volume: 26, Issue: 2, pp. 243–262.

İş Kanunu. (2003). T.C. Resmi Gazete, 4857 sayı, 10.06.2003.

Özler, Derya E., Şahin, Meltem D., Atalay, Ceren G. (2010). "Teorik Bir Çerçevede Whistleblowing – Etik İlişkisi", Eskişehir Osmangazi Üniversitesi Sosyal Bilimler Dergisi, Sayı: 11, Cilt: 2, ss. 169–194.

Türk Borçlar Kanunu. (2011). T.C. Resmi Gazete, 6098 sayı, 04.02.2011.

http://www.tdk.gov.tr/ (Erişim Tarihi: 24.07.2018).

Selcuk Yalcin[1]

Customer Focused New Product Design Process

1 Introduction

While successful new product designs provide significant benefits to businesses, failure to design new products can bring significant risks and losses to businesses. In the first place, all the designs which were made cannot be produced as a product. At any stage of the design, the product design can be abandoned. On the other hand, some of the designs that are decided to be produced with the thought of being successful in the market may fail in the market.

In this part, a model that will allow businesses to design and launch products with the quality and functions that customers want and the prices at a level that they can accept to pay has been proposed. In this model, pre-existing target costing, quality function deployment, analytic hierarchy process, value engineering and activity based costing methods are used together.

2 New Product Design

In an environment where competition is intense, customers are conscious, communication is fast, and products and production processes can be imitated rapidly, the success of businesses depends on designing and launching products with the quality and functions that customers want and the prices at a level that they can accept to pay.

3 Tools for New Product Design Process

There are many methods that can be used in new product design in the engineering and accounting literature. Some of them are target costing, quality function deployment, analytic hierarchy process, value engineering and activity based costing.

1 Department of Accounting, Kutahya Dumlupinar University, Turkey, selcuk.yalcin@dpu.edu.tr.

3.1 Target Costing

Traditional new product design methods deal with costs after they come to the conclusion that the concept of the product emerges and the product can be produced. This causes the costs to be taken as data. However, it is not possible to make very significant changes in product costs without re-designing after the product launch.

Target costing (TC) is the discipline that ensures that new products are profitable when they are launched. There are two major steps in target costing. The first is to determine a product's target price and target margin so that its target cost can be determined (Cooper, 1994, p.22). Target Costing was developed in Japan by companies such as NEC, SONY, NISSAN, and above all, TOYOTA as an instrument to plan costs and combine the instruments of cost management and cost engineering (Arioti et al., p.629). Target costing views meeting or exceeding customer requirement for quality, functionality and prices as key to attaining and sustaining product competitiveness (Lockamy III and Smith, 2000, 214). The TC process is presented in Fig. 1.

3.2 Quality Function Deployment

The success of a product or service largely depends on how they meet the customers' needs and expectations. Consequently, more effort is involved in getting the information necessary for determining what the customer truly wants. This tends to increase the initial planning time in the project definition phase of the development cycle, but it reduces the overall cycle time in bringing a product to market (Bouchereau and Rowlands 2000, p.8). Customer requirements, product functions and cost may be seen as three vital elements of the target costing process. Hence tools like (Quality Function Deployment) and VE (Value Engineering) play a very vital role in supporting the target costing process by way of maintaining functional requirements and customer satisfaction (Gandhinathan et al., 2004, p.1004). Quality Function Deployment (QFD) has mainly been used as a methodology for describing the inter-relationships between customer requirements and technical attributes. Attribute interdependencies are usually represented in the relationship matrix which depicts the impact of technical attributes on customer requirements, and the correlation matrix which illustrates interdependencies among technical attributes (Bode, 1998, p.587). This relationship and mutual relations must be taken into account to achieve high customer satisfaction.

Probably the most widely described and used model in the United States is a four-level model known as the Clausing model or the ASI model. ASI model is the American Supplier Institute, an organization that has done much to

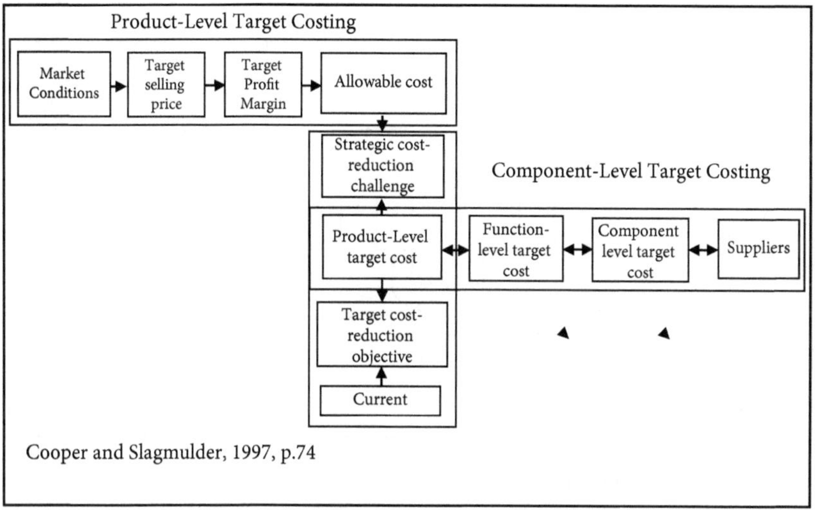

Fig. 1: The Target Costing Process

popularize QFD (Cohen, 1995, p.311). The Four Phase approach is more popular. It uses a series of charts and inter-related matrices which transform the voice of the customer at four phases of the product development cycle. The four phases are planning, design, process and production (Omar, 1999, p.200). The four-stage QFD model is shown in Fig. 2.

The QFD process involves four phases: (Bouchereau and Rowlands 2000, p.10):

(1) Product planning: house of quality.
(2) Product design: parts deployment.
(3) Process planning.
(4) Process control (quality control charts).

QFD is a tool that is not simple to develop and use. It takes a lot of time to prepare the QFD tables. Furthermore, more subjective assessment of information gathering and analysis is another disadvantage of QFD.

3.3 Other Techniques

In the new product design, priorities of customer demands and needs from market research are not the same. It is important to set priorities according to each other. An analytic hierarchy process can be used for this purpose. The use of Activity Based Costing (ABC) in the management of costs during

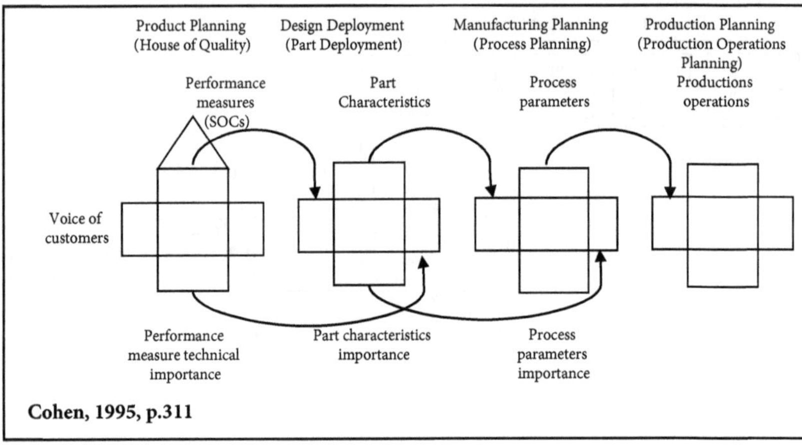

Fig. 2: Four-Phase QFD Model

design is necessary for more accurate distribute of overall production costs and production processes and products. ABC evaluates the costs of a firm based on actual resources and time consumed when doing so. Value engineering (VE) is an important tool in determining the value-adding product/service and business processes of a business. VE accomplishes the design of the products by analyzing them so as to find effective ways to achieve their function and basic characteristics. The necessary functions define which product needs to be made.

4 Approaches to New Product Design

Two approaches can be mentioned in the new product design. These can be specified as traditional new product design process and customer focused new product design process.

4.1 Traditional New Product Design Process

Design activities and all of the approaches that carry out without customer focus and different anxieties and priorities can be considered as traditional methods. The traditional new product design process takes place at successive stages and one that cannot be overcome without result. In this approach, the product development effort is initiated by marketing, which specifies the product functions, features, and approximate cost. Design engineering then designs a prototype and prepares documents detailing specifications of the desired product. These specifications are then used by manufacturing engineering to design and configure the needed tools, fixtures, and manufacturing equipment. Then, production manufactures the product in volume. Finally, the product becomes the responsibility of sales, distribution, and service groups (Tatikonda L.U. and Tatikonda M.V., 1994, p.22–23).

In the Traditional New Product Design Process, it is often tried to get the customer's reaction to the trial sales before the product is launched. If it is thought that the product can provide enough income for the business, it can be started to manufacture and sell. As a result of all these studies, the actual success of the product launched to the market can only be seen on the market. This is the main disadvantage of the traditional design approach that initiates design work from within the business.

4.2 Customer Focused New Product Design Process

Customer focused new product design both allows the design of new products that meet customer needs better and provides opportunities that enable to make production economically and quickly. The customer focused new product development process was created with the thought of combining pre-existing quality function deployment and target costing methods in new product design. The process is called "Customer Focused New Product Design Process" because both methods start with customer demands and needs.

Effective new product design requires the mutual and close relationship of many business functions. Therefore, in the customer focused new product design process, design activities should be conducted by a cross-functional new product design team. In order to design products that are constantly being renewed, the marketing function should be included in the team. Also, cost accounting should also be included in the team to manage product and process costs during design. The procurement unit will be responsible for providing the functions and properties of the product specified during the design at the target costs. However, the success of the team in new product design depends on the coordination and cooperation of the team, the tactics used to create new products from concept to product launch.

At the customer focused new product design process, design activities are initiated by the demands and needs of the customer. This is the reason why the process starts with market research. In this process, the business collects firstly the probable needs and demands of the customers by means of survey and interest groups. Then, these demands and needs are evaluated by QFD. In this way, the product concept is created in accordance with the characteristics that the customers want and do not want on the product, technical competence of the business and competitive evaluations of customers about competitors' products and the existing products of the business. With the customer focused new product design process, the design process will be continued in the direction of the product specifications and operational qualifications, whereas the management process of the costs that will enable the other party to sell the product at the price that the customer will be willing to pay will be continued. In this process, the management of the costs will be achieved with the TC. The team will determine product level and component level target costs in the direction of target selling price obtained from market research with TC, simultaneously, set forth the concept of product by evaluating product characteristics and business competencies together with QFD. The determined target costs will lead to the team during design and will be used as the goals that must be accomplished when determining the product functions and features by the team.

These goals will be also available for procurement function of the business. Thus, the procurement unit will cooperate with suppliers to achieve these goals. In case of inconsistency between the designed product functions and features and the target cost shares allocated for them, the product features and functions will be redesigned and, if this is not possible, the share of other functions and features will be transferred without exceeding the product level target costs.

Simultaneously with these studies, production and design engineers in the team will investigate the manufacturability of the product concept that has started to be produced from the industrial point of view.

Despite all work done, if the designated functions and features cannot be reached with the shared target costs, the new product design will be abandoned, or – if the product indispensable for the business – target costs will be increased or product functions and features will be reduced. At the end of the mentioned process, when product is produced with success, customer demands will be met both in terms of product features and price. On the other hand, if the process fails, the new product design will be abandoned. Although the decision of abandonment is perceived as a failure, no fixed investment is made in the product; only the product is being designed, until the production decision is made in the mentioned process. Thus, the risks and losses that the business will undertake in the design of new products will at the lowest level. In Fig. 3, Customer Focused New Product Design Process is presented.

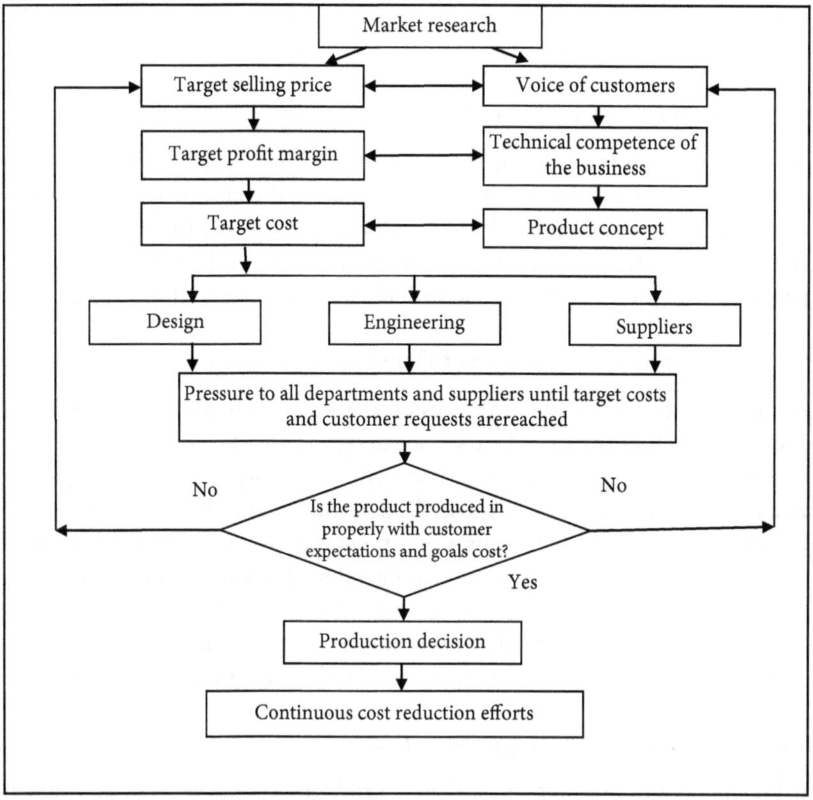

Fig. 3: Customer Focused New Product Design Process

4.3 Customer-Focused New Product Development Steps

4.3.1 Organizing the Customer-Focused New Product Development Team

The first step in developing a customer-focused new product is to create the design team. The new product design requires a simultaneous engineering and cross-functional team, which includes cost and management accountants. This team is required to have expertise and responsibility in marketing, new product design, production, purchasing and cost accounting. The team will work on new product design work together, in communication and interaction, make joint evaluations of the designed product and take decisions. However, each member of the team will have different areas of activity and responsibility. Procurement unit must negotiate to obtain the best materials, parts and services at the best price. Suppliers of goods and services must fully meet the features and functions that allow designers to offer product and service features that their customers will prefer.

4.3.2 Determination of Target Customer Segment

The second step in the customer-focused new product development phase is to identify the target customer segment. At this stage, the business determines the marketing strategy within the framework of vision and mission definitions and enterprise level strategies. Then the business determines the target market and the target customer segment in line with the identified marketing strategy.

4.3.3 Determination of Customer Demands and Needs

The most important feature of the customer focused new product development process is that it enables product/service design in the direction of the product function and features that the designated target market segment wants or does not want on the product. For this purpose, the demands and needs of the target market segment about the product features and functions are investigated by methods such as questionnaire and face-to-face interview. Such inquiries will be made by the marketing manager in the team and will reach the needs and demands of customers to the business. In addition, customer demands and needs will be made available to the QFD applications of the new product design process at this stage.

4.3.4 Determination of Target Sales Price

In the course of customer focused new product development, in addition to meeting customer demands and needs, it is also important that the customer is satisfied with the purchase price at which the customer is willing to pay. This is the reason why the marketing manager explores this price in market research. Thus, this will determine the target selling price for which the target customer segment is voluntary to pay.

4.3.5 Determination of Target Profit Margin

At this stage, the target profit margin to be achieved from the product to be designed is determined by taking into account the situation of the competitors in line with the business strategies.

4.3.6 Determination of Product Level Target Cost

At this stage, the product level target cost is obtained by subtracting the target profit margin expected from the product from the target selling price.

4.3.7 *Determination of Component Level Target Cost*

For the production of each product, raw material, direct labor and manufacturing overhead costs are required. In the customer focused new product development process, the sum of these costs must not exceed the specified product level target cost. Therefore, the product level target cost is shared among each cost item required for production. In the product design, the product is tried to be manufactured without exceeding the target costs determined for each component.

4.3.8 *Priority of Customer Demands and Needs*

The intensity of request of customer' demands and needs obtained during market research are not equal to each other. Therefore, it has to be put in order of priority. For this purpose, customer demands and needs can be prioritized using analytic hierarchy (AHP).process

4.3.9 *Create Product Concept on Quality Home*

In the design of customer focused new products, the product concept is built on the quality house matrix from the QFD matrices. For this, the customer demands and needs determined in the previous step and their AHP values are placed in the rows of the quality house. Then the business functions that the business has to fulfill to meet these customer requests are placed in the columns of the quality house matrix. Relations between rows and columns on the matrix are scored so that the percent importance of each business function is reached.

4.3.10 *Comparison of the Percent Importance of Each Business Functions and Component Level Target Costs*

In this step of the customer focused new product development process, the previously determined component level, the target costs and the comparison of the importance percentages of these components determined in the quality home are made and harmonized. Thus, it is possible to re-adjust the cost shares in line with the percentage of importance determined in the direction of customer demand. This adjustment allows the shaping of the product costs in line with customer requests.

4.3.11 *Industrial Design of Product*

At this stage, the manufacturability of the product from the industrial point of view is provided. The design team must work together at this stage, beginning with drawing the product's technical drawings, continuing with the creation of the prototype of the product, until the production decision is taken.

At this stage, the new product design manager will work with the marketing manager to harmonize customer needs and demands with the technical competence of the business and to design the customer's preferred product. It is also important that the design made at a price that the customer will be willing to pay should be produced within the target costs to be determined for sale. Therefore, the design manager will not exceed the target costs determined during the process in the direction of customer demands, competition on the market and strategic and tactical decisions of the business. This will ensure that the product being designed has the features and prices that can meet customer expectations.

Besides, the cost accounting manager will investigate ways of making cost calculations with the design of the product, customer demands and needs of the designed product, and the production costs at the target costs determined in this process. In this context, customer value analysis and value engineering studies that can be used to transform target costs into component level target costs will work together with production responsibility.

4.3.12 Cooperation with Suppliers

The procurement at this stage will look for ways to ensure that the required raw materials and materials are available at the specified component-level target costs; provide communication and cooperation and contracts with suppliers. During these studies, the components that cannot be achieved in the target costs can be changed or the target cost shares can be increased. Such decisions are among the most important decisions the new product design team will make. At this stage, the component adds value to the product and the customer's thinking about the component will lead the team.

4.3.13 Production Decision-Making

At the end of the design process, it can be decided to produce products that meet customer needs and demands at the target costs. On the other hand it can be decided to produce designs that cannot be produced at the target costs. If the product is important for the strategic objectives of the management, the business may decide to produce this product by sacrificing the target profit margin. The designs for which the decision not to be made can be kept in operation for later evaluation.

5 Conclusion

In this part, a customer focused new product design process is proposed. The process will be carried out by a multifunctional team. In this process, target costing, quality function deployment, analytic hierarchy process, value engineering and activity based costing methods will be used. It is possible to make designs in which the customer demands and needs at the prices they are willing to pay are provided in accordance with the qualifications of the business before the fixed capital investment is made by using the recommended process. Also, with this method, the business can give up production of designs without incurring significant risks and costs.

References

Arioti, A., Fantozzi, C., Granchi, M. and Vettori, E. (1999). "A Methodology to Diagnose the Target Cost in a Manufacturing Process", IEEE 0-7803-5489-3/99, pp. 629–633.

Bode, J. and Fung, R.Y.K. (1998). "Cost Engineering with Quality Function Deployment", Computers Industrial Engineering, Vol: 35, No: 3–4, ss. 587–590.

Bouchereau, V. and Rowlands, H. (2000). "Methods and Techniques to Help Quality Function Deployment (QFD)", Benchmarking: An International Journal, Vol: 7, No: 1, pp. 8–19.

Cohen, L. (1995). Quality Function Deployment How to Make QFD Work for You, Davison Wesley Longman, Massachusetts.

Cooper, R. (1994). "Japanese Cost Management Practices", CMA – The Management Accounting Magazines, October-, Vol: 68, pp. 20–26.

Cooper, R. and Slagmulder, R. (1997). Target Costing and Value Engineering, The IMA Foundation for Applied Research Inc., Productivity Press, Portland-Oregon.

Gandhinathan, R., Raviswaran, N. and Suthakar, M. (2004). "QFD- and VE Enabled Target Costing: A Fuzzy Approach", International Journal of Quality & Reliability Management, Vol: 21, No: 9, ss. 1003–1011.

Lockamy, A. III. Smith, W.I. (2000), "Target Costing for Supply Chain Management: Criteria And Selection", Industrial Management & Data Systems, Vol: 100, No: 5, pp. 210–218.

Omar, A.R. and Harding, J.A. (1999). "Design for Customer Satisfaction: An Information Modelling Approach", Integrated Manufacturing Systems, Vol: 10, No: 4, pp. 199–209.

Tatikonda, L. Tatikonda, M.V. (1994). "Tools for Cost-Effective Product Design and Development", Production and Inventory Management Journal, Second Quarter, pp. 22–28.

Serkan Çelik[1]

Basel IV: Reform or a New Era?

1 Introduction

Especially with the recent global banking crisis, the whole world has once again experienced that the most important player of the financial sector is the banks, and that the distresses of the banks deeply affect all the other components in the sector. In particular, the integration process that accelerated with the 70's, risky investment opportunities and complex financial transactions brought about by the diversification of banking products and services brought about by the rapidly developing technologies, led to undertake high risks while triggering their high profit desire. Because of the fact that it is the nature of the business taking risks and managing them correctly and even placing the concept of "risk" in the centers, the banks taking overmuch risk have led to the disruption of not only their banks but also the country economies on a global scale in terms of size of the bank.

At this point, the BASEL consensus emerged as an arrangement for capital that should hold to the risks that banks face due to their operations. In the most crude terms, BASEL consensus, which can be explained in the form of calculation of the capital amount, that the bank has to deal with the liquidity risk faced by the bank in the event that the loans which are the most important activity items of the banks cannot be paid by the customer, is not a necessity but a recommendation text. However, in terms of the sector, it has been accepted and applied as a necessity over time.

The inadequacy of BASEL consensus to take loan risk to the center alone, the need to update the regulations in parallel with the market due to the crises experienced by banks due to the fact that the existing risks of the banks are not only loans but also due to the existence of internal and external risks. While BASEL II calculated the capital adequacy required for the risks related to loan risk, then the market risk with BASEL II was also included in the consensus, then the developments related to the strong capital adequacy of the banks continued along with BASEL III.

1 Research Asistant, Kırklareli University, School of Applied Sciences, serkancelik@klu.edu.tr.

Since the BASEL IV consensus we are facing at the last point means a new period for banks and it will bring many changes together, the positive side of the new consensus may cause confusion and difficulties as well as even negative effects on the profitability due to the effects of the banks 'capital structure as well as many issues have been discussed.

2 Why We Needed to BASEL

2.1 Basel I

Due to the collapse of the Bretton Woods system in 1973 and the contraction in the foreign currency triggered by the Herstatt Bank crises, the G10 countries later established the "Committee on Banking Regulations and Supervisory Practices", which will be changed as "Basel Committee on Banking Supervision", which will become one of the most important institutions in banking history (Akkizidis & Kalyvas, 2018). The main objective of the BASEL Committee, established by the heads of the central banks of 10 Member States and 28 Member States as of 2018, is to develop and sustain financial stability, and to develop banking activities on the basis of all Member States, meaning the strengths and weaknesses of banking activities.

In 1988, the Committee published its first study, which was not binding to "International Convergence of Capital Measurement and Capital Standards, but highly recommended, and which, over time, would become a must for the industry. Although there is no obligation to implement any of the Committee Member States, the Committee considered it a necessity to apply the relevant decisions to their banking systems. The first consensus focused on the loan risk. The committee preferred to leave other risk management to its own regulatory agencies. Although loans are the main operating items of the banks, it was clear that the Banks were at significant risk if the loans were not repaid to the banks. It is also clear that the banks cannot fulfill their obligations to face liquidity risk if the loans are not paid, since the banks are involved in the redistribution of the money in the market.

The first BASEL text, published in 1988, roughly sets the standards for the calculation of the amount of "Capital" that must be held instantaneously in the bank's vault for the status of the "Active" and "Passive" positions of the bank (Balthazar, 2006). Countries would be able to raise capital standards if their own regulatory bodies wanted. Although it is considered necessary for the committee's decisions to be complied with by internationally operating banks, many countries have made it mandatory for decisions to be implemented in order to be able

Tab. 1: Capital Structure According To Basel I (Balthazar, 2006)

Tier 1 Capital	Tier 2 Capital	Deductions
• Paid-Up Capital • Disclosed Reserves	• Undisclosed Reserves • Asset Revaluation Reserves • General Provisions • Hybrid Instruments (Must be unsecured, fully paid-up) • Subordinated debt (Max. 50 %Tier 1)	• Goodwill • Investments in Unconsolidated Subsidiaries

Tab. 2: According to Basel I Risk Weight of Assets (Balthazar, 2006)

0 (%)	20 (%)	50 (%)	100 (%)
• Cash • Claims on OECD central governments • Claims on other Central governments if they are denominated and funded in the national currency	• Claims on OECD banks and multilateral development banks • Claims on banks outside OECD with residual maturity • Claims on public sector entities of OECD countries	• Mortgage Loans	• All other Claims

to build a strong structure against possible crises in their own banking sectors on a national basis.

The first requirement to determine the capital adequacy of a bank was to determine what the bank could calculate as capital. The committee separated the capital into 2 groups as Tier 1 and Tier 2 Capital (Tab. 1). Tier 2 capital is limited to not exceeding Tier 1. Tier 2 Capital is limited to not exceeding Tier 1. Risk weights were created through the balance sheet items of the Bank (Tab. 2) and capital was calculated as equivalent to 8 % of these risky assets.

After the structure and definition of capital was understood, the Committee weighed the risk weights of balance sheet items in 4 groups. According to the account here, if a bank buys a corporate bond at a value of 400 EU from the capital market, the amount of capital that the bank should hold for it;

- It is located in 400 EU x 100 % zone. (Since it is Corporate bond)
- 400 EU x 8 % = 32 EU is the amount of capital required to be separated.

Finally, the Committee determined the risk weights in the off-balance sheet items and determined the amount of capital that should be reserved for these items according to the weights.

3 Why We Reformed Basel?

3.1 Basel I Criticism

The most important criticism of the first Basel consensus is the fact that the only risk in the banking sector is not just the loan risk. In the banking sector, many risk items from domestic and foreign sources should be mentioned. Exchange rate, interest, market, liquidity, operational risks are the main risk items that can cause banks to risk their business lives or even end. Apart from all these important risk items, only the first text on loan risk seemed inadequate in terms of risk-taking, making it especially inevitable for Basel I to be referred to as inadequate, especially in the period conjuncture because of the increasingly complex and complicated banking operations and the introduction of high but equally risky products.

The second important criticism of Basel I concerns the inadequacy of capital adequacy calculations. The capital adequacy calculation is not calculated adequately in the worst-case periods, and the efficiency is being reduced and calculated excessively during periods when a good financial climate is expected (AYKUT, 2008, p. 2).

Another important criticism was that while calculating the risk weights for the BASEL consensus, the calculation process is considered to be a non- risky if the party to the calculation is an OECD member country while it is considered to be 100 % risky if it is a non-OECD member country. This could almost be regarded as a direct or even positive discrimination. While it is considered as a zero-risky according to BASEL I if you are an institution in an OECD member country even if it is a risky institution, it is considered as a 100 % risky if you are in non-OECD member country even if it is a party to the agreement (AYKUT, 2008, p. 2).

3.2 Basel I Market Risk Management

After the criticism of the lack of risk definition of the BASEL I consensus in 1996, the first consensus was defined as "losses due to market risk in on-balance sheet and off-balance sheet positions" and capital adequacy calculation related to "Market Risks" was added. "Tier 3 Capital" has also been defined to calculate the capital adequacy of market risk. The market risk capital of 28.5 % of Tier 3 capital is limited to be supported by Tier 1 Capital (Balthazar, 2006, p. 27).

4 BASEL II

In addition to Basel II Loan and Market risks, it also added solutions for managing operational risks. For Basel II consensus, the most important change that we need to mention for the "Identify-Assess-Monitor-Control/Mitigate" BASEL II

Tab. 3: Differences Between BASEL I and BASEL II. Reference: (BIS, 2004)

Basel I	**Basel II**
• Focused only on a single risk group	• Management of the Bank's internal risks and Audit and market risks.
• Same application solution for all risks	• More flexible structure. It includes capital incentives for less risky institutions. Risk profiles have been created to make appropriate calculations.
• Focuses on the overall structure of the Bank	• Focuses separately on all operational parts of the Bank.

consensus for these risk groups is to include the concept of "Operational Risk" within the capital calculation.

In June 1999, the Basel Committee issued the framework for the new capital adequacy standard to replace BASEL I. Due to the deficiencies mentioned earlier in the first consensus published in 1988, the transition to BASEL II consensus has become inevitable in order to manage the needs of the sector and the risks in which the current text is insufficient. Eighteen months later, the first text published in January 2001 was re-edited and published by integrating the comments and needs from the industry. After that Basel II, which was reorganized in 2003 and 2004, became the final version (Balthazar, 2006, p. 39).

Basel II was constructed on three structural blocks (Pillar). The main objective of this three-block structure is to implement a more efficient risk management and to increase financial efficiency on a global and sectoral basis.

5 BASEL III

The global economic crisis, which emerged in 2008 as a banking center and set the whole world on fire, clearly revealed the inadequacy of Basel II and its structural blocks, which came into force in 2004. This, in turn, led to why the measures to be taken in the banking sector were never sufficient and the adequacy of BASEL practices was also discussed. The crisis will last for many years and will cause the Basel consensus to be updated within the framework of the crisis.

Basel III recommendation text was first published by the Committee in 2010. In June 2011, the revised final version entered into force. The committee called the new text "BASEL IIIA Global Regulatory Framework for More Resilient Banks and Banking Systems" (Ramirez, 2017, p. 1). In the years following the crisis, the Committee was aware that a new need to study to ensure that banking activities are more stable, robust and transparent. This awareness was also the origin of the recommended text known as BASEL III (Ferretti, 2016, p. 46).

Tab. 4: BASEL II Pillars. Reference: (BDDK, 2004, p. 18)

BASEL II		
Financial Activity – More Effective Risk Management		
• Calculation of minimum capital adequacy 1. Loan risk ❖ Standard approach ❖ Internal rating ❖ Securitization 2. Operational Risk 3. Market Risk	• Screening of the audit authority	• Market Discipline

Tab. 5: BASEL III Capital Adequacy Ratio. Reference: (Mermod & Ceran, 2011, p. 36)

Risk Weighted Assets (%)	**Capital Adequacy**						
	Common Equity			**Tier 1 Capital**		**Total Capital**	
	Minimum	**Buffer Capital**	**Required Capital**	**Minimum**	**Required**	**Minimum**	**Required**
Basel II	2 % 1 % Level for International Banks			4 % 2 % Level for International Banks		8 %	
Basel III	4,5 %	2,5 %	7 %	6 %	8,5 %	8 %	10,5 %

While the minimum capital adequacy ratio on the basis of total capital in BASEL II is 8 %, the discussions on the fact that the amount reserved for capital adequacy together with BASEL III has negative effect on the profitability of the bank, is also called as Buffer Capital we can see that the minimum capital adequacy ratio of BASEL III has been raised to 10.5 % with the addition of 2.5 %, which is optional. Basel III, as in its predecessor, introduced important regulations on the items that play an important role in the formation of the 2008 economic crisis, such as liquidity, leverage ratios and risky assets, as well as the minimum capital adequacy while working on 3 structural blocks, and also increased the capital adequacy ratio with the application of buffer capital without necessity but optional.

6 Section III BASEL IV a Reform or a New Era

6.1 Basel IV What Is Next?

In 2014, the Basel Committee shared with the sector the need to update the methods (IRB approach to capital requirements) used by banks to calculate risk-weighted capital adequacy within themselves. The objective of the Committee is to ensure that the Bank's internal risk estimation and capital adequacy calculations reach a certain standard and by the way of this to provide comparativeness.

In addition to the very complicated and misleading practices of existing applications,

- The risk profiles of banks are prevented from being understood by investors,
- Prevents the bank from understanding whether the Bank's capital is sufficient by regulatory agencies,
- For the bank's management, it is difficult to calculate the risk profile of the bank and to make capital planning difficult,
- It was believed that making the risk estimates difficult to compare (Aksel, Geraskin, & Izrailov, 2017, p. 37).

The arrangement, which brings with it great discussions and which is almost unanimous about the fact that it is not BASEL III accessory due to its impact, was called BASEL IV in the sector. The general expectation and desire of the banking sector was that the new application called BASEL IV, which is actually the continuation/end point of BASEL III, was not able to raise the capital adequacy standards of the banking sector because of the innovations it would bring to the sector. While raising the capital adequacy ratio obliges banks to keep the amounts they can give as loans in their vault case, it is argued by the sector that they will have negative effects on the banks ' profitability, as the loan amount is seen as economic size and that they will have negative effects on the economies.

Tab. 6: BASEL III vs BASEL IV. Reference: (TBB&EY, 2016, p. 9)

Capital Adequacy Regulations		
	Equity Capital	**BASEL III** It is based on strengthening the quality and quantity of equity, liquidity and leverage ratios.
Need 1. Loan risk standard approach 2.Loan Risk -IEB 3.Loan Risk Reduction 4.Securitisation 5.Counterparty Loan Risk 6.Operational Risk 7.Market Risk 8.Loan Valuation Regulation		
Loan Limits	Large	**BASEL IV** It is based on the share of capital adequacy (**risk weighted assets**) and the **risk of concentration.**
Risk Transfer	Loan	
	Liquidity	
	Leverage	
Notes	Marginal	

Tab. 7: BASEL IV Outlines/Actions. Reference: (TBB&EY, 2016, p. 10)

Loan Risk Standard Revision **1.** External Rating **2.** Internal Due- Diligence procedure **3.** Housing project, etc. special calculations in risks **4.** Risk Reduction	**Revision Of Loan Risk Calculation Methodology** **1.** In sovereign risk and low-default portfolios the internal model will remove. **2.** Parameter adaptation and estimation implimentation
Expected: Higher risk weight and conversion to loan	**Expected: Transition to standard method**
Market Risk Framework Revision **1.** Banking purchase/sale distinction **2.** Transition from internal model VaR to Expected Shortfall **3.** More precise approach in standard method	**Operational Risk Revision** **1.** Standardization of operational risk methods **2.** Starting to use activity indicators
Expected: Expected to create additional liabilities of 40 % to the bank	**Expected: Standard method calculation methodology**
Counterparty Risk and KDA Revision **1.** Margin and guarantee calculation changed **2.** Effect of market risk on the Loan Policy	**Revision of Securitization Regulations** **1.** Hierarchy will be renewed. **2.** Transparency and comparability will be ensured by standardizing securitization methods.
Expected: Relief of banks with transparency	**Expected:?**

With BASEL IV implementation, it is possible that many European banks will experience a lack of capital. It is envisaged that BASEL IV will require additional capital of 120 billion euros and that the profitability of the equity will decrease as a result of the adequacy ratios, risky assets and internal ratings regulations that will enter into force (Schneider, Schrock, Koch, & Schneider, 2017, p. 1).

Although BASEL III is based on raising the liquidity and leverage ratios of the equity quality, it is thought that this will lead to significant changes in the sector due to focusing on risk Weighted Assets (RWA) calculations in BASEL IV (PWC, 2017, p. 3).

6.2 BASEL IV Outlines

The impact of the economic crisis due to the concern that these crises will not be experienced again, Basel IV brings significant and very harsh changes to the sector compared to previous implementations. While it is argued that the changes that will be experienced will affect the sector in many respects, especially in the period of the full enforcement of the regulations, due to the complexity of transactions, and also the need for extra capital to be provided by the sector to create new calculation methods can create difficulties, in fact, it is argued that due to the decrease in loan amount, it can cause negative positions in terms of the global economy, while the Committee states that there is an increase and expectation in the capital markets.

References

Akkizidis, I., & Kalyvas, L. (2018). Final Basel III Modelling Implementation, Impact and Implications. Switzerland: Palgrave Macmillan.

Akkizidis, I. S., & Bouchereau, V. (2005). Guide to Optimal Operational Risk and BASEL II. Auerbach Publications. Boca Raton/New York.

Aksel, K., Geraskin, P., & Izrailov, I. (2017). Basel IV the Next Generation of Risk Weighted Assets. Germany: Wiley.

Aykut, C. (2008). BASEL II Standartları. Uluslararası Ekonomik Sorunlar Dergisi, 30.

Balthazar, L. (2006). From Basel 1 to Basel 3 The Integration of State of the Art Risk Modelling in Banking Regulation. Great Britain: Palgrave Macmillan.

BDDK. (2004). Sermaye Ölçümü ve Sermaye Standartlarının Uluslararası Düzeyde Uyumlaştırılması. from https://www.tbb.org.tr/Content/Upload/Dokuman/1391/Basel_II_Yeni_Sermaye_Yeterliligi_Duzenlemesi.pdf. Retrieved 15.07.2018.

BIS. "History of the Basel Committee", Retrieved 15.07.2018, from https://www.bis.org/bcbs/history.htm

BIS. (1988). International Convergence of Capital Measurement and Capital Standards. Retrieved 15.07. 2018, from https://www.bis.org/publ/bcbs04a.pdf

BIS. (2004). International Convergence of Capital Measurement and Capital Standards. Retrieved 15.07. 2018, from https://www.bis.org/publ/bcbs107.pdf

Ferretti, P. (2016). New Perspectives on the Bank-Firm Relationship Lending, Management and the Impact of Basel III. Palgrave Macmillan Studies, Springer, Switzerland.

Mermod, A. Y., & Ceran, M. (2011). BASEL III Doğrultusunda Bankacılık Riskleri ve Sermaye Yeterliliği; Türk Bankacılık Sektörü Üzerine Karşılaştırmalı Bir Analiz Finansal Araştırmalar ve Çalışmalar Dergisi, 2(4), 29–38.

PWC. (2017). Basel IV: Big Bang or The the Endgame of Basel III. Retrieved 15.07.2018, from https://www.pwc.com/sg/en/publications/assets/basel-iv-big-bang-or-endgame-of-basel-iii-201712.pdf

Ramirez, J. (2017). Handbook of Basel III Capital Enhancing Bank Capital in Practice. Wiley. United Kingdom.

Schneider, S., Schrock, G., Koch, S., & Schneider, R. (2017). Basel IV What's Next For Banks. McKinsey&Company. Retrieved 15.07.2018, from https://www.mckinsey.com/~/media/mckinsey/business%20functions/risk/our%20insights/basel%20iv%20whats%20next%20for%20european%20banks/basel-iv-whats-next-for-banks.ashx

TBB&EY. (2016). Basel IV: Bankaları Bekleyen Zorluklar.

Yavuz Gul[1], Basil Okoth[2], and Serpil Altinirmak[3]

Comparative Analysis of Web-Based Investor Relations of Companies in the Telecommunication Sector Traded in Istanbul and New York Stock Exchanges

1 Introduction

In today's competitive environment, firms should seek to utilize the financial markets efficiently. In these markets, businesses are always engaged in battles with others, and it is the nature of this competition that accentuates the significance of the firm's ability to attract the attention of market investors, establish a trust environment, increase the prestige of the business as well as its aptitude to raise its recognizability, and to convince the investors of its performance and potential. Businesses are in constant interaction with existing and potential investors, analysts, banks, creditors and financial market units, putting the concept of investor relations at top of their agenda. When the aim of the business is taken to be the maximization of shareholder value, the activities undertaken within the context of investor relations in order to attain the high market value play important roles as strategic tools. As far as investor relations is concerned, businesses that offer sound, timelier and more descriptive information to these market units reap more advantages over their competitors.

2 Investor Relations

Investor relations, which is a concept that describes the relationship between publicly traded firms and the financial markets, is a new concept that has developed substantially in recent years. The term 'investor relations' refers to the legal and voluntary continuous communication that companies operating in or intending to operate in the capital markets conduct with existing and potential investors, intermediary institutions, regulatory financial institutions and the

1 Masters Student, Anadolu University, yavuz.gul@outlook.com.
2 PhD Student, Social Science Institute, Anadolu University, basils.okoth@gmail.com.
3 Associate Professor, Eskişehir Vocational School, Anadolu University, saltinirmak@anadolu.edu.tr.

media they interact with (Sayılır, 2012, p.4). Investor relations may be said to be one of the fastest growing areas of corporate communication. The National Institute of Investment Associations defines investor relations as "... a strategic management responsibility using the disciplines of finance, communication and marketing to manage the content and flow of company information to financial and other constituencies to maximize relative valuation" (Hockerts and Moir, 2004, p.86).

The ability to raise the required funds and at minimum costs from the financial markets is squarely tied to the reputation and credibility of the business in the market. From this point of view, it is possible to say that the level of development and professionalism of the investor relations practices of the enterprise strengthens the owner's position relevant to the market. In the existence of an effective market, where all investors can access all information freely, instantly and cost-effectively, the role of investor relations is considerably reduced, since all the market units have access to all the information they need whenever they do. As desirable as this may seem in theory, this situation is not fully achievable in real life, even in developed markets like the US and UK. We can, therefore, assert that one of the objectives of the investor relations practices is the strengthening the trust between the investors and the business by reducing the problem of asymmetric information. Asymmetric information in financial markets can arise in the form of adverse selection, moral hazard and monitoring costs (Bebczuk, 2003, p.7). One point that should be stressed is that the business should give adequate weight to its relations with all financial units, not only the investors.

One of the fundamental and perhaps the most important objectives of investor relations may be said to be the establishment a trust environment between investors and the business. This means that investors have access to clearer and more reliable information about the business firsthand, putting them in a position to take more sound actions in the face of current or anticipated adverse developments on the business. In addition to the trust aspect, the other areas of concern for the investor relations practices include to persuade investors about the strength and success of the business as well as create a sense of prestige in the business. Other activities within the purview of investor relations also include communicating with investors and informing them of the various regulatory changes effected by the regulatory authorities in the financial markets. The availability of these practices will enable the business to be evaluated more accurately. Yet another purpose of investor relations practice is to provide a two-way communication by sharing the views of investors regarding the actions and performance of the business with the top management (Türkiye Yatırımcı İlişkileri Derneği, 2016, p.7). Craven and Marston (1997) argued that institutional investors may be more willing to invest in businesses that provide well-organized and controlled investor relations programs (Craven and Marston, 1997, p.138).

There are several groups to be considered when talking about the target population of investor relations practices. These groups include individual and corporate investors, as well as a variety of other players such as regulators, analysts, rating agencies, banks and intermediaries. Analysts however need to be looked at in a different light from the others because they have the capacity to positively or negatively influence the prestige value of business, and have a strong significance in attracting new investors with their opinions and commentaries in the written and visual media (Kuperman, Athavale and Eisner, 2003, pp.74–80). Intermediaries also play an important role as information conduits between the management and investors. These institutions receive and transmit the views and concerns of investors concerning the business and in turn relay notices and feedbacks from the business.

3 The Importance of Internet in Investor Relations

When debate first started on investor relations, the associated practices were perceived as costs to the business. This perception has evolved into the realization that more value than expected can be created from the practice of sound investor relations. With respect to investor relations, businesses try to keep investors informed in a variety of ways. Annual reports, financial reports, meetings, press releases, presentations can be cited as examples of these ways. While the Internet can be used to provide investors with a copy of the traditional, printed annual reports, it also offers new opportunities for presenting and communicating the information (Geerings, Bollen and Hassink, 2003, p.568).

Information Technologies, which has found its way into every aspect of life today, plays a major role in making the communication between businesses and their stakeholders easier. It is an accepted fact that the developments in technology have made information about organizations more transparent, accessible and understandable. Every developing organization is currently engaged in activities that seek to access and attract customers and investors more easily through the internet and internet-based applications. Businesses that keep pace with the times and technology have increased their usage of the internet and other web-based technology. With Web-based investor relations, investors have become able to access information easily and effortlessly, and businesses have also been able to save on costs. In other words, while businesses had to incur large costs with regards to printing and distribution of different business reports, information process conducted over the internet and other investors relations practices conducted in this form ensure that businesses avoid such costs. Once the information has been published on the internet, businesses have the opportunity to stay in communication with investors at all times, not only when financial reports are published or when meetings are held. The data and information published on the internet can be accessed at any time.

The organizations which own these websites also have the ability to update the site, data, and reports whenever they desire. While the fact that websites are capable of responding to most of the demands by investors increase the degree of transparency, well-designed and attractive websites make it easier for investors to find them when they need to. The interaction that can be created with investors through the internet will also help strengthen the bond between the investors and the business. Geerings, Bollen, and Hassink found in one of their studies that the size of the firm has an influence on the investor relations: large firms use the internet more frequently for investor relations practices and they have better quality websites (Geerings, Bollen and Hassink, 2003, p.572). Another study conducted by Bollen and Hassink with contributions from Bozic purposed to examine the quality of the websites in investor relations. The collected detailed explanations of the *characteristics* of the investor relations websites and explanatory variables from 270 firms in 6 countries. The results showed that the investor relations pages were used to disclose financial reports and other general information, and to facilitate direct communication between investors and the investor relations department (Bollen, Hassink and Bazic, 2006, pp. 296–297).

Collison (2003) reviewed the websites of Fortune 500 companies in 2001 to identify how these companies used their websites to feed the informational needs of journalists. The results show that firms are making some efforts to help the media through their websites. However, there is a need for further development of these efforts (Collison, 2003, pp.29–41) A fair and more efficient information access and sharing opportunity may be created for investors and other users of the financial reports provided over the internet by including keyword searches of the contents of the reports, thereby instituting a more interactive experience (Fisher, Oyelere and Laswad, 2004, p.414). In their study examining the use and role of the internet in investor relations, Deller, Stubenrath and Weber (1999) scrutinized the web-based investor relations practices of American, British and German companies. The sample was taken from the 100 indexes of the relevant stock markets of the countries (S & P, FTSE, DAX). The results revealed that American companies engaged in more internet investor relations practices (91 %) than their English (72 %) and German (71 %) counterparts. In addition, American companies were found to use the internet more broadly with respect to corporate reporting. While corporate reporting through the internet appeared to have become a standard feature in investor relations strategies in the United States, it was established that only about two-thirds of companies in Germany have embraced the internet as an alternative means of disseminating financial information (Deller, Stubenrath and Weber, 1999, pp.351–364). In a related study, Hamid looked at the Malaysian market and took his sample from 100 Index of The Kuala Lumpur Stock Exchange. In his results, he emphasized the huge differences that exist between developed and developing countries in the use of the internet for investor relations purposes with a finding that only 70 companies in his sample had materials on investor relations on their websites. He emphasized the need for the regulatory bodies in East Asia to encourage the publishing of information on investor relations on the company websites (Hamid, 2005, pp.5–14).

4 Telecommunication Sector

The telecommunications sector is one of the sectors with the highest brand equity, not only in Turkey but globally as well. The telecommunication sector has experienced rapid development in the recent past and managed to rise to the pinnacle of business significance, with many countries making great investments in the sector through research and development.

Telecommunication, by way of facilitating effective information transmission, forms the infrastructure of the information society (http://www.bilgitoplumu.gov.tr/wp-content/uploads/2014/04/Telekomunikasyon_Alt_ Komisyonu _ Raporu pdf Access Date: 29.04.2018).

Information and communication technologies increase the output per employee by reducing transaction costs. In addition, the rapid dissemination of information occasioned by effective ICT has helped to immensely reduce market irregularities to the minimum. (https://www.tasav.org/media/k2/attachments/bf_rapor_no.16_telekom_sektoru_ejderoruc_07.03.2015.pdf Access Date: 29.04.2018).

In today's rising and evolving technological environment, with the appropriate infrastructure, telecommunication services are able to access, use and transmit information available anywhere in the world. Hence, it can be said that the telecommunication sector holds special value in the eyes of investors.

İçöz (2003, p.20) classified the telecommunication sector in terms of its basic services. He grouped them as those which provide only carrying capacity by means of transmission lines; value-added services which are information-intensive services, and telecommunication devices as telephone devices (like mobile devices) added at the end of the network.

In general, after 1980, globalization and liberalization tendencies in the economies around the world increased raising with them the importance of the telecommunications sector. The demand for information increased, and with it the advancement of technology; telecommunication services started to become global. With this regard, the telecommunication sector also began to play a role in the development of many other sectors. The 1990s can be termed as a period in which telecom operators of many countries were privatized and government monopoly telecom was replaced by autonomous institutional regulators as private companies started to operate (http://home.ku.edu.tr/~kyilmaz/papers/Y_Atiyas2000.pdf, Access Date: 29.04.2018)

5 Data and Methodology

In this research, 8 companies that are currently trading in Istanbul Stock Exchange, either providing telecommunication services or conducting production activities related to telecommunication services, and 8 companies with the same qualifications in the New York Stock Exchange were considered. Since the number of telecommunications companies in the New York Stock Exchange was more than eight, the eight companies with the highest market value during the study period were selected. The companies covered in the study include, alphabetically (from BIST), Alcatel Lucent Teletaş Telecommunication Co. (ALCTL), Anel Telecommunication Electronik Sistemleri Sanayi ve Ticaret AS (ANELT), Karel Elektronik Sanayi ve Ticaret AS (KAREL) Kron Telekomünikasyon Hizmetleri A.Ş (KRONT), Netaş Telekomünikasyon AS (NETAS), Turkcell Communication Services Inc. (TCELL), Türk Prysmian Kablo ve Sistemleri A.Ş (PRKAB), Türk Telekomünikasyon AS (TTKOM), and (from NYSE) America Movil (AMX), American Telephone and Telegraph Company (T), Bell Canada Enterprises (BCE), China Mobile LTD (CHL), Nippon Telegraph and Telephone Docomo (DCM), Orange SA (ORAN) Telefonica SA (TEF) and Verizon Communications (VZ).

The study, in evaluating the investor relations websites of the companies, made use of the score card developed by the Turkish Investor Relations Society (TUYID) for this purpose. The scorecard takes into account and assesses the investor relations websites of companies in terms of how open, transparent and rich they are, and the extent to which they satisfy the needs of the investors.

The scorecard is comprised of 3 basic sections which include the annual report, the financial disclosures and the website format. There is a total of 66 questions in the first section which looks at the annual report. Under this heading, an evaluation is made on the most recent annual report published to check whether all the necessary data are included and then the data is examined, and its sufficiency interrogated. Both the English and Turkish annual reports were examined during this research. The financial disclosure section has 45 questions which help in the scrutiny of the company's annual reports, financial reports, press releases, presentations and websites. The last section which deals with the website format has 59 questions and focuses on the website itself and the extent and ease with which investors can access the information they need.

In the analysis of the web-based investor relations practices of companies using the scorecard scale, 0 points are awarded when the response is 'not found' or 'doesn't exist', 1 point when the answer is 'found' or 'exists' and 2 points awarded when the answer is 'not applicable'. Some of the questions in the scale developed by the Turkish Investor Relations Society may not be relevant or viable for implementation in companies listed on the New York Stock Exchange. In such cases, the companies were exempted from the question by being awarded 2 points. The scores obtained in each company in the three sections were then added to determine the final scores of the companies. The number of questions that were considered 'not applicable' was then deducted from these totals and the new total was divided by the remaining number of questions to get the companies' card scores and hence the evaluation.

During the study, some problems were experienced in the application of the scale developed by TÜYİD and these problems were expressed as 'limitations'. That is to say, there may be some differences between the companies in the two countries either in terms of public disclosure practices or reporting. Some of the elements included in the annual reports of BIST companies may not appear on the annual reports of NYSE companies. For instance, some reports like the 'sustainability report' or the 'corporate responsibility report', may have been published within other reports rather than the annual reports, or the information on the companies' websites may be found under different headings or in different locations. In such cases, when the relevant information was found the company was given 1 point for the related question.

6 Findings

6.1 Examination of Annual Reports

As already mentioned, this section had 66 questions that were all considered in the examination. These questions were further divided into two parts that consisted of 42 questions regarding corporate governance principles and 24 questions on contents of the report and its visual quality.

Tab. 1: Results of Annual Reports

Companies	Corporate Governance Principles	Contents and Visualization	Total Annual Report Score	Ranking
TTKOM	42	22	64	1
TCELL	33	22	55	2
NETAS	35	17	52	3
PRKAB	34	16	50	4
KAREL	36	13	49	5
ANELT	35	14	49	6
ORAN	30	17	47	7
CHL	28	18	46	8
AMX	25	17	42	9
KRONT	28	13	41	10
DCM	21	18	39	11
TEF	20	17	37	12
BCE	19	16	35	13
ALCTL	24	9	33	14
T	14	14	28	15
VZ	9	13	22	16

Türk Telekomünikasyon A.Ş. was found to have the highest score in this section. With 42 full points from the corporate governance principles sub-section, it was the only company to obtain the full score in this section. In terms of *content and visualization, Turkish Prysmian Cable & Systems Inc.* performed even better than AT & T and Verizon Communications, which have a market value of more than 200 billion dollars. The differences in the reporting standards between the countries may be thought to have led to this situation. It should be noted that since the requirement by the Article 199 of the Turkish Commercial Code on what to be included in the report does not apply to companies in the NYSE, these companies were awarded two points in this question as a means of compensation.

6.2 Examination of Financial Disclosures

There was a total of 45 questions in the three-part financial disclosure section which included 12 questions on information concerning the relevant accounting period, 14 questions on financial tables and 19 questions on other important information about the company. The questions were examined relevant to the

Tab. 2: Financial Results Explanations

Companies	Other Important Developments and Information about the Company	Financial Tables	Important Information on the Relevant Accounting Period	Total Financial Reports Points	Ranking
TTKOM	16	14	11	41	1
TCELL	14	14	11	39	2
BCE	16	13	9	38	3
TEF	14	13	8	35	4
VZ	15	11	8	34	5
T	13	12	8	33	6
NETAS	11	12	10	33	7
ORAN	13	11	8	32	8
CHL	13	11	6	30	9
AMX	12	11	7	30	10
DCM	12	11	6	29	11
KRONT	8	11	7	26	12
PRKAB	8	10	7	25	13
KAREL	8	8	9	25	14
ALCTL	9	8	7	24	15
ANELT	8	9	6	23	16

information available in the annual reports, financial reports, press bulletins, website and presentations.

When the results from the evaluation of financial disclosure are compared to the results from the annual reports section, the first two positions appear not to have changed with Turk Telekom maintaining its first position and Turkcell its second position. There are however significant changes in the order of the other companies. In this section, only two of the first six companies are traded in the BİST as opposed to the annual reports section. AT & T and Verizon Communications which ranked last in the annual reports section rose to sixth and fifth place in this section. Likewise, Bell Canada Enterprises and Telefonica rose to take positions three and four. Turkish Prysmian Cables and Systems, Karel Electronics and Anel Telecommunication experienced significant declines from positions four, five, and six in the previous section to thirteen, fourteen, and sixteenth respectively in this section. While Turk Telekom and Turkcell continued their successes, AT & T, Verizon Communications, Bell Canada Enterprises and Telefonica were more successful when the financial reports, press releases, presentations and websites were considered besides the annual reports.

All the companies got positive scores in areas like accounting policy, availability of historical data, operation areas, cash flow statement and availability of full and comprehensive balance sheets. Only three of the companies traded in NYSE had information on foreign exchange-based debt whereas it was available for all BIST companies. On the other hand, while all the NYSE companies had information on profit margins, only four of the BIST companies had this information. Another area of concern was whether or not teleconferencing/webcasting was used in the companies and whether transcripts and presentation were provided. Apart from Turk Telekom, no other BIST company had teleconference records and even Turk Telekom did not have the transcripts for these teleconference records. Four NYSE companies included their teleconference records with their transcripts. In this respect, NYSE companies were much more successful than BIST companies.

6.3 Evaluation of Websites

This section had 59 questions on three main concerns i.e. content, website traffic and the nature of the technology used.

The first and second places remained unchanged in this part of the scorecard examination. However, of the first six companies on the list, three are traded at BIST while the other three are traded at NYSE. Türk Prysmian Kablo and Sistemleri A.Ş. recorded a huge leap compared to its performance in the financial disclosure section and ranked fifth. Alcatel once again remained in the last position. A deeper scrutiny reveals that the sub-sections on content and website traffic had great influence on the existing gap among companies. Companies that scored lower in these two areas ended up losing positions.

The questions in this section that concerned the existence of a Central Registry System were of no significance to companies in NYSE hence these companies were compensated for these questions by awarding two points.

When all three parts in this section were considered together, it was observed that Turk Telekom and Turkcell showed considerably good performance and obtained 28 of the 30 possible points in the first part. Türk Prysmian Cable and Systems followed with 24 points, Netaş got 22 points followed by Telefonica with 21 points. Alcatel only managed 9 of the 30 points. In the second part, Türk Telekom managed to maintain its leadership by getting 18 of the 23 points available. China Mobile and NTT Docomo which are both traded at the NYSE followed with 14 points each. Karel Electronics, Kron Telecommunication, Alcatel and Anel Telecommunication were the worst performers in this part. Karel Elektronik received 4 points as Kron Telecommunication and Alcatel each got 2 points while Anel Telecommunications surprisingly received no points

Tab. 3: The Results of Examination of Websites

Companies	Content	Traffic	Technology	Total Website Points	Ranking
TTKOM	28	18	5	51	1
TCELL	28	12	5	45	2
CHL	19	14	4	37	3
DCM	19	14	4	37	4
PRKAB	24	8	3	35	5
TEF	21	11	3	35	6
BCE	17	11	4	32	7
T	16	10	5	31	8
NETAS	22	7	2	31	9
VZ	14	12	4	30	10
AMX	13	8	4	25	11
KAREL	19	4	2	25	12
ORAN	15	8	2	25	13
ANELT	19	0	1	20	14
KRONT	15	2	1	18	15
ALCTL	9	2	1	11	16

from this part. None of the details sought in the questions could be found on Anel Telecommunication's website. When the poor scores from this part are combined with the scores from the other parts of the internet review, Kron Telecommunications, Alcatel and Anel Telecommunication ranked in the last three places. Questions from the technology part of the website review did not influence the general scores in this section by much, but this could be attributed to the existence of only six questions in this part.

7 General Overview

The final part of the study consisted of a final evaluation of the total score of the companies based on the scores from all the sections of the scorecard. For the three sections of concern, a total of 170 questions were presented. Three of these questions were considered to be of no significance to companies trading in the NYSE hence the companies were exempted from these questions.

As can be seen Türk Telekom did not relinquish its first place in any of the categories going on to earn a total of score of 159 points. It was followed by Turkcell with 139 points and Netaş with 116 points in the second and third positions

Tab. 4: General Overview of Companies

Companies	Annual Report	Financial Disclosure	Website	Total Score	Scorecard	Ranking
TTKOM	64	41	51	156	0,917	1
TCELL	55	39	45	139	0,817	2
NETAS	52	33	31	116	0,682	3
CHL	46	30	37	113	0,676	4
PRKAB	50	25	35	110	0,647	5
TEF	37	35	35	107	0,640	6
BCE	35	38	32	105	0,628	7
DCM	39	29	37	105	0,628	8
ORAN	47	32	25	104	0,622	9
KAREL	49	25	25	99	0,582	10
AMX	42	30	25	97	0,580	11
T	28	33	31	92	0,550	12
ANELT	49	23	20	92	0,541	13
VZ	22	34	30	86	0,514	14
KRONT	41	26	18	85	0,500	15
ALCTL	33	24	12	69	0,405	16

respectively. China Mobile's 113, Türk Prysmian Kablo ve Sistemleri A. Ş's 110 and Telefonica's 107 points landed them in positions, 4, 5 and 6 respectively. Out of the first six companies, four companies were listed on the BIST while two were on NYSE. Verizon Communications and AT & T remained in the lower ranks due to their bad performances in the annual report section. Kron Telecommunication and Alcatel on the other hand performed quite poorly in the website section leading them to rank in the last two positions. Alcatel showed a particularly bad overall performance. Table 5 shows the ranking of the companies in terms of their scores in the different sections and general overview.

According to the table, Türk Telekom and Turkcell appear to have a very firm hold on their positions while the other companies have fluctuating performances on different sections. Alcatel is the worst performing company in almost all the sections.

8 Conclusion

Despite being considered by business managers as a cost element in the early days, investor relations has been accorded the deserved recognition as a result

Tab. 5: Ranking based on all Scores

Companies	Annual Report	Financial Disclosure	Website	Total
TTKOM	1	1	1	1
TCELL	2	2	2	2
NETAS	3	7	9	3
CHL	8	9	3	4
PRKAB	4	13	5	5
TEF	12	4	6	6
BCE	13	3	7	7
DCM	11	11	4	8
ORAN	7	8	13	9
KAREL	5	14	12	10
AMX	9	10	11	11
T	15	6	8	12
ANELT	6	16	14	13
VZ	16	5	10	14
KRONT	10	12	15	15
ALCTL	14	15	16	16

of developments that have taken place in the recent years. Business managers, who have become aware of the importance of investor relations with regard to both institutional and individual investors, as well as the other actors in financial markets, have started to pay more attention to investor relations practices.

This study sought to compare the web-based investor relations practices of 8 companies that are currently trading in Istanbul Stock Exchange, either providing telecommunication services and conducting production activities related to telecommunication services, and 8 companies with the same qualifications in the New York Stock Exchange. To achieve this objective, the study used a scorecard scale developed by the Turkish Investor Relations Society to evaluate the web-based investor relations practices with a total of 170 questions in 3 sections. The result of the examinations revealed that Türk Telekom obtained the highest scores in both the individual sections and in the overview ranking. As the overall leader, Turk Telekom obtained a total of 156 points and a card score of 0.917 while Turkcell İletişim Hizmetleri A.Ş. followed with a total of 139 points and a score of 0.817. The third place went to Netaş Telekomünikasyon A.Ş. with 116 total points and 0.682 card score. The remainder of the first six positions was taken by, respectively, China Mobile, Türk Prysmian Kablo ve Sistemleri A.Ş. and Telefonica. It was observed that 4 of the first 6 companies are traded in

BİST. Looking at the last six positions we find America Movil, AT & T, Anel Telecommunication, Verizon Communications, Kron Telecommunication in the eleventh, twelfth, thirteenth, fourteenth and fifteenth positions respectively. In the last place is Alcatel which had a very low performance with only 69 total points and 0.405 card score. Three of the last six companies are traded at BİST.

A look at the overall results of the study revealed that companies traded in the BIST are more successful than their NYSE counterparts with respect to their web-based investor relations practices and that they are more open and transparent regarding the exchange of information with existing and potential investors and other elements of the financial markets.

References

Bebczuk, R.N. (2003). *Asymmetric information in financial markets.* United Kingdom: Cambridge University Press.

Bollen, L.H.H., Hassink, H.F.D. and Bozic, G. (2006). Measuring and explaining the quality of internet investor relations activities: a multinational empirical analysis. *International Journal of Accounting Information Systems*, 7(4), 273–298.

Collison, C. (2003). Media relations and the internet: how Fortune 500 company web sites assist journalists in news gathering. *Public Relations Review*, 29(1), 29–41.

Craven, B.M. and Marston, C.L. (1997). Investor relations and corporate governance in large UK companies. *Corporate Governance: An International Review*, 5(3), 137–151.

Deller, D., Stubenrath, M. and Weber, C. (1999). A survey on the use of the internet for investor relations in the USA, the UK and Germany. *The European Accounting Review*, 8(2), 351–364.

Fisher, R., Oyelere, P. and Laswad, F. (2004). Corporate reporting on the internet: audit issues and content analysis of practices. *Managerial Auditing Journal*, 19(3), 412–439.

Geerings, J., Bollen, L.H.H. and Hassink, H.F.D. (2003). Investor relations on the internet: a survey of the Euronext zone. *The European Accounting Review*, 12(3), 567–579.

Hamid, F.Z.A. (2005). Malaysian companies' use of the internet for investor relations. *Corporate Governance*, 5(1), 5–14.

Hockerts, K. and Moir, L. (2004). Commucating corporate responsibility to investors: the changing role of the investor relations function. *Journal of Business Ethics*, 52(1), 85–98.

İçöz, Ö. (2003). Telekomünikasyon sektöründe regülasyon ve rekabet (uzmanlık tezleri serisi no:16). Ankara: Rekabet Kurumu Yayınları.

Kuperman, J.C., Athavale, M. and Eisner, A. (2003). Financial analysts in the media: Evolving roles and recent trends. *American Business Review*, 21(2), 74–80.

Sayılır, Ö., Yılmaz, S., Bayram, F., Sarıkaya, M. (2012). *Yatırımcı İlişkileri Yönetimi* (1.baskı), Eskişehir: Anadolu Üniversitesi Açıköğretim Fakültesi Yayınları.

Türkiye Yatırımcı İlişkileri Derneği. (2016). *Beyaz Kitap V: Yatırımcı İlişkilerinin Önemi ve Fonksiyonu.*

http://www.bilgitoplumu.gov.tr/wpcontent/uploads/2014/04/Telekomunikasyon_Alt_Komisyonu_Raporu.pdf (Access Date: 29.04.2018).

https://www.tasav.org/media/k2/attachments/bf_rapor_no.16_telekom_sektoru_ejderoruc_07.03.2015.pdf (Access Date: 29.04.2018).

http://home.ku.edu.tr/~kyilmaz/papers/Y_Atiyas2000.pdf (Access Date: 29.04.2018).

Meltem Dil Sahin[1]

Industry 4.0: What about Human Resources?

1 Introduction

The socio-economic developments of societies have changed with technological evolution throughout history. With the development of the steam machine in 1770, the 1st Industrial Revolution took place and the steam machine took the place of the arm power. After World War II, there was a new Industrial Revolution with automation; mechanization has increased in the factories and the products have spontaneously passed from one stage to another. In this sense, technology has started a thinking process rather than a human being. However II. The Industrial Revolution lasted fairly short, III. The Industrial Revolution has begun with the emergence of computers in the 1970s. Unlike the previous two revolutions, this period symbolized by the computer, takes the creative power of man. At this stage, which is nowadays referred to as information technology, technology has become a complex structure that can self-program, start, develop, repair and terminate without the need for human beings (Akgeyik, 2009).

On the other hand, in the process of socio-economic development, the agriculture revolution is called the first wave, the industrial revolution is the second wave, the information revolution or the information society is called the third wave (Emiroğlu, 2009). In agrarian societies, the power of organizations depended on productive landmarks and demographics, while in industrial society they depended on organizations, machinery and material capital. The agrarian society has brought "aristocracy" to the forefront, while industrial society foregrounded "bourgeoisie" and information society foregrounded "individual". In the information society, organizations take their strength from human resources that represent humanity. So while landowners are in agriculture society and capital-employers in industrial society are in possession of power, power in the information society belongs to the information class as human resources (İnce, 2009).

Nowadays, it can be said that with the transition phase to the industry 4.0, the digital society will foreground the "internet" and the power in society will pass to those who have accessibility.

---

1 Assistant Professor, Kütahya Dumlupınar University, meltem.sahin@dpu.edu.tr

2 Industry 4.0

The emergence of the word Industry 4.0 took place with the German government`s introduction of high-tech project and for the first time has come to the agenda in 2011 Hannover Fair. The project dealed with the matter of the computerization of manufacturing and the term Industrial 4.0 was used to be described as a new industrial revolution and to figure out how this revolution transformed the organization of global value chains (Banger, 2018:79, Schwab, 2017:16).

The base of the 4. Industrial Revolution is the use of information technologies in all areas of life, with the emergence of intelligent and connected machines and smart factories. The significant difference of it from other industrial revolutions is the fusion of high-tech interactions of biological, physical and digital fields such as gene sequencing, nanotechnologies, renewable energies, quantum computing, sensors, artificial intelligence and robots (Schwab, 2017:17). Therefore, the distinctive feature of the industry 4.0 is to internalize information, communication, internet, automation and data collection technologies in every aspect of life, especially in the business sectors (Banger, 2018:83).

According to the research of Schwab (2017), which is prepared on the basis of the works of World Economic Forum, the driving forces of the 4th Industrial Revolution are technological innovations realized with digital power. These innovative megatrends are examined under three clusters as physical, biological and digital. The technological advances in the physical arena are the development of sensors and artificial intelligence and autonomous machines, the use of responsive drones that can perceive their environments, the ability to make custom productions with 3D printers that create a physical object using a 3D design, advanced robotics studies such as the development of robots that can mimic the patterns and strategies of nature, self-programmable and accessible to remote information via the cloud, and the emergence of new, lightweight, powerful, recyclable and adaptable new materials (Schwab, 2017:23–27). Progresses in the field of biology are listed as: ability to regulate biology therefore regulation of genetics, cell studies, the determination of appropriate diagnosis and treatment possibilities with the rapid determination of our genetic structure by sequencing machines (Schwab, 2017:30–33).

As the third megatrend that accompanies physical and biological innovations, the digital domain is in itself the focal point of the 4th Revolution. With the digitalization, it is possible to have the internet of objects where everything interacts. Objects of the internet, described as a relationship that is possible by the interconnected technologies between objects (such as products, services, spaces, information, etc.) and people and various platforms. Digitalization, not only the products or services, but also transforms the economy by technology-based platforms and operationalizes the demand economy where the customer is the focus point. With the demand economy, the companies without having any physical presence (Goodwin, 2015, as indicated in TechCrunch's article: Uber without a tool, Facebook without content, Alibaba without a stock, Airbnb without a real estate) that create value by providing services through the use of assets showed up and reliable platforms have emerged that enable the supply and demand to be met quickly, easily and cost-effectively (Schwab, 2017:27–30).

The vision of Industry 4.0 is that in the future, industrial businesses will build global networks to connect their machinery, factories, and warehousing facilities as cyber-physical systems, which will connect and control each other intelligently by sharing information that triggers actions. This will bring about improvements in the industrial processes within manufacturing as a whole, through engineering, material usage, supply chains, and product lifecycle management. As a result the vision of Industry 4.0 will deeply integrate with each stage in the horizontal value chain to provide tremendous improvements in the industrial process (Gilchrist, 2016:195).

Although the vision of the 4th Industrial Revolution seems to be focused on changes in the industry and the manufacturing sector with the use of digitalization and intelligent production systems, as in other industrial revolutions the 4th Industrial Revolution will lead to changes in the ways of doing business, organizational structures, and even social life as a whole.

In addition to the structure of the 4th Industrial Revolution that presents virtual-physical-mechanical environments such as internet, cyber-physical structures, artificial intelligence, cloud technologies, the features of it such as the combination of network-based strategic collaborations, virtual business platforms, combination-based business forms combining value-added features, substitution of labor into capital by robots and algorithms, rapid delivery of supply and demand, transition from ownership of assets to accessibility, will change business comprehension, professions, organizations, and therefore societies (Schwab, 2017). Sociological reflections naturally also have psychological consequences. As the activities that should be carried out for adoption of human resources to this changes is a separate study theme, this section is trying to foresee the changes and expectations that are experienced in human resources in the digital transition phase.

3 Human Resources X.0 Loading

The individual is more important than ever, but in the near future an individual with innovative, creative, problem-solving skills will be more valuable in business life. It is foreseen that the individual shaped according to new values will be tolerant to different cultural features, different life styles and traditions, sensitive to all religions and different beliefs (Asunakutlu, Baydur, 2001:13) Easily communicating with people or groups on the other side of the world through the Internet facilitates the learning about the characteristics, perspectives, cultures of different people or communities and enhances this sensitivity.

For the individual to achieve success in the information society, qualifications such as critical thinking, good communication, high level of creativity, taking responsibility, using authority, being open to constant development, acting flexibly, being in peace with technology, having participatory spirit and effective teamwork are required beyond the educational status and quantitative values. In addition to these features, concepts such as computer literacy, lifelong learning, internet literacy, information literacy will be superior features (Gürdal, 2004:56–57; İnce, 2009:320) not only for the information society but also for the digital society. Also social media literacy becomes important along with internet and computer literacy.

With the 4th Industrial Revolution, the competencies of having the knowledge and skills about developed and featured technologies, and also using and developing them are at the forefront. Hence, it is inevitable that there will be a rapid and strong change in the structure of human resources as well as in the way of doing business and economy. In the simplest case, through the use of virtual networks and the Internet, accessing to the human resources who is trained and has specific experience and expertise, and even temporary project-based operation of this human resources, will increase competition between both businesses and human resources among themselves. Human resources are expected to be competent, expert, fast, mobile and accessible, like a computer which has a software with the latest version and an equipment compatible with the latest technology. Similar to the information society, in the digital society of Industry 4.0, the individuals will want to increase their level of awareness, focus on the need for self-realization, achieve continuously learning and self-development. However, in the mobile environment of Industry 4.0, human resources will be in demand of being faster and accessible.

3.1 Awareness

According to Self-Determination Theory people are active organisms with an innate tendency to develop and have inherent psychological needs, such as autonomy, competence and social interaction with others. However, this tendency does not arise spontaneously but emerges with the support of the social environment. In this respect, human activities are sometimes facilitated by the social environment, sometimes it gets harder (Kart, Güldü, 2008:187–207).

Self-determination is associated with increased creativity, conceptual learning, self-esteem. Organizationally self-identification studies have shown that organizations that offer the opportunity to satisfy the high level of human resource needs have improved performance in a positive way. However, the form of management and organizational structuring, which provides flexibility in the conduct of business and allows participation in decision-making, has a positive effect on employees' job satisfaction, quality of work life and organizational effectiveness (Deci vd., 1989:580). Besides, in the Self-Determination Theory, the ability of an individual to identify his own goals and to take initiative to achieve those goals is defined as autonomous decision-making. This is possible by showing the individual's own existence, informing others of its own needs, that is, by self-defense if necessary. In order to be able to defend ownself individual must know his/her individual needs, interests, existing power and limitations in order to meet them, and in a different way reach "individual awareness". (Kart, Güldü: 2008:187–200). Individual awareness is expressed as self awareness, and there are two dimensions as public self and personal self. While public self-awareness creates the direction that others can see and react to; self-awareness creates the internal direction of the individual that cannot be observed by others. Personal self-awareness is the mirror of the individual; public self-awareness can be explained by the presence of the audience in front of the individual. (Froming et al., 1985:1223–1224). In the digital society process, public self-awareness has been given more attention through social media and individuals have almost created a separate virtual personality by improving the public self-awareness by direction of the audiences.

Nowadays, according to their interests and the topics they are curious about, individuals are developing both internal and external awarenesses with tools such as researches on the internet, information messages coming from mobile phones, e-mail groups, e-books, member sites. Although there are opinions that the virtual environment is misleading because of the lack of face to face interaction and the validity of the information obtained, it is positively affecting the development of awareness of individuals with accessing to various and rich sources of information. However, in the digital society like in the information society, human resources will act for self-development and gaining different skills because of increased career competitiveness and the need for both special and multiple expertise in the work to be done (egitimportali.com, 2009).

As a result, in Industry 4.0, individuals who have completed their personal awareness and have developed awareness of others that can't be same with them, will get the edge over. In addition, human resources who can reach the most reliable and accurate information among the information load offered by the internet and can use mobile communication effectively, will be able to direct their awareness exactly.

3.2 The Need for Self-Realization

Self-realization involves developing the character of the individual, creating a rich, supreme and harmonious personality. The need for self-realization in the moral sense is associated with virtue (Stuart,1898:328). According to Maslow, self-realization is to experience life as a whole, alive and self-sacrificing, with complete concentration and inclusion in the self (Maslow, 1965:111).

It is stated that for the need of self-realization, the individual must first self-define and realize his/her experiences. Self-realization involves individuals to be free, to choose, to determine their own destiny and their efforts to demonstrate their individual development. In general, people in the process of self-realization need to obtain information about themselves and the outside world and to understand what is happening within themselves and around them. In this process, individual is in the effort of and willing to achieve own goals and reach the desired position with using his/her abilities to the end. According to this, self-realization is not only a process of increasing competence and maturity but also a process of orientation towards self-direction and autonomy at the same time. (Çırak, 2006:46–48).

Therefore, the need for self-realization requires a different sense of work with autonomy request. Regardless of partly static differences (such as age, gender, seniority, status), people need an environment where everyone can exhibit multiple areas of expertise, and this environment should not be limited. In this understanding, the human resource idea that is subject to the company is changed and the companies pay attention to mutual relations while carrying out their operations. (Lewis, 1998:1). In fact in the digital society of Industry 4.0, human resources that are linked to information and transactional technologies, but which are autonomous to any authority, will come to the forefront.

In terms of the information society, people who seek information in the process of self-realization and who value it by processing the information they have acquired have become important. In the digital society of Industry 4.0, not just looking for information, people who know how to find it as soon as possible and who can access the information will be valuable. The idea of combining and interpreting multi-disciplinary information to produce a new synthesis knowledge will become even more important than equipped ownself with knowledge and adding value by processing it (which will provide by computers and artificial intelligence). As a result, the process of adding value to knowledge will change, but still the individuals will need to be open to continuous learning and develop themselves.

3.3 The Desire for Continuous Learning and Self-Development

In the information society, with the constant renewal of technology and the rapid change of the skills required by this technology, full-time education in the school or similar official institutions, acquired in the first stages of life is inadequate, so new skills such as lifelong education and professional skills in the workplace by learning by doing methods come to the forefront (Güder, Taşcı, 2006:236). In order to prepare human resources for ongoing development, businesses take advantage of e-learning opportunities for rapid acquisition of knowledge and experience and for employees to adapt to rapid changes (Duran, Önal, Kurtuluş, 2009:1). Accordingly, in electronic environments such as the internet, which are always accessible from anywhere with a network connection, the interactive aspect of information increases the power of human logic and learning (Tokman, 2000).

Parallel to these explanations, with the emergence of new and unforeseen professions in Industry 4.0, it will be important to have new skills and to acquire these skills in different and richer ways. Mobile, dynamic, simulated learning methods will be used more intensively in the form of learning at home, traveling and sports, rather than learning by doing at work.

However, the employees, especially the creative staff, mostly work on project basis and organize their professional and personal lives according to the projects. As the training and skills required for each project can be relatively different, education and especially continuous learning will be one of the basic dynamics in the digital society as it is in the knowledge society. Human resources have to constantly improve and diversify their skills and be prepared to do more than one profession throughout their working lives. Otherwise, even well-educated people face the danger of unemployment in the new economy (Tonta, Küçük, 2005).

Human resources will want to improve themselves in order to advance both in the career process and to improve their quality of life. Through continuous learning, human resources will be able to develop multiple expertise areas, will have strategic information, and will also led him to develop himself. Particularly quick and easy access to information resources contributes to the ability of individuals to improve themselves and learn at the right time and with the desirable quality, about the subjects they are interested in.

3.4 Homo-Digitalis

Anthropologists look at whether there is evidence of a serious instrument construction around the research in determining whether a skull belongs to a human. Because, as an effort to create something, to have knowledge for doing anything, technology creates the cultural orientation of people's heritage. Thus, technology development is regarded as a phenomenon specific to human beings. In addition, technology develops and directs people's brains. According to this, it is stated that it is better to call the human kind as homo-technologicus or technical person instead of as homo-sapiens or logical person (Lienhard, 1988–1999).

But the human type of industrial society is called "Homo-Economicus" (Nair, 2009:335). It can be expressed as the idealized human type of economic principle based on the relation of blessings and burdens, which is revealed as the criterion of rationality in business activities (Müftüoğlu, 1999:8). This type of human being is presented as a person who carries economic interests in a rational manner and whose life passes through efforts to produce and consume and carry no moral value concerns. However, with the financial behavior researches it has been revealed that people do not behave rationally or even act with irrational expectations (Kahneman, Tversky, 1979; Kahneman, 2003).

On the other hand, individuals who are called white-collar workers in the information society, especially in the service sector, are referred to as "Homo-Technologicus" in another variation "Homo-Digitalis". It is expressed that Homo-Technologicus is self-developed, open to learning and information, has both internal and external high level awareness, has planning and programming skills, and can establish a work-life balance. They are professional individuals, professional producers, professional equipment, professional audiences and interpreters and they are aware of this situation. They dominate computer technology and guide them (Nair, 2009:335). With Industry 4.0, homo technologicus will come to the forefront with its fast, mobile, accessible and connected features and will be a colleague with artificial intelligence and robots as well as computer technologies. In this respect human resources in the digital world of 1s and 0s, will evolve from homo technologicus which emphasizes the human-technology relationship, into a homo-digitalis that reflects human and technology co-operation.

4 Conclusion

Although the Industry 4.0 has emerged as a project of the German Government, it has been taken into consideration by many researchers that the proposed predictions are in line with the spirit of the time and started to take place on the agenda of other countries. Industry 4.0, that deals with innovative technologies (such as intelligent factories, internet of objects, nanotechnology, use of artificial intelligence and robots) as to be dynamics that can be used primarily in business life and in all areas of life afterwards, will also change the life of society and the individual, as it is in every industrial revolution, while first changing the industry and the economy.

It is valuable to examine the measures to be taken by states for changes in social order and regulations on digital and virtual processes in another study. In this section, the changes that Industry 4.0 can create towards human resources have been tried to be explained with the changes in information society. Here, the basic point of view is not that every industrial revolution introduces completely new features by destroying the properties of the previous period; at every period more specialized, more knowledgeable, more developed human resources are emerging by articulation of the characteristics of each period to the characteristics of previous periods.

In this context, individuals who are aware of their boundaries and who are able to test their boundaries, who can not only be self-directed or have only an awareness of the immediate environment, but can develop awareness without the boundaries of space, will become a digital community member of Industry 4.0. These individuals will feel the desire for self-realization, continuous learning and self-development as the dominant and will try new ways and methods offered by the virtual world and innovative technologies to meet their desires. As Homo-Digitalis, they will be able to carry out all kinds of work that robots and artificial intelligence can do to them or work collaboratively with them to develop and collaborate through information processing technologies that can be accessed from anywhere. Assuming that all the features are gathered in Homo-Digitalis, we can say that we will be faced with an accessible, connected, fast and mobile human resources structure.

The fast, mobile, accessible and connected features of human resources can be seen as a reflections towards society of Industry 4.0, and we can discuss various issues and debates in Digital Society such as work-life balance, privacy and security issues, need for break-idle, need for residence or belonging. Although it is necessary to carry out detailed researches on each problem, it is especially important that states, societies, educational institutions, NGOs come together to develop preparation strategies including solutions to these problems for Industry 4.0.

References

Akgeyik, T. (07.05.2009). Teknolojik Değişim, Postfordist Eğilimler ve Endüstri İlişkilerinde Yeni Arayışlar, Çimento İşveren Dergisi, http://www.ceis.org.tr/dergiDocs/1mak20003.pdf.

Asunakutlu, T., Baydur, C.M. (2001). Ekonominin Yeni Trendleri Üzerine Bir Değerlendirme, Muğla Üniversitesi SBE Dergisi, 3, Bahar: 1–15.

Banger, G. (2018). Endüstri 4.0 ve Akıllı İşletme, 2. Baskı, Dorlion Yayınları, Ankara.

Çırak, G.K. (2006). Üniversite Öğrencilerinin Ahlaki Yargı Yetenekleri ve Ahlaki Yargı Yetenekleri ile Kendini Gerçekleştirme Düzeylerinin Karşılaştırılması, Çukurova Üniv. S.B.E. Eğitim ABD., Yayımlanmamış Yüksek Lisans Tezi, Adana.

Deci, E.L. Connell, J. P. & Ryan, R. M. (1989). Self-Determination in a Work Organization, Journal of Applied Psychology, 74(4): 580–590.

Duran, N. Önal, A. & Kurtuluş, C. (01.06.2009). E-Öğrenme ve Kurumsal Eğitimde Yeni Yaklaşım Öğrenim Yönetim Sistemleri, http://ab.org.tr/ab06/bildiri/165.pdf.

Emiroğlu, B.G. (07.05.2009). Türkiye ve Dünya`da Bilgi Toplumu ve Ekonomisi: Süreçler ve Değişimler, http://inet-tr.org.tr/inetconf12/sunum/42.doc.

Froming, W.J. Allen, L. & Jensen, R. (1985). Altruism, Tole-Taking and Self-Awareness: The Acquisition of Norms Governing Altruistic Behavior, Child Development, 56(5): 1223–1228.

Gilchrist, A. (2016). Industry 4.0-The Industrial İnternet of Things, Apress, DOI 10.1007/978-1-4842-2047-4_13.

Güder, G., Taşçı, K. (2006). Avrupa Birliği ve Türkiye`de Bilgi ve İletişim Teknolojileri İstihdam İlişkisi, 5. Bilgi, Ekonomi ve Yönetim Kongresi, Bildiriler Kitabı 1, Kocaeli Üniv. İ.İ.B.F., 3–5 Kasım.

Gürdal, O. (2004). Bilgi Ekonomisi ve/veya Yeni Ekonomi`nin Reddettikleri, Bilgi Dünyası, 5(1): 48–73.

İnce, M. (07.05.2009). Değişim Olgusu ve Örgütlerde İnsan Kaynakları Yönetiminin Değişen Fonksiyonları, http://www.sosyalbil.selcuk.edu.tr/sos_mak/makaleler/Mehmet%20 %C4 %B0NCE/319-340.pdf.

Kahneman, D. (2003). A Psychological Perspective on Economics, 93(2), Views of Economics from Neighboring Social Sciences, May: 162–168.

Kahneman, D., Tversky A. (1979). Prospect Theory: An Analysis of Decision under Risk Econometrica, 47(2): 263–292.

Kart M.E., Güldü, Ö. (2008). Özerk Benlik Yönetimi Ölçeği: Uyarlama Çalışması, Ankara Üniv. Eğitim Bilimleri Fakültesi Dergisi, 41(2):, ss. 187–207.

Lewis, J. (1998). Self-Realisation as a Human Resources Tool, New Straits Times, Main/Lifestyle, 2nd Edt. Nov.7, Kuala Lumpur.

Lienhard, J.H. (24.05.2009). Homo Technologicus, http://www.uh.edu/engines/epi16.htm.

Maslow A. (1965). Self-Actualization and Beyond, Conference on the Training of Counselors of Adults, May 22–28, The New England Board of Higher Education, The Center for the Study of Liberal Education for Adults, Chatham, MA.

Müftüoğlu, T. (1999). İşletme İktisadı, 3. Baskı, Turhan Kitabevi, Ankara.

Nair, C.Ü. (07.05.2009). Bilgi'nin Değişen Anlamı ve Kavram Tartışmaları, Cumhuriyet Üniv. İ.İ.B.F. Dergisi (Doç.Dr. Feramuz AYDOĞAN'ın Anısına), http://eskidergi.cumhuriyet.edu.tr/makale/108.pdf.

Schwab, K. (Çev. Dicleli Z.) (2017). Dördüncü Sanayi Devrimi, Optimist Yayım Dağıtım San. ve Tic. Ltd. Şti., İstanbul.

Stuart, H. (1898). Self-Realization as a Working Moral Principle, International Journal of Ethics, 8(3): 328–345.

Tokman, L.Y. (2000). Bilgi Çağının Gücü: Internet, Eğitim ve Demokrasi, VI. Türkiye'de Internet Konferansı, 9–11 Kasım 2000 Askeri Müze/Harbiye Kültür Sitesi, İstanbul, inet-tr.org.tr/inetconf6/tammetin/tokman-tam.doc.

Tonta, Y., Küçük, M.E. (2005). Sanayi Toplumundan Bilgi Toplumuna Geçiş Sürecinde Temel Dinamikler, Bilgi Çağı ve Teknolojik Gelişmeler Işığında Toplum, Yönetim, Yönetici ve Lider Yaklaşımları Uluslararası Sempozyumu, 12–13 Mayıs, İstanbul, http://yunus.hacettepe.edu.tr/~tonta/yayinlar/tonta-kucuk-bilgi-toplumu.pdf.

Mehmet Emre Unsal[1]

Macroeconomic Determinants of Economic Growth in Latin American Countries

1 Introduction

Economic growth, which is defined as the annual increase rate of gross domestic product, is one of the most important macroeconomic indicators for a state. Based on the production function of Solow's growth model, the raises on employment, capital stock and the level of technology are indicated as the traditional sources of economic growth. Moreover, the increases on exports, imports, foreign direct investment, labor productivity and money supply have positive effects on economic growth (Nelson, 2000). This study aims to determine the factors that influence the economic growth in Latin American countries. For this purpose, primarily, the changes of the macroeconomic indicators in Argentina, Bolivia, Brazil, Chile, Colombia, Mexico, Paraguay and Uruguay will be revealed in the period of 1991–2016. Following that, the effects of the macroeconomic indicators on economic growth in Latin American countries will be investigated by using Panel Data Analysis.

2 Macroeconomic Indicators in Latin American Countries

2.1 Gross Domestic Product

Gross domestic product of a country is measured by the help of three approaches: Expenditure, income and production. These approaches measure the annual monetary amount of the final goods and services in a country by using different methods. The importance of GDP is based on presenting data about the greatness and performance of an economy (Callen, 2008). The annual gross domestic product levels of Latin American countries are seen in Tab. 1. According to Tab. 1, while Brazil has the biggest GDP level in the period of 1991–2016, Mexico, Argentina, Colombia, Chile, Uruguay, Bolivia and Paraguay follow it respectively. Considering the annual average increases in the same period, Colombia comes first with the rate of 8.95 %. While Chile follows

1 Asst. Prof. Dr., Istanbul University, Faculty of Political Sciences, Department of Economics, mehmet.unsal@istanbul.edu.tr

Tab. 1: GDP (Current Million US$). Source: World Bank Data

Years	Argentina	Bolivia	Brazil	Chile	Colombia	Mexico	Paraguay	Uruguay
1991	189720	5343	602860	37835	41240	314454	6984	11206
1992	228789	5644	400599	45964	49280	363609	7157	12878
1993	236742	5735	437799	49298	55803	500736	7250	15002
1994	257440	5981	558112	57008	81704	527813	7871	17475
1995	258032	6715	769305	73447	92507	360074	9062	19298
1996	272150	7397	850426	78040	97160	410976	9788	20516
1997	292859	7926	883200	84952	106660	500413	9965	23970
1998	298948	8498	863723	81577	98444	526502	9025	25386
1999	283523	8285	599389	75174	86186	600233	8393	23984
2000	284204	8398	655421	77861	99887	707907	8196	22823
2001	268697	8142	559372	70980	98204	756706	7663	20899
2002	97724	7905	507962	69737	97933	772106	6325	13606
2003	127587	8082	558320	75643	94685	729336	6588	12046
2004	164658	8773	669317	99210	117075	782241	8034	13686
2005	198737	9549	891630	122965	146566	877476	8735	17363
2006	232557	11452	1107640	154788	162590	975387	10646	19579
2007	287531	13120	1397084	173606	207416	1052696	13795	23411
2008	361558	16674	1695825	179638	243982	1109989	18504	30366
2009	332976	17340	1667020	172389	233822	900045	15930	31661
2010	423627	19650	2208872	218538	287018	1057801	20031	40284
2011	530163	23963	2616202	252252	335415	1180490	25100	47962
2012	545982	27084	2465189	267122	369660	1201090	24595	51264
2013	552025	30659	2472807	278384	380192	1274443	28966	57531
2014	526320	32996	2455994	260584	378196	1314385	30881	57236
2015	594749	33000	1802214	243999	291520	1169623	27283	53274
2016	554861	33941	1793989	250036	280091	1076912	27424	52688

Colombia with the rate of 8.50 %, the sorting of Bolivia, Uruguay, Argentina, Paraguay and Brazil comes next. In addition, with the rate of 5.99 %, Mexico has the minimum growth in Latin America. The annual average growth rate of all of the region has become 7.31 % from 1991 to 2016.

2.2 Employment

Economic theory claims that an increase in employment causes a growth in the size of total economy of a country. Also, according to the theoretical and applied studies, there is a bidirectional causality between employment and gross domestic

Tab. 2: Employment (Thousand). Source: World Bank Data

Years	Argentina	Bolivia	Brazil	Chile	Colombia	Mexico	Paraguay	Uruguay
1991	13021	2663	55482	4816	10807	30501	1664	1274
1992	13230	2740	59431	5059	11233	31750	1708	1307
1993	12984	2804	61388	5265	11769	33043	1765	1316
1994	13003	2974	60157	5279	12184	33547	1835	1343
1995	12173	3045	65079	5342	12612	33416	1909	1358
1996	12671	3083	66357	5333	12669	34875	1869	1342
1997	13322	3282	67599	5473	13127	36984	1983	1362
1998	13936	3348	68619	5599	13206	37888	2042	1401
1999	13909	3384	70008	5491	12907	38639	2012	1390
2000	13985	3458	68512	5505	13324	39304	2113	1369
2001	13798	3528	74026	5605	14789	39670	2175	1372
2002	13530	3634	76730	5683	15228	40385	2163	1328
2003	14560	3765	77857	5845	16043	40733	2295	1323
2004	15219	3899	81025	6092	16697	42121	2378	1379
2005	15708	3980	82449	6199	17647	43237	2484	1400
2006	16244	4120	85113	6404	18055	44749	2524	1462
2007	16558	4127	86351	6721	18965	45840	2614	1498
2008	16698	4345	86635	6884	19557	46597	2672	1543
2009	16877	4432	89335	6805	19976	46895	2749	1572
2010	16902	4544	89166	7331	20781	47849	2751	1590
2011	17503	4652	90610	7669	21548	49009	2816	1624
2012	17620	4574	91141	7821	22268	50754	3025	1620
2013	17886	4689	92584	7975	22704	51611	3037	1617
2014	17859	4951	93893	8065	23162	52187	3004	1638
2015	18146	4708	93667	8185	23650	53588	3080	1620
2016	18050	4829	91231	8246	23848	54780	3149	1617

product. Moreover, employment is taken as a traditional source of economic growth by both of the exogenous and endogenous growth theories (Mankiw, 2014). The annual employment levels of Latin American countries are seen in Tab. 2. According to Tab. 2, while Brazil has the biggest employment level in the period of 1991–2016, Mexico, Colombia, Argentina, Chile, Bolivia, Paraguay and Uruguay follow it respectively. Considering the annual average employment increases in the same period, Colombia comes first with the rate of 3.24 %. While Paraguay follows Colombia with the rate of 2.61 %, the sorting of Bolivia, Mexico, Chile, Brazil and Argentina comes next. In addition, with the rate of 0.97 %, Uruguay has the minimum employment rise in Latin America. The annual average employment increase rate of all of the region has become 2.15 % from 1991 to 2016.

2.3 Gross Capital Formation

With labor and technology, gross capital formation is one of the main sources of production based on the Solow's growth model. In accordance with the theory, there are also many applied studies which show the causality from gross capital formation to economic growth. This causality especially depends on the positive effects of the gross capital formation on the production potential of a country (Ünsal, 2007). The annual gross capital formation levels of Latin American countries are seen in Tab. 3. According to Tab. 3, while Brazil has the biggest gross capital formation level in the period of 1991–2016, Mexico, Argentina, Colombia, Chile, Uruguay, Bolivia and Paraguay follow it respectively. Considering the annual average gross capital formation increases in the same period, Colombia comes first with the rate of 12.4 %. While Bolivia follows Colombia with the rate of 10.7 %, the sorting of Argentina, Chile, Uruguay, Paraguay and Mexico comes next. In addition, with the rate of 6.4 %, Brazil has the minimum gross capital formation rise in Latin America. The annual average gross capital formation increase rate of all of the region has become 8.9 % from 1991 to 2016.

2.4 Exports

Depending on the export led growth perspective and expenditure approach of measuring GDP, economic theory and econometric studies have proved the positive effects of exports on economic growth. These effects are come to exist by means of foreign trade multiplier, new technologies and productivity growth (Kavoussi, 1984). The annual exports levels of Latin American countries are seen in Tab. 4. According to Tab. 4, while Mexico has the biggest exports level in the period of 1991–2016, Brazil, Argentina, Chile, Colombia, Paraguay, Uruguay and Bolivia follow it respectively. Considering the annual average exports increases in the same period, Bolivia comes first with the rate of 9.76 %. While Mexico follows Bolivia with the rate of 9.13 %, the sorting of Chile, Colombia, Uruguay, Argentina and Brazil comes next. In addition, with the rate of 5.96 %, Paraguay has the minimum exports rise in Latin America. The annual average exports increase rate of all of the region has become 7.83 % from 1991 to 2016.

2.5 Imports

The view of import led growth depending on most particularly endogenous growth theories claims that the raises in imports cause expansion in production

Tab. 3: Gross Capital Formation (Current Million US$). Source: World Bank Data

Years	Argentina	Bolivia	Brazil	Chile	Colombia	Mexico	Paraguay	Uruguay
1991	27769	832	119180	8838	6578	73358	1335	1695
1992	38213	943	75852	11518	8237	84691	1324	1981
1993	45115	950	91265	13799	11875	115272	1426	2347
1994	51331	860	128329	14619	20866	131549	1922	2774
1995	46285	1024	133031	20165	23866	75493	1996	2973
1996	49211	1201	146843	21734	21522	88656	2166	3127
1997	56727	1556	156891	23599	22317	113078	2284	4038
1998	59595	2006	156893	21980	19421	124745	1744	4401
1999	51074	1555	104231	15689	11101	135525	1476	3616
2000	46020	1524	123895	17220	14879	162523	1293	3300
2001	38099	1162	104837	15876	15744	157660	1207	2994
2002	11688	1288	88635	15574	16895	159871	952	1779
2003	19314	1069	94114	15916	17689	153860	1119	1832
2004	28900	967	119892	19623	22761	168143	1336	2391
2005	37538	1361	153404	26856	29637	194152	1486	3073
2006	43443	1588	197342	32220	36425	222612	1825	3810
2007	57791	1993	276893	36189	47762	243371	2176	4571
2008	70767	2927	366627	48175	57305	267583	3042	7047
2009	53453	2943	313335	36302	52470	206011	2199	6213
2010	75005	3342	481563	50570	63506	241106	3242	7818
2011	97542	4748	571019	62162	80085	274832	4281	10016
2012	90098	4787	527975	70652	88173	286899	3708	11747
2013	95532	5831	536445	71338	92419	286665	4463	12936
2014	90858	6940	504668	60553	99384	287921	5031	12136
2015	101528	6693	313795	58024	77895	272193	4593	10498
2016	94476	7147	276045	55623	69196	255709	4930	9378

structure of an economy. This positive interaction depends on the technology transfers and the raises in international competition and productivity (Parasız, 2008). The reasons of this theoretical The annual imports levels of Latin American countries are seen in Tab. 5. According to Tab. 5, while Mexico has the biggest imports level in the period of 1991–2016, Brazil, Argentina, Chile, Colombia, Uruguay, Paraguay and Bolivia follow it respectively. Considering the annual average imports increases in the same period, Colombia comes first with the rate of 11.5 %. While Argentina follows Colombia with the rate of 11.1 %, the sorting of Bolivia, Chile, Mexico, Uruguay and Brazil comes next. In addition, with the

Tab. 4: Exports (Current Million US$). Source: World Bank Data

Years	Argentina	Bolivia	Brazil	Chile	Colombia	Mexico	Paraguay	Uruguay
1991	14561	1148	52310	11843	8802	51460	3551	2319
1992	15096	1131	43538	13312	8727	55406	3567	2633
1993	16357	1094	45983	12759	9168	61497	4344	2869
1994	19385	1296	53942	15656	12254	70636	4787	3454
1995	24979	1514	57920	21025	13445	86955	5598	3666
1996	28381	1670	57235	20794	14768	106874	5162	4035
1997	30928	1673	61680	22487	15830	121765	4830	4185
1998	31137	1674	60724	20819	14774	129490	5079	4168
1999	27862	1399	57331	21625	15812	147853	3800	3621
2000	31224	1535	66775	23772	15897	179856	3839	3811
2001	31113	1626	69204	22997	15111	171521	3459	3512
2002	27737	1710	72286	22876	14509	174129	3403	2806
2003	33084	2069	84757	26974	15694	177670	3626	3304
2004	39267	2732	110744	39488	19634	222269	4372	4395
2005	46198	3395	135919	49382	24696	266558	5084	5279
2006	53550	4784	159216	67790	28677	266526	6252	5932
2007	65162	5484	186199	78242	34305	289778	7818	6810
2008	79763	7488	229513	74414	43403	307484	9994	9172
2009	65133	6194	180895	63854	37484	244407	8210	8580
2010	80209	8093	237193	82487	45739	314142	11036	10612
2011	97811	10566	299977	95255	62844	366385	13186	12673
2012	88656	12775	288502	91147	67495	387539	12278	13288
2013	80690	13518	287592	89638	66807	398973	14357	13435
2014	75819	14285	270453	86267	60271	419248	13955	13475
2015	63672	10187	232489	71655	44453	404586	11537	11975
2016	69823	8312	224152	70469	41335	399776	11449	11290

rate of 7.60 %, Paraguay has the minimum imports rise in Latin America. The annual average imports increase rate of all of the region has become 9.31 % from 1991 to 2016.

2.6 Foreign Direct Investment

The positive effect of foreign direct investment on economic growth is especially explained through the diffusion of technology, knowledge and technical progress. In line with this endogenous growth framework, the productivity increasing influences of foreign direct investment are indicated by many applied

Tab. 5: Imports (Current Million US$). Source: World Bank Data

Years	Argentina	Bolivia	Brazil	Chile	Colombia	Mexico	Paraguay	Uruguay
1991	11531	1441	47710	10137	5736	60603	2675	2002
1992	18607	1640	33591	12545	7765	73709	2839	2527
1993	22050	1628	39822	13669	10468	77848	3892	2934
1994	27300	1627	53957	14681	17092	91455	4900	3562
1995	26038	1826	72742	19347	19393	79835	5101	3686
1996	30148	2017	75734	21947	20253	100336	4923	4074
1997	37414	2327	84721	24191	22138	122323	4730	4854
1998	38667	2769	81260	23494	20576	139005	4369	4879
1999	32763	2261	68434	19982	15343	155972	3091	4386
2000	33070	2295	81611	22412	16733	191319	3135	4568
2001	27604	2056	81470	21822	18181	185388	2727	4076
2002	13066	2191	68005	21332	17792	186428	2298	2641
2003	18773	2131	72356	23190	18881	188499	2624	2930
2004	27737	2310	87898	29695	22353	234750	3308	4019
2005	34392	3065	105595	38681	27531	280629	4018	4944
2006	40481	3752	129233	45358	33390	280595	5221	6202
2007	52568	4496	167160	54405	41049	308104	6462	7051
2008	66316	6330	232728	70716	49437	333835	9166	10630
2009	48269	5706	187616	50504	42671	259328	7130	8325
2010	67938	6745	260188	68443	50988	328581	10313	10215
2011	88839	9199	320106	86885	66858	382868	12622	12866
2012	78014	10233	322009	91222	74070	402385	11980	14939
2013	81240	11386	344504	91238	76518	413674	12984	15168
2014	73692	13849	335819	83795	80870	434741	13242	14621
2015	70065	12231	253273	72190	68136	428462	11319	12173
2016	75118	10832	216708	68333	60802	421081	10839	10476

researches (Borensztein, De Gregorio, & Lee, 1998). The annual foreign direct investment levels of Latin American countries are seen in Tab. 6. According to Tab. 6, while Brazil has the biggest foreign direct investment level in the period of 1991–2016, Mexico, Chile, Argentina, Colombia, Uruguay, Bolivia and Paraguay follow it respectively. Considering the annual average foreign direct investment increases in the same period, Paraguay comes first with the rate of 166 %. While Uruguay follows Paraguay with the rate of 61.8 %, the sorting of Brazil, Colombia, Argentina, Chile and Mexico comes next. In addition, with the rate of -12.7 %, Bolivia has the minimum foreign direct investment rise in Latin America. The

Tab. 6: Foreign Direct Investment (Current Thousand US$). Source: World Bank Data

Years	Argentina	Bolivia	Brazil	Chile	Colombia	Mexico	Paraguay	Uruguay
1991	2439000	52000	1103000	822700	456900	4742000	86100	32340
1992	4430978	93100	2061000	936100	728700	4393000	117500	11300
1993	2793085	123800	1292000	1034300	959100	4389000	75000	101500
1994	3634932	130200	3072000	2582100	1446497	10972500	137100	154500
1995	5609423	392700	4859000	2957000	968368	9526290	103200	156600
1996	6948537	474100	11200000	4814616	3111677	9185600	149400	136800
1997	9160272	730600	19650000	5271400	5562216	12829800	235800	126400
1998	7290657	949300	31913000	4627818	2828826	12756765	341900	164100
1999	23987696	1010500	28576000	8761016	1507907	13880523	94500	235300
2000	10418314	736350	32994719	4860016	2436460	18382285	107800	262825
2001	2166137	705756	23225846	4199763	2541943	30060020	99200	310403
2002	2148910	676543	16586600	2549923	2133698	24055125	90400	179852
2003	1652010	197400	10123014	4026498	1720493	18223514	-57700	402717
2004	4124710	65430	18181191	6797253	3115636	24916054	93979	352713
2005	5265250	–238620	15459982	7462207	10235419	26018160	7300	826627
2006	5537340	280763	19378093	7586190	6750618	20663137	187800	1508350
2007	6473150	366294	44579492	13474760	8885768	33070051	105000	1358737
2008	9725560	512336	50716403	18473103	10564151	32187777	337856	2141969
2009	4017159	423040	31480932	13855126	8034566	19454803	26913	1602592
2010	11332719	621998	88452079	16019683	6429772	20989870	555544	2191068
2011	10839931	858941	101157818	24149599	14646780	24320407	463994	2690094
2012	15323934	1059965	86606503	30292555	15039359	17570374	727144	6043903
2013	9821662	1749613	69686088	20824865	16209296	47228942	312567	755137
2014	5065336	656566	97179590	23736253	16167023	30286843	549690	3830457
2015	11758994	554644	74718045	21050770	11735726	36518545	529859	2435422
2016	3260164	335366	78248380	12373873	13848995	34775685	411466	–379109

annual average foreign direct investment increase rate of all of the region has become 42.3 % from 1991 to 2016.

3 Panel Data Analysis for Latin American Countries

In this part of the study, a Panel Data Analysis is performed through the regression model seen in Tab. 7, by using the data of Argentina, Bolivia, Brazil, Chile, Colombia, Mexico, Paraguay and Uruguay. While gross domestic product is the dependent variable in this analysis, employment, gross capital formation, exports, imports, foreign direct investment, labor productivity and money supply are identified as the independent variables. The results of the unit root test and the other required econometric tests for Panel Data Analysis are also seen in Tab. 8 and Tab. 9.

According to the results of Im-Pesaran-Shin Unit Root Test seen in Table 8, in order to provide the stationarity condition for Panel Data Analysis, the first difference values of the series should be used in 5 % significance level. In addition, the results of F Test and Breusch-Pagan LM Test seen in Tab. 9 show that there is no need to use the models of fixed or random effects. Moreover, as seen in Tab. 9, while White's Test determines heteroscedasticity, there is not an autocorrelation problem in the model. According to results of these econometric tests,

Tab. 7: Regression Model

GDPit = β0 + β1 EMPit + β2 CAPit + β3 EXit + β4 IMit + β5 FDIit + β6 LPit + β7 Mit + Uit

Variable	Explanation
GDP	Logarithm of the gross domestic product of the relevant country in the relevant year.
EMP	Logarithm of the employment of the relevant country in the relevant year.
CAP	Logarithm of the gross capital formation of the relevant country in the relevant year.
EX	Logarithm of the exports of the relevant country in the relevant year.
IM	Logarithm of the imports of the relevant country in the relevant year.
FDI	Logarithm of the foreign direct investment of the relevant country in the relevant year.
LP	Logarithm of the labor productivity of the relevant country in the relevant year.
M	Logarithm of the money supply of the relevant country in the relevant year.
U	Error term.

Tab. 8: Im-Pesaran-Shin Unit Root Test

Variable	Level		First Difference	
	Test Statistic	P-Value	Test Statistic	P-Value
GDP	2.1444	0.9840	–5.1730	0.0000
EMP	1.6446	0.9500	-7.0669	0.0000
CAP	1.3428	0.9103	–6.4270	0.0000
EX	1.0701	0.8577	–5.6354	0.0000
IM	0.4045	0.6571	–6.2370	0.0000
FDI	-3.0875	0.0010	–7.1974	0.0000
LP	1.4412	0.9252	–6.8782	0.0000
M	0.2112	0.5837	–7.3839	0.0000

Tab. 9: Model Determination, Heteroscedasticity and Autocorrelation Tests

Test	Test Statistic	P-Value
F Test	0.11	0.9974
Breusch-Pagan LM Test	3.35	0.0674
White's Test	162.91	0.0000
Wooldridge Test	2.715	0.1434

Tab. 10: Results of the Panel Huber-Eicker-White Estimation

Number of Obs: 200				
F: 69.57		Prob > F: 0.0000		
R^2: 0.8392				
Variable	**Coefficient**	**t**	**P > |t|**	**Robust Std. Err.**
EMP	0.2296323	0.75	0.455	0.3067487
CAP	0.6285257	5.80	0.000	0.10845
EX	0.2061897	2.43	0.016	0.0849979
IM	–0.1477507	–1.19	0.236	0.1243292
FDI	0.0027897	1.44	0.150	0.0019308
LP	2.563231	1.30	0.194	1.965552
M	-0.1023521	–1.71	0.090	0.0600006

Huber-Eicker-White Estimation is suitable for this model of Panel Data Analysis (Tatoğlu, 2013). The results of this estimation is shown in Tab. 10.

According to the results of Huber-Eicker-White Panel Data Estimation seen in Tab. 10, F test is significant and the coefficient of determination is adequately high, therefore, there is not a suspicion about the significance of the model. On the other hand, only the coefficients estimated for gross capital formation and exports are significant on the level of 5 % (Gujarati, 2011). Consequently, while gross capital formation and exports affects economic growth positively, employment, imports, foreign direct investment, labor productivity and money supply do not have a statistically significant effect on economic growth in Latin American countries. In accordance with the results of Panel Data Analysis that is conducted by using the datasets of Latin American countries for the application part of this study, if gross capital formation increases by 1 %, gross domestic product increases by 0.63 % and if exports increase by 1 %, GDP increases by 0.23 %.

4 Conclusion

The aim of this study is to find how the macroeconomic factors affect the growth of gross domestic product in Latin American countries. For this aim, firstly, the changes of the macroeconomic indicators in Argentina, Bolivia, Brazil, Chile, Colombia, Mexico, Paraguay and Uruguay were investigated in the period of 1991–2016. After that, by the help of Panel Data Analysis, the effects of the macroeconomic indicators on economic growth were examined by using the datasets of these Latin American countries.

The necessary econometric tests such as Im-Pesaran-Shin Unit Root Test, F Test and Breusch-Pagan LM Test showed that the series of the panel became stationary after getting first difference and they were suitable for the classic model of pooled ordinary least squares. Moreover, although Wooldridge Test did not determine an autocorrelation problem in the model, the series involved a heteroscedasticity problem as a result of White's Test. As a consequence of these outcomes, Huber-Eicker-White Estimation was identified as the suitable method for Panel Data Analysis.

According to the results of Huber-Eicker-White Panel Data Estimation, while there is not a statistically significant effect of employment, imports, foreign direct investment, labor productivity and money supply on economic growth in Latin American countries, gross capital formation and exports affect economic growth positively. Such that, if gross capital formation increases by 1 % in Latin American countries, economic growth occurs by 0.63 % and if exports increase by 1 %, economic growth takes place by 0.23 %.

References

Borensztein, E., De Gregorio, J., & Lee, J. W. (1998). How does foreign direct investment affect economic growth? *Journal of International Economics*, *45*(1), 115–135.

Callen, T. (2008). What is gross domestic product? *Finance & Development*, 48–49.

Gujarati, D. N. (2011). *Econometrics by example*. Hampshire: Palgrave Macmillan.

Kavoussi, R. M. (1984). Export expansion and economic growth: further empirical evidence. *Journal of Development Economics*, 14(1), 241–250.

Mankiw, N. G. (2014). *Principles of macroeconomics*. Stamford: Cengage Learning.

Nelson, R. R. (2000). *The sources of economic growth*. Cambridge: Harvard University Press.

Parasız, İ. (2008). *Ekonomik büyüme teorileri*. Bursa: Ezgi Kitabevi Yayınları.

Tatoğlu, Y. F. (2013). *Panel veri ekonometrisi: Stata Uygulamalı*. İstanbul: Beta Yayıncılık.

Ünsal, E. (2007). *İktisadi büyüme*. Ankara: İmaj Yayınevi.

M. Said Ceyhan[1], Ahmet Kamaci[2], and Mehmet Akif Pece[3]

Impact on Economic Growth of Military Expenditures: An Application Turkey

1 Introduction

Defense spending has been the largest share of public budget almost all countries and since very long periods of history. The spending has been growing steadily nowadays. A global state of insecurity dominates the world today. Despite the end of the cold war period, there are still internal and external threats that every country today feels confronted with. For this reason, all countries, both large and small, demonstrate an endeavor to sustain their existence by devoting a large part of their economic means to the survival question. In doing so, they have to shift their economic resources from the prosperity target to the survival target. For this reason, defense spending, which has a high share in public expenditures, has a great prospect for countries. Because the success of capturing the aims of an economic, social, cultural, political, etc. area depends on the protection of the bachelor of that country and its national security.

Especially after World War II, it seems that countries have a big increase in their defense spending. In the last hundred years, major changes and developments in weapons technology and production have led to an increase in defense spending on a global basis, and each country has taken its share in various measures without this development.

On the other hand, national security must be provided first of all to ensure economic growth in a country. Therefore, defense spending is a prerequisite for the development of an country. Nevertheless, it is always a matter of curiosity about the effect of the increase or decrease of defense spending on economic growth. as a result of various scientific researches carried out in this respect in the world, it has been found that defense expenditures are affected in two ways as negative and positive on the national economy. According to one opinion, the use of resources allocated for the increase of wealth in defense spending negatively affects economic development, in other words it is stated that the resources allocated for defense spending generally contribute to economic development.

1 Assistant Professor, Bartın University, Department of Economics
2 Assistant Professor, Bartın University, Department of Economics
3 Research Assistant, Bartın University, Department of Economics

On the other hand, it is estimated that military expenditures affect economic growth differently depending on the development status of the country and the status of exporter or importer. A considerable part of developing countries, even though some of their defense expenditures are covered by domestic firms in the defense industry operating in their own structures, have suffered serious deterioration in the current account balance because they use high import inputs in their productions, which has a negative effect on economic growth.

2 Basic Characterıstıcs of Relatıonshıp between Defense Expendıtures and Economıc Growth

It is quite difficult to determine the limits of spending and investments in defending a state in order to deflect its own security and continuation threats. Therefore, governments cannot ignore the issue of dividing a significant part of the national income of the country into defense spending when it comes to the security and continuation of the country.

The economic effects of defense expenditures, which have great effects both nationally and regionally, are emphasized. What economists particularly emphasize is the impact of defense spending on economic growth. There are many scientific studies in the scientific studies that investigate the relation between defense expenditures and economic growth in different countries and different periods.

While it is known that this relationship is very important and strong, it has come to various and different conclusions about its content, effect and direction of influence. According to the results of studies investigating the relationship between defense spending and economic development, defense spending has not affected economic growth. It has also come to the conclusion that defense spending accelerates economic growth and, on the contrary, reduces economic growth.

The level of optimal defense expenditure is very important for countries. Excessive defense spending adversely affects economic growth by delaying growth, but by increasing internal and external security, allowing more investment into the country, reducing unemployment and thus increasing economic growth. Giving less resources to defense spending leads to unstable growth and chaos(Gökbunar and Yanıkkaya, 2004:161; Canbay and Mercan, 2017:89).

Defense spending includes the purchase of weapons systems, tools and supplies used in this sector, the large and small maintenance and repair expenses, various service procurements, building facilities and construction, such as buildings, environment, infrastructure, expropriation leases and expenses such as expenditures are made up a lot.

When the classification of defense expenditures is examined, it is seen that all of the classification types of public budgets are included in defense budget more intensively in some of their items. Defense spending includes current and personnel expenditures, investment expenditures and transfer expenditures. While the transfer expenditures are relatively less compared to other expenditures, the largest spending model creates current and personnel work investment expenditures.

The relationship between defense spending and economic growth is discussed in theory as Military Keynesian Approach and Neo-Classical Approach in two groups. In the Military Keynesian Approach, defense spending is seen as a public expenditure and increases economic growth. In the Neo-Classical approach, defense spending negatively affects growth by reducing scarce resources and human capital (Durgun and Timur, 2017:129–130).

Although it is seen that the accelerating effect of investment expenditures is considerably higher than the current and transfer expenditures, it can be said theoretically that the accelerating effect of current expenditures is higher than transfer expenditures. In terms of multiplier effect, it is seen that the effect of defense investment and current expenditures on macroeconomic growth is considerably higher than the effect of transfer expenditures. In other words, the multiplier effect of transfer expenditures theoretically occurs at a lower level than other expenditures. Therefore, it is evaluated that the effect of investment and current defense spending on economic growth is higher than transfer expenditures.

3 Literature Search

There is a wide literature covering the relationship between military spending and economic growth. The results of these studies are shown in Tab. 1.

Tab. 1 gives the result of 14 different studies. According to the results of these studies, there cannot be a meaningful relationship between military spending and economic growth in developed countries; whereas in the underdeveloped countries a positive relationship was found between the two variables.

4 Empirical Approach and Data

4.1 Research Method

In this study, to cover the period 1961–2016, the impact of military spending on economic growth in Turkey will be analyzed using the ARDL model. Before the ARDL model is applied, the unit root test should be applied to the variables. In

Tab. 1: Literature Survey on Military Spending and Economic Growth Relation

Writers	Countries	Method	Variables	Result
Benoit (1978)	44 least developed countries (1950–1965)	Regression analysis	Military expenditures and economic growth	A positive correlation was found between the two variables.
Biswas and Ram (1986)	14 OECD countries (1956–1969) and 44 less developed countries (1950–1965)	Panel data analysis	Defense spending and economic growth	There was no statistically significant relationship between the two variables.
Kollias and Makrydakis (2000)	Greece (1955–1993)	Causality analysis	Military expenditures and economic growth	There was no statistically significant relationship between the two variables.
Aizenman,and Reuven (2006)	99 countries (1989–1998)	Panel regression analysis	Military expenditures and economic growth	A positive relationship was found between military spending and economic growth.
Lee and Chen (2007)	A total of 89 countries, 27 of which are OECD countries (1988–2003)	Panel cointegration and causality analysis	Military expenditures and economic growth	A positive correlation was found between the two variables.
Heo (2009)	USA (1954–2005)	Time series-Feder-Ram model	Defense spending and economic growth	Defense spending does not have a significant effect on economic growth.
Yılancı ve Özcan (2010)	Turkey (1950–2006)	Causality analysis	Defense spending and GNP	A one-way causality relationship from GNP to defense spending was identified.
Yurttançıkmaz et all. (2012)	Iran (1965–2008)	ARDL Model	Military spending and economic growth	In the long run, it has been determined that military expenditures have positive effects on economic growth. In the short term, military expenditures have statistically significant and positive effects on growth.

Na and Bo (2013)	Bangladesh, India, Pakistan, Nepal and Sri Lanka (1990–2006)	Panel regression analysis	Military expenditures and economic growth	Military expenditures negatively affect economic growth.
Duyar and Koçoğlu (2014)	6 Sub-Saharan African countries (1990–2012)	Panel regression analysis	Military expenditures and economic growth	They found positive effects of military spending on economic growth not to be taken into consideration in terms of macroeconomics.
Destek (2016)	14 NATO countries (1988–2014)	Panel cointegration and causality analysis	Military expenditures and real national income	Bi-directional causality between military spending and real national income for the United States Canada, England, Italy and Norway from military spending to real GDP unidirectional causality and Turkey, Portugal and Denmark was found unidirectional causality from the real GDP to military spending.
Kesgingöz ve Olcay (2016)	Turkey and selected Middle Eastern countries (1991–2014)	Panel regression analysis	Defense spending and economic growth	A negative relationship between defense spending and economic growth has been found.
Korkmaz ve Bilgin (2016)	Turkey and the United States (1961–2015)	Cointegration and causality analysis	Military expenditures and economic growth	Whereas here it is not detected any causal relationship between military spending and economic growth for the US, while for Turkey it can be said that there is bidirectional causal relationship between the two variables.
Canbay and Mercan (2017)	Turkey (1986–2016)	Time series-VECM model	Defense spending and industrial production index	Defense spending has been found to be a shrinking effect of economic growth.
Tuncay (2017)	7 countries in connection with Turkey and Turkey (1996–2014)	Dynamic panel data analysis	Defense spending and economic growth	There was a negative relationship between defense spending and growth.

Tab. 2: Unit Root Test Results

Variables	Stationary Grade	ADF Test Statistic	Critical Value	Probability Value
LOGMX	I (0)	−1.000909	−2.915522	0.7470
DLOGMX	I (1)	−5.399224	−2.916566	0.0000
LOGGPC	I (0)	−5.299096	−2.915522	0.0000

the analysis, military spending is shown as "LOGMX" and economic growth as "LOGGPC".

5 Empirical Results

In studies using time series data, it should be tested whether the data used in the study have a static structure. Because, when non-stationary time series are used, a fake regression problem occurs and the results obtained with regression analysis do not reflect the actual relationship(Granger and Newbold, 1974:111).
In this study, ADF unit root test was performed to determine the stability of the series. Tab. 1 gives the results of unit root test.

Tab. 2 shows the results of the unit root test. Military spending is stable at the level of economic growth, although it is gaps of the first. The ARDL model was established because the variables studied are stable at different grades.

The ARDL model has several advantages. One of them is that the variables used in the model are I (0) or I (1), which is not a problem to perform the boundary test. It gives statistically more meaningful and more reliable results than classical cointegration tests. It also includes short and long term dynamics(Yilanci and Gazel, 2014:30–31). Furthermore, in the ARDL model, the components of data generation processes are included in the estimates and give consistent results even if the number of observations is not much (Narayan, 2004:199).

In the framework of the ARDL model, the existence of a long-term relationship will be searched through the boundary test. Tab. 3 shows the results of the ARDL boundary test.

It is seen that there is a cointegrated relationship between the variables because F statistic value according to Tab. 3 is higher than all critical values. Long term coefficients are given in Tab. 4 by the ARDL cointegration test results.

Tab. 4 shows that the system has been rebalanced in the short term and long term coefficients are shown. The error correction coefficient is -0.84 and is significant. When we examine long term coefficients, the coefficient of LOGMX

Tab. 3: Results of ARDL Boundary Test

Test Statistic	Value	k
F-statistic	27.61849	1
Critical Value Bounds		
Significance	I0 Bound	I1 Bound
10 %	4.04	4.78
5 %	4.94	5.73
2.5 %	5.77	6.68
1 %	6.84	7.84

Tab. 4: ARDL Cointegrating and Long Term Form

Cointegrating Form				
Variable	Coefficient	Std. Error	t-Statistic	Prob.
D(LOGMX)	-5.938660	1.289541	-4.605251	0.0000
CointEq(-1)	-0.847949	0.114414	-7.411234	0.0000
Cointeq = LOGGPC – (0.4554*LOGMX + 1.5449)				
Long Run Coefficients				
Variable	Coefficient	Std. Error	t-Statistic	Prob.
LOGMX	0.455426	0.132603	3.434514	0.0012
C	1.544926	0.121953	12.668203	0.0000

Tab. 5: VECM Casuality Analysis Results

	Coefficient	**Std. Error**	**t-Statistics**	**Prob.**
C(1)	-1.005417	0.267362	-3.760500	0.0005
	Coefficient	**Std. Error**	**t-Statistics**	**Prob.**
C(7)	0.025050	0.022094	1.133811	0.2626

is 0.455. Accordingly, 1 unit increase in military spending increases economic growth by 0.455 units.

Finally, the VEC causality model was established. Tab. 5 gives the results of the causality analysis in the VECM framework.

According to the results of the VECM causality analysis in Tab. 5, since the coefficient C (1) is negative and statistically significant, a one-way causality from military spending to economic growth has been determined. Since C (7) is statistically insignificant, there is no causality from economic growth to military spending.

6 Conclusion

In our analysis, we first found the results of unit root test. Military spending is stable at the level of economic growth, although it is gaps of the first. The ARDL model was established because the variables studied are stable at different grades.

As a result of the ARDL estimator made, 1 unit increase in military spending was found to increase economic growth by 0.455 units. On the other hand, according to the results of causality, a one-way causality relation was found from military expenditures to economic growth.

These results show the importance of military spending in economic growth of countries. Hence, it also emphasizes the importance of the share of policy makers that allocate military spending in the country budget.

References

Aizenman, J. and Reuven, G. (2006), "Military Expenditure, Threats, and Growth" Journal of International Trade & Economic Development, 15(2), ss. 129–155.

Benoit, E. (1978), "Growth and Defense in Developing Countries" Economic Development and Cultural Change, 26 (2), pp. 271–280, Published by: Sage Publications Ltd.

Biswas, B. and Ram, R. (1986), "Military Expenditures and Economic Growth in Less Developed Countries: An Augmented Model and Further Evidence" Economic Development and Cultural Change, 34 (2), pp. 362–364.

Canbay, Ş. and Mercan, D. (2017), "Savunma Harcamalarının Ekonomik Büyüme Ve Cari İşlemler Dengesine Etkisi: Türkiye Örneği" Journal of Emerging Economies and Policy, 2 (2), pp. 86–104.

Destek, M.A. (2016), "NATO Ülkelerinde Askeri Harcamalar Ve Ekonomik Büyüme İlişkisi: Yatay Kesit Bağımlılığı Altında Panel Veri Analizi" Uluslararası Yönetim İktisat ve İşletme Dergisi, 12 (28), pp. 209–223.

Durgun, Ö. and Timur, M.C. (2017), "Savunma Harcamaları ve Ekonomik Büyüme İlişkisi: Türkiye Analizi" Dumlupınar Üniversitesi Sosyal Bilimler Dergisi, 54. Sayı/Ekim 2017, pp.126–137.

Duyar, M. and Koçoğlu, M. (2014), "Askeri Harcamaların Ekonomik Büyüme Üzerine Etkisi: Sahra Altı Afrika Örneği" Uluslararası Sosyal Araştırmalar Dergisi, 7 (33), pp. 702–722.

Gökbunar, R. and Yanıkkaya, H. (2004), "Savunma Harcamalarını Belirleyen Faktörler ve Ekonomik Büyümeye Etkileri" Ankara Üniversitesi, SBF Dergisi, 59-1, pp. 159–179.

Granger, C.W.J. and Newbold, P. (1974), "Spurious Regressions in Econometrics" Journal of Econometrics, 2 (1974) s. 111–120, NorthHolland Publishing Company.

Heo, U. (2009), "The Relationship between Defense Spending and Economic Growth in the United States" Political Research Quarterly, 63(4), pp. 760–770.

Kesgingöz, H. and Olcay, T. (2016), "Türkiye ve Seçilmiş Ortadoğu Ülkeleri için Benoit Hipotezinin Sınanması: Panel Veri Analizi" Çankırı Karatekin Üniversitesi, İktisadi ve İdari Bilimler Fakültesi Dergisi, 6 (1), pp. 585–607.

Kollias, C. and Makrydakis, S. (2000), "A Note on the Causal Relationship between Defence Spending and Growth in Greece: 1955–93" Defence and Peace Economics, 11(1), pp. 173–184.

Korkmaz, Ö. and Bilgin, Tuba (2016), "Askeri Harcamalar İle Ekonomik Büyüme Arasındaki İlişki: Türkiye Ve Amerika Birleşik Devletlerinin Karşılaştırmalı Analizi" UİİİD-İJEAS, 2017 (18), pp. 289–316.

Lee, C. C. and Chen, S. T. (2007), "Do Defence Expenditures Spur GDP: A Panel Analysis from OECD and Non-OECD Countries" Defence and Peace Economics, 18(3), pp. 265–280.

Na, H. and Bo, C. (2013), "Cooperation for a Peaceful and Sustainable World Part 2: Military Expenditure and Economic Growth in South Asia" Contributions to Conflict Management, Peace Economics and Development, 20, pp. 213–223.

Narayan, P.K. (2004), "Fiji's Tourism Demand: The ARDL Approach to Cointegration" TourismEconomics, 2004, 10 (2), 193–206.

Tuncay, Ö. (2017), "Finansal Serbestleşme Sonrası Dönem Savunma Harcamalarının Ekonomik Analizi" Uluslararası Ekonomik Araştırmalar Dergisi, Mart 2017, 3 (1), pp. 23–37.

Yılancı, V. and Özcan, B. (2010), "Yapısal Kırılmalar Altında Türkiye İçin Savunma Harcamaları İle GSMH Arasındaki İlişkinin Analizi" C.Ü. İktisadi ve İdari Bilimler Dergisi, 11 (1), pp. 21–33.

Fusun Celebi Boz[1]

Industry 4.0 and Energy Politics

1 Introduction

Economic crisis, which the developed economies have experienced since 2008, has directed those economies to a new search. Within the scope of that search, a new industry has emerged, which information communication Technologies has come into prominence in industry in order to be able to develop manufacturing industries and transform the cheap labor force based production model. As a result of the fact that digital elements are in manufacturing industry within the framework of the new industrial revolution, it can be said that production costs shall diminish and competition levels of countries shall rise through fast production. Accordingly, it can be stated that economic growth shall rise and levels of per capita income shall go up, depending on the increase in productivity of the countries that speed up the digitalization in industry through that revolution.

Industry 4.0 or Fourth Industrial Revolution, which firstly appeared in Hannover city of Germany, are described as smart factories, the internet of objects, smart industry, big data and advanced manufacturing. This revolution covers cyber physical systems, simulation, network connections, big data collection at the same time upon the application of information communication Technologies by both intra-company and firms to which the company is affiliated from all the phases of production to the usage (Schwab, 2016:16–17). Through this revolution, it can be said that robotics, considered to take away the job of unskilled labor force, also comes into prominence and a new labor force structure shall appear.

While it is estimated, through Industry 4.0, that there shall be productivity increases by 6–8 % per annum in manufacturing industry, it is considered that investments in the internet industry shall reach 500 billion dollars by 2020 and the added value shall rise and turn out to be 1.3 billion dollars. It can be said that investments of the countries in the Asian region shall rise from 10 billion dollars to 60 billion dollars and the United States of America has allocated 1 billion

1 Assisstant Professor Dr. Füsun Çelebi Boz, Bayburt University, Faculty of Eonomics and Administrative Sciences, Economic Development and International Economics Department,fcelebi@bayburt.edu.tr

dollars of public fund in order to bring together the research agencies that work in the digital industry (EBRS, 2015:2–3).

As a result of technological progresses, important developments were provided in industrial production area following the industrial revolution and productivity rose. While the use of hydraulic and steam-powered machinery started in the first industrial revolution, mass production became possible depending on electric power in the second industrial revolution. In the third industrial revolution, automation in industry became widespread through the electronic and information Technologies. It is seen that, today and in the near future, we shall be faced with the fourth industrial revolution in which connection between physical and digital systems has been provided, the use of cyber physical systems; namely, the computers that monitor and check the physical processes based on the feedback cycle, has come into prominence (TÜSİAD, 2016:19).

The Fourth Industrial Revolution can be said to deeply affect the developing countries, which have focused the cost decreases on cheap labor force based production, and the countries of the Far Eastern Asia. Within this context, it can be possible for the developed countries (the USA, Germany, Japan) that have lost their competitiveness to come into prominence again within the world economy through their advancements in industry. Since investment costs shall decrease especially as a result of the developments in robotics, more opportunities of providing saving emerge for firms and it is thought that the production volume of the developed countries shall gain momentum depending on the increasing savings (Alçın, 2016:22).

Energy is one of the most important inputs of all the industrial revolutions. Developments in energy sector have positively influenced the development of industrial sector and directed it. It is thought that the energy sector shall head towards digitalization through Industry 4.0 in the next periods and the limited energy resources shall be able to be used more effectively and efficiently. Within this context, it is necessary to put forth Energy 4.0, in which the changes in energy sector and the developments in industry appear together, and to accordingly evaluate the economic policies. In the present study I have carried out, it shall be tried to reveal the role of digitalization in energy sector and also the role of energy resources in Industry 4.0 and the policies in this direction shall be determined.

2 Industry 4.0 and Energy 4.0

By the 2000s, production processes of firms became complex based on the change of expectations and requests. Therefore, since firms need interdisciplinary study, a revolution has emerged, in which the objects get in contact with each other over the internet and high-level technology has appeared as a result of the fact that factories are self-managed through moving up into a higher level in production (Yıldız, 2018:0547, Bulut and Akçacı, 2017: 53). Through the mentioned revolution called Industry 4.0, the machine power has taken the place of manpower and a system has emerged, in which information communication Technologies, such as cyber physical systems, the internet of objects, big data, smart product, work in coordination with machinery. Accordingly, in one sense, Industry 4.0 emphasizes the digitalization process in all the areas from production phase of the product to marketing phase.

One of the areas, in which Industry 4.0 or the Fourth Industrial Revolution shall make a change, is energy sector. Especially as a result of digitalization that has occurred in manufacturing industry, it can be said that savings shall be made in energy sector and accordingly the alternative energy resources shall come into prominence for increasing the energy productivity. In this regard, as a result of the mentioned change emerging in industrial sector, it becomes inevitable that energy sector and information services conspire with each other. This situation we call as Energy 4.0, in one sense, indicates digitalization in energy sector. Digitalization in energy sector contributes to conversion of wind and solar energy to electric energy and tries to find solutions for the problems that occur in integration process of those resources (UNIDO, 2017:26).

It is seen that rapid changes in both physical and commercial world also cause the changes in Energy 4.0. Physical changes are the cuts related to renewable energy resources, the start of falling of nuclear energy into disuse, the new transmission and distribution Networks, the start of falling of resources, such as lignite, hard coal, oil and gas, into disuse and storage. Decomposition, trade, new products and new firms in the market are the commercial changes (http://www.endustri40.com/enerji-4-0-enerji-sektorunde-dijitallesme/). When it is considered that fossil fuels shall deplete and the effectiveness of nuclear energy shall diminish in the next period, the share of renewable energy resources shall rise and the necessity of storage activities shall come into prominence for decreasing the costs. Moreover, it is stated that as a result of developments related to the digital use, energy resources shall be able to be included into the production flexibly and thus access to both clean and reliable energy resources can be gained.

2.1 Industry 4.0 and Renewable Energy Resources

The resources we describe as fossil fuels form an important part of energy inputs in the world. However, in order to decrease the effect of greenhouse gas which those resources emit into the environment on the climate and vegetation; the importance of renewable energy resources is increasing day by day. In the next periods, many countries have a tendency to decrease nonrenewable energy resources[1] and to increase the share of renewable energy resources[2]. It is important to obtain renewable energy resources continually and in a sustainable way in order to both decrease the effect of greenhouse gases and effectively use the current energy resources.

Although the share of renewable energy resources rises in the world, it has not still reached the desired level. In 2015, while the share of energy consumption within fossil fuels was 78.4 %, it was estimated that the share of renewable energy resources was 19.3 %; the share of nuclear energy was 2.3 %. Furthermore, it has been stated that 10.2 % of all the renewable energy resources consists of modern renewable energy resources and 9.1 % of them consists of conventional biomass. Within the modern renewable energy resources, the total of biomass, geothermal and solar heat is 4.2 % and the share of water power is 3.6 %. The remaining part of modern renewable energy resources consists of wind, sun, biomass and geothermal power with 1.6 % and of biofuels with 0.8 % (REN21, 2017:30).

Electricity consumption is one of the most important components of energy consumption. A large part of electricity consumption is obtained from fossil fuels. When the share of renewable energy resources is examined, it is considered that the 23 % of electricity generated by 2015 was obtained from renewable resources, and that rate shall rise to 28 % by 2021. Based on renewable energy resources generated by 2015, 153 gw of electricity was generated at the same time. 63 GW of the generated electricity was obtained from wind energy and 49 gw of it from solar energy (IEA, 2016:16). In line with the recent investments of the developed countries in wind and solar energy of China, Chile, India, the USA, Spain, Austria, North Africa and the Middle East countries, it can be said that the share of renewable energy resources in electricity generation shall rise (UNIDO, 2017:23). Thus, in line with the investments made, the energy dependency on fossil fuels is decreased and a sustainable growth is provided in the economy by transferring those environmental resources to next generations. In Tab. 1 below, the developed and developing countries' electricity generation capacity based on renewable energy resources, except hydroelectricity, is seen by years.

According to Tab. 1, the countries' electricity generation capacity by years based on renewable energy resources has increased and it is seen that the countries in which the most production occurred became China and the United States of America by 2015. Based on the increasing demand of those countries for energy, it can be said that they benefit from solar and wind energy and make investments in those areas. When the share of Germany, another developed

Tab. 1: Renewable Energy Resources and Electricity Generation (Billion Kilowatt hours). Source: https://www.eia.gov/beta/international/data (Date of access: 25.07.2018) Table shows the amount of renewable energy resources except hydroelectricity

	2000	2005	2006	2007	2008	2009	2010	2011	2012	2013	2014	2015
Australia	1.2	4.8	5.7	6.7	7.8	6.8	8.3	9.7	13	15	19	21
Austria	1.7	4.2	5.6	6.7	6.8	6.9	7.1	7.1	8.1	8.9	9.5	11
Brazil	7.8	14	15	19	21	24	34	35	40	47	58	70
Canada	8.5	11	11	12	11	15	19	21	22	29	37	42
China	3.1	4.6	6.5	8.3	30	48	79	111	143	206	243	295
Denmark	6.1	11	11	10	11	11	13	15	16	17	19	20
France	4.2	6.5	7.7	10	12	15	18	22	27	28	31	37
Germany	20	45	54	72	78	81	90	112	128	136	150	175
Russia	2.6	3.1	3.2	2.5	3	3.1	3.3	3.3	3.5	3.4	3.8	3.8
Finland	8.8	9.8	11	10	11	9.2	11	12	12	13	13	14
India	3	8.5	11	14	23	30	34	43	53	60	68	75
Japan	19	29	29	31	27	27	41	44	47	55	71	85
South Korea	0.1	0.4	0.6	1	1.3	1.9	2.7	3.4	3.7	5	6.3	8.8
Norway	0.3	0.9	1.1	1.4	1.4	1.3	1.4	1.8	2.1	2.4	2.7	2.9
Turkey	0.3	0.3	0.4	0.7	1.2	2.3	3.9	5.8	7.3	9.7	12	16
United Kingdom	5.4	15	16	16	18	22	24	31	38	51	61	81
United States	80	100	109	117	138	156	180	208	232	267	304	323

country, is examined, it is seen that its electricity generation based on renewable energy resources increased. In Russia, by 2015, 3.8 billion kilowatts of electricity generation were obtained from renewable energy resources and they were obtained mainly from nonrenewable energy resources. The other countries following those countries were respectively Japan, England, India, Brazil and Canada. When the share of Turkey is examined, although it has shown a significant increase in the last 15 years, it can be stated that it is still not at the desired level.

When we evaluate electricity consumption based on renewable energy resources except hydroelectricity according to Tab. 2, while the use of those resources in electricity consumption of countries except the USA was 0 million kilowatt by 2000, it is seen that it showed an increase in the other years. It can be said that the most increase was in China and the USA and a large part of electricity generated based on renewable energy resources is used in consumption

Tab. 2: Renewable Energy Resources and Electricity Consumption (Billion Kilowatt hours). Source: https://www.eia.gov/beta/international/data (Date of access: 25.07.2018) Table shows the amount of renewable energy resources except hydroelectricity

	2000	2005	2006	2007	2008	2009	2010	2011	2012	2013	2014	2015
Australia	0	1.5	1.7	2.2	2.3	2.6	3.1	4.4	5.8	7.3	8.6	9.4
Austria	0	2.8	3.3	3.6	3.6	3.8	3.9	4.2	4.5	4.6	5	5.7
Brazil	0	6.1	6.5	6.6	7.4	6.7	8.8	10	12	15	18	22
Canada	0	2.4	3.2	3.5	4.1	5.1	5.9	7.4	8.7	11	14	16
China	0	3.1	4.7	7.3	12	23	36	56	73	101	132	183
Denmark	0	4.1	4	3.8	4.1	4.6	5.1	5.3	6.1	6.7	6.9	7.3
Finland	0	1.8	1.8	1.9	2	1.9	1.9	2	2	2.3	2.4	2.8
France	0	2.1	3	3.9	5	6.4	8.5	12	14	16	18	20
Germany	0	25	28	31	37	44	53	63	73	81	88	95
India	0	6.3	7.5	9.4	12	14	16	20	24	27	31	36
Japan	0	4.7	5.5	5.5	5.9	6.7	8.6	10	12	19	29	40
South Korea	0	0.2	0.4	0.4	0.8	1	1.3	1.5	1.8	2.8	4.2	5.7
Norway	0	0.4	0.5	0.5	0.6	0.6	0.6	0.7	0.9	1	1.1	1.1
Russia	0	-	-	-	-	-	1.3	1.3	1.3	1.3	1.5	1.6
Turkey	0	0.1	0.2	0.3	0.5	1	1.6	2	2.6	3.3	4.4	5.7
United Kingdom	0	3.2	3.7	4.3	5.2	6.4	7.8	11	14	18	23	29
United States	16	21	24	30	38	49	54	61	77	83	98	113

in the mentioned countries. When Germany, another developed country and where Industry 4.0 appeared, is evaluated, it can be stated the share of renewable energy resources in electricity consumption increased by years. When Turkey is examined, the fossil fuels and hydroelectric power plants are mainly at the forefront in electricity consumption. In Japan, another developed country, the share of renewable energy resources has increased in electricity consumption in recent years.

Information and communication technologies of today face with difficulties in obtaining electricity consumption from different resources and inspecting and distributing the obtained resources. Accordingly, firms should benefit from technological innovations in order to be able to make the necessary infrastructure investments for solving the problems in reliable transfer of energy. Thus, the generation, distribution and consumption of electricity are solved without any problem via smart meters emerging as a result of technological innovations and leakage of electricity can be prevented (UNIDO,2017:26). Furthermore, some problems can be encountered in integration of renewable energy resources, which have limited production compared to other fossil fuels. The flexible and interdependent Industry 4.0 smart devices shall be utilized in order to overcome those problems (Nath, 2018).

One of the digital elements related to distributed energy generation is virtual power plants. Those virtual power plants are the heterogeneous coalitions of distributed energy resources. Discontinuous renewable energy resources, which generally need to negotiate some bilateral agreements before participating in the day-ahead market, consist of storage systems, flexible currents and small conventional power plants (Shabanzadeh et.al, 2015). In virtual power plants, there are cloud based center, distributed control center, the internet of objects and other digital Technologies. As a result of analysis and simulation carried out by German scientists, it was stated that the use of tailor-made energy resources shall appear later on through union of virtual power plants and renewable energy resources (UNIDO:2017:27).

2.2 Industry 4.0 and Energy Efficiency and Energy Saving

It is important to efficiently use energy resources, as well as to be able to obtain those resources. Energy efficiency is the situation that firms decrease the energy amount without decreasing the production quality and amount and also the service which the buildings got. Decrease of that energy amount occurs in line with developments in technology (https://www.eia.gov). In order to increase the energy efficiency within this context, it is necessary to obtain energy data from smart meters, sensors and other tools and to integrate the obtained data into production management. Smart meters and sensors enable the remote observation of energy consumption data in the factory. Results and error messages, which appear as a result of the fact that the observed data are kept in cloud and can be analyzed, can be transferred to administrator at the base via mobile applications. Thus, energy management can carry out a realist evaluation about energy consumption and make a decision in this direction. Thus, more production is made with lower costs and effective use of energy resources is provided (Shrouf et al., 2014:700).

Except productive use of energy resources, the truth that the produced resources are not unlimited and continuous brings the energy saving into the forefront. Energy saving is affected by digitalization of the processes in manufacturing industry as well. The use of new software tools by means of substitution or optimization of specific Technologies reveals functionality and adaptation of energy optimization in the economic activity process. Specific technology optimization is provided as a result of the control of a large number of interdependent robots by an algorithm and it decreases energy consumption (UNIDO, 2017:28). Accordingly, energy consumption can be reduced up to 40 % by minimizing the acceleration of robots and without increasing the production time (Ackerman, 2015).

When we evaluate the developed countries, those countries can be said to take remarkable steps in digitalization. However, some companies benefit from digital Technologies with respect to energy efficiency. A German car firm obtains more than 30 % of energy efficiency than the previous one by using Industry 4.0 technologies for a robot system (Daimler, 2017). Similarly, a forest products company in Canada has decreased the use of energy by 15 % by increasing the controls in production process. In this process, it utilized the internet of objects component (Thilmany, 2018). Accordingly, it is ensured that energy is obtained efficiently and reliably by means of smart meters. At the same time, carrying out Industry 4.0 activities and sustainable energy policies together also decreases the energy consumption of the developed countries and the emission of greenhouse gases which they emit into the environment.

Although the developing countries increase the share of renewable energy resources in order to provide their economic developments, they significantly use nonrenewable energy resources. Within this context, based on the thought that these resources shall run out, making savings happens through the digital technology. The fact that these developing countries become important supplier countries in the global production line leads to adoption of flexible production structure depending on customer demands. Reducing the production costs is also possible with the decrease of the energy costs as a result of cooperation of Industry 4.0 tools with energy resources. Accordingly, according to the result of questionnaire applied to industrial companies that carry on a business in China holding a large part of trade in the world, 83.5 % of companies stated that the saving in energy consumption shall be provided as a result of digitalization. Furthermore, 89.8 % of the mentioned companies emphasized that energy efficiency is an important component (Beier, 2017:231).

3 Conclusion

While hydraulic and steam-powered machinery came into prominence in the First Industrial Revolution, electric energy came into prominence in the Second Industrial Revolution, the automation in industry process became important depending on electronic and information Technologies in the Third Industrial Revolution. The fourth industrial revolution is described as overall systems in which the objects are connected to each other through the internet, the big data related to the increase in data supply are collected and stored, smart machinery and intelligent robots take place in business world. Accordingly, it can be described as the fact that digital components come into prominence in many fields, such as production, manufacturing, marketing, sales, and they are intensively used by companies, through the union of virtual world and physical world.

Industry 4.0 presents the effective and reliable use of energy, an important input in production process. Ensuring the problem-free production, distribution and consumption of energy resources is associated with the technological developments in that sector. Accordingly, in one sense, Energy 4.0 presents the digitalization process which occurs in energy sector. Integration of energy resources produced via smart devices and sensors becomes easy and production amount can show an increase based on decreases in costs since energy consumption declines. Furthermore, after the data of energy are observed and later the observed data are stored via smart devices, they can be analyzed in the cloud. By transferring the results and error messages, emerging as a result of the analyses carried out, to the relevant units, the error rate in production process can be reduced and the effective use of energy resources can be ensured. Thus, energy management can take rational decisions about energy resources they have and change their production structure in this direction.

It is necessary to decrease energy amount used in order to decrease the greenhouse gas emissions and the climate change or turn towards renewable energy resources. However, since renewable energy resources are not continuous resources although they are clean and reliable, it is important to integrate the mentioned resources into production process. Important information can be provided as a result of the analysis of the provided resources by using Industry 4.0 tools and that information enables firms to take realist decisions in increasing the energy generation. Accordingly, it becomes possible though Industry 4.0 to decrease the cut encountered in energy resources and also to save on those resources.

Energy resources are of vital importance in terms of both industrial production and domestic use in the developed and developing countries. In this regard, the countries should efficiently use their limited energy resources against the increasing energy demand. Those countries should also reduce the emission of greenhouse gases they emit into the environment with regard to the climate change and regulate their energy politics to find solutions to that problem. Accordingly, it is necessary for countries to use digital components in terms of both energy and energy consumption against environmental pollution and to make the investments towards the Industry 4.0 tools. Moreover, since the developed and developing countries shall use their energy resources more economically through digitalization in energy sector, the unit production costs shall decrease. In this case, since the production volumes of the countries shall increase, their competitiveness and welfare levels shall also increase rapidly. Along with the decrease of energy costs, the R&D investments shall be focused on in developing the technological infrastructure and the resources, which the economy has, shall be able to be used in different sectors.

References

Ackerman E. (2015), Robots with Smooth Moves Are Up to 40 % More Efficient, Https://Spectrum.İeee.Org/Automaton/Robotics/İndustrial-Robots/Robots-With-Smooth-Moves-Are-More-Efficient (28.07.2018).

Alçın S. (2016), Üretim İçin Yeni Bir İzlek: Sanayi 4.0, Journal of Life Economics, Volume 3, No:2, pp. 19–30

Beier G., Niehoff S., Ziems T. & Xuel B., (2017). Sustainability aspects of a digitalized industry – a comparative study from China and Germany, International Journal of Precision Engineering And Manufacturing-Green Technology Volume 4, No. 2, pp. 227–234

Bulut E. & Akçacı T (2017). Endüstri 4.0 ve İnovasyon Göstergeleri Kapsamında Türkiye Analizi, Assam Uluslararası Hakemli Dergi, Volume 4, No:7, pp. 55–70

Daimler (2017), Industrial Robots Are Learning to Save Energy. https://3blmedia.com/News/Industrial-Robots-Are-Learning-Save-Energy (28.07.2018)

EPRS (2015), Industry 4.0 Digitalisation for productivity and growth, European Parliamentary Research Service, Briefing, http://www.europarl.europa.eu/RegData/etudes/BRIE/2015/568337/EPRS_BRI(2015)568337_EN.pdf (28.07.2018).

IEA (2016), Renewable Energy: Medium-Term Market Report 2016.Executive Summary. http://www.iea.org/publications/freepublications/publication/MTRMR2016.pdf (Erişim Tarihi 25.07.2018).

REN21 (2017), Renewables Global Status Report, http://www.ren21.net/wp-content/uploads/2017/06/17-8399_GSR_2017_Full_Report_0621_Opt.pdf (25.07.2018).

Schwab K. (2016), The Fourth Industrial Revolution (trans. Zülfü Dicleli), Optimist Publishing, İstanbul.

Shrouf F., Ordieres J. & Miragliotta G. (2014), Smart factories in industry 4.0: a review of the concept and of energy management approached in production based on the Internet of things paradigm, 2014 IEEE International

Conference on Industrial Engineering and Engineering Management, Malaysia.

Thilmany, J. 2018, "Industrial Internet of Things: Empowering Big-Time Energy Savings" https://www.emersontopquartile.com/z-featureditems/featured-2/industrial-internet-of-things-empowering-big-time-energy-savings (28.07.2018).

TÜSİAD (2016), Industry 4.0 as a Necessity for Turkey's Global Competitiveness Developing Economy Perspective, http://www.tusiad.org/indir/2016/sanayi-40.pdf

UNIDO (2017). Accelerating Clean Energy through Industry 4.0: Manufacturing the Next Revolution, Nagasawa, T., Pillay, C., Beier, G., Fritzsche, K., Pougel, F., Takama, T., The, K., Bobashev, I., United Nations Industrial Development Organization, Vienna, Austria.

Yıldız A. (2018), Endüstri 4.0 ve Akıllı Fabrikalar, Sakarya Üniversitesi Fen Bilimleri Enstitüsü Dergisi, 22 (2), 546–556.

http://www.endustri40.com/enerji-4-0-enerji-sektorunde-dijitallesme/(Erişimtarihi: 25.07.2018).

https://www.eia.gov/beta/international/data (Erişim tarihi: 25.07.2018).

https://www.eia.gov/energyexplained/index.php?page=about_energy_efficiency (25.07.2018).

Esra Yildirim Soylemez[1]

Approach of Theory of Constraints in Production Process of Enterprises

1 Introduction

Globalization era is defined as an increasing change in every part of social, cultural and economic life. This growing and continuous change increase its effect of globalization on economic life and business world. Intense competition environment forces executives to both increase the competition capacity today and to foresee the future developments. Flexibility, the rapid reaction for changes and also a timely intervention have been the strongest weapons for the enterprises besides providing price and quality advantage. In line with these changes, using a new approach and tools in business management have become a requirement, even an obligatory. One of these new approaches is the Theory of Constraints (TOC) that also used in production processes which is the most important functions in enterprises.

TOC is a systematic management approach that managing the constraints which inhibit enterprise to reach the goals like maximum profit and efficient use of resources. The main goal of TOC is to develop a process that defines, analyzes and applies the requirement changes to eliminate the constraints which limit the adding value process of the enterprise. Accordingly, TOC works to reach the system efficiency by using the capacity of limited sources at the highest level instead of ignoring and activating the constraints in all activities of the system. Theory of constraints that aims to reach to business goals and has a problem solving and thinking process in direction is frequently used in fields such as production, logistics, distribution, project management, research and development, finance, sales and marketing, strategy, change management in several small and large scaled profit oriented and nonprofit organizations.

2 Theory of Constraints

Theory of constraints was developed by Dr. Eliyahu M. Goldratt in the early 1980s. This theory is defined as a method and management philosophy that is used in business management and improvement (Pozo et al., 2012:3). Theory

1 Asst.Prof., Dumlupinar University, esra.yildirim@dpu.edu.tr

of constraints that contributes to the continuous development of the enterprise accepts the enterprises as a chain (or chains network) of the interconnected resources, departments, processes, and functions in which a number of inputs are turned into several goods and services. Accordingly, this theory emphasizes the cross-functional nature of the organizational processes. Much as it is possible to see the production/operation functions as a functional area with a set of input and output group, in concept of TOC the role of the operations should be evaluated within the scope of whole organization (Gupta and Boyd, 2008:993). While it was focusing on especially functional activity areas such as production in the beginning, it has now become an approach that is adopted to manage an entire enterprise or entire supply chain is managed (Kolinska and Domanski, 2017:110).

Theory of constraints expresses that the capacity of an enterprise is bounded by the bottleneck that is defined as the constraint limits the flow in the production process. Moreover, the same theory argues that the bottleneck needs to be described and eliminated to develop the capacity (Yüksel, 2010:210). The bottleneck is defined as a capacity constrained resource that limits the organization's ability to meet the market demand (Krajewski et al., cited: Birgün, 2013:264).

Following hypotheses are argued by the theory of constraints; each system has a purpose; it is expected from a system to increase the success about the goal; the success of each system is limited by the constraints (Kolinska and Domanski, 2017:110). According to hypotheses, these constraints and obstacles need to be known and defined well for business system or process success. Constraint types are differently defined in the literature. Ruhl (1996:44) defined the constraints as the internal constraints (management constraints, workers' attitudes, the capacity of the production process) and external constraints (variables like the market demand that the enterprise cannot interfere). Atwater and Gagne (1997:7) defined the constraints by five different categories; market constraints (lack of the enough market demand to completely use the production capacity to produce the relevant product); resource constraints (lack of the capacity of a resource to meet the market demand); politic constraints (management rules that limit the ability of using the opportunities); raw material constraints (shortage of raw materials or materials supplied externally); logistical constraints (transmitting the required materials to the company and also transmitting the orders completed). The most frequently used constraints are as follows; physical constraints (machine, manpower, job station capacity, lack of material, etc.); managerial constraints (policies, criteria of thoughts caused constraints in workflow); market constraints (inadequate demand) (Krajewski et al., cited: Birgün, 2013:264; Pozo et al.,2012:8).

Theory of constraints contributes to business management and development by two significant components. One of this component is the thinking process (a number of tools that looks for systematic solutions to problematic and complicated situations). Another component powerful applications based on systematic thinking and operational research (production, operations, processes, supply chain, project management, stock, decision making, etc.) (Pozo et al., 2012:3). In this chapter, rather than the thinking process component of the theory of constraints, enterprises' applications, especially in the production process, were analyzed.

2.1 Fundamental Principles and Steps of Theory of Constraints

Eliyahu Goldratt developed Optimized Production Technology (OPT) software with his friends in the late 1970s by asserting that the production managers behave wrongly on programming and controlling the stocks. OPT software provides to be scheduled the works in all the production processes by considering constrainted machines, facilities, personnel, devices, materials other constraints that will affect adaptability of the company with schedule planned. Thus, bottleneck resources will not limit the sales revenue and production of sellable products (Chase et al., 2006:721; Sevindirici, 2009:149). The underlying principles behind the OPT scheduling logic are defined by Goldratt as the fundamental principles of production scheduling rules (Tab. 1) (Chase et al., 2006:721;Gupta et al., 2010:2094).

With reference to Goldratt, these principles form a productive basis for TOC. They are also described as worth to be emphasized because of the importance of management approaches need to be adopted by the enterprises.

Tab. 1: Fundamental Principles of TOC

- Don't balance capacity, balance the flow
- Level of utilization of a non-bottleneck is determined not by its own potential but by some other constraint in the system
- Utilization and activation of a resource are not synonymous
- An hour lost at a bottleneck is an hour lost for the total system
- An hour saved at a non-bottleneck is just a mirage
- Bottlenecks govern both throughput and inventory in the system
- A transfer batch may not and many times should not be equal to the process batch
- The process batch should be variable both along its route and in time
- Schedules should be established by looking at all of the constraints simultaneously. Lead times are a result of a schedule and cannot be predetermined

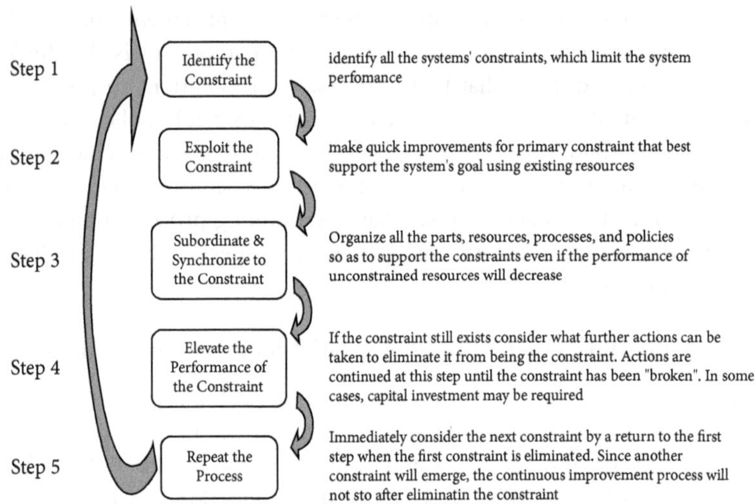

Fig. 1: Steps of Theory of Constraints (Five Focusing Steps)

Even though OPT software was used by big business, it did not attract the attention expected. Therefore Goldratt started to introduce OPT main logic under the name of Synchronous Manufacturing in the mid-1980s. Synchronous Manufacturing is defined as running production processes together and harmonizingly to reach the goals. The main goal is to prepare programs that synchronize the flow rate of dependent parts so as to comply with the production rate in the resource with a bottleneck. It is focused on the success of the entire system rather than partial success measures such as manpower and machine utilization in a synchronized production environment for providing coordination to run all the resources together and accordantly at the same time (Üreten,1998:289).

Following the publication of these principles, Goldratt and Jeff Cox have developed an innovative method based on a five-stage continuous improvement process in their book The Goal (Goldratt and Cox, 1984), written in 1984 on production management, to disseminate ideas about the theory of constraints that have not received much attention. This process argues a system management by focusing on physical constraints (like machine capacity) and nonphysical constraints (like management policies) (Balakrishnan et al., 2008:5). In this respect, the following steps are being followed in this five-step process, which forms a framework for the application and use of TOC, which aims to continuously improve and perfection of the system (Fig. 1) (Mishra et al., 2005:447;

Kolinska and Domanski, 2017:111; Institute of Management Accountants, 1999:6):

Five focusing step continuous improvement model of TOC provides management to focus on system-oriented constraints in the enterprise. Constraints are the pioneers of the whole system; this is because they are the crucial goals. The power of the system that is accepted as a chain is determined by the constraint that is the weakest link, not by the other components. In this direction, the five-step process ensures to remove the bottleneck and constraints to improve the system and reach the goals.

Continuous improvement model (Fig. 1) brings profit growth in a short time in the production process where mostly the physical constraints available. The thinking process model that was developed by Goldratt has been used to define and eliminate the nonphysical constraints about management and market like an inadequate demand.

3 Theory of Constraints in Production Management

TOC accepts the enterprise as a chain where the interdependent functions, processes, departments or resources are turned into goods and services. Much as is it possible to see the production/operations function as a functional area with a different input and output group, the role of the activities should be evaluated within the frame of TOC.

Production/operations strategy should be consistent with other functional area strategies just as both work unit strategy and marketing, human resources. TOC moves beyond the stability emphasize that focuses on money making purpose in both today and future by paying sufficient attention to the rules required for customer satisfaction and satisfactory work environment for the employees. This aspect of TOC creates a common mission to be actualized by all the functional areas including work unit and production/operations function (Gupta and Boyd, 2008:995).

The primary objective of TOC as a production management method is to provide the optimization of an organization's performance by focusing on the constraints that limit the activities. Especially when the production process is concerned, all activities are united for business purposes and it is clear that the factory floor must be optimized while reducing the costs and operating costs to increase performance and efficiency and therefore increase profits. This improvement process starts by constituting performance measuring criteria that are directly related to this target and a clear definition of the goal of the institution (Pozo et al., 2012:5).

Goldratt and Fox (1984) describe three important performance indicators that are used in operational evaluation and also will ensure a synchronized and conscious production: Throughput, Inventory, and Operational Expenses. Throughput is defined as the rate at which the manufacturing business sells its finished products. Inventory is the storage cost of the raw material components and finished goods which have not been sold, and Operational expenses are the cost incurred in turning inventory into throughput (Mishra et al., 2005:446).

Throughput is a proportion; time is an essential factor in measuring the throughput. Similarly, inventory is a broad concept that is defined as everything that a company sells. The investments like construction, property, and machines are classified as the inventory. Operational expenses mean the money that is spent by the company without noticing short or long-term expenses or direct or indirect expenses. The enterprise criteria used in all these definitions is money (Gupta et al., 2010: 2093). As Eliyahu Goldratt said the main goal of organization is not an effectiveness production or high quality products, but it is to "make more money now as well as in the future". And that is why all three measures are determine by money. If we want to check whether conducted action caused the positive effect it is necessary to check whether at least two measures are improved (Trojanowska and Pajak, 2010:2).

TOC that emerged as a production management method was analyzed by Gupta ve Boyd (2008) under four categories; processes, quality, capacity, and inventory. In this section, the use and application of TOC in production management, based on Gupta and Boyd's four categorical approaches, will be examined in four titles; Process management, Capacity management, Inventory management and Quality management.

3.1 Process Management

Process management is the achievement of higher customer satisfaction and competitive advantage through the development and management of the performance of all processes of the organization (Özveri and Kabak, 2016:102).

TOC that focuses on managing an available process submits three levels to manage the processes (Gupta and Boyd, 2008:997):

1. at the highest level; TOC thinks that the entire system consists of a series of interconnected processes, in which the output of a process is input for another process or processes. The number and type of available dependencies will be a function of the range of products, production processes and a set of other factors. There is a constraint that is significant and has an effect on the whole

system in any complicated framework; this constraint mentioned is discussed by following five focusing step.
2. at the operation level, TOC reveals logical product structure (LPS) and V-A-T analyses.
3. at a detailed level, TOC submits drum-buffer-rope (DBR) (production scheduling method) and buffer method.

LPS concept that is used by TOC for each of the products or product family is a combination of material tree and crop rota. Besides, this concept shows the flow of raw material within the facility to create a final product. LPS defines the part numbers, operations performed and resources used in different steps in a transformation process for a product or the product family. VAT analysis approach is a constraint management process that determines the flow from beginning to end in an organization. Three general process structure can be revealed when the organization is discussed from this perspective. T structure that is mostly used in organizations is the structures in which obtaining more than one final process output is possible. V structure is the structures where a single type of resources is used to meet the demands expected. While the T structure prioritizes the guidance points, V structure mostly considers the differentiation points. A structure is a structure in which solely a number of final process outputs are produced by the combination of several activities. Using a large variety of resources to optimize the process is one of the most prominent attributes of this process (Gürses, 2007: 14). VAT analysis helps to define the obstacles in each of the production processes by separating different production processes into category or structures.

3.2 Capacity Management

The capacity approach in operations management splits long term, medium term, and short-term capacity problems. TOC defers consideration of long-term capacity issues until after short-term capacity issues have been dealt with the five focusing steps framework (Gupta and Boyd, 2008:999).

One of the applications of this five steps process within the scope of the theory of constraints is DBR (drum-buffer-rope) scheduling. DBR is a finite capacity planning method that provides the production program to fulfill the capacity planning functions such as rough capacity planning and capacity requirements planning (Gupta and Boyd, 2008:1000). The primary goal is to facilitate the business enterprise to optimize the use of a capacity constrained resource (CCR) and use time buffers to create schedules that help deliver products on time (Trojanowska and Pajak, 2010:3). Capacity constrained resource (CCR) is a resource that is

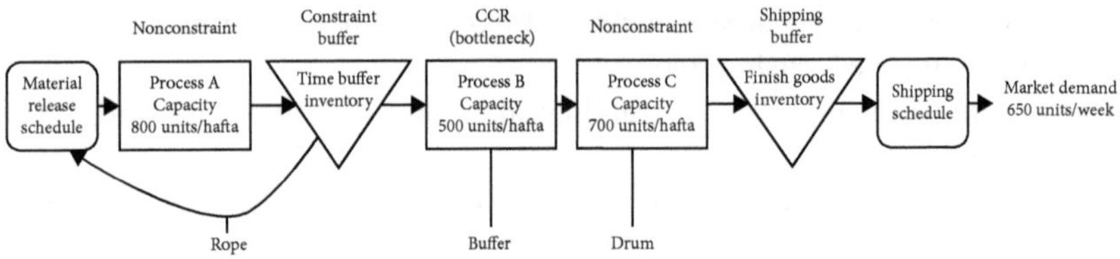

Fig. 2: Drum-Buffer-Rope System. Source: Krajewski et al., cited: Birgün, 2013:273

close to capacity and can be a bottleneck if not carefully programmed. A bottleneck is also called as CCR under some specific conditions. If its output is less than the market demand, the process with minimum capacity is a bottleneck. If it is the resource with the minimum capacity in the system, but yet it has a higher capacity than the market demand, it is defined as CCR (Krajewski et al., translated by Birgün, 2013:264). The DBR works by regulating the in-process material flow at the bottleneck or at the CCR.

The drum in DBR is a bottleneck that is defined as a resource which has not a capacity to meet the demand; the bottleneck continuously works. The bottleneck is a drum, namely a control point. Drum is CCR if there is not a bottleneck in the system. A buffer is a time buffer that plans the early flows to the bottleneck. It protects the bottleneck from disruptions and provides it to stay full. Inventory buffer can be placed in front of the shipment point to keep the customer shipment schedule. The rope is information 'link' from the drum to the raw material release schedule so that the constraint is always kept supplied with just the right amount of work (Chase et al., 2006:730; Trojanowska and Pajak, 2010:3).

Buffer management that completes DBR cycle controls conducting of bottleneck running. While the buffer management increases both the contribution and delivery on time by working with DBR, it helps managers about creating a production schedule that reduces the inventory (Krajewski et al., cited: Birgün, 2013:273)

The drum-buffer-rope system is shown in detail in Fig. 2. Process B, with a capacity of only 500 units per week, is the bottleneck because the up-stream Process A and downstream Process C have capacities of 800 units per week and 700 unitsper week, respectively, and the market demand is 650 units per week, on average. In this case,because the capacity at process B is less than the market demand, it is the bottleneck. A constrainttime buffer, which can be in the form of materials arriving earlier than needed, is placed rightin front of the bottleneck (Process B). A shipping buffer, in the form of finished goods inventory,can also be placed prior to the shipping schedule in order to protect customer orders that arefirm. Finally, a rope ties the material release schedule to match the schedule, or drum beat, at the bottle neck. The material flow is pulled forward by the drum beat prior to the bottleneck, while it ispushed downstream toward the customer subsequent to the bottleneck (Krajewski et al., cited: Birgün, 2013:273).

DBR tries to develop an output by using the bottleneck resource better and by also protecting from the problems with the help of a time buffer and a protector buffer in another place. DBR system that necessitates being understood the principles of TOC can be used in different types of production and service enterprises that are combined with other planning and control systems.

3.3 Inventory Management

Inventory that is one of the performance criteria has particular importance in the theory of constraints. Inventory concept is defined as everything that a company sells. Meanwhile, the focus of DBR is accepted as the approach of TOC towards planning, timing, and buffer management.

Goldratt accepts the theory of constraints as a system with low inventory rather than a system without the inventory. The main goal of the product inventory is to keep the productiveness of the system; having too many inventories may decrease the output because of several reasons. Accordingly, Goldratt offers to be used as the buffers before the shipment and during the shipping to eliminate these constraint problems (Gupta and Boyd, 2008:1000).

In operation management, while the inventory working is divided into two as dependent and independent demand, the dependent demand is called as DBR in TOC. DBR that is a finite planning method plans the constrained resource at first. Thereby, it is assumed that the resources without any constraint will not have excess capacity. So, waiting period on ranks without constraints will be minimum. Moreover, since the goods produced are not accepted as an output till selling, the parts that wait in a constraint ordered by the customer is accepted as the base for any lot-sizing in TOC. However, it benefits from the second step constraint in five steps improvement process; namely, it provides to be optimized the constraint capacity. This circumstance mentioned ensures to be minimized the nonproductive time including the setups on the constraint (Gupta and Boyd, 2008:1001).

3.4 Quality Management

TOC that is one of the continuous improvement approaches developed to gain more competitive advantages to enterprises can also be defined as process development policy within the scope of quality improvement (Kasemset, 2011:327).

TOC is assimilated to the Total Quality Management (TQM) approach in that including a continuous improvement cycle and considering production line or service area as the whole process to be improved for finding the next problem. There are studies that tried to reveal the differences and similarities between TOC and TQM. Some of those researches pointed out that there is not a superiority between TOC and TQM however, the TOC approach can be built on the basis that is constituted by TQM.

TOC and TQM try to improve the products and results instead of accepting the current situation. Because of this similarity, TOC is assimilated to the process improvement processes such as TQM, Six Sigma, and Lean production.

TQM does not differentiate between the goal and the necessary conditions. TQM proponents appear to argue that employee satisfaction leads to customer satisfaction and retention which leads to company financial success and which in turn provides employees with security and satisfaction. Viewed as a loop, it may not matter what we call the goal as long as the other two are considered as necessary conditions. However, according to the approach of TOC, the major difference between the goal and necessary conditions is that the goal is something a company wants to increase continually whereas the necessary conditions must simply be met, i.e., a threshold level must be achieved but increasing the level beyond the threshold does not result in an increase in profit. The TOC focuses on what is the constraint that prevents an increase in performance that will provide the business with the goal of earning money (Gupta and Boyd, 2008:998).

Much as TOC is a system development methodology that helps enterprises to think about their problems and apply the solutions, there is a need for some of the improvement concepts to correct the quality problems. Besides, TOC can be assimilated to TQM application as a mechanism to help TQM and generalize its application area. With reference to many of the investigators, the approaches like JIT, Six sigma should be considered with TOC to obtain a better result.

4 Conclusion

TOC that was developed as a new management philosophy by Goldratt encourages enterprises to maximize the profitability by satisfying the customer needs better than the rival firms. In this way, the continued optimization of expected performance will be encouraged at the same time. This theory tries to reach the desired system effectiveness by using the capacity of limited sources at maximum instead of accepting the constraints in all the activities of the system. It is aimed to maximize the profit by determining the contributions obtained from the resources cause to the bottleneck in the enterprise.

TOC is a beneficial method for the executives to understand how the bottlenecks can be understood and managed. Besides, this theory teaches them how the information is used to specify the best service of the company. Furthermore, TOC ensures increasing the current output by expediting the material flow in an operational manner. The profitability increases due to the decrease in inventory and cycle time by this mean. In conclusion, TOC is one of the methods that contribute to the enterprises by optimizing the production process, using the resources better and also decreasing the production costs.

TOC has an extensive usage area by being compatible with each kind of company and market structures, understandable, applicable and an effective technique. In addition to this, investigators confirm that TOC methods give better results when being used with lean manufacturing, JIT, and ERP.

References

Atwater, B. and Gagne M.L., (1997). "The Theory of Constraints Versus Contribution Margin Analysis for Product Mix Decisions", *Journal of Cost Management*, Vol. 11, No. 1, pp. 14–22.

Balakrishnan, J., Cheng, C.H. and Trietsch, D., (2008). "The Theory of Constraints in Academia: Its Evolution, Influence, Controversies, and Lessons", *Operations Management Education Review*, Vol. 2, pp. 97–114.

Chase, R.B., Jacobs, F.R, Aquilano, N.J., (2006). *Operations Management for Competitive Advantage*, Boston, McGraw-Hill.

Goldratt, E.M. and Cox, J., (1984). *The Goal: Excellence in Manufacturing*, Great Barrington, MA., North River Press.

Gupta, M.C. and Boyd, L.H., (2008). "Theory of Constraints: A theory for Operations Management", *International Journal of Operations & Production Management*, Vol. 28, pp: 991–1012.

Gupta, A., Bhardwaj, A., Kanda, A., (2010). "Fundamental Concepts of Theory of Constraints: An Emerging Philosophy", *International Scholarly and Scientific Research & Innovation*, Vol: 4, No: 10, pp. 2089–2095.

Gürses, M., (2007). *Kısıtlar Teorisi ve Proje Yönetiminde Bir Uygulama*, Master Thesis, İstanbul Teknik Üniversitesi – Fen Bilimleri Enstitüsü, İstanbul.

Institute of Management Accountants (IMA), (1999). *Theory of Constraints (TOC) Management System Fundamentals*, USA, Institute of Management Accountants Publishing.

Kasemset, C., (2011). "A Review on Quality Improvement and Theory of Constraints (TOC)", *International Conference on Quality and Reliability*, 14–17 Sept. 2011, Bangkok, Thailand.

Kolinska J., Domanski, R., (2017). "The Analysis of Production Lines Bottlenecks - Identification and Ways of Management", *The 17th International Scientific Conference Business Logistics in Modern Management*, 12–13 October 2017, Osijek, Croatina.

Krajewski, L.J., Ritzman, L.P., Malhotra, M.K., (2013). *Üretim Yönetimi Süreçler Ve Tedarik Zincirleri* (cited. Semra Birgün), Ankara: Nobel Akademik Yayıncılık, 2013.

Mishra, N., Tiwari, M.K., Shankar, R., Chan, F.T.S., (2005). "Hybrid Tabu-Simulated Annealing Based Approach to Solve Multi-Constraint Product Mix Decision Problem" *Expert Systems With Applications*, Vol. 29, No. 2, pp. 446–454.

Özveri, O., Kabak, M., (2016). "Süreç Yönetimi Olgunluk Modelleri ve Bir Organizasyonun ve Süreç Yönetimi Olgunluğunun Değerlendirilmesi", AKÜ İİBF Dergisi, Cilt:18, Sayı: 1, pp. 101–110.

Pozo H., Tachizawa, T., Soares,W.L., (2012). "The Theory Of Constraints as a Manufacturing Strategy: a Case Study in A Small Manufacturing Company", *POMS 23rd. Annual Conference*, 20–23 April 2012, Chicago, USA.

Ruhl, J.M., (1996). "An Introduction to the Theory of Constraints", *Journal of Cost Management*, Vol. 10, No. 2, pp. 43–48.

Sevindirici, İ., (2009). *Üretim Teknikleri*, İstanbul, Kum Saati Yayınları.

Trojanowska J., Pająk E., (2010). "Usıng the Theory of Constraınts to Productıon Processes Improvement", *7th International Daaam Baltic Conference "Industrıal Engıneerıng"*, 22–24 April 2010, Tallinn, Estonia.

Üreten, S., (1998). *Üretim İşlemler Yönetimi Planlama Denetim Kararları Karar Modelleri ve İyileştirme Yaklaşımları*, Ankara: Gazi Üniversitesi İktisadi İdari Bilimler Fakültesi Yayını.

Yüksel, H., (2010). *Üretim/İşlemler Yönetimi Temel Kavramlar*, Ankara: Nobel Akademik Yayıncılık.

Bayram Akay[1]

The Impact of Generic Competition Strategy on Performance: A Research in Car Rental Sector

1 Introduction

The car rental industry has a very competitive structure. The sector is shaped by intense price and service competition. Competition is primarily based on other factors such as price, reliability, vehicle status, national distribution, availability of reservation systems, renting and returning convenience and customer service. Competition in the car rental sector is strongly influenced by advertisement, marketing and brand reputation (Datamonitor, 2011:7), other transportation systems such as planes and taxis (Marijanovic, 2010: 113), fuel and plane ticket prices, vehicle size and type (Mancini, 2012: 175).

In the tourism literature, there is almost no focus car rental establishments while there is a considerable interest in topics such as hotels, food and beverage or gastronomy, tour operators, railways, roads and destination management (Marijanovic, 2010). On the other hands, Enright and Newton, (2015); Lo, (2012); Garcia et al., (2017) have done researches on the impact of competition strategies on performance in tourism literature.

2 Conceptual Framework

The car rental sector provides billions of dollars of income to the economy of many countries. In the US with 19.643 car hire locations, more than 2.1 million cars in service in 2017, the car renter sector's contribution to the economy was about $28.626 billion (www.autorentalnews.com). In the world, the car rental industry is most prevalent in the US, Europe and other developed countries. The sector is also growing in developing countries such as India, China and Brazil (Tyya, 2007). In Turkey, car rental companies operating in airports and big city centers in the past years provides services in many tourism regions as a result of rapid developments in the tourism sector (MEB, 2006).

The car rental sector takes place in two forms: long-term car rentals (more than 12 months) and short-term car rentals (hourly/daily /monthly). Long-term

1 Department of Travel Management & Tourism Guidance, Kırklareli University, Faculty of Tourism, Kayalı Campus, Kırklareli 39100, Turkey.

car rental activities are mainly divided into operational renting and financial renting. Short-term car rental activities take place in two forms: daily car rental and one-year minimum rental (Gençler, 2012).

In Turkey, 6–7 % of the operational rentals are made by the public, although there is no clear data regarding the sector's operational and daily rental market. The market share of the top 10 largest firms in Turkey is 69 % and the remaining 31 % is shared by hundreds of various-sized firms (Karaboğa, 2012). In the car rental sector, Istanbul takes the first place with 70 % share, followed by Ankara at the second Izmir at the third. However, in summer, the trend reverses and there is a shift towards tourism centers such as Antalya, Muğla and Aydın (www.turizmgazetesi.com).

2.1 Cost Leadership Strategy

Cost leadership requires the establishment of operational facilities with efficient scale, obtaining strong cost reductions from experience, strict cost and overhead control, avoiding small client accounts, and the reduction of costs in areas such as R&D, service, sales force and advertisement (Porter, 2000: 44). By creating a cost advantage in this way, it is possible to increase the number of customers and hence the market share via shifting towards a wider market (Bahar and Kozak, 2012: 98). The business sense of the companies in the car rental sector can be divided into groups according to these competition strategies. For example, companies operating outside the airport follow the cost leadership principle. To maintain this strategy, businesses need to reduce costs, overhead, R & D, the service sales force and advertising costs and require strict cost control. In fact, although all companies pay the same price for their vehicles, businesses operating outside the airport can rent cars at low prices (Pachon, 2000: 65).

2.2 Differentiation Strategy

The differentiation strategy is the ability to offer a unique product or service. By differentiating the product or service offered by the business, the business will be in a more advantageous position compared to the products, technologies, images and services offered by its competitors in all sectors (Aktan and Vural, 2004: 47). The businesses that anticipate the changes in the customer profile and requests in due time and determine the appropriate differentiation will further increase their market share by preserving their competitive position (Bahar and Kozak, 2012: 98). In the differentiation, brand loyalty of the customer is created and the price sensitivity decreases. In the maturing car rental sector, the eligibility necessary for high-priced service differentiation is not clear (Pachon, 2000: 65).

2.3 Focusing Strategy

The focusing strategy is to focus on a specific buyer group, a segment of the product range or geographical market. The business that achieves the focus can potentially earn above the sector average (Porter, 2000: 48). In focusing, it is important to identify the areas where the service providers in the sector place less emphasis or where the customer requests are not adequately responded to (Bahar & Kozak, 2012: 98). In the car rental industry, Enterprise has specialized in insurance. Applications such as nostalgic, limousine, hourly car rental are the focus of the car rental business (Pachon, 2000: 66).

2.4 Stuck in the Middle

Porter describes the businesses that are not in included any group among cost leadership, differentiation and focusing as "stuck in the middle" between the three generic competitive strategies. If the company fails to develop one of the three strategic behaviors mentioned above, it will have a fuzzy organizational culture and conflicting organizational arrangements (Cronshaw et al., 1994: 20). These businesses almost guarantee low profitability. Either they lose high volume customers who demand low prices or they have to give up their profits to get the business from low cost enterprises (Porter, 2000: 52).

3 Research Methodology

Survey technique from the quantitative research methods was used in the research. The survey includes questions that measure demographic and competitive strategies variables. The 15 questions that measure the level of implementation of the companies' competitive strategies and 15 questions financial and non-financial firm performance were taken from Türkay (2007) and Taşkın et al. (2011). All questions were measured using the 5-point Likert scale (1: very low; 5: very high). According to the procedure suggested by Wilson (2010) the questionnaires were pretested on 30 respondents. After analyzing the pretest results, was modified the wordings of some statements in the questionnaire.

The research was conducted face to face and online questionnaire technique with car rental managers in Turkey's Istanbul and Antalya provinces between January and October of 2016. Convenience sampling method, one of the non-random sampling methods, was preferred in the research (Altunışık et al., 2005: 132). Each car rental business responding to the survey was included in the sample. A total of 200 people was reached and since no missing data was found, all questionnaires were included in the analysis. In the evaluation of the

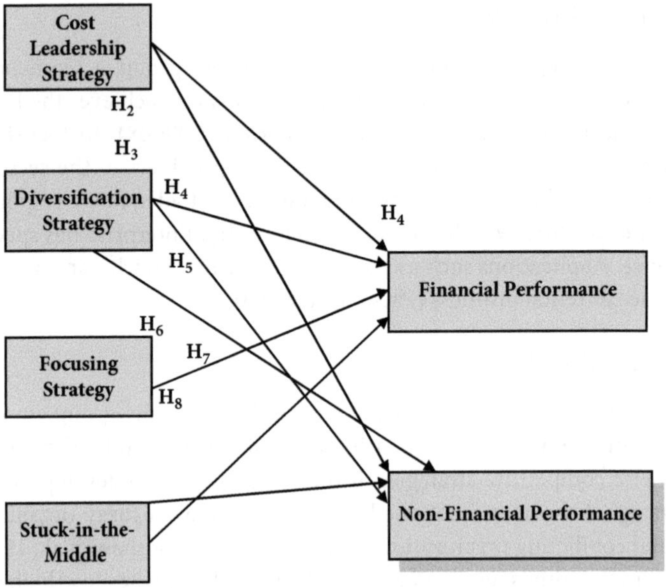

Fig. 1: Model of the research

measurement model, the Smart PLS 3 package program using the partial least squares method was used (Ringle et al., 2015).

3.1 Model of the Research

The research model created in line with the objectives of the research is shown in Fig. 1. differentiation, focusing, cost leadership among competitive strategies of companies and stuck in the middle and its (financial and non-financial) effect on performance of companies are determined by research model.

4 Findings of the Research

4.1 Demographic Findings of the Research

The majority of the managers participating in the research are male (90.5 %) and senior managers (56.5 %). 57.5 % of the managers are married and 42.5 % are single. Businesses prefer both daily and operational renting (70.5 %) among market segments. 38,5 % of the managers have associate degree, 33,0 % are high school graduates and 14,5 % are undergraduates. It can be said that the car rental sector in Turkey is managed by well-trained managers. In businesses, tourism graduates account for only 10.5 %. Besides, the ratio of business graduates is 20,5 %, automotive 8,5 %, economy 7,5 % and percentage of the individuals marking the option "other" is 53 %. Other graduated fields are sociology, philosophy, history, geography, foreign trade, graphic design, computer, public administration, finance, public relations, construction-machinery and electronics engineering. Despite being a tourism activity, it is observed that the areas where the managers take education are different. It is noted that 21.5 % (43) of the vehicle rental companies operating in Istanbul and Antalya have between 3 and 17 vehicles, 26.5 % (53) have between 18 and 31 vehicles, 26.0 % (52) have between 32 and 73 and 72 % and 26 % (52) have between 73 and 125 respectively. It is also observed that 49.5 % (99) of these enterprises have 0–1 branches and 50.5 % (101) of them have 2–90 branches in terms of the number of branches. The survey of 200 people was conducted in Istanbul (50 %) and Antalya (50 %).

4.2 Measurement Model Findings

Internal consistency is used to assess the suitability of the measurement model. Cronbach's alpha coefficient and combined reliability values are used in controlling the internal consistency (Fornell and Larcker, 1981). Each construct must have a Cronbach's alpha coefficient greater than 0.6 (Nunnally and Bernstein, 1994) and a combined reliability value greater than 0.8 (Werts et al., 1974). Tab. 1 shows the Cronbach's alpha coefficient and combined reliability coefficient for each structure. These results indicate that internal consistency is achieved.

The validity of the measurement model depends on the provision of convergent validity and discriminative validity criteria. Standardized factor loadings and t values are used in evaluating convergent validity (Fornell and Larcker 1981). The fact that the factor loads are greater than 0.4 and all t-values are significant at $\alpha = 0.001$ level indicate that the convergent validity criterion is achieved.

In the evaluation of discriminant validity, the correlation values and the square root values of the mean variance are compared. In Tab. 2, the correlation values have been found to be lower than the diagonal values and it has been found that discriminant validity is achieved.

4.3 Testing of Structural Model and Hypothesis

The structural model has been assessed using standard path coefficients, significance (t-statistic) and R^2 estimates (See Fig. 2). Tab. 3 shows the results of the hypothesis tests. The R^2 for financial and non-financial performance are 0.584 and 0.684, respectively. This shows that the exogenous variable of each structure constitutes approximately 58 % and 68 % of the variance of each structure.

Tab. 1: Reliability and validity

Structure and Statements	Factor Loading	t-value	*a* Cronbach	Comp. R.	AVE
Diversification Strategy			*,81*	*,87*	*,64*
DS-1	,783	17.088			
DS-2	,860	33.079			
DS-3	,877	52.468			
DS-4	,764	20.154			
Cost Leadership Strategy			,68	,81	,59
CLS-1	,420	4.107			
CLS-2	,820	29.026			
CLS-3	,777	18.012			
CLS-4	,710	12.290			
Focusing Strategy			,82	,88	,64
FS-1	,829	28.992			
FS-2	,817	31.193			
FS-3	,781	21.388			
FS-4	,801	24.036			
Stuck-in-the-middle			,76	,86	,67
SMS-1	,832	29.594			
SMS-2	,777	16.643			
SMS-3	,776	20.471			
Financial Performance			,86	,89	,61
FP-1	,824	31.974			
FP-2	,754	18.777			
FP-3	,811	21.747			
FP-4	,894	52.967			
FP-5	,792	25.223			
Non-Financial Performance			,92	,93	,67
NFP-1	,627	9.317			
NFP-2	,822	29.718			
NFP-3	,823	25.168			
NFP-4	,866	44.705			
NFP-5	,862	41.632			
NFP-6	,859	35.108			

Note: All loadings are significant at level $p < 0.001$.

Tab. 2: Correlations of variables

Discriminant Validity	Cost Leaders.	Financial Perform.	Focus	Stuck-in-the-middle	Non-Finan. Perform.	Service Divers.
Cost Leaders.	0,79[a]					
Financial P.	0,58	0,82				
Focus	0,71	0,71	0,81			
Stuck-in-the-middle	0,59	0,60	0,67	0,80		
Non-Financial P.	0,62	0,82	0,77	0,65	0,81	
Service Divers.	0,55	0,68	0,73	0,65	0,74	0,82

a = The values on the diagonal are the square root of the mean variance

The r^2 values should be greater than the recommended value of 0.10 (Falk and Miller, 1992).

In the Fig. 2, t values and β coefficients for explaining the relations between variables are indicated on the arrows. Parameter estimates have a significance of 0.05 if t values exceed 1.96 and of 0.01 if they exceed 2.56 (Çokluk et al., 2012: 304). In order to examine whether competitive strategies have an effect on firm performance, the relationships shown in the structural model have been examined. When the t values were analyzed, the relations between cost leadership, financial and non-financial performance are significant at a level of 0.05 the relationship between differentiation and focusing strategies and financial and non-financial performance are significant at a level of 0.01.

In the structural model, the paths with a t value less than 1.96 (red colored paths and figures) are not statistically significant and should be deleted (Taşkın and Akat, 2010: 60). Since the effect of being stuck in the middle on both financial and non-financial performance is statistically insignificant ($\beta = 0.098$ and 0.124, $t < 1.96$), these paths are shown in red and deleted.

These hypotheses have been accepted as the relevant variable effect of hypotheses H_1, H_2, H_3, H_4, H_5 and H_6 ($t > 1.96$) have been found according to the results of the hypothesis tests in the above table. Hypotheses H_7 and H_8 have been rejected due to the fact that their effects on the related variable ($t < 1.96$) have not been found.

5 Conclusion and Assessment

The car rental establishments within the highway transportation, one of the transportation sub-systems of the tourism industry and which presents

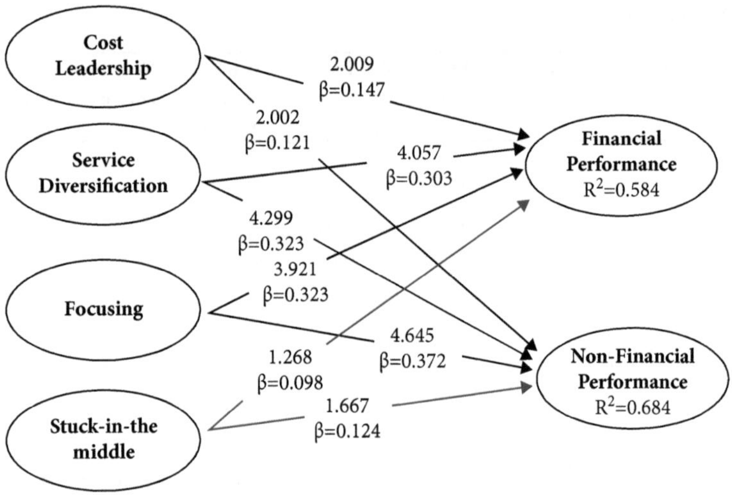

Fig. 2: Estimated results of the model

Tab. 3: Hypotheses tests

Hypothesis			**t-Value**	**p-Value**	**Results**
Cost Leadership	→	Financial Performance	2.009	0.045*	Supported
Cost Leadership	→	Non-Financial Perform.	2.002	0.045*	Supported
Service Divers.	→	Financial Performance	4.057	0.000**	Supported
Service Divers.	→	Non-Financial Perform.	4.299	0.000**	Supported
Focusing	→	Financial Performance	3.921	0.000**	Supported
Focusing	→	Non-Financial Perform.	4.645	0.000**	Supported
Stuck-in-the-middle	→	Financial Performance	1.268	0.205	Not Supported
Stuck-in-the-middle	→	Non-Financial Perform.	1.667	0.096	Not Supported

$p < .01$**, $p < .05$*

speed, flexibility, comfort and individuality for the tourists while reaching a destination, emerged with the start of the serial production of the automobile in 20th century. These establishments play a big role in moving the tourists from the tourism market and tourist destinations and in their trips within the destination. Although there have been important developments in the researches on tourism recently, there are a few number of works regarding the car rental establishments which have an important role in tourism transportation.

This empirical study focused on relationships between service differentiation strategy, cost leadership strategy, focusing strategy, stuck in the middle and organization performance within the car rental sector. As a result of the study, it has been empirically tested that the financial and non-financial performances of the car rental establishments that follow the cost leadership, service differentiation and focusing strategies have increased. It is also empirically supported that there is no increase in the performance of companies that have not followed these strategies and are stuck in between. These results confirm the hypothesis of Porter (2000) that businesses implementing the three general strategies will increase in performance, while those that are stuck in between without implementing are "almost guaranteed to have low profitability".

It can be stated that establishments implementing cost leadership, service differentiation and focusing strategies may provide important contributions and gains towards their performance. There will be no positive effect on the performances of the establishments that are not directed towards any of these strategies and that are stuck in between. No studies that examine the relationship between being stuck in between and financial and non-financial performance have been encountered in the tourism literature. It can be stated that the research is unique with that aspect.

In line with these findings, it is suggested that car rental managers should give importance to service differentiation, cost leadership and focusing strategies, and adapt these strategies systematically. Besides, it is important to systematically measure the performances of the establishments. It should be borne in mind, however, that the strategies applied and the dimensions used for performance evaluation are only tools, but they can help improve business performance when implemented and managed correctly.

References

Aktan, C. Coşkun & Vural, Y. Istiklal (2004). Rekabet gücü ve rekabet stratejileri, Ankara: TISK Yayınları.

Altunışık, R., Coşkun, R., Bayraktaroğlu, S. & Yıldırım, E. (2005). *Sosyal bilimlerde araştırma yöntemleri (SPSS uygulamalı)*, 4. Baskı, Sakarya: Sakarya Yayıncılık.

Auto Rental News (2018). Fact Book 2017, www.autorentalnews.com/fileviewer/2689.aspx, Retrieved from: 10.02.2018.

Bahar, O. & Kozak, M. (2012). Turizm ve rekabet. Ankara: Detay Yayıncılık.

Cronshaw, M., Davis, E. & Kay, J. (1994). On being stuck in the Middle or Good Food Cost Less at Sainsbur, Biritish Journal of Management, 5 (3), pp. 19–32.

Çokluk, Ö; Şekercioğlu, G & Büyüköztürk, Ş. (2012). Sosyal bilimler için çok değişkenli istatistik SPSS ve LISREL uygulamaları, Ankara: Pegem Akademi.

Datamonitor (2011). Avis Budget Group Company Profile, www.datamonitor.com, Retrieved from: 01.01.2013.

Enright, M. J., & Newton, J. (2004). Tourism destination competitiveness: A quantitative approach, Tourism Management, 25 (12), pp. 777–788.

Falk, R.F. & Miller, N.B. (1992). A Primer for Soft Modelling. USA: OHIO: University of Akron Press.

Fornell, C., & Larcker, D. F. (1981). Evaluating structural equation models with unobservable variables and measurement error, Journal of Marketing Research, 18 (1), pp. 39–50.

Garcia, M., Cortes, E., Marco-Lajara, B. & Zaragoza-Sáez, P. (2014). Strategy, training and performance fit, International Journal of Hospitality Management, 42 (11), pp. 100–116.

Gençler, G. (2012). Beyaz filo faaliyet raporu. www.beyazfilo.com, Retrieved from: 12.12.2012. http://www.turizmgazetesi.com/news.aspx?id=71446. Retrieved from: 20.10.2013.

Karaboğa, K. (2012). Araç kiralama sektörünün 1.6 milyarlık yatırımı. www.dunya.com/print.php?type, Retrieved from: 12.02.2013.

Lo, Y. H. (2012). Back to hotel strategic management 101: An examination of hotels' implementation of Porter's generic strategy in China, The Journal of International Management Studies, 7 (1), pp. 56–69.

Mancini, M. (2012). Access: Introduction to Tourism and Travel, USA: Wiley Publishing.

Marijanovic, K. (2010). Differentiation of car rental services in the Croatian market, Preliminary Communication, XX (II), pp. 113–128.

MEB (Milli Eğitim Bakanlığı) (2006). Konaklama ve seyahat hizmetleri rezervasyon sistemleri, mesleki eğitim ve öğretim sisteminin güçlendirilmesi projesi, Milli Eğitim Bakanlığı Yayınları, Ankara.

Newton, S., Gilinsky, A. & Jordan, D. (2015). Differentiation strategies and winery financial performance: An empirical investigation. Wine Economics and Policy, 12 (4), pp. 88–97.

Nunnally, J. C. & Bernstein, I. H. (1994). The assessment of reliability. Psychometric Theory, 3 (1), pp. 248–292.

Pachon, E. J. (2000). Strategic and Tactical Fleet Planning for the Car Rental Industry, Doctoral Theses, USA: University of Miami.

Porter, M. (2000). Rekabet stratejileri sektör ve rakip analizi teknikleri, (Çev. Ulubilgen, Gülen), Istanbul: Sistem Yayıncılık.

Ringle, C. M., Wende, S. & Becker, J. M. (2015). Smartpls 3. Boenningstedt: SmartPLS, http://www.smartpls.com, Retrieved from: 10.11.2016.

Taşkın, E., Kayabaşı, E. & Kiracı, H. (2011). Rekabetçi yöntemlerin işletme performansı üzerinde etkisi: İnegöl'de faaliyet gösteren ve ihracat yapan işletmeler üzerine bir alan araştırması, *Pazarlama ve Pazarlama Araştırmaları Dergisi*, 8 (2), pp. 105–122.

Taşkın, Ç & Akat, Ö. (2010). Araştırma yöntemlerinde yapısal eşitlik modelleme, Bursa: Ekin Yayınevi.

Türkay, O. (2007). Pazara dayalı örgütsel öğrenme: Konaklama işletmelerinde pazara dayalı örgütsel öğrenmeyi etkileyen değişkenler ve pazarlama performansına etkileri, Doktora Tezi, İzmir: Dokuz Eylül Üniversitesi,S.B.E.

Tyya, N. T. (2007). Hospitality & tourism industry employers, USA: Vault Inc.

Werts, C. E., Linn, R. L., & Jöreskog, K. G. (1974). Intraclass reliability estimates: Testing structural assumptions. Educational and Psychological Measurement, 34 (1), pp. 25–33.

Wilson, J. (2010). Essentials of Business Research: A Guide to Doing Your Research project, England: Sage Publishing.

Bengü Hırlak[1] and Ergün Kara[2]

Organizational Change and Leadership

1 Introduction

In the face of the socio-cultural, economic, political and technological developments that are taking place in today's business world, the structures of businesses are becoming more and more complicated and management approaches are changing, and the changes in organizations are accelerating. Businesses shall be able to achieve sustainable competitive advantage, shall make their change plans that shall allow them to adapt to these changes and developments, and they shall develop their change strategies, management and leadership approach and style in order to survive. Because, while some changes experienced may solve problems, sometimes they may cause new problems to arise. Effective leaders shall be required in order to be able to initiate change and to resume it in a successful manner, without ignoring the condition when the elements that may affect the change of a business have emerged. Effective leaders are leaders who do not use power to resist the change, but who may accelerate the change with the strong personal qualities, inspire their followers and manifest a vision. In short, the role of the leaders in managing change is too important that it cannot be denied.

The aim of this study is to underline the importance of leadership in the process of change by addressing the skills and roles that the leaders shall have in order to manage organizational change by identifying the link between change, organizational change, change management and leadership literature.

2 Conceptual Framework

2.1 Change, Organizational Change and Change Management

Change is a concept that affects every aspect of life. Change may happen on everything and everywhere, as the philosopher Herakleitos says, the only thing that does not change is change itself. Economic, socio-cultural, political, technological

1 Kilis 7 Aralık University, Faculty of Economics and Administrative Sciences, Department of Business Administration, benguhirlak@hotmail.com.tr
2 Osmaniye Korkut Ata University, Faculty of Economics and Administrative Sciences, Department of Business Administration, ergunkara@osmaniye.edu.tr

and legal structures are constantly changing besides the individuals. In today's competitive business environment, businesses shall follow and even anticipate these changes occurring around them and determine their plans and strategies accordingly in order to achieve sustainable competitive advantage. While experiencing change in such a rapid pace may sometimes lead to conflicts in organizations, it may cause a great deal of stress for the individuals. Therefore, organizations shall understand what factors affect change, how they shall respond to change, how they shall initiate and manage the change in order to respond to change effectively (Cornell, 1996, p. 23).

Change is defined as the process by which individuals, groups and organizations respond to the dynamic internal and external factors that change the current facts, and process of dealing with the process of moving from the current condition to the desired condition (Singh, 2009; cited by: Goswami, 2015, p. 136). Organizational change, on the other hand, is related to optimizing performance standards of an organization, and this may usually arise depending on the proactive capabilities of the managers of the organization or on the peripheral changes or in response to the presence of a crisis. Regardless of the situation, organizations shall always need a very skilful, good management team to be able to trigger a change and to ensure that this change will be successful (Ebongkeng, 2018, p. 3). Organizational change management is expressed as the application of new procedures or technologies aimed at reorganizing a business environment with changing requirements or taking advantage of business opportunities that emerge (Markovic, 2008, p. 7; Cited by: Goswami, 2015, p. 136).

Change may be caused by many factors, and these factors may be mainly collected in two groups, namely internal and external. These factors are shown in Fig. 1.

Change may be performed proactively and as planned for creating the future, or reactively and adaptively, i.e. in an unplanned manner (Attah, Obera and Isaac, 2017, p. 39). Planned change may take place in two ways: gradual or radical change. In order to adapt to changing conditions, all businesses may make gradual changes from time to time. These changes may cover a wide variety of decisions and actions. For example, roles of organization members may be redefined, new roles may be specified, activities may be re-grouped, organizational structure may be changed, existing systems or procedures may be changed, abandoned, or new ones may be presented (Dawson, 1994, pp. 14–15; Cited by: Bubshait et al. 1998, p. 5). The purpose of radical change is to transform the organization radically into a different style. This type of change involves creating change in values, attitudes and beliefs, which are the elements of organizational

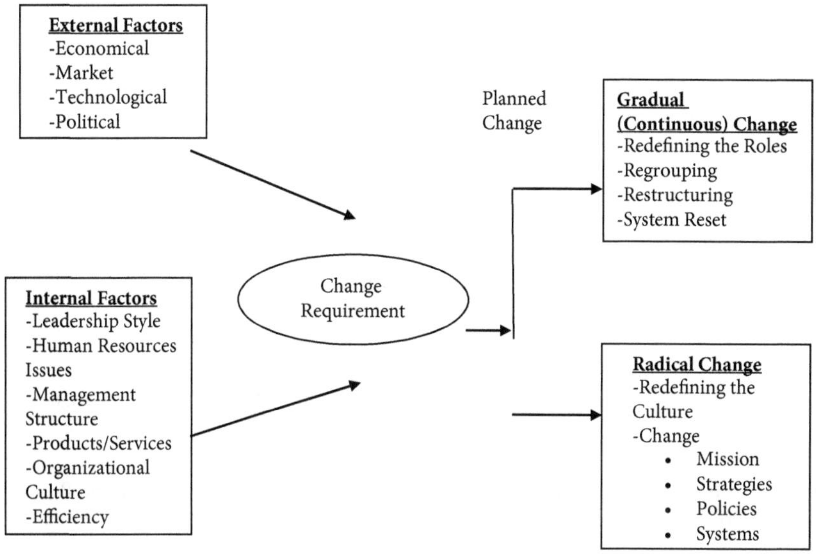

Fig. 1: Change Requirement. Source: Dawson, 1994, pp. 14–15; Cited by: Bubshait, Burney and Nadeem, 1998, p. 5

culture. All attempts to realize a radical change may fail unless a cultural change takes place (Roberts and Hunt, 1991, p. 321; Cited by: Bubshait et al. 1998, p. 5).

Furthermore, Kerber and Buono (2005, pp. 29–30) state that each of these change approaches are guided by two main factors: complexity of the task and the socio-technical uncertainty. The complexity of the task indicates the complexity of the system, the number of essentially different components and the degree of differentiation in the organizational system where the change shall be applied. As you may see in Fig. 2, the optimal situation for the managed change approach is that both levels of the complexity of the task and the socio-technical uncertainty are less. If it is possible to implement change in a relatively simple, routine environment, and if the change involves well-known and accepted actions, managed change may ensure optimal use of limited organizational resources. In this context, ethical and persuasive communication by the change expert/strategist is essential for achieving integrity and credibility. Because the members of the organization shall be less likely to accept the change if they do not trust the person implementing the change and his/her messages. In planned change, the bottom line is complexity of the task. When the complexity of a task is increased, it shall be better to adopt a planned change approach. And for the guided change,

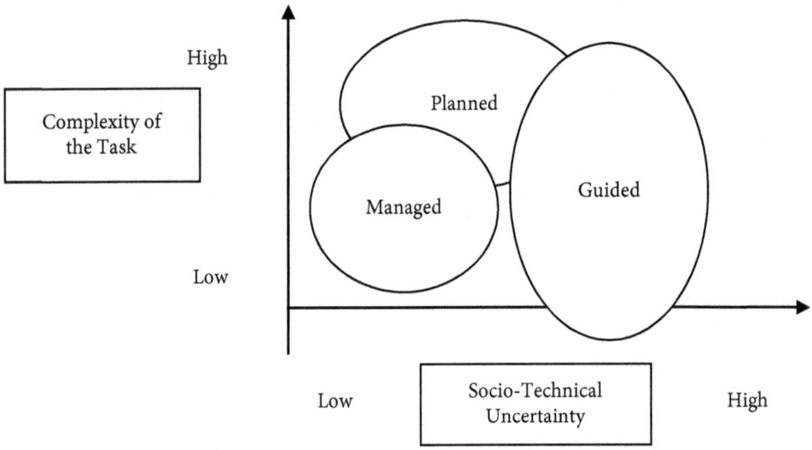

Fig. 2: Complexity, Uncertainty and Approaches of Change. Source: Kerber and Buono, 2005, p. 30

what matters is the socio-technical uncertainty. If the future condition or the solution for the change is not known, managers may not be able to plan the change process carefully and may be able to guide change in a meaningful way even in simple conditions faced. It would be more appropriate to adopt a guided change approach rather than a managed change in such a case.

The process of change in organizations consists of three stages. The first stage is being ready for change and indicates that the members of the organization are ready for change and that they support change. The second stage is adoption. At this stage, change has occurred and the employees have adopted the new methods. However, this adoption process is a trial process and employees deny the change at the end of this stage. The third stage is institutionalization, and change is reinforced until employees internalize the change and consider it as a norm, and required efforts are made to ensure that the adoption stage is resumed (Armenakis and Harris, 2002, p. 169). Organizations may receive four different types of responses to change, change messages, or just to possibilities of change. These are as follows (Cornell, 1996, p. 25):

- **Withdrawal**: This behaviour is related with the thought that the change has not occurred and that the things shall always continue as usual.
- **Resistance**: This behaviour covers sabotaging of the change by opposing to change directly, delaying the implementation of the change, and refusing to cooperate, etc.

- **Acceptance**: This means submitting to the change reluctantly considering that change is inevitable.
- **Embracing/adoption**: This means truly volunteering for change in order to implement the new order of things by looking at new opportunities positively.

Organizations shall always respond to change in the face of change being experienced and adapt themselves to their environment. Businesses, which cannot adapt to this change, shall have their existence under threat after a while (Waddell and Sohal 1998, p. 543).

The management of the organization shall not focus on the requirements of the organization only, and shall not neglect the requirements of its employees in order to reduce the resistance to change and to ensure adoption of the change by the members of the organization. Because, change programs are crucial for the survival and success of the organizations. Neglecting the requirements of the employees may be a serious mistake at this point. If employees are neglected in the planning and implementation of organizational change, this process shall probably very stressful for all employees and the negative impacts of this condition shall be reflected on the organizations as some kind of a cost (McHugh, 1997, pp. 345–359).

As a result of many researches conducted, it has been shown that an important variable for the success of the change is the human factor, and it has been found that the change programs are not successfully implemented without the support of the persons, no matter how well the change program was developed. In this context, it is not required that persons are ready for organizational change only, but they shall also participate in the change (Herscovitch and Meyer, 2002; Cited by: Mangundjaya, Utoya, and Wulandari, 2015, p. 472). In other words, the success of the organizational change is related with the participation of the employees in the change. What is essential is to determine the variables that may increase the participation rate of employees to the change (Mangundjaya et al. 2015, pp. 472–477).

However, although we know that there are many studies related to organizational change in the literature, the studies investigating the effects of change on the individual level and its effects on the behaviour of employees are less in number unfortunately (Rafferty and Griffin, 2006, p. 1154). Yet, perceptions and attitudes of employees against change have a great effect in the implementation of change successfully (Eby, Adams, Russel and Gaby, 2000, p. 420). These perceptions may facilitate or weaken the effectiveness of an intervention aimed for change (Armenakis, Harris and Mossholder, 1993, Lewin, 1951, Cited by: Susanto, 2008, p. 51).

There are many studies that address the importance of the leader in initiating of the change in the literature. Transformational leadership style, which is closely bound up with change, draws more attention in the execution of the change in these studies. This style of leadership is discussed under the next heading, "leadership", in this study.

2.2 Leadership

Leadership term is of English origin, and "Lead" as a verb is described to guide, to direct; and "Leader" is described as chief, guide, head, commander, captain, pioneer (Redhouse, 2005). Leadership has been the subject of many studies in popular and academic literature as a concept and a whole body of applications. It is stated that leadership may be defined infinitely under eleven main categories, namely "focal point of the group process, art of assuring obedience, influencing, behaviour, form of persuasion, relation of power, means of achieving goals, result of interaction, differentiation of roles, activator of a structure and combination of different elements" (Bass, 1990a, pp. 19–20). Leadership is the ability to instil support and confidence in people who need to achieve organizational goals (Dubrin, 2012, p. 346). Leadership is guiding the persons in the organization in a proactive work for ensuring motivational process, inspiration, and following up of organizational goals (Hill and McShane, 2008, p. 404). The main task of the leaders consists of the realization of the organizational goals. Thus, leadership means directing a group of people toward the accomplishment of a task or the reaching of an endpoint through various ethically based means (Rowe and Guerrero, 2011, p. 2).

Leadership is being capable of influencing others in order to achieve the specified goals, leading the organization to become more consistent and harmonious (Sharma and Jain, 2013, p. 310), Management is also a process used to reach organizational goals successfully just as leadership (Bohoris and Vorria, http://www.ep.liu.se/ecp/026/076/ecp0726076.pdf, p. 2). However, while there are similarities between the leaders and the managers in terms of the goals to be achieved, it may be said that there are differences in terms of the means they use. Some of these differences are provided in Tab. 1.

Developments and changes experienced have revealed new leadership approaches such as transformational, charismatic and interactional leadership, etc. One of the most comprehensive leadership theories for organizational transformation is transformational and transactional leadership theories. While Burns (1978) has brought forth initial ideas about transformative and transactional leadership in political terms, Bass (1985) has improved these leadership

Tab. 1: Comparison of a Leader and a Manager. Source: Bennis, 1989, p. 7; Lunenburg, 2011, p. 2

Leader	Manager
Is innovative	Manages
Is genuine	Is a copy
Improves, provide strength, creates the future	Protects, supervises, develop the current condition
Has a long-term perspective	Has a short-term perspective
Asks what and why	Asks how and when
Challenges status quo	Accepts status quo
Focuses on persons	Focus on the job, system and structure
Looks at external environment	Looks at internal environment
Creates a vision	Applies plans
Sees the whole forest	Sees trees
Considers employees as colleagues	Considers employees as subordinates
Trusts and improves employees	Directs and controls employees
Does the right things	Does things in the right way
Creates change	Manages change
Serves his/her subordinates	Serves his/her superiors

approaches and defined them in organizational terms (Eisenbach, Watson and Pillai, 1999, pp. 83–85). These approaches may be described as follows:

- ***Transformational Leadership***: Transformational leadership is a style of leadership that emerges as a result of the transformation process between the leaders and their followers. Leaders offer awards for their followers' performances. Transformational leaders shall apply the change after developing a vision first. This may only be achieved with intellectual stimulation, i.e. leaders set challenging targets for their employees and encourage them to rethink about their old ways of doing business. Leader may render the change attractive and achieve the change successfully by ensuring that it addresses the achievement and improvement requirements of the employees only. If the leader may provide support, coaching and guidance for his/her employees with an individualized approach in this process, this may facilitate the change. These coaching and guidance actions are particularly important for achieving large-scale transformations and ensuring the creation of self-managing teams. And many of the modern businesses are adopting teamwork for the construction of an organization, which is an important cultural transformation in itself. (Eisenbach et al. 1999, pp. 83–85). Transformational leadership has some key qualities that allow it to be distinguished from other types of leadership. These features are listed as follows (Bass, 1990b, p. 22):

- **Charisma**: Determination of mission, vision and culture, taking pride, gaining respect and confidence.
- **Inspiration**: Using symbols that direct efforts, expressing important goals with simple methods.
- **Intellectual stimulation**: Providing support for resolution of problems in intelligent, rational, and careful manner.
- **Individualised consideration**: Offering personal interest, coaching and counselling for each individual.

- ***Transactional Leadership***: Transactional leadership is a model based on mutual exchange. In this type of exchange, the followers are awarded with a prize when they fulfil their duties and face a punishment when they do not. The leader uses organizational resources to ensure his/her followers are obedient and willing to work (Grundstein, 1999, p. 150). Transactional leaders have certain features. These are listed as follows (Bass, 1990b, p. 22):
  - **Contingent reward**: Promising prizes for good performances and recognition of the successes.
  - **Management by exception (active)**: Investigation of deviations from rules and standards, taking corrective measures.
  - **Management by exception (passive)**: Intervening when standards are not met only.
  - **Laissez-faire**: Not taking responsibility, avoiding making decisions.

  According to Burns (1978), transactional leadership occurs when a person or a leader makes an attempt to make changes and communicate by going making a deal on some issues and taking decisions together (Kuhnert and Lewis, 1987, p. 648). According to Bass (1990b, pp. 19–21), transformational leaders inspire and provide energy to their employees, are charismatic, cause intellectual stimulation, and may meet the emotional requirements of their employees. Bass also suggests that leaders may learn the skills they need to become a transformational leader trough training and that they may learn the techniques required. A transformational leader is defined as a source of vision, creativity and inspiration that drives the change (Al-Qura'an, 2015, p. 1).
- ***Charismatic Leadership***: Max Weber described charisma as an effect that is not based on authority of an office, or the condition of followers ascribing extraordinary qualities to their leaders. Charismatic leaders usually emerge during transition periods of organizations and under stressful conditions (Edwards 2012, p. 14). Charismatic leadership is related to values that the

followers attribute to their leaders and the personal characteristics of leaders (Pawar and Eastman, 1997, p. 84).

2.3 The Role of Leadership in Organizational Change

Organizational change is defined as a deliberate effort by the leader or manager of the organization aimed at improving the organization. While it is possible that internal and external factors such as technological, social or economic or motivational factors may lie behind the change process, it is also possible that visions and innovative ideas of organization leaders may lie behind it, too (Abbas and Asghar, 2010, p. 18).

Curry (1992, pp. 23–25) has cited many different authors to identify various roles that the leaders may play to facilitate the change. These are (Cited by: Gray, 1997, pp. 8–9):

Leaders play an important role in the institutionalization of organizations, creating an environment where change can take place or affecting the perceptions and attitudes of members of the organization.

- Leaders help to identify and to shape the issues that lead to innovation, to define the organization as an environment, to facilitate discussions, and to encourage more participation in innovative activities. They ensure participation of other members of the organization to the decision making process.
- Leaders create coalitions to support change, and they follow the important processes.
- Leaders may provide finance and other incentives for participation in the change process.
- Leaders are the sponsors of change sponsors, and they attempt to create a synergy.
- Leaders perform tasks that may facilitate change such as collecting information, communicating with other members of the organization, developing new coalitions, and identifying existing coalitions that perceive their members as stakeholders within this process.
- Leaders shall have a vision so that they may initiate the change. Moreover, decision-making and communication processes shall be mutual. Otherwise, the culture that was created as a result of the change shall not be shared.

According to Pagon et al. (2008, p. 4), competencies that shall be found in the leaders for a successful and effective change management are given in Fig. 3.

According to Gill (2002, pp. 307–309), if we consider change as taking an organization to a journey from its current condition to the future, dealing with

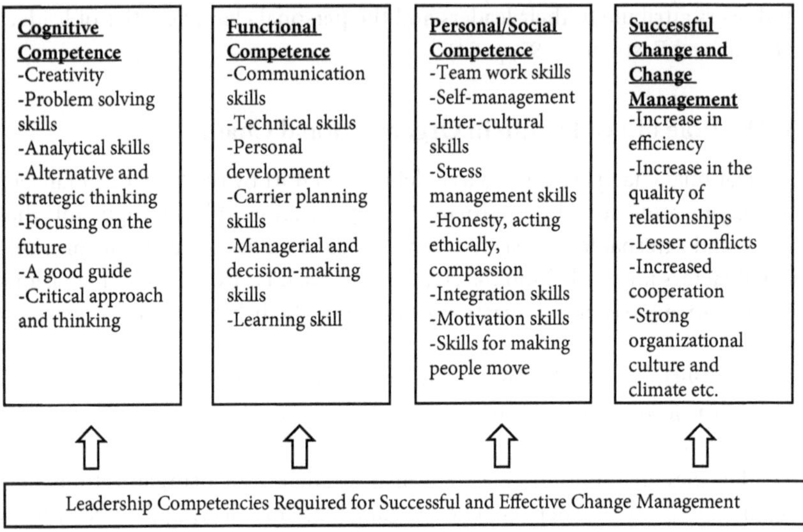

Fig. 3: Competencies Required in Leaders for Successful and Effective Change Management. Source: Pagon et al. 2008, p. 4

problems that occur in course of the journey shall be related with leadership besides being related with management. Change shall be well managed, planned, organized and inspected. Effective leadership is required to be able to accomplish the change successfully, i.e. it is the leader that makes the difference. In order to manage change successfully, an effective leader shall meet some different aspects and requirements. These are as follows (Gill, 2002, p. 311):

- **The intellectual/cognitive aspects and requirements of leadership (thinking)**: Effective leaders shall understand the information using their intellectual and cognitive skills, and they shall reason with knowledge, imagine the possibilities, make judgements, solve problems and make decisions.
- **The spiritual/moral aspects and requirements of leadership (meaning)**: The spiritual aspect of leadership is about the desire to have a meaning and to feeling of being esteemed that motivate people on what they are doing and searching for. This feeling of having a meaning and being esteemed depends on the vision and values shared. For example; Xerox PARC's guru John Seely Brown described the purpose of leader today as creating meaning and winning people's souls, not just to make money (Dess and Picken, 2000).
- **The emotional aspects and requirements of leadership (emotions)**: Effective leadership also requires a well-developed emotional intelligence. Emotional

intelligence is expressed as the ability to understand oneself and other people, to ensure self-control and self-confidence, and to respond to others in appropriate forms. Leaders with high emotional intelligence use their personal power instead of their official power or authority.

- **The behavioural aspects and requirements of leadership (actions)**: Behavioural skills required for leadership covers, for example, both using emotions and responding to emotions using body language, as well as communicating by writing, speaking, listening and physical behaviour using personal power.

3 Conclusion and Discussion

Change is an essential concept, which never goes out of date and always continues to be discussed, in the field of management. Today, we experience continuous change in all kinds of structures as an inevitable condition due to vital reasons. The developments in the field of science and technology, which have an important role in satisfaction of human requirements in particular, force organizations to undergo a serious structural change. Therefore, it is only possible for organizations to sustain their existence in line with their missions, only by keeping up with current developments and changes. Organizations are trying to meet the demands that arise as a result of all developments that are experienced, and to adapt to change. Leaders shall have a significant effect on achieving this adaptation. However, it is almost impossible that these continuous organizational changes may be succeeded by managers with lesser visions. Thus, managers with leadership qualities are required in order to ensure a successful transformation in the organizations. Managers with different leadership qualities are employed in today's organizations. It is not enough for a leader just to motivate his or her employees on work, to take steps to improve their performance or to motivate them. The leader shall also have the knowledge and technique to ensure that the organizational change is carried out successfully.

Many researches on the role of leaders in organizational change show that leaders who attach importance to participation in organizational decisions, who are agreeable with a democratic approach, and who keep their communication channels always open are more successful in the works for achieving change. This leadership style, which may keep up with the changes that may occur around the business while keeping its organizations at the top level in terms of efficiency, is named as the "Transformational Leadership Model" within the literature. Thus, transformational leadership has become the most preferred and accepted leadership model for organizational change. Transformational leaders work to determine the most appropriate vision for the organization and to realize radical changes that shall be performed in economic, social and technological terms to reach their goals in line with this vision. A transformational leader shall create a detailed plan of change and manage the process in the best way to bring the organization to the future in the most appropriate way for its current condition. Failure shall be inevitable if the organizational change process can not be planned and managed properly.

When the need for change arises, it shall be ensured that the necessary infrastructure conditions are met and that the change is perceived positively in both personal and organizational contexts in order to realize the change. In such a condition, it would also be possible to remove any resistance that may cause the change to fail. At this point, leaders shall ensure the harmony and consistency of the change process with the strategies, policies, visions, goals, objectives, values, and beliefs of the business in order to manage the change well. They shall take necessary precautions to prevent resistance against change, to keep communication channels open, and to support the development of the skills and knowledge required for change. Differences in organizational structure shall also be considered in the change. Because the structure of each organization is different and the change made in one organization may not be suitable for another organization. All differences shall be considered when you are managing a change. Changes applied regularly and properly by considering organizational culture and structure will be successful.

References

Abbas, W. and Asghar, I. (2010). The Role of Leadership in Organisational Change: Relating the Successful Organisational Change to Visionary and Innovative Leadership. Masters Thesis. Faculty of Engineering And Sustainable Development, University of Gavle.

Al-Qura'an Atif. (2015). "The Impact of Transformational Leadership on Organizational Change Management: Case Study at Jordan Ahli Bank", IORS Journal of Business and Management, 17 (12): 1–7.

Armenakis, A. A., Harris, S. G. and Mossholder, K. W. (1993). "Creating Readiness for Organizational Change", Human Relations, 46 (June): 681–703.

Armenakis, A. A. and Harris, S. G. (2002). "Crafting a Change Message to Create Transformational Readiness", Journal of Organizational Change Management, 15 (2): 169–183.

Attah, E. Y., Obera, V. A. and Isaac, S. (2017). "Effective Leadership and Change Management for Sustainable Development in Nigeria", International Journal of Public Administration and Management Research, 4 (2): 37–42.

Bass, B. M. (1985). Leadership and Performance beyond Expectations, Free Press, New York, NY.

Bass, B. M. (1990a). Bass and Stodgill's Handbook of Leadership: Theory, Research and Managerial Applications, Free Press, New York, NY.

Bass, B. M. (1990b). "From Transactional to Transformational Leadership Learning to Share Vision", Organizational Dynamics, 18 (3) 19–31.

Bennis, W. G. (1989). "Managing the Dream: Leadership in the 21st Century", Journal of Organizational Change Management, 2 (1): 6–10.

Bohoris, G. A. and Vorria, E. P. "Leadership vs Management: A Business Excellence/Performance Management View", Helsingborg: Lund University. http://www.ep.liu.se/ecp/026/076/ecp0726076.pdf, 1–8, Erişim: 10.07.2018.

Bubshait, K. A., Burney, M. A. and Nadeem, I. A. (1998). "An Integrated Model for Managing Organizational Change", Journal of King Abdulaziz University: Islamic Economics, JKAU, Econ. & Adm. 11: 3–14.

Burns, J. M. (1978). Leadership, Harper & Row, New York, NY.

Cornell, J. (1996). "Aspects of the Management of Change", Journal of Management in Medicine, 10 (2): 23–30.

Curry, B. K. (1992). Instituting Enduring Innovations: Achieving Continuity of Change in Higher Education. ASHE-ERIC Higher Education Report, No. 7. Washington, D.C. School of Education and Human Development, George Washington University.

Dawson, P. (1994). Organizational Change: A Processual Approach, London: Paul Chapman Publishing Company.

Dess, G. G. and Picken, J. C. (2000). "Changing Roles: Leadership in the 21st Century", Organizational Dynamics, 28 (3): 18–34.

Dubrin, A. J. (2012). Essentials of Management, Ninth Edition, South-Western Cengage Learning.

Ebongkeng, H. (2018). Organizational Change and Performance. Case Study: African Financial Company SOFINA S.A, Cameroon, Thesis Centria University Of Applied Science Business Management.

Eby, L. T., Adams, D. M., Russel, J. E. A. and Gaby, S. H. (2000). "Perceptions of Organizational Readiness: Factor Related to Employees' Reactions to the Implementation of Team Based Selling", Human Relation, 53 (March): 419–442.

Edwards, E. R. (2012). Charisma, and the Fictions of Black Leadership. University of Minnesota Press, London, UK.

Eisenbach, R., Watson, K. and Pillai, R. (1999). "Transformational Leadership in the Context of Organizational Change", Journal of Organizational Change Management, 12 (2), 80–88.

Gill, R. (2002). "Change Management or Change Leadership?", Journal of Change Management, 3 (4): 307–318, DOI: 10.1080/714023845.

Goswami, M. (2015). "Employee Specific Attributes for Managing Organisational Change: An Empirical Study", The International Journal of Business & Management, 3 (8): 135–141.

Gray, P. J. (1997). "Viewing Assessment as an Innovation: Leadership and the Change Process", New Directions for Higher Education, 100: 5–15.

Grundstein, R. A. (1999). "Bilateral Transformational Leadership an Approach for Fostering Ethical Conduct in Public Service Organizations", Administration & Society, 31 (2): 247–260.

Herscovitch, L. and Meyer, J. P. (2002). "Commitment to Organizational Change: Extension of a Three-Component Model", Journal of Applied Psychology, 87, 474–487.

Hill, C. W. L. and McShane S. L. (2008). Principles of Management, The McGraw-Hill Companies Publication, Boston.

Kerber, K. and Buono, A.F. (2005). "Rethinking Organizational Change: Reframing the Challenge of Change Management", Organization Development Journal, 23 (3): 23–38.

Kuhnert, K. and Lewis, P. (1987). "Transactional and Transformational Leadership: Constructive/Developmental Analysis", Academy of Management Review, 11 (4): 648–657.

Lewin, K. (1951). Field Theory in Social Science. New York: Harper and Row.

Lunenburg, F. C. (2011). "Leadership Versus Management: A Key Distinction—at Least in Theory". International Journal of Management, Business, and Administration, 14 (1): 1–4.

Mangundjaya, W., Utoya, D. and Wulandari, P. (2015). "The Role of Leadership and Employee's Condition on Reaction to Organizational Change", Procedia - Social and Behavioral Sciences, 172: 471–478.

Marković, R. M. (2008). "Managing the Organizational Change and Culture in the Age of Globalization", Journal of Business Economics and Management, 9 (1): 3–11.

McHugh, M. (1997). "The Stress Factor: Another Item for the Change Management Agenda?", Journal of Organizational Change Management, 10 (4): 345–362.

Pagon, M., Banutai, E. and Bizjak. U. (2008). Leadership Competencies for Successful Change Management, A Preliminary Study Report, University of Maribor, Slovenia, 1–25.

Pawar, S. B. and Eastman, K. K. (1997). "The Nature and Implications of Contextual Influences on Transformational Leadership: A Conceptual Examination", Academy of Management Review, 22 (1): 80–109.

Rafferty, A. and Griffin, M. (2006). "Perceptions of Organizational Change: A Stress and Coping Perspective", Journal of Applied Psychology, 91 (5): 1154–1162.

Redhouse Sözlüğü (2005). Redhouse Sözlüğü Yeni, El Sözlüğü, İngilizce-Türkçe/Türkçe-İngilizce, Redhouse Yayınevi, İstanbul.

Roberts, K. H. and Hunt, D. M. (1991). Organizational Behavior, Boston: PWS-Kent Publishing Company.

Rowe, W. G. and Guerrero, L. (2011). Cases in Leadership, Second Edition, Ivey Casebook Series, Sage Publications, United States of America.

Sharma, M. K. and Jain, S. (2013). "Leadership Management: Principles, Models and Theories", Global Journal of Management and Business Studies, 3 (3): 309–318.

Singh, K. (2009). Organizational Behaviour: Text and Cases, Pearson Education India.

Susanto, A. B. (2008). "Organizational Readiness for Change: A Case Study on Change Readiness in a Manufacturing Company in Indonesia", International Journal of Management Perspectives, 2 (1): 50–61.

Waddell, D. and Sohal A. S. (1998). "Resistance: A Constructive Tool for Change Management", Management Decision, 36 (8): 543–548.

Erkan Alsu[1] and Bilge Apaydin[2]

Prediction of the Gold Price per Ounce Using Artificial Neural Networks

1 Introduction

Gold is a precious metal that has been in use for a long time, either as an ornament, an investment tool or raw material in many fields of the industry (electronics, dentistry, medicine, decoration, and engineering). Gold is traded by investors instantly in gold exchanges in many countries. It is also used as an investment or saving tool through the gold funds provided by banks.

Persons wishing to make investments want to have the tools to make sound estimates of macroeconomic variables such as inflation rates, share prices, the exchange rates and gold prices (Benli and Yildiz, 2014). Gold prices are prone to fluctuations due to economic and political reasons (Yuksel and Akkoc, 2016). Gold prices constantly change all around the world and for gold investors, making accurate estimates of gold prices is vital (Kocatepe and Yildiz, 2016). Estimates for gold prices are made in the short term (hourly, daily, weekly), medium term (monthly and quarterly) and long-term (annual and longer) (Dolgun, Saracbası and Yeniler, 2014).

Gold is a precious item on the markets, which still makes it a valuable investment tool and that in itself makes investors keep a close eye on fluctuations in gold prices. Any changes in gold prices impact on financial markets with changes in real and financial markets causing fluctuations in gold prices (Doganalp, Konya and Kabaloglu, 2016).

For many years, the Turkish public has seen gold as a reliable investment tool. Gold is also seen as the safest investment tool especially in times of crises and war. For investors who wish to make high returns on their investments, the importance of making a correct estimate of gold prices cannot be overrated.

Artificial neural network (ANN) is a data processing system inspired by biological neural networks that simulate neural networks of the human brain (Kaynar and Tastan, 2009). Artificial neural networks create their own experiences with

1 Assit. Prof. Dr., Gaziantep University, Department of Business, alsu@gantep.edu.tr
2 PhD Student, Gaziantep University, Department of Business, apaydin.bilge@gmail.com

the information they obtain from samples and make generalizations to make similar decisions in similar situations (Erkaymaz and Yasar, 2011). The most important feature of ANN is their ability to learn. Thanks to this feature, it is successfully used in many fields such as industry, commerce, finance, meteorology, education, military, defense, and health (Zeren and Erguzel, 2014). Artificial neural network model is also used in the field of finance generating accurate estimates for the future and helping achieve successful results. Especially in stock price estimation, this model produces more satisfactory results compared to other traditional models (regression etc.). As a matter of fact, there are many studies in the literature about the estimation of stock prices and the price trends using ANN model (Caliskan and Deniz, 2015). It is also seen that the model is applied to estimate the gold prices and determine the factors affecting the gold price.

In this study, the closing price of gold per ounce was predicted using ANN Model. The opening price of gold per ounce, and the highest and lowest price of gold per ounce during the trading day were the input variables whereas the estimated closing price of gold per ounce was the output variable. This study will show to what extent the closing price of gold per ounce estimated with ANN model is close to the actual closing price of gold per ounce. Thus, it will be seen that ANN model is capable of producing successful results in estimating the closing price of gold per ounce. Also, when the correlation between the actual closing price of gold per ounce and the forecasted closing price of gold per ounce is examined, the extent of ANN model's capability in making correct estimates will be more clearly understood.

All data related to the model was taken from the Istanbul Stock Exchange. In the study, gold per ounce data for a total of 2323 working days covering the dates between January 2, 2009 and December 1, 2017 were analyzed.

The first chapter of the study is the "Literature Review", the second chapter is the "Artificial Neural Networks Model", the third chapter is the "Findings", and the final chapter of the study is "Results".

2 Literature Review

In a study conducted by Yuksel and Akkoc (2016) using ANN model, the price of gold per ounce was forecasted using the variables (oil prices, silver prices, US dollar/EUR parity, EuroNext 100 index, US Dow Jones Index, 13-week US dollar bond interest rate and US CPI index) that can affect gold prices as independent variables. In the analysis section of the study, it was seen that the independent variables had been chosen correctly. Thus, it has been understood that ANNs are a successful model that can be used for estimating the price of gold. In addition, a sensitivity analysis was conducted and it was seen that the price of gold per ounce was most influenced by the silver price, followed by Brent oil, the Dow Jones Index, Euro/US Dollar parity, EuroNext100 Index, US treasury bills and US CPI values.

In his study, Kilic (2013) predicted the gold price trends by combining the Markov chain model with ANN model. He used the Markov chain method to model the average daily returns on gold and ANN model to estimate the next day's gold prices. This study came to the conclusion that ANN provides significant information about the next day's gold returns.

In an article titled "Estimation of Trends in Gold Prices with Economic Indices using Artificial Neural Networks", Kocatepe and Yildiz (2016) tried to predict the trend in gold prices using ANN model. While the price of gold per gram was accepted as the dependent variable, silver and copper prices, the dollar index and the US dollar exchange rate, crude oil price, Standard and Poor's 500 index, BIST 100 index, inflation, bond and interest rates in Turkey, inflation, bond and interest rates in the US were chosen as independent variables to be used in the model. The study correctly estimated the trend changes in the price of gold per gram at a rate of 75.24 % using ANN model.

Dolgun, Saracbasi, and Yeniler (2014) forecasted daily TRY-based gold closing prices in the short term between January 3, 2011 and June 30, 2014. Artificial Neural Networks and Time Series Methods were compared and it was seen that ANN model made much more successful estimates.

Cam and Kilic (2018) tried to estimate the daily returns on gold by combining ANN algorithm and the Markov Chain Models. With the new method, the daily estimates of gold prices were successful by 70 % in the study.

In their study called "Gold Price Estimation using the Time Series Methods and Artificial Neural Networks", Benli and Yildiz (2014) made estimates using the weighted average monthly gold prices from the Istanbul Stock Exchange covering the period from January 1996 to December 2013. When the root mean square errors were compared, it was seen that the ARIMA model yielded better results than ANN model while the predictive power of ANN model was found to be higher than the time series methods, the simple exponential smoothing method and Holt's linear trend method.

Kucukaksoy and Yalcin (2017) examined the factors that could affect the gold prices using the VAR model. The analysis showed that any shock impact from the independent variables could affect the gold prices for a maximum of 3 months. On the other hand, the most important finding was that while data on past price trends of gold can be an important indicator, the price history of gold accounts for 97 % of the spot gold prices.

Guresen, Kayakutlu, and Daim (2011) forecasted the approximately seven-month NASDAQ index daily data on the basis of the output from a multi-layered ANN model and several hybrid models, and concluded that the multi-layered ANN model had a high predictive power.

In an article titled "Forecasting the Direction of BIST 100 Returns with Artificial Neural Networks Models", Kilic, Paksoy, and Genc (2014) used ANN model to forecast the trends in the BIST 100 index. During the training period for ANN model, the weekly deferred value of interest rate returns and exchange rate returns are used as the input data. Forecasts using ANN model provide valuable information for investors.

Kara, Boyacioglu, and Baykan (2011) performed analyses on the future trends of the BIST 100 index (a downward or an upward trend) using ANN model. The analyses provided correct estimates of the trends in the BIST 100 index by 75.4 %.

Toraman (2008) forecasted the 22-day closing values of Erdemir company and Kardemir company stocks in the iron and steel sector using ANN model. While the price trend forecast for the Erdemir company shares was done with an accuracy rate of 95 %, the same rate was 90 % for the Kardemir company shares.

Vaisla and Bhatt (2010) observed that ANN model performed 9 times better than the performance criteria regression model in the forecasting of Indian stock prices. Furthermore, Carvalhall and Riberio (2008) made price forecasts for the stock market indices of Latin American countries (Argentina, Brazil, Mexico, Chile) with the ARIMA, GARCH, ANN and the RW (Random Walk) models using daily data covering the years 1994–2006, and found that ANN model yielded the best results among these 4 models.

Erdogan and Ozyurek (2012) tried to make daily price forecasts for white goods companies whose shares are traded in the Istanbul Stock Exchange 100 using ANN model. In the study, factors affecting stock prices were integrated into the model only later and the analysis showed that ANN model could be used as a tool for forecasting stock prices.

In a study called "Forecasting Stock Prices and Trends using Artificial Neural Networks", Caliskan and Deniz (2015), tried to forecast the daily prices of 27 shares traded in the BIST 30 Index and the price trends using ANN model. The subsequent analysis showed that the model forecasted the price trends of these 27 shares with an accuracy rate of 58 %.

In a study called "Prediction of Gold Prices Using Artificial Neural Networks", Adem, Comert, Zengin, and Hekim (2017) used multi-layer ANN to make forecasts of gold prices per ounce. The input variables were the Brent oil price, US dollar price, BIST100 index, the weekly interest rate of Central Bank of the

Republic of Turkey, and silver and copper prices and a high degree of correlation was found between the gold prices and the input variables used in the study. Artificial Neural Networks model forecasted the gold prices with an accuracy rate of 98.17 %.

3 Artificial Neural Networks Model

The human brain can be regarded as the most complex machinery in the world. While computers can solve many complex problems, they are not quite so adept at defining and using knowledge gained with experience. Although it is difficult to develop a system that is an exact replica of the human brain, there are new systems entering our lives that can partly emulate the human brain. Today, we are at a stage where we see lots of intelligent products from driverless cars to servant robots being produced thanks to such studies (Birgili, Sekmen, Esen, 2013). Systems such as Expert Systems, Fuzzy Logic, Genetic Algorithms, and ANN, which are the sub-branches of artificial intelligence, are engineering methods that can react according to human behavior (Elmas, 2003). Artificial Neural Network is a data processing system inspired by biological neural networks that emulate the human brain system and shows similarities to biological neural networks (Kaynar and Tastan, 2009). In other words, ANN finds solutions to problems that require natural human skills for thinking and observation. A person's capability in finding solutions to problems that require thinking and observation lies in the fact that the human brain, and therefore human beings, learn by experience or trial. ANN builds up its own experiences using the information obtained from samples and then makes similar decisions in similar situations (Erkaymaz and Yasar, 2011). ANN is a data processing system of collaborating components, each of which has its own data processing skills and memory. The most important features of ANN are their ability to learn (Yildiz, 2009). Thanks to this feature, ANN is successfully used in many fields such as industry, commerce, finance, education, military, and defense.

Artificial Neural Networks are mathematical processes consisting of several neurons assembled and interconnected. Generally speaking, neurons are almost similar to real biological neurons, picking up, combining, and changing signals from other neurons to generate a numerical result. While neurons connect to each other in a network to form ANN, neurons are grouped into layers in ANN model.

ANN consists of 3 layers: the entry layer, the hidden layer, and the exit layer. Artificial neural networks are modeled on the basis of data obtained from training and the test. Training data consists of training input and output. On

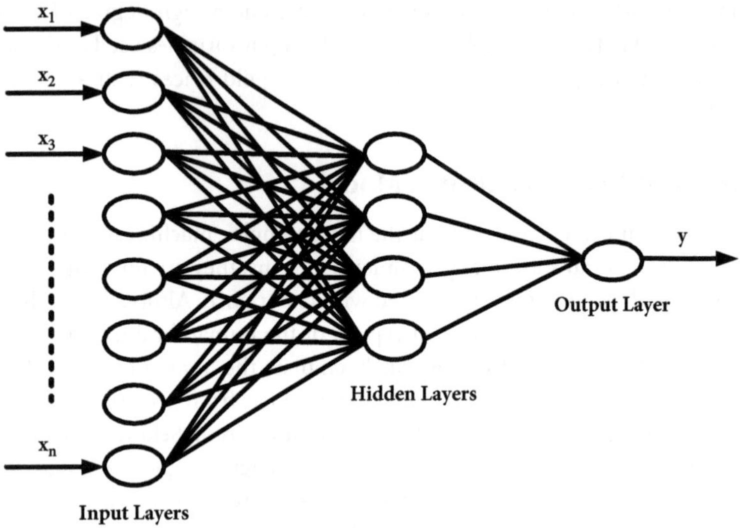

Fig. 1: Overall structure of ANN.

the other hand, the test data only consists of the test input. The system tries to estimate the output of the generated model test by using the learning process required by the training process. Input data resembles the independent variable whereas the output data resembles the dependent variable. The neurons in the other hidden layer do not have any relation to the external environment. All they do is take the signals from the entry layer and pass them on to the exit layer. In terms of the network performance, it is important to determine the number of neurons in the hidden layer (Cuhadar and Kayacan, 2005).

Fig. 1 shows the overall structure of ANN. During the training period, the nature of the relationship between the input and the output is taught. During the testing period, the system is required to predict test outputs on the basis of the test inputs. At this stage, the input types to be presented to the model are important. Because these input variables are the identifiers of the outputs, and the correct input will increase the chances of achieving the correct results (Zeren and Erguzel, 2014).

Artificial Neural Networks are divided into two according to their mode of operation. These are feedforward ANN and feedback ANN.

i) Feedforward Artificial Neural Networks
   With feedforward ANN in Fig. 2, the given signal always moves forward. In other words, the information fed first enters the entry layer and then moves

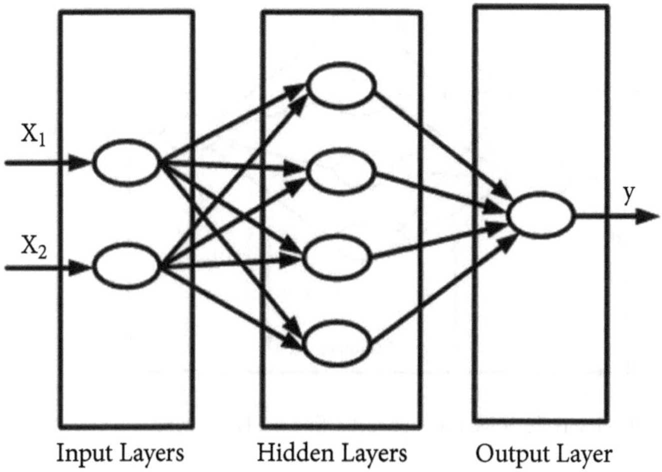

Fig. 2: Feedforward Artificial Neural Networks. Source: Firat and Gungor, 2004

forward toward the exit layer. The number of hidden layers in between depends on the type of data trying to be resolved.

ii) Feedback Artificial Neural Networks
In feedback ANN (see Fig. 3), the information from the output is firstly transmitted to the hidden layer through a buffer and then to the output layer. In such networks, the signal sent from the previous layer is important in terms of achieving more accurate results.

4 Results

In the study, gold per ounce data for a total of 2323 working days covering the dates between January 2, 2009 and December 1, 2017 were analyzed. 85 % of the total data (1975 work days) was used for training purposes while the remaining 15 % portion (348 work days) was used for testing purposes. With the feedforward ANN model, the opening price of gold per ounce, and the highest and lowest value of gold per ounce during the trading day were used as input variables, while the closing price of gold per ounce was predicted as the output variable.

Fig. 4 contains the closing prices of gold per ounce between January 2, 2009 and December 1, 2017, the dates for which the model made its forecasts. The section in blue is for training, while the red section is for testing purposes.

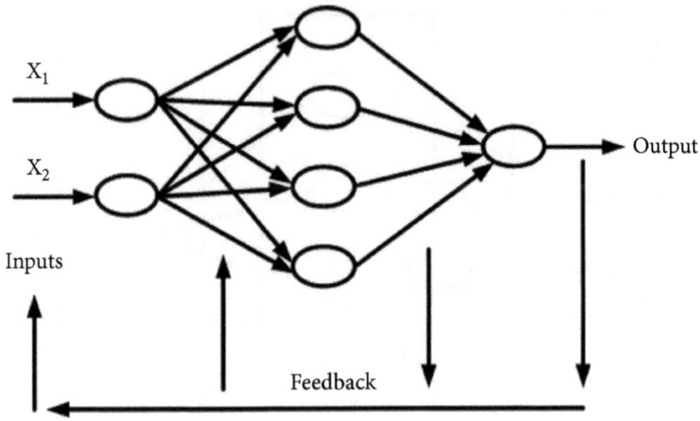

Fig. 3: Feedback Artificial Neural Networks. Source: Diler, 2003

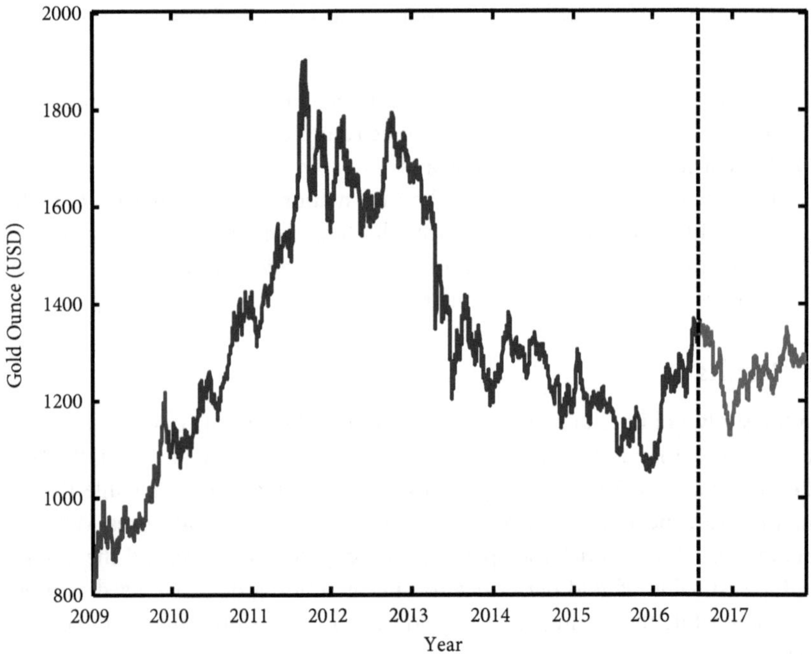

Fig. 4: Closing price of gold per ounce.

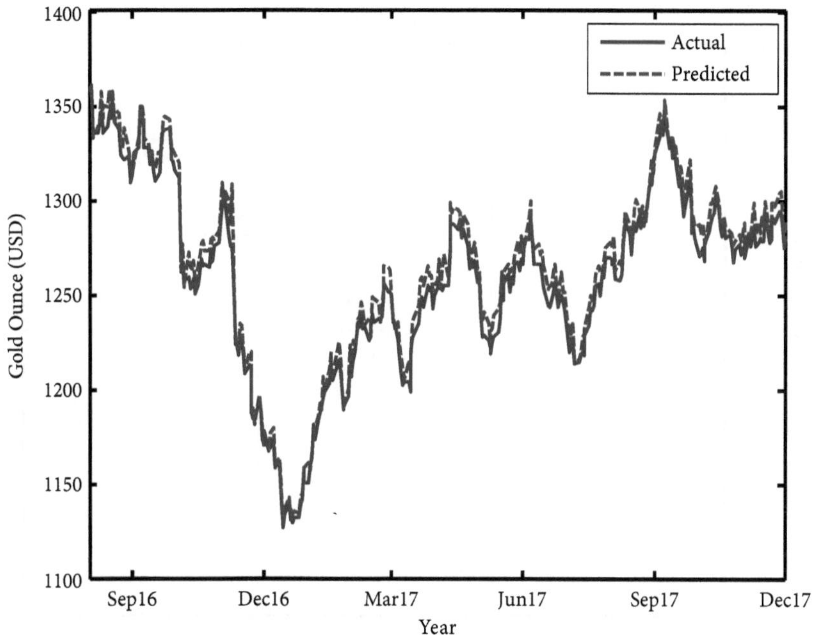

Fig. 5: Price forecast for the closing price of gold per ounce

Fig. 5 shows a close correlation between the actual closing price of gold per ounce and the predicted value generated by the model.

Fig. 6 shows a strong correlation between the closing price of gold per ounce as forecasted by ANN model and the actual closing price of gold per ounce. The R^2 was 0.99057 and the model predicted the closing price of gold per ounce with an accuracy rate of 99 %.

5 Conclusion

Forecasting gold prices is highly important for decision makers wishing to invest in gold so that decision makers wish to maximize their returns by correctly predicting gold prices.

While various methods have been used for predicting gold prices, there are also many studies worthy of note on the use of ANN model for predicting gold prices. Through an analysis of data on the price of gold per ounce between January 2, 2009–December 1, 2017, which corresponds to 2323 work days, we tried to

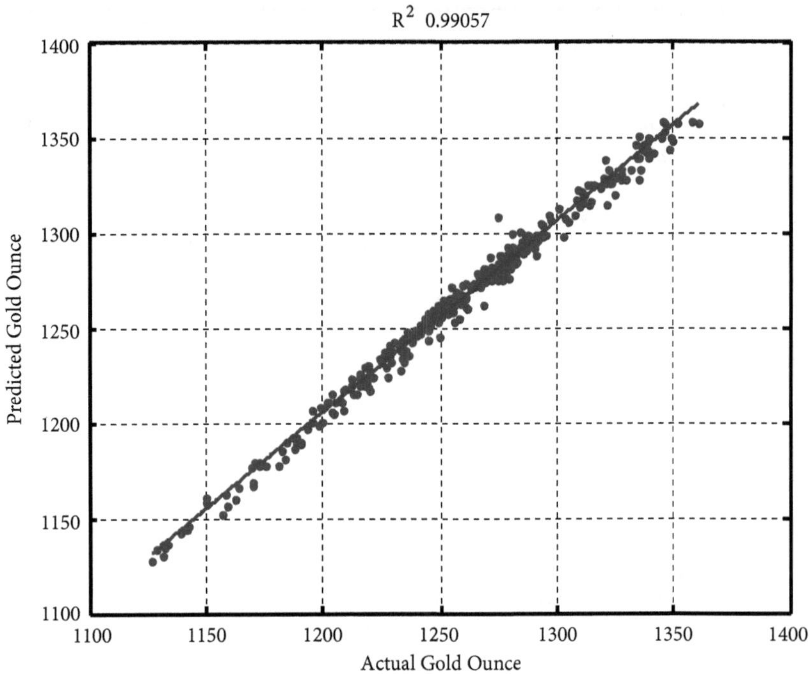

Fig. 6: Correlation between the actual and the predicted closing price of gold per ounce

predict the closing price of gold using ANN model. The analysis result showed a strong correlation between the predicted and the actual price of gold. For that reason, the ANN can be used to predict the closing price of gold using daily data.

The strong correlation between the actual closing price of gold per ounce and the predicted closing price of gold per ounce attests to the reliability of the model in predicting the price trends. The study has shown how ANN model can be used to make reliable estimates of the closing price of gold per ounce.

References

Adem, K., Comert, O., Zengin, N., and Hekim, M. (2017). Prediction of gold prices using artificial neural networks. *International Journal of Engineering Research and Development*, 9(3), 84–89.

Benli, Y. K., and Yildiz, A. (2014). Altin fiyatinin zaman serisi yontemleri ve yapay sinir aglari ile ongorusu. *Dumlupınar Universitesi Sosyal Bilimler Dergisi*, (42), 213–224.

Birgili, E., Sekmen, F., and Esen, S. (2013). Bulanık mantık yaklasimiyla finansal yonetim uygulamaları: Bir literatur taramasi. *Uluslararasi Yonetim Iktisat ve Isletme Dergisi*, 9(19), 121–136.

Caliskan, M. M. T., and Deniz, D. (2015). Yapay sinir aglariyla hisse senedi fiyatlari ve yonlerinin tahmini. *Eskisehir Osmangazi Universitesi Iktisadi ve Idari Bilimler Fakultesi Dergisi*, 10(3), 177–194.

Cam, S., and Kilic, S. B. (2018). Altin fiyat gunluk getirilerinin yapay sinir aglari algoritmasi ve markov zinciri modelleri ile tahmini. *Uluslararasi Iktisadi ve Idari Incelemeler Dergisi*, 681–694.

Carvalhal, A., and Ribeiro, T. (2008). Do artificial neural networks provide better forecasts? Evidence from Latin American stock indexes. *Latin American Business Review*, 8(3), 92–110.

Cuhadar, M., and Kayacan, C. (2005). Yapay sinir aglari kullanilarak konaklama isletmelerinde doluluk orani tahmini: Turkiye'deki konaklama isletmeleri uzerine bir deneme. *Anatolia: Turizm Arastirmalari Dergisi*, 16(1), 24–30.

Diler, A. I. (2003). IMKB ulusal-100 endeksinin yonunun yapay sinir aglari hata geriye yayma yontemi ile tahmin edilmesi. *IMKB Dergisi*, 7(25–26), 66–81.

Doganalp, N., Konya, S. and Kabaloglu, G. (2016). Turkiye'de altin fiyatlarinin belirleyicileri uzerine ampirik bir uygulama. *ODU Sosyal Bilimler Arastirmalari Dergisi*, 6(15), 412–424.

Dolgun, M. O., Saracbasi, O., and Yeniler, A. (2014). Zaman serisi verilerinin yapay sinir aglari yaklasimi ile cozumlenmesi: Altin fiyatinin tahmini. *XVI. Ulusal Biyoistatistik Kongresi*. Antalya, Turkiye.

Elmas, C. (2003). *Yapay sinir aglari: (kuram, mimari, egitim, uygulama)*. Seckin Yayincilik.

Erdogan, E., and Ozyurek, H. (2012). Yapay sinir aglari ile fiyat tahminlemesi. *Sosyal ve Beseri Bilimler Dergisi*, 4(1), 85–92.

Erkaymaz, H., and Yasar, O. (2011). Yapay sinir agi ile hava sicakligi tahmini. *5th International Computer and Instructional Technologies Symposium*, 22–24 September, Firat University, Turkey.

Firat, M., and Gungor, M. (2004). Aski madde konsantrasyonu ve miktarinin yapay sinir aglari ile belirlenmesi. *IMO Teknik Dergisi*, 219, 3267–3282.

Guresen, E., Kayakutlu, G., and Daim, T. U. (2011). Using artificial neural network models in stock market index prediction. *Expert Systems with Applications*, 38(8), 10389–10397.

Kara, Y., Boyacioglu, M. A., and Baykan, O. K. (2011). Predicting direction of stock price index movement using artificial neural networks and support vector machines: The sample of the Istanbul Stock Exchange. *Expert systems with Applications*, 38(5), 5311–5319.

Kaynar, O., and Tastan, S. (2009). Zaman serisi analizinde MLP yapay sinir aglari ve arima modelinin karsilastirilmasi. *Erciyes Universitesi Iktisadi ve Idari Bilimler Fakultesi Dergisi*, 33, 161–172.

Kilic, S. B. (2013). Predicting the direction of gold price returns: Integrating composite artificial neural network models by markov chain process. *Cukurova Universitesi Iktisadi ve Idari Bilimler Fakultesi Dergisi*, 17(2), 15–28.

Kilic, S. B., Paksoy, S., and Genc, T. (2014). Forecasting the direction of BIST 100 returns with artificial neural network models. *International Journal of Latest Trends in Finance and Economic Sciences*, 4(3), 759–765.

Kocatepe, C. I., and Yildiz, O. (2016). Ekonomik endeksler kullanilarak Turkiye'deki altin fiyatindaki degisim yonunun yapay sinir aglari ile tahmini. *Duzce Universitesi Bilim ve Teknoloji Dergisi*, 4, 926–934.

Kucukaksoy, I., and Yalcin, D. (2017). Altin fiyatlarini etkileyebilecek faktorlerin incelenmesi. *Ekonomik ve Sosyal Arastirmalar Dergisi*. 13(2), 1–19.

Toraman, C. (2008). Demir-celik sektorunde yapay sinir aglari ile hisse senedi fiyat tahmini: Erdemir as ve kardemir as uzerine bir tahmin uygulamasi. *Muhasebe ve Finansman Dergisi*, (39), 44–57.

Vaisla, K. S., and Bhatt, A. K. (2010). An analysis of the performance of artificial neural network technique for stock market forecasting. *International Journal on Computer Science and Engineering*, 2(6), 2104–2109.

Yildiz, B. (2009). *Finansal analizde yapay zeka*. Ankara: Detay Yayincilik.

Yuksel, R., and Akkoc, S. (2016). Altın fiyatlarinin yapay sinir aglari ile tahmini ve bir uygulama. *Dogus University Journal*, 17(1), 39–50.

Zeren, F., and Erguzel, O. S. (2014). Forecast share prices with artificial neural network in crisis periods. *Journal of Business Research-Turk*, 6(3), 16–28.

Murat Karahan[1]

The Activity Audit as Approach to Improved Operations and Profitability: Literature Review

1 Introduction

In a competitive world today, the ability to make sound decisions between businesses and those using the information produced by these businesses is first and foremost closely related to the importance given to auditing. It is very wrong to see the audit only as the review of the financial statements. There is also a need for the operator to examine all its activities instead of just accounting and economic areas. This type of audit is related to a specific review field called activity audit. Especially as businesses grow, it will be difficult to measure the success of business policies, the efficiency of activities, and determine the effectiveness of business management. However, the result of the activity audit will affect the stable future of the business.

The audit is gaining higher importance in the world recent years, especially with globalization, the concept and scope of the review are expanded and become more active. Auditing involves a systematic process of collecting and evaluating claims related to economic activity and operations, investigating the appropriateness of information presented in the framework of accepted criteria, and managing and assessing relevant evidence to report.

In this article, the author will present the concept of activity audit and its consequences.

2 Activity Audit

The activity audit is a naturally developed extension of internal audit. The growth of businesses increases the number of holdings, and the tendency to decentralization led to the development and spread of audit operations. The accelerated growth of all companies, the complexity of processes, difficulty of supervision and control over them, and the difficulties of measuring the success of governance and policies, constitute the most important reasons for an operational audit (Balkaran, 2014).

---

1 Assist. Prof. Dr., Gaziantep University, karahan@gantep.edu.tr

Activity supervision involves the effective and efficient use of resources by systematically monitoring some or all the business activities (Messier, 1997).

The activity is a measure of operator reaching its goals, which are determined based on departments. Productivity is a ratio of resources used to achieve these defined goals (Kızılboğa and Özşahin, 2013).

Although an auditor can do activity auditing, in practice this audit is usually carried out by internal auditors and state auditors (Güredin, 2000). Independent (external) auditor provide an operational review in the form of management consultancy service. Management consultancy is the service which includes "business strategy, organizational structure, methods of doing business, identification of problems in private/public and other businesses by independent and experienced individuals or persons, and support for the implementation of the research and appropriate proposals" (IIA, 2013). It is more rational to conduct the activity audit by internal auditors because he knows better than the independent auditor. They are more informed about the characteristics of the business and how their activities are carried out. Because of this feature, it is more comfortable and more useful for the internal auditor to perform an activity audit according to the independent auditor.

3 The Objective of Activity Audit

It is difficult to say that an activity audit has a defined purpose with boundaries. Activity audit is an audit based on practical and efficiency concepts. If there is a general framework for it (Özer, 1997; Althani, 2008):

- To measure the success of business management,
- To measure the efficiency and success of business policies,
- To measure the ability and success of internal auditing,
- To measure the success and effectiveness of any activity which will affect the achievement of the specified objectives of the business,

To beneficial audit, it must define the goals of the review and establish a reliable and valid system (Karahan, 2017).

The auditor can summarize as having management advice to ensure that the business grows steadily and healthily achieves its objectives.

The purpose of the activity audit is to assess performance and provide recommendations by identifying areas of improvement (Messier, 1997).

As a result of such auditing, there is a function to determine the situation and make proposals to the management. In this respect, activity auditing considered as a consultancy service (Bozkurt, 1998).

Although the information on the past and ongoing operations of the entity reviewed during the activity audit, the purpose is not to confirm this information.

The aim is to increase profitability (Chambers and Rand, 2012). Improving the profitability will be through the suggestions brought to the end of the audit.

Therefore, activity audit is for the future. In the case of an audit work to be done, the purposes mentioned above may be considered all at once, or one of these objectives may treat as a priority over the other. Depends entirely on the auditor who has undertaken the audit task.

4 The Scope of Activity Audits

Activity audit is also known as performance or management audit and is often more difficult than financial inspection and compliance audit. Because it is necessary to evaluate and determine the measurable criteria of efficiency and productivity and to demonstrate their suitability for the specified purposes, which is slightly tricky to understand (Messier, 1997; Dittenhofer, 2001).

An activity audit involves the monitoring of the implementation of the procedures and methods related to these activities to assess the efficiency and effectiveness of the events in an enterprise (Raaum and Morgan, 2009).

Activity audit is not concerned only with financial events. Any event, whether commercial or non-financial, will enter the issue of activity audit, which will affect the subjects we regard as the above. One of these matters is the internal control. The relation of the operational review to the internal control system is essential in this direction (Messier, 1997; Dittenhofer, 2001).

Activity audit also includes other functions of the entity including financial transactions. There can be many different events or different factors affecting management's success. The activity audit separately covers each of these. For this reason, the application area is quite extensive. For example, management decisions and policies regarding purchasing, production, personnel, marketing and financing issues are investigating whether they are in harmony with the outcome of the activity (Raaum and Morgan, 2009).

The organization's structure, production methods, marketing policies, information processing activities can enter the scope of the activity audit. Therefore, implementation of activity audit is more complicated than other audit types (Bozkurt, 1998; Balkaran, 2014).

Comparison criteria are more complicated than others. In such audits, auditors use budgets, success measures, ratios and sector averages as predefined measures (Ataman, et al., 2001).

5 Elements of Activity Audits

The aspects of activity audits can be listed as follows:

1) **Auditing is a process**: Auditing is carried out in various stages, and all activities between the initial results are carried out in a plan.
2) **Claims on economic activity and events**: Reports on the financial operations of the business issued for business purposes and these reports are prepared for market and presented to interested groups. Audit activity investigates the truthfulness and credibility of these advocated claims.
3) **Audit uses pre-agreed criteria**: The auditor decides on the accuracy and reliability by comparing the financial statements of the entity's claimed feature with predetermined criteria. The requirements determined by laws, generally accepted accounting standards, agreements or management.
4) **Evaluation of impartial evidence and evidence**: To investigate the correctness of the claims made by the operator, auditors independently collect proof from relevant persons and institutions.
5) **Notification to interested parties**: The auditor will disclose the audit to those interested in the form of a written report at the end of the financial information operator.
6) **Provide information about the future**: Providing information about whether future business continuity can maintain by comparing past data. For this reason, the audit also contributes to having information about the future of the business.

6 Time of Activity Audit

Activity audit is a natural extension of internal audit. It is not possible to consider activity audit utterly independent of internal audit. It is evident that it is more accurate to conduct the review within the activity period when the objective of the audit taken into consideration, as well as the absence of a definite time, suggested in the inspection of the activity as it is in the internal audit (Özer, 1997).

When we say that the goal of activity audit is to measure the success and effectiveness of the management policies, it is not just to measure what we want to tell. The primary purpose is to identify the factors that cause failure and to remove these factors. The effectiveness of the audit to be performed after the closing of the operating period will be considerably lower than the efficacy of the review of operations to complete during the operating period. Because it is not possible to eliminate the factors that affect the success while the activity is finished (Balkaran, 2014).

Fig. 1: Activity audit Process. Source: Whittington and Pany, 1997

As a result, it is necessary to determine the time required for the operation to be achieved within the operational period of it to reach the desired effect in the activity audit work and to identify the factors that affect the management as soon as possible (Raaum and Morgan, 2009).

7 The Process of Activity Audits

There is no fundamentally different between the process that an auditor conducting an activity audit can follow and the procedure to follow in the review of financial statements. This process sound in 7 steps (Whittington and Pany, 1997):

I. **Goal Description**: This is the first phase of the activity audit. The auditor broadly sets out the purpose of the activity audit, with the intention to evaluate the specific activities and functions carried out in operation. The auditor should specify which policies and procedures are to assess and how they relate to specific objectives of the business (Whittington and Pany, 1997).

II. **Recognition**: Before commencing an activity audit, the auditor should obtain comparative information about the operational characteristics, organization structure, and objectives of the supervised items. This recognition process should include activity policies and procedures, management's policies and directives, expressions of defined responsibilities and functions, and organizational schemes (Whittington and Pany, 1997).

III. **Preliminary Research**: At this stage, the auditor should seek answers to the questions "What should be the function of activity when collecting information" and "Which control procedures should include in the study?" The primary purpose of the preliminary study is to identify problem areas. For this purpose, three types of procedures used in this phase: review interviews, observations and internal reports (IIA, 2013; Carlos, 2008).

IV. **Program Development**: The activity auditor develops the program in the stage following the preliminary research phase. Here, the auditor undertakes the following two primary tasks to study the responsibilities set out in the agreements, contracts, authorities, and activities, also, to define and develop the relevant activity criteria.
- During the examination of contracts and agreements, the auditor conducts studies to determine the goals and objectives set in the business.
- When establishing the performance criteria, the auditor should determine whether the policies and procedures set by the management as an initial business complied with and whether they are sufficiently compelling. At this phase, the auditor may want to test and analyze the need to assess the operations of the operator (Whittington and Pany, 1997). The auditor may write in his/her program:
  - o Examine the conformity of contracts and agreements with the specified objectives and targets.
  - o Making sure whether the management's policies and procedures will comply.
  - o Examine the effectiveness of internal control.
  - o Examine the performance measurement for internal control.
  - o And what will be the necessary tests and analyzes to evaluate the business operations.

V. **Working Field:** After the program developed, the auditor starts working. The auditor's track here is the business management and related audits. Within these controls, management audit is more critical for activity audit. An activity auditor should consider the following points when examining controls (Balkaran, 2014).
- Whether the designated responsibilities, given authorities and necessary agreements are by the policies of the employer, and
- Whether the policies and procedures are successful in management audit in the context of efficiency and affordability.

- The management and accounting auditing have provided sufficient credibility to the operator's resources, revenue, and expenses.

VI. **Reporting and Presentation of Findings**: In this phase, the auditor develops suggestions for the problems have identified before and reports them to the relevant information users. These information users are other business-related parties, particularly business management.
To be able to report the findings of the inspector and develop suggestions, he must have gathered evidence and various information in the previous steps and should discuss the matter with the business management and be meeting with other managers. If additional information obtained as a result of this meeting, it should be followed by an approach as follows (Balkaran, 2014):
- Identifying of the problem, fault, and deficiency.
- Perceptioning of the loss magnitude, performance degradation and other factors in the cost system.
- Investigate the reasons for the situation.
- Determining the persons responsible for correcting faults.
- Determination of corrective and protective activities and the establishment of constructive suggestions.

An audit report should write in line with this approach. The activity audit report does not have a standard format, but it can be composed of five parts in evaluating the activity and suggestions related to them (Whittington and Pany, 1997), which are the criteria, conditions, purpose, the approaches used, and findings used.

VII. **Monitoring:** The auditor examines whether the report is reachable and whether there are any deficiencies in it. This phase of the activity audit usually involves the auditor as well as the relevant audit firm, because the monitoring stage is the responsibility of the entire group undertaking the review. After the audit report is submitted, during the monitoring phase, the audit firm sends auditors to examine whether the proposed changes made or not, and if so, it discusses how it did and, in this way, it takes the work to monitor even after the control is over (Balkaran, 2014).

8 Results and Conclusions

During the activity audit, the findings compared with the standards and efforts are made to measure the effectiveness and success of the activities. However, the identification of these standards may not always be as easy as it may seem.

Tab. 1: Typical Areas to Analyze in an activity Audit. Source: Balkaran, 2014

Sub-sets of areas in procurement	Reviews of the following
Management	Vision and Mission Statement Procurement plan and its alignment with the organization's overall strategic plan Organizational structure—span of control, levels of authority and responsibility Staff—job descriptions, qualifications, performance, and appraisals Management—style, performance, and control Memberships of recognized supply management associations.
Financial activities	Risk, governance, analysis of control environment Procurement risk and management Financial Procurement budgeting process Budget vs. actual costs and variance analysis Operations, Procurement policies and procedures Process maps and narratives Reports—produced and received Changes in operations, systems, and personnel since the last review.
Performance	Contract management Vendor management and control Performance Functional Performance Benchmarking, key performance indicators, and other metrics.
Information Technology	Quality measures used Information Technology Systems in place—state, appropriateness, use, performance, and access security
Effectiveness	The extent to which procurement objectives are achieved Efficiency Reviewing methods of operations
Economy Compliance	Cost and use of procurement resources Compliance The degree of compliance with regulations

Standards related to non-business sectors may not be appropriate for the efficiency and success of the enterprise. However, it is important to note that progress and effectiveness are subjective concepts such as length and brevity (Özer, 1997). For these reasons, activity audit includes partial or even subjective aspects in assessing audit results.As mentioned above, activity audit is more difficult and comprehensive than financial and compliance audit. The most important reason why it is difficult; Decisions, regulations, and criteria against which findings can compare in financial and conformity checks, but there are no precise and objective rules measure the success of the entity in the audit of activities, as well as in other audit types, as the management policies and internal control activities are not measured. The auditor, however, must be impartial in the judgments and decisions that he or she has.

The ability of firms to survive and grow in the future depends on the decisions they will make today. At the focal point of the decisions they receive, their weaknesses corrected, and their strengths maintained. The information obtained as a result of the activity audit made reveals the weaknesses and strengths of the business. If it is difficult to do so, the benefits of activity audit to the company cannot underestimate. The ability of the auditors to provide a benefit to the activity depends, among other things, on the correct recommendation in place. The activity audit tries to measure whether the operator has achieved its designated goals and objectives. In this, all the factors that may affect the achievement of the goals and objectives and their contribution to the management (goals) carefully examined.

References

Al Athmay, A. (2008). Performance auditing and public-sector management in Brunei Darussalam, International Journal of Public Sector Management. 21(7). 798–811.

Ataman, Ü. Hacırüstemoğlu, R. and Bozkurt, N. (2001). Muhasebe Denetimi Uygulamaları. İstanbul. Alfa Yayınevi. 1. Baskı.

Balkaran, L. (2014). Unleashing the power of an operational audit. EDPACS: The EDP Audit, Control, and Security Newsletter. 50:4, 13–20, DOI 10.1080/07366981.2014.952528 To link to this article: http://dx.doi.org/10.1080/07366981.2014.952528

Bozkurt, N. (1998). Muhasebe Denetimi, İstanbul: Alfa Yayınevi, 1. Baskı.

Chambers, A. and Rand, G. (2012). The Operational Auditing Handbook. Wiley: London. ISBN: 978-0-470-74476-5.

Dittenhofer, M. (2001). Performance auditing in governments. Managerial Auditing Journal. 16(8). 438–442.

Elder, C. Aquino. (2008). Six steps to an effective continuous audit process. International auditor: https://iaonline.theiia.org/six-steps-to-an-effective-continuous-audit-process The Access date: 25.05.2018.

Güredin, E. (2000). Denetim. İstanbul. 10. Baskı. Beta Yayınları.

Karahan, M. (2017). "Türkiye, ABD ve AB'de Muhasebe Denetiminin Karşılaştı rılması", Al Farabi Sosyal Bilim Dergisi. 1(2). pp: 273–288.

Kızılboğa, R. and Özşahin. F. (2013). Etkin Bir İç Kontrol Sisteminin İç Denetim Faaliyetine ve İç Denetçilere Katkısı. Niğde Üniversitesi İİBF Dergisi. 6(2), 220–236.

Messier, W. F. (1997) Auditing, New York: The McGraw-Hill Comp.

Özer, M. (1997). Denetim. Ankara. Özkan Matbaa. 1. Baskı.

Raaum, Ronell B. and Morgan, Stephen L. (2009). Performance Auditing: A Measurement Approach. 2nd ed. (IIA: Altamonte Springs: 2009).

The Institute of Internal Auditors. (2013). The IIA's Global Internal Audit Competency Framework. (IIA: Altamonte Springs: 2013). To link to this article: (https://na.theiia.org/about-us/Public%20Documents/The%20 IIA%20Global%20Internal%20Audit%20Competency%20Framework.pdf)

Whittington, Ray and Pany, Kurt (1997). Principles of Auditing & Other Assurance Services (Irwin Accounting). McGraw-Hill Education. 2nd Edition. New York.

Fulya Misirdali Yangil[1]

Social Sustainability in Businesses

1 Introduction

Many problems in the world have arisen due to the fact that people are not born under equal conditions. People come into the world in countries with different environmental, cultural and economic conditions as children of families with different conditions. This equality, which could not be initially provided, is acknowledged as destiny by some countries and families, and a luck by some others in the forthcoming periods, and effort is being made to be able to live under existing conditions. This problem has led to the rapid growth of hostility between people and societies and become insurmountable after the hunting and collecting period of humanity making effort to maintain their life for their living spaces and food. Moreover, every living condition that can not be equalized today poses a threat to the continuity of humanity, and the equalization of these living conditions for individuals was discussed within the concept of social sustainability.

Sustainability first emerged with the idea of that nature will keep living without decreasing. However, sustainability, reaching today a broader meaning than its first released meaning, has evolved into a different understanding and reality comprising other environments that people involved in (cultural, economic, social, etc.). The concept of sustainability is defined from economical, social and ecological dimensions, which are called triple bottom line in the literature. It is stated in the definitions that sustainability can not be provided if one of these aspects falls behind, or problems encountered in one of these dimensions can not be solved. In the light of this statement, sustainability can be defined as " to make effort to protect cultural heritage and create equal living conditions, providing both the transportation of natural habitat resources to the future, and economic welfare for the future generations". But, sustainability's focal point is future generations, the resolution of today's problems lies at its essence. In other words, to leave a "livable and beautiful world" to the future generations seems impossible without struggling with today's problems.

Studies on the environmental and economic sustainability dimensions of triple bottom line are supported more, and conducted more easily in comparison

---

1 Assist. Prof. Dr., Dumlupınar University.

to social sustainability dimension in order to leave a livable and beautiful world for future generations. However, this situation negatively affects the achievement of the sustainability studies. In this context, it is important to examine social sustainability concept.

2 Social Sustainability Dimension of Sustainable Development

Global significant changes and developments took place after the second world war. Economic activities rapidly increased in this period, but the effects it created were ignored for a long time. Development disrupted ecological balance, caused environmental disasters to increase and created negative social effects, which has led to establish a connection between environment, society and economic development. Organizations on a global scale have brought forward a new understanding for the fulfillment of activities aimed at protecting the ecological environment, as well as ensuring social justice and supporting economic development sustainability efforts, and this has been called as sustainable development. One of the three dimensions of the concept of sustainable development is considered as social sustainability. However, it is more difficult to define this aspect according to ecological and economic aspects, and accurately determine its limits.

The social sustainability dimension deals with the creation of humanistic living conditions, and establishment of equality in all segments and practices. In other words, while social sustainability refers to the social aspect of sustainability, it also provides a basis for codes of conduct in social life. Accordingly, the basic element of social sustainability is social integration of societies, encouragement of citizens to participate in public affairs, as well as oppose to social exclusion and discrimination (including sex). In social sustainability, there is a critical tendency to social processes and access to the benefits of modern society for most societies, including the right to an honorable standard of living for all citizens (Omann & Spangenberg, 2002: 5). However, despite this important definition, the social dimension of sustainability is regarded as the weakest "leg" of sustainable development, especially in respect to analytical and theoretical basis. One of the main reasons for this is the fact that the founders of the concept of sociology try to define social science apart from natural sciences. Until the Brundtland report published in 1987, the social sciences perspective was not discussed in the analysis of natural habitat. Secondly, sustainable development emerged primarily on the basis of ecological-centered perspective. So, the issue of how to integrate ecological anxiety into economic decision-making processes was discussed, focusing on economic growth and industrialization at the beginning, and social sustainability excluded from discussions and described economically (Parra, 2013: 144). Moreover, the fact that social sustainability has an abstract nature and that it is bipolar including both individual and collective, which make difficulties in defining its content, or reaching a consensus of its content (Lehtonen, 2004: 202).

The concept of social sustainability can be considered as a system that enables the provision of social services such as health, education, that provides distribution and gender equality, political accounting, and participation (Harris, 2000: 6). Sharma and Ruud define social sustainability as humanistic behavioral rules that should be realized in a fair, inclusive and prudent way (Mani, Agrawal & Sharma, 2014: 100). Besides, Bansal (2005: 198) considered social sustainability as a social equality, and defined it as equal access of all members of society to resources and opportunities. In this sense, social sustainability refers to meet humanistic needs such as protection, freedom, understanding and participation, which are universal social-psychological concepts (Kallströrm & Ljung, 2005: 377).

Most of the definitions of social sustainability focuses on the criteria or characteristics of social sustainability rather than being general and inclusive. It appears that topics and themes, appropriate for sustainability, are mostly attempted to be created in these definitions. In this context, it is beneficial to establish new and clear definitions to assess social sustainability (Ajmal, Khan, Hussain & Helo, 2017: 2029).

Tab. 1: Fragmented scope of social sustainability. Source: Ajmal, Khan, Hussain & Helo, 2017: 2028–2029

Authors	Scope
(Sachs, 1999)	Basicvalues of equity and democracy
(Koning, 2010)	Culture, equity and social justice
(United Nations. Department of Economic& United Nations. Department of Public Information, 2009)	End of extreme poverty and hunger, universal primary education, promoting gendere quality and empowerment of women, reduced child mortality, improved maternal health and fighting HIV/AIDS and malaria
(McKenzie, 2004)	A life-enhancing condition within communities, and a process within communities that can achieve that condition
(Gilchrist & Allouche, 2005)	Basic needs, capacity of individual/community
(Littig & Grießler, 2005)	Satisfy human needs and to fulfill social justice, human dignity and engagement
(Marafa, 2002)	Social and cultural consequences to the society

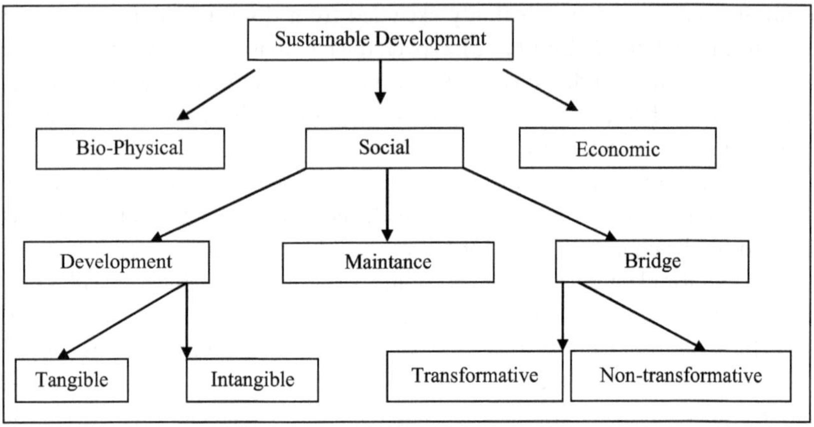

Fig. 1: Three strands of 'social sustainability'. Source: Vallance, Perkins & Dixon, 2011: 345

Vallance et al.'s (2011: 342–343) definitions of social sustainability and a three-layered literature schema are given in Fig. 1. According to this, social sustainability can be mentioned in three stages as "development sustainability", "bridge sustainability" and "maintance sustainability". They refer to; Development sustainability; provison of basic needs such as social capital, justice, equality; Brigde sustainability; provision of the changes in human behaviors to achieve environmental goals and obtain better environmental outcomes; Maintance sustainability; protection of socio-cultural characteristics when people actively accept or resist change.

Social sustainability is neither absolute nor fixed. It should be considered as a dynamic concept that will change somewhere in time (Boström, 2012: 4),and include human welfare, social justice, social adaptation, cultural diversity, democratic rights, social gender issues, employee rights, broad participation, social capital development and individual skills (Vifell & Thedvall, 2012: 50). This actually suggests four fundamental problems in deriving social sustainability goals and their corresponding indicators. These are as follows (Omann & Spangenberg, 2002: 4):

- There is a lack of conceptual explicity on social sustainability. For example; while the issues such as labor, employment opportunities, business prospects, health and safety are mostly discussed in Germany; consumption, gender, and aging society are discussed in the Netherlands, poverty issues constitute the major part of discussions in the UK. Employment, employability education,

education and training, and women's participation in the labor market in the information society were emphasized in the European Commission.

- The complexity of the concept of social sustainability likely can not be managed in existing institutional environments. While sustainability is degraded into a kind of "21 th century environmentalism; the non-environmental aspects of sustainability are either ignored, or degraded into the side effects of environmental policies to be controlled. In the best case, social sustainability, including social objectives, is specified separately, but can not be fully integrated into sustainability frame.
- Easily understandable targets should be created to discuss social sustainability on an equal level with other aspects of sustainable development. Indicators and targets are proposed for the small segments of social development, but too little is mentioned about the general tendency.
- Defining social goals as a part of a general sustainability concept questions the basis of current European development model, which is basically a productive model of a society. That is, this model ackowledge gainful occupation as a valuable source of income; it consideres that only market transactions contribute to the standard of living. In this way, it leads to systematic prejudice of social welfare towards women, ignoring the tremendous value of unpaid work.

3 Principles and Characteristics of Social Sustainability

Although the definition of social sustainability can not be absolutely made, the studies of social sustainability meet in a common set of principles. These principles also reveal a visionary perspective that will provide social sustainability. The first of these principles is equality. According to the principle of equality, the community provides fair opportunities and results for all its members, especially for the poorest and most vulnerable prople. Equality takes on a task of a filter where all other principles are satisfied. There must be some features to satisfy the principle of equality. These are equality of opportunity for all members, equality for community, equality for human rights and equality for disadvantaged groups. The second principle is diversity. Community encourages and supports diversity. The third principle is interattachment. Community provides processes, systems and structures that encourage formal, informal and institutional interrelationship both within and outside the community. The fourth principle is quality of life. Quality of life ensures to meet the basic needs of the society. The fifth principle is democracy and governance. Society provides democratic processes, open and accountable governance structures (McKenzie, 2004: 18–19).

Omann and Spangenberg (2002: 6) expressed their social sustainability criteria in a similar way to McKenzie's principles in their study of defining goals and criteria for social sustainability.

Basic supply: minimum basic needs (residence, food, clothing, health) and assurance against central risks (illness, disability) should be provided for all members of a society.

Independent livelihood security: Livelihood security of all members of a society should be guaranteed with voluntarily realized activities.

Equal opportunities: All members of a society should have equal opportunities in education, employment and access to information.

Social resources: Strengthen social cohesion, indulgence, solidarity, integration capability, social welfare tendency and potentials to control non-violent conflict.

Based on the principles of social sustainability, McKenzie (2004: 13), in his study, set forth the indicators of the features of social sustainability and steps for its establishment and implementation as follows.

- Equality of access to key services (including health, education, transport, housing and entertainment),
- Providing equality between generations. In other words, providing future generations not to fall into a disadvantaged situation due to current generation's activities,
- A cultural relations system in which positive aspects of different cultures are assessed and protected, and cultural integration of individuals and groups are supported at any time, or a supported cultural relations system.
- Citizens' extensive participation especially at local level, in not only electoral procedures but also in other areas of political activity,
- A system to transmit social sustainability awareness from one generation to another,
- A communal responsibility feeling to sustain this transmission system,
- Mechanisms existing to collectively define the strengths and needs of a community,
- Mechanisms that enable a community to meet its own needs through community action,
- Political advocacy mechanisms to meet needs that can not be met through social action.

When considered from the perspective of sustainable development, social sustainability has principles and criteria dealing with the establishment of a sub-structure that will realize unity and solidarity among people. In this context, it reveals factors that abalienate society, cause its dissociation and that will harm public awarenes in the future, and it involves an effort to create a world order in which there are no barriers for future generations.

4 Social Sustainability Dimension of Corporate Sustainability

The consideration of sustainable development in the dimension of businesses and establishment of balance in triple bottom lines are explained by the concept of "corporate sustainability". Corporate sustainability is expressed for businesses to adapt economic, social and environmental factors to their operations and strategies to create long-term value. Corporate sustainability has also led to changes in the profit-oriented perspective of businesses, causing them to deal with social and environmental issues (Tuna & Besler, 2015: 174–175). The fact that especially managers and shareholders aware that the success of businesses depends on the welfare of the different sources involved in operations, and that the depletion of resources will restrict the alternatives in their own operations (Kira & VanEijnatten, 2007: 2) have increased the importance of corporate sustainability.

Businesses do not operate in a limited market area as it used to be in previous periods. As a result of this, the effects created by businesses are on a global scale, and their areas of responsibility are increasing accordingly. Regarding the relations that the businesses develop with the society, it is seen that expectations of the society from businesses are increasing. Today's society, which is especially called as knowledge society, have expectations for businesses to take an active role in the solution of both ecological, economic and social problems that they have caused during economic value creation process (MısırdalıYangil, 2015: 361). At this point, the social dimension of corporate sustainability enables businesses to understand their influences on society and people (http://esg.adec-innovations.com/about-us/faqs/what-is-social-sustainability/), thus leading to businesses for solution. But, the needs and expectations of societies differ depending on development level of societies. It is therefore necessary for businesses to analyze the needs and expectations of the society in which they operate, and identify solutions for them.

As well as the topic of social sustainability cover anthropocentric approaches such as labor, empowerment of women, social gender equality, poverty, education and health, the main task in these studies belongs to governments. However, businesses are expected to actively participate in these fields. For example,they are expected not to create a negative influence on human rights while performing their activities.In this context, social sustainability deals with managing

Tab. 2: Social Sustainability Indicators from Companies' Perspective. Reference: Ajmal, Khan, Hussain & Helo, 2017: 2033

Indicators	Indicators
Equal Opportunities	Indigenous Rights
Education and Training	Labor Practices
Governance	Fair Operating Practices
Health and Safety	Cultural Heritage
Employment	Community Involvement and Development
Job Security	Technology Development
Human Rights	Consumer/Product Responsibility

everything that affects businesses' relationships with their stakeholders, such as employees, customers, suppliers, society, and becomes a proactive way in developing these relationships (https://www.unglobalcompact.org/what-is-gc/our-work/social). Corporate social sustainability literally refers to enterprices' engage in activities and practices as having common social concerns with society.

The best social sustainability practices in businesses involve a range of work practices, extending especially from workplace diversity to occupational health and safety, education and training, to provide a quality work environment. These practices involve human rights and human development concerns, and take institutional interaction with society into account. It also consider product or service performance, customer health and safety, marketing standards and compliance with ethical rules and reflect this with its product responsibility (http://sustainability.sbp360.com/triple-bottom-line/social-sustainability). The operation topics of social sustainability are also seen as its indicators. Businesses especially benefit from these indicators when they prepare sustainability reports, and can create a standard for businesses.

When study topics of social sustainability examined, it is seen that it have both individual and collective characteristics, and that it creates a wide space in which businesses will be a pressure element for their stakeholders, which has led the importance of social sustainability to increase for businesses over the past decade. According to the United Nations Global Principles Contract, targeting social sustainability will help businesses (https://www.unglobalcompact.org/what-is-gc/our-work/social); to enter new markets, to protect business partners and attract new ones, to be the source of innovation for new products or service line, to be an internal moral resource and increase employee's attachment, to improve risk management, to improve conflicts between company and society.

Social sustainability reduces risks for businesses. Mismanaged social sustainability can lead to situations such as improper working conditions and making production ignoring public health, which primarily damage to product quality and also brand image (http://esg.adec-innovations.com/about-us/faqs/what-is-social-sustainability/). Furthermore, businesses' social sustainability-related deficiencies such as poverty, inequality, and poor legal rules can inhibit their operations and growth (https://www.unglobalcompact.org/what-is-gc/our-work/social).

In order for businesses to make use of the benefits of social sustainability, it is first necessary for them to identify existing social sustainability situations. To fulfill this, there are two questions that businesses should ask. The first one is what are the negative effects that businesses create on their stakeholders? In other words, it is necessary to determine to which need of stakeholders and at which level was damaded. Secondly, how they will contribute to meet these needs that they have damaged, in a sustainable way (https://www.triplepundit.com/2015/08/social-sustainability-well-organization/). The answers to these questions will guide businesses for strategies and practices to be followed.

Eş (2008: 24) listed strategies and practices that businesses can socially perform as follows:

- Helping employees in their own development and career studies, offering them safety work environments, not making discrimination in the fields such as wages and promotion (sex, race, religion, language), providing health insurance, etc.
- Being in communication with shareholders and ensuring transparency in decision-making processes and information retrieval, and publishing annual activity reports at the end of each year,
- To contribute to the development of universal principles such as SA 8000 Social Responsibility Standard.

When these strategies and implementations are considered, it is necessary for businesses to revise human resources policies within the scope of sustainability, and voluntarily apply institutional governance principles and standards. In addition, in respecct to any individual (employees, customers, etc.) -intended decision, they should acknowledge universal principles in their own internal structure, and adopt them in their own business policies.

5 Conclusion

Despite the fact that sustainability has been defined by ecological, economic and social aspects since the 1980s, its social aspect has been more ignored than other ones. Many studies, both singly and holistically, have been done in respect to the aspects of ecological and economic sustainability. However, the social sustainability aspect has been studied alongside these concepts, and examined singly in very few studies, which suggests that its content and definition is general and noninclusive. Besides, the fact that priorities of societies change according to their level of development, and societies and individuals have dynamic characters, which leads to a different approach to social sustainability.

While social sustainability includes the criteria that address people's social and institutional relationships starting from their basic needs in the perspective of sustainable development; it deals with the management of relations with stakeholders in the perspective of corporate sustainability, and aims to meet the expectations of future stakeholders, not just today's. In this sense, social sustainability has the ability to create a vision of stakeholder expectations for businesses.

Many social problems in the world cause expectations from businesses to increase, and stakeholders create pressure on businesses to solve these problems. While employees expect from businesses to offer a quality job environment in which balance between business and life is established, job security is ensured, skills are developed and discovered through training activities in addition to fair and equitable behaviors; society expect from businesses to take part in the solution of social problems such as poverty, corruption, inequality in income distribution, establishment of justice in education and health, development of backward segments of society. The customers of enteprises have many expectations in many fields such as provision of customer's health and safety in products and services with the awareness of product responsibility, product performance improvement. Meeting all these expectations is social sustainability. However, today, there are still many people who work long hours for very low wage and in non-humanistic working environments and there are workers who are seriously injured or die because of not being taken necessary precautions, there are still women in the world or in a significant part of our country who have difficulty finding employment and getting promotion due to their gender, there are people who see poverty as a fact of life and do not try to fight it, people lose their health because of the use of faulty products or health-damaging substances. The costs of the above mentioned negative conditions are very high in society and businesses. Today, businesses are not only paying high sum of money to abandon or ignore social sustainability, but also hamper their future by preventing the formation of a healthy society.

References

Ajmal, M., Khan, M.,Hussain, M. & Helo, P. (2017). Concepting social sustainability in the business operations. Proceedings of the International Conference on Industrial Engineering and Operations Management. April 11–13, 2017. Rabat, Morocco. 2027–2040.

Bansal, P. (2005). Evolving sustainably: a longitudinal study of corporate sustainable development. Strategic Management Journal, 26, 197–218.

Boström, M. (2012). A missing pillar? Challenges in theorizng and practicing social sustainability: introduction to the special issue. Sustainability: Science, Practice and Policy, 8(1), 3–14.

Eş, A. (2008). Sürdürülebilirlik ve firma düzeyinde sürdürülebilirlik performans ölçümü. Abant İzzet Baysal Üniversitesi, Sosyal Bilimler Enstitüsü, Yayınlanmamış Yüksek Lisans Tezi, Bolu.

Harris, J. M. (2000). Basic principles of sustainability development. Global Development and Environment Institute Working Paper 00-04. Tufts University, Medford, MA. http://ase.tufts.edu/gdae/publications/working_papers/Sustainable%20Development.pdf (Accepted: 30.06. 2018).

Kallström, H. N. & Ljung, M. (2005). Social sustainability and collaborative learning. Ambio, 34(4/5), 376–382.

Kira, M. & Van Eijnatten, F.M. (2007). Socially sustainable work organization. Seventh Annual Meeting of the European Chaos and Complexity in Organisations Network ECCON Hotel Nassau, Bergen aan Zee, The Netherlands.

Lehtonen, M. (2004). The environmental-social interface of sustainable development: capabilities, social capital, institutions. Ecological Economics, 49, 199–214.

Mani, V., Agrawal, R. & Sharma, V., (2014). Supplier selection using social sustainability: AHP based approach in India. International Strategic Management Review. 2 (2), 98–112.

McKenzie, S. (2004). Social Sustainability: Towards Some Definitions. Working Paper Series No 27. Hawke Research Institute for Sustainable Societies, University of South Australia, Magill.

Mısırdalı Yangil, F. (2015). Kurumsal sürdürülebilirlik kapsamında sürdürülebilirlik raporlarına ilişkin içerik analizi: Türkiye'deki en büyük 100 sanayi işletmesi. İşletme Araştırmaları Dergisi, 7(3), 356–376.

Omann, I. & Spangenberg, J.H. (2002). The social dimension of sustainability in a socio-economic scenario. Paper presented at 7th Biennial Conference of the International Society for Ecological Economics in Sousse (Tunisia). March 8–10, 2002.

Parra, C. (2013). Social Sustainability: a competing to social innovation?. In Frank Moulaert, Diana MacCallum, Abid Mehmood & Hambouch Abdelillah (eds.) The International Handbook on Social Innovation: Collective Action, Social Learning and Transdisciplinary Research. Northampton, MA: Edward Elgar.

Tuna, Ö. & Besler, S. (2015). Kurumsal sürdürülebilirlik anlayışı ve uygulamaları: Örnek olay çalışması. İ. Ü. Siyasal Bilimler Fakültes Dergisi, 52, 173–199.

Vallence, S., Perkins, H.C. & Dixon, J. E. (2011). What is social sustainability? A clarification of concepts. Geoforum, 42, 342–348.

Vifell, A. C. & Thedvall, R. (2012). Organizing for social sustainability: governance through bureaucratization in meta-organizations. Sustainability: Science, Practice and Policy. 8(1), 50–58.

http://esg.adec-innovations.com/about-us/faqs/what-is-social-sustainability/ (Erişim tarihi: 30. 06. 2018)

https://www.unglobalcompact.org/what-is-gc/our-work/social (Erişim tarihi: 30. 06. 2018)

https://www.triplepundit.com/2015/08/social-sustainability-well-organization/ (Erişim tarihi: 30. 06. 2018)

http://sustainability.sbp360.com/triple-bottom-line/social-sustainability (Erişim tarihi: 30. 06. 2018)

Fikret Yaman[1]

Subliminal Advertising

1 Advertisement

Advertisement is an extremely important marketing component for companies and consumers. Companies are able to "tell" their products to consumers with the help of advertisement, inform them, persuade them, and remind them about their products. For consumers, on the other hand, advertisement is a "tool" that helps them identify products by guiding their preferences for products.

Advertisement is one of the marketing elements prepared by receiving the help of advertising agencies or their own departments of advertisers by using communication means such as television, radio, newspaper, internet; and are published in return for a certain price, aiming to promote a person, a product, an enterprise, an institution or an idea to the public.

The importance of advertisement is understood better with each passing day; and businesses which do not care for advertising are facing the danger of being withdrawn from the market in time.

Even if they do not want this, people are exposed to advertisements in their everyday lives. People are interacting with advertisements with the help of open air advertisements they see when they go to work, on the radio they listen to, on the Internet in their workplaces, on the television they watch at home, and in the newspaper or magazine they read at cafés. They show a reaction to the advertisements, which have become an indispensable part in our lives, in this situation. This reaction may sometimes be positive or sometimes negative; and sometimes people who are under the effects of advertisements reflect the things they acquire in advertisements on their behaviors.

There are many components in the creation and presentation of the advertisement on the market. Firstly, the person or the business that wants to promote a product will either contact the advertising department -if there is an advertising department in the business- or will start looking for an external advertising agency. Today, the advertising agencies' using technology and changing the viewpoints prepares the ground for advertisements that were never thought of previously. Once the preparation of the advertisement is completed, the selection

1 Assist. Prof. Dr., Afyon Kocatepe University.

of the advertisement tools becomes important. Here, the decision is up to the advertise-giver. The advertise-giver of the agency has the status of being a "guide" in this stage. Once the advertisement tool is selected, the advertisement meets consumers. The consumer may react to the advertisement positively or negatively. The positive reaction of the consumer is buying the product s/he watches in the advertisement; and the negative reaction appears in the form of escaping from the advertisement and not buying it.

The main purpose of advertisement is to promote sales of the advertised product. For this purpose, advertisers make use of several concepts like fear, humor, music, religion, and sexuality. While they are making use of these concepts, they mostly try to contact the subconscious of people with their messages.

2 Subliminal Advertisement

Subliminal Advertisement is a technique in which consumers are exposed to the pictures of products, names of the brands or other stimuli used in marketing without being conscious Trappey (1996, pp. 517).

Subliminal advertising has been applied from the past until our present time. Such advertisements are successful in selling the product but are unethical advertisements. For this reason, subliminal advertising, which cause that consumers are manipulated in a defenseless manner, are forbidden in many countries Özdemir and Yaman, (2015, ss. 199).

It was claimed by some authors that subliminal materials are usually very weak and the receiver is not aware of them with no sensory effects, which makes the effect of such advertisement negligible. However, some authors also claimed that "subliminal advertisement" might be influential and its use to affect the purchase behaviors of consumers is justified Tsai, Liang and Liu (2007, pp. 4).

Dues to its hidden characteristics, and because of the ethical concerns, the subliminal advertising is underestimated in previous studies Moore (1982, pp. 38–39).

A subliminal message usually appears in the form of a reminder; and does not cause the same recalling about the product when the "visible advertisement" is considered. For this reason, subliminal advertisement is limited to the cognition of products that are recalled in a very limited manner Rose (1958, pp. 280).

It is clear that many people know the "subliminal advertising". They also understand this concept; and believe that such advertisement is used by advertisers in a successful manner to influence the brand preference and purchase behavior Rogers and Smith (1993, pp. 11).

In New Jersey, in September 1957, the audience of a theatre who were blinded to the experiment were invited to "drink Coca-Cola" and "eat popcorn" in a short show which was super-imposed on the film that was on. The exposure time for the audience was very short and the audience did not become aware of any messages. The company which was involved in this experiment reported later that there was a huge increase in coke and popcorn sales; however, they did not provide any documents on these effects Moore (1982, pp. 38). This is considered to be among the first examples for subliminal advertisement.

Fechner and Helmholtz in the late 19th century conducted the first study on sensations and perceptions in the field of psychology. The "subliminal perception" field emerged in this way and has become a controversial field in our present time Broyles (2006, pp. 393).

For many years now, advertisers have used the subliminal advertisement. When the audience changes the station on the radio, the spot radio and TV announcements are subliminal especially when the audience starts a conversation during the advertisement or walks to the fridge at home. Most of the time, advertisers increase the volume when the advertisements start to improve the chance of catching the attention of the listener Klass (1958, pp. 150).

Subliminal advertising is the placing of the elements, words, pictures and shapes included in the advertisement in a way that cannot be traced at first sight by people and only understood at subconscious level Bişkin (2014, ss. 180).

Collective subconscious consists of elements that are called archetypes. An archetype expresses the learning of a certain topic by experiences. Archetype is a conscious that undertakes the organizing principle role as a result of the things we do or see. The functioning of it follows the same route mentioned in Sigmund Freud's theory for the activation of the instinct. It is like a baby's first desire to eat something but not knowing what s/he wants, and as s/he grows up, shaping his/her wishes and asking for things with their names Darıcı (2013, ss. 79). In archetypes, people behave like a newborn baby. As they gain experience, they discriminate between these behaviors. Advertisers use different archetypes like birth, death, and family in their advertisements.

A subliminal message is conveyed in such a way that the receiver is not aware of receiving, which means that the symbols are very "weak" or very "short" to be comprehended Wells, Burnett and Moriarty (1992, pp. 49).

Subliminal advertisement means conveying persuasive messages below the perception threshold "buried" in a material that may be perceived. It is possible to name the message that flashes between images in a video advertisement and that is not perceivable, or a message which may only be heard when played backwards. Subliminal advertisement differs completely from simple "exposure" to a

Picture 1: The difference between looking and seeing. Source: https://pbs.twimg.com/media/CfR5A74WAAQdL92.jpg 12.08.2016

message, which means stimulus is perceivable even if not effective. Subliminal advertisement claims that a certain stimulus is intelligible even if it is not perceived in a normal manner Tellis (1997, pp. 105).

The 3 types of the subliminal stimulation are as follows Dunn, Barban, Krugman and Reid (1990, pp. 81);

- Stimulus presented at a fast pace in images like films or advertisements,
- The speech in an accelerated manner as low-volume audio message,
- Stimulus like a word or sexual image embedded in printed material.

Most of the time, the words "look" and "see" do not mean the same. Our previous experiences may affect our perception. when people are asked what they see when they look at the above picture, many of them may answer like "eggs and fried potatoes". However, when we look more carefully, it is seen in the picture that there is a piece of peach on yogurt and apple slices next to. For this reason, if people want to be influenced less by the subliminal advertisements, they must be aware of the importance of looking.

A belief is dominant in the society claiming that subliminal advertising is performed. In a telephone questionnaire performed by Rogers and Smith, 45 % of the participants said that subliminal advertising was influential in making them purchase the products advertised. In a questionnaire performed by the Roper Group, 57 % of the participants in 1992, and 80 % of the participants in 2011 mentioned their belief in the existence of subliminal advertising Bişkin (2014, ss. 184).

3 Subliminal Message Techniques

Advertisers make use of many messages to reach the subconscious of people, which are conveyed to people through certain techniques. Among these techniques, there are the 25th Frame Technique, Fovea Spot, Tachistoscope Device and Eye-Tracking Techniques are the most well-known ones.

3.1 The 25th Frame Technique

The 25th Frame Technique was used in old times. Its effect was less than the other techniques; and nowadays it is not used much. The technique influences the subconscious. However, it is simple when compared to the techniques that are used today. The 25th Square Technique, which was employed in old days when computers and technology were not so influential; and when the effects of the cinema and television were more in people's lives, may be immediately understood with the help of the new broadcasting systems and technologies Darıcı (2013, ss. 168–169).

3.2 Fovea Centralis

Fovea Centralis is a structure that sees what the eye cannot see. The eye, which is constantly scanning, "casts" the objects, the events and the information it scans to the subconscious without even being aware of it. One remembers very few things that are stored in the brain with Fovea Movements Sungur (2007, ss. 178).

A sharp and central vision is the task of the Fovea Centralis. This is required for reading in which visual details are very important Kessler and Guenther (2017, pp. 309).

The fovea, or the Fovea Centralis with its other name, takes the visual detail as it is and transfers it to the mind. However, people cannot perceive all of the elements that are transmitted to the mind in a conscious manner. If we consider the fovea as if it is a camera, we may say that everything we see is recorded; however, not all of them are perceived, in other words, they go to the subconscious (http://pentangle.blogcu.com/bilinc-altina-yonelik-etkileme-ve-subliminalreklamlar/2416061). In this situation, the messages that are desired to be conveyed by advertisers are positioned in our subconscious without willingly.

3.3 Tachistoscope

In the past, a specific device, which could emit the white light flash at a speed of 1/60.000th of a second, was developed and was called as "Tachistoscope". The white light flash in the Tachistoscope was very fast and was imperceptible

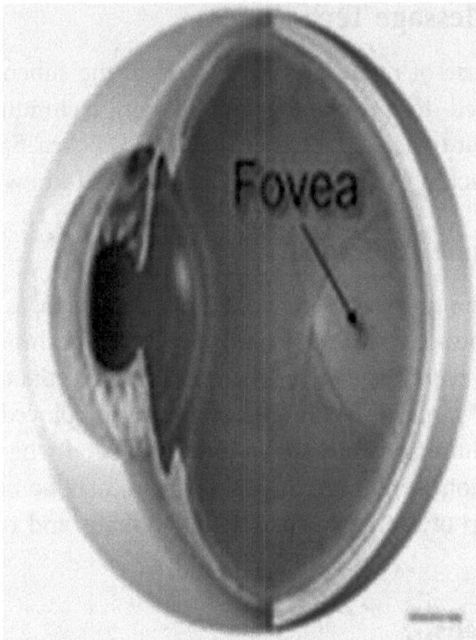

Picture 2: Fovea Centralis. Source: http://bp0.blogger.com/_WbS9_NPw4jU/RwTYhRO9bCI/AAAAAAAAAPg/07rRWUekmvY/s1600-h/001.jpg

for the human consciousness, which was called "subliminal" to mean "below", i.e. "sub" and to mean "threshold", i.e. "limen" for the perception of humans. Tachistoscope was used in a work that was prepared for Kodak and provided lighting in a pitch-dark studio for a camera with a large lens that had an open aperture. The flash of the Tachistoscope was triggered in an electronic manner by a rifle shot sound; and the image of the flying bullet was frozen on a color film Rogers (1992, pp. 12).

The Tachistoscope reflects images, which are invisible to the eye but may be perceived by the subconscious, was found in 1859 by the German physiologist A. W. Volkmann. The device was used for trainings during the World War II; and successful results were reported (http://subliminal-mesaj-nedir.blogspot.com/2015/04/subliminal-mesaj-nedir.html#!/2015/04/subliminal-mesaj-nedir.html).

3.4 Eye-Tracking Techniques

Increased eccentricity of the Fovea affects the acuity across the retina of human eye and is the central and most sensitive part of the retina that is opposite the

Picture 3: The Tachistoscope. Source: http://2.bp.blogspot.com/pCQWaNKsASM/VSVcdQ4neDI/AAAAAAAAAG0/HENMwoJV8M0/s1600/takiskop-cihazi1.jpg

lens. For this reason, eye-tracking provides better understanding in terms of visual data acquisition behavior and attention Ma, Campos, Shanshi, Gardiner and Scott (2016, pp. 57).

In recent years, studies on human-computer interaction have made use of Eye-Tracking Techniques; and investigated the user behaviors on webpages and the visual attention and cognitive processes of users Bayram and Yeni (2011, pp. 223).

4 Subliminal Advertisement Examples

There are many examples of subliminal advertising that affect people. These effects are applied by different methods. These different examples are given below. Ads, sometimes sexuality, sometimes fear, sometimes unexpectedly, comes out and sends a message to my unconscious.

In the advertisement given, there is a perfume which was released by Joop brand to the market with the name "Nightflight". The blue color of the product has been used in the front line. However, the most noticeable thing in subliminal terms is the use of a naked male figure. The advertisement was not only limited with this, and the bottle of the product was combined with men's sexuality; and a subliminal message was given in the form of "becoming a strong man through

Picture 4: Joop Advertisement. Source: https://fragrances.bg/en/product/product/joop-nightflight-edt-125ml-for-men-without-package

Picture 5: Skıttles Advertisement. Source: https://mediastudiesmeetsmarketing.files.wordpress.com/2014/09/subliminal-skittles.jpg

Picture 6: Domestos Advertisement. Source: https://www.sanalmarket.com.tr/kweb/prview/73159944-31053-domestos-camasir-suyu-dag-esintisi-2x2000-gr-mikrop-oyuncak-set-hediyeli-paket

the use of this perfume". The strong male figure was placed ahead of the product in this advertise.

In Picture 5, there is an advertisement image of a candy company. In the advertisement, the letter "S" placed in front of the "explosion" sends a subliminal message to the subconscious of people. With this letter, which is placed before the word, sexuality is evokes, and this message is conveyed to the consumers.

The image given above is from an advertisement. The message to be conveyed in this advertisement is that if the product is not used, the germs will surround you; and you may only be saved from them with this product. The advertisement aims to sell the product by bringing the unconscious fears of people to the conscious.

References

Bayram, S. ve Yeni, S. (2011). "Web Tabanlı Eğitsel Çoklu Ortamların Göz İzleme Tekniği ile Kullanışlılık Açısından Değerlendirilmesi". *Ahi Evran Üniversitesi Eğitim Fakültesi Dergisi*, Cilt 12(2): 221–234.

Bişkin, F. (2014). *Subliminal A.Ş.* Ankara: ElmaYayınevi.

Broyles, S.J. (2006). "Subliminal Advertising and the Perpetual Popularity of Playing to People's Paranoia". *The Journal of Consumer Affairs*, 40(2): 392–406.

Darıcı, S. (2013). *Bilinçaltı Reklamcılık ve İletişim Teknikleri*. İstanbul: İstanbul Gelişim Üniversitesi Yayınları.

Dunn, S.W., Barban, A.M., Krugman, D.M. and Reid, L.N. (1990). *Advertising*. USA: The Dreyden Press.

http://bp0.blogger.com/_WbS9_NPw4jU/RwTYhRO9bCI/AAAAAAAAAPg/07rRWUekmvY/s1600-h/001.jpg

http://2.bp.blogspot.com/pCQWaNKsASM/VSVcdQ4neDI/AAAAAAAAAG0/HENMwoJV8M0/s1600/takiskop-cihazi1.jpg

https://fragrances.bg/en/product/product/joop-nightflight-edt-125ml-for-men-without-package

https://mediastudiesmeetsmarketing.files.wordpress.com/2014/09/subliminal-skittles.jpg

https://pbs.twimg.com/media/CfR5A74WAAQdL92.jpg

http://pentangle.blogcu.com/bilinc-altina-yonelik-etkileme-ve-subliminalreklamlar/2416061.

https://www.sanalmarket.com.tr/kweb/prview/73159944-31053-domestos-camasir-suyu-dag-esintisi-2x2000-gr-mikrop-oyuncak-set-hediyeli-paket

http://subliminal-mesaj-nedir.blogspot.com/2015/04/subliminal-mesajnedir.html#!/2015/04/ subliminal-mesaj-nedir.html

Kessler, S.H. and Guenther, L. (2017). "Eyes on the frame: Explaining people's online Searching Behavior in Response to TV Consumption". *Internet Research*, 27(2): 303–320.

Klass, B. (1958). "The Ghost of Subliminal Advertising". *American Marketing Association*, 23(2):146–150.

Ma, J., Campos, A.C., Shanshi, L., Gardiner, S. and Scott, N. (2016). "Attention, Emotion and Hedonic Service Experiences: Managing and Delivering Services in the Asian Century". *Worldwide Hospitality and Tourism Themes*, 8 (1): 53–60.

Moore, T.E., (1982). "Subliminal Advertising: What You See Is What You Get". *Journal of Marketing*, 46: 38–47.

Özdemir, Ş. and Yaman, F. (2015). *Türkiye'de Reklam Ahlakı Sorunlar ve Çözüm Önerileri*. İstanbul:İgiad.

Rogers, M. and Smith, K.H. (1993). "Public Perceptions of Subliminal Advertising: Why Practitioners Shouldn't İgnore This İssue". *Journal of Advertising Research*, 33(2): 10–18.

Rogers, S. (1992). "How a Publicity Blitz Created The Myth of Subliminal Advertising". *Public Relations Quarterly*, 37(4): 12–17.

Rose, A.W. (1958). "Motivation Research and Subliminal Advertising". *Social Research*, 25(3): 271–284.

Sungur, S. (2007). "Bilinçaltı Reklamcılık ve Toplumsal Etkileri". *İstanbul Üniversitesi İletişim Fakültesi Dergisi*, 29(1):169–182.

Telis, G.J. (1997). *Advertising and Sales Promotion Strategy*. USA: Addison-Wesley Educational Publishers.

Trappey, C. (1996). "A Meta-Analysis of Consumer Choice and Subliminal Advertising". *Psychology & Marketing*, 13(5): 517–530.

Tsai, M., Liang, W. and Liu, M. (2007). "The Effects of Subliminal Advertising on Consumer Attitudes and Buying İntentios". *International Journal of Marketing*, 24(1): 3–14.

Wells, W., Burnett, J. and Moriarty, S. (1992). *Advertising Principles and Practice*. New Jersey: Prentice Hall.

Muhammet Atalay[1]

Industry 4.0: Its Development and Pioneers

1 Introduction

There is a common agreement that 4 major transformations in the economy have come into question after the agricultural revolution. These are the first major transformation in which water and steam powered mechanical production plants were engaged, the second major transformation in which electricity-based mass production based on division of labor was engaged, the third major transformation in which electronic and information technology, which carried the automation of manufacturing to the advanced stage, was engaged, and the fourth major transformation in which production based on cyber-physical systems has been engaged. These transformations are called "industrial revolution" since their effects have been mainly felt in the fields of technology, industry and trade. The latest one of them, unlike the others, is progressing at an unprecedented pace with intensive technologies such as internet, sensors, artificial intelligence, cyber systems and wearable technologies so that information and network technologies will intensely encircle almost every area of life. The transformations and developments experienced with reference to this progress are probably summarized by the concept of "Industry 4.0".

The source that constitutes the raw material of the developments emerging in all these transformations experienced has also undergone a transformation. For instance, mechanization and the sources, such as oil, that will provide energy to the machines were very important in the first industrial revolution. For this reason, the leap which was experienced with the engagement of electricity is regarded as a new industrial revolution. At this point, the data generated consisted of the records kept accordingly. However, because of the engagement of computers along with the third industrial revolution, it became easier to store the data kept, and the steps regarding the storage and analysis of larger volume data were accelerated. Although the data generated were human-induced, the data generated by the machines were also analyzed. The use of artificial intelligence techniques besides statistics in data analysis was also encountered as of

1 Assist. Prof., Kırklareli University Faculty of Economics and Administrative Sciences Department of Business Administration Quantitative Methods Department, atalay@klu.edu.tr

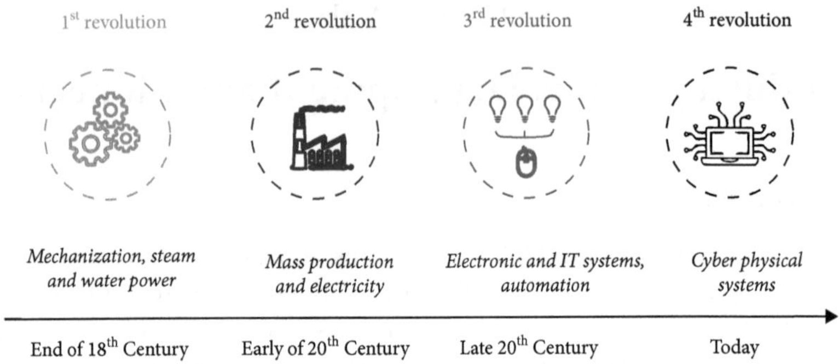

Fig. 1: Milestones of Industrial Revolutions. Source: Holtkamp and Iyer, 2017, p. 7

these years. Whichever tool is used, the results obtained are evolved into "information" which becomes more valuable as the analysis becomes deeper. Here at this stage, we face with a new source of energy, Data. The Fourth Industrial Revolution is progressing with a stage in which data is used as a very important source and big data stacks are analyzed with the dimensions such as volume, diversity, speed and value. In the processing of these data, the techniques classified as data mining, artificial intelligence, machine learning (artificial learning) and deep learning, as well as statistical methods, are used.

The Fourth Industrial Revolution is a transformation containing many components. These components, which will be explained in the following sections, are experienced simultaneously with this transformation in the areas such as daily life, politics, economy, sports, and physical life. The competition conditions of global economy requires that the countries that want to keep up with the modern age are prepared for the developments that are being experienced/will be experienced, and that the businesses comply with the developments brought/to be brought by Industry 4.0.

2 Industry 4.0 and Its Components

Industry 4.0, which came to the fore for the first time in Germany, generally projects the use of information and network technologies in all sectors, especially in industry, the renewal of industrial processes in connection with digital networks and synchronized with data analysis, and the integration of production with smart factories. There are systems in which industry is connected to each other by network technologies such as sensors, and cloud computing, data transfer and simultaneous data analysis not only in the phases of production but also in all phases from raw material procurement to after sales services. On the other hand, factories are expected to be transformed into new generation smart factories and then all functions integrated with them are also expected to be transformed into smart systems.

The concept, which was declared to be one of the main initiatives of the high-tech strategy by the German Government by bringing to the agenda at the Hanover Fair in 2011, started to be used as "Industry 4.0" by referring to the Fourth Industrial Revolution with the report prepared by a working group in 2013 (Kagermann, Wahlster and Helbig, 2013). It was supported by the business world, and the world of politics and academia as an approach to strengthen the competitive power of the German manufacturing industry (Kagermann, Lukas and Wahlster, 2011). The "Plattform Industrie 4.0" portal, which was formed based on this vision and makes suggestion on how to implement transformation, describes Industry 4.0 as "a new value chain organization and management throughout the life cycle of products" (Plattform Industrie 4.0, 2014). The same concept is called as the "Industrial Internet" by General Electric and is defined as the "integration of complex physical machines and devices, enabling smart industrial operations, using advanced data analytics to which the objects, machines, computers and people connect via internet" (Industrial Internet Consortium, 2013). Since then, many articles, congresses and academic publications have addressed this issue. When the literature is reviewed, it is seen that the studies carried out have focused on four main elements of Industry 4.0: Cyber Physical Systems, Internet of Things (IoT), Internet of Services (IoS) and Smart Factories (Herman, Pentek and Otto, 2015). These concepts are used in a way to involve other components such as big data, cloud computing, integration of machines, and smart production.

The Industry 4.0 vision contains a combination of different applications both in the economy and in other areas of life by expanding from the days during which it was put forward until today. The main ones of them (Kesayak, 2017, Coşkunoğlu, 2016) can be listed as the Internet of things (IoT), cloud computing, cyber physical systems, cyber security, autonomous robots, horizontal and vertical software integration, integrated systems, big data analytics, data mining, artificial intelligence and machine learning, augmented reality, simulation, additive manufacturing, and 3D software. The sensors, unmanned air vehicles, genetic and block-chain technologies can also be added to them.

2.1 Internet of Things

The concept of Internet of Things was first used in a presentation (Ashton, 2009) prepared by Kevin Asthon in 1999 (Kutup, 2011) and constituted one of the foundations of the Industry 4.0. The Internet of Things (IoT) can be described as a network in which cyber physical systems collaborate with each other through unique addressing schemes (Herman, Pentek and Otto, 2015). IoT allows the "things" and "objects" such as RFID, sensors, actuators and mobile phones to collaborate with their neighboring "smart" components in order to interact with each other and to achieve common goals through addressing schemes (Giusto, Lera, Morabito and Atzori, 2010, pp. V). In other words, it is possible that various things are in communication with each other through network technologies and manage their affairs by themselves. The system machines and programs that communicate and collaborate with each other and with people are described with IoT, which project a system that connects all subsystems, processes, internal and external objects to suppliers and customer networks (MÜSİAD [Independent Industrialists' and Businessmen's Association], 2017: pp. 51). Smart factories, smart homes, smart cities and intelligent networks are the examples of IoT's applications.

2.2 Cyber Physical Systems

An important component of Industry 4.0 is the Cyber Physical Systems (CPS), which combine the physical and cyber worlds and refer to the integration of calculations and physical processes. Embedded computers, monitors and networks usually monitor and control the physical processes in feedback cycles in which the physical processes influence the calculations (Herman, Pentek and Otto, 2015). They describe the systems that consist of software embedded in the hardware such as sensors, processors and communication technologies, and that can autonomously exchange information, initiate actions, and independently control each other (MÜSİAD [Independent Industrialists' and Businessmen's Association], 2017: pp. 52). Cyber-physical systems are the systems in which the basic principles in production processes such as observation, coordination and control are managed by the mixed technology consisting of computation and communication. The relevant mixed technology, more clearly, makes physical machines much smarter through integration with cyber technology. In this context, the process is referred to as cyber physical systems as a whole (Davutoğlu, Akgül and Yıldız, 2017).

Cyber physical systems (CPS) are the engineering systems that are formed by the seamless integration of calculation and physical components and that are connected to them. The advances in CPS will ensure the capability, adaptability, scalability, flexibility, safety, security and availability that will expand the horizons of these critical systems. CPS technologies transform the ways people interact with engineering systems, just as changing the way people interact with information. The new smart CPS promotes innovation and competition in a range of application areas such as agriculture, aviation, building design, civil infrastructure, energy, environmental quality, health and individualized medicine, production and transportation. Moreover, the integration of artificial intelligence with CPS creates new research opportunities with great social influences (National Science Foundation, 2018).

2.3 Big Data Analytics

The big data, which is described as "the data sets that are too large to be analyzed and cannot be managed by traditional data processing tools" (Ohlhorst, 2013: 1), is described by five concepts that we can briefly call 5V: Volume, Velocity, Variety, Verification, and Value. Along with the increase in data sources and data types, this definition can be extended in a way to include the concepts of 7V consisting of Volume, Velocity, Variety, Value, Veracity, Volatility and Validity (Khan, Uddin and Gupta, 2014), and 10V by adding Vulnerability, Variability, and Visualization to them (Firican, 2017) (Atalay and Çelik, 2017k). While the source of big data can be individual components such as people, machines and things, they are mostly used in interconnected systems. The data generated by one of them can be analyzed and transferred to make it possible for another component to decide and act wisely. For instance, the information coming from sensors such as log records of web servers, internet statistics, social media publications, blogs, microblogs, and climate sensors, and various and ever-changing data such as call records obtained from GSM operators fall within the definition of big data. This also allows for real-time and simultaneous decision making.

All business sectors from retailing to automotive and energy sectors store big data generated by interconnected objects, from all aspects of daily life (health, education, etc.). Big Data involves the processing, collection, storage, visualization and analysis of large amounts of data. It is predicted that the value creation for the Big Data will constitute 8 % of the European GDP until 2020 (Republique Française, 2016, pp. 51).

2.4 Cloud Computing

Cloud computing is the common name given to services providing common information sharing between the objects (IoT devices), and it is not a product but a service with this aspect. It is the use of existing information service via information network (usually internet) by providing the sharing of software and information in the main source. By storing the applications, programs and data owned in a virtual server, in other words in the cloud, and storing the data coming from IoT devices, it is possible to easily access these information, data and programs in any environment when the internet is connected (Aegean Region Chamber of Industry, 2015). Cloud computing model enables access to remote, distributed and scalable information processing sources according to needs instead of using a local infrastructure of the server and software.

Sector players improve themselves around important issues for the growth of cloud computing services, including standardization and data security. Cloud computing promises to increase business competition and to ensure the introduction of new innovative services. In addition to these economic facts, cloud computing also brings the issues related to security (such as the protection of personal data and the security of critical business data) to the agenda. This situation, which is expressed by the concept of cyber security, leads to another area of expertise. When devices are further connected to each other through the Internet, security and privacy become the primary concern between consumers and businesses, and cyber attacks are regarded as a growing threat. According to a report on cyber attacks and threats prepared by Vormetrik in 2016, it was stated that data are not only lost by those leaking information but mostly by externally financed attacks. These attacks consist of cybercrimes (data stealing etc.) by 44 %, hacker attacks by 17 %, cyber terrorism by 15 %, attacks carried out by states by 12 %, and commercial competing attacks by 12 % (MÜSİAD [Independent Industrialists' and Businessmen's Association], 2017, pp. 56).

Data processing is one of the most important information resources of Industry 4.0. Therefore, the data sharing must be adequately realized, thus the confidence that the shared data will be protected must be fully established. For this reason, data protection policies should be determined in advance and should be supported with protocols so that the data can be protected and customer and employees' information is not disclosed by a cyber attack. If customer information cannot be protected as a result of data breach, this may lead to the reduction and loss of customer confidence. For this reason, regulations that protect intellectual property rights and ensure information security should be made and updated continuously. Because the rapid developments in the field can make the measures taken inadequate in a short time.

2.5 Integrated Systems (Horizontal and Vertical System Integration)

With Industry 4.0, companies, departments, functions and capabilities will become more compatible as universal data integration networks are developed and really activate the automatic value chains. To ensure the integration of information technologies systems will enable that companies, suppliers and customers will be closely connected and will fully integrate them from business to the workshop level, from products to factories and automation. Along with the digitalization of information, information and communication technologies will be used intensively for the integration of systems in the stages of product creation and use. The machines will transmit the information to the integrated machines in order to initiate the next process step in any process of the business when other processes are completed or information is received from customers and stakeholders. The system integration, which will increase both coordination and productivity, appears to have evolved into new systems such as smart factories, smart houses, and smart cities.

2.6 Autonomous Robots and Smart Factories

Autonomous Robots can be defined as robotic systems with certain intelligence rather than the robots capable of doing the job automatically. Some of the robots may be in interaction with the environment. Pre-programmed robots are mechanical devices that work as previously described in their software, without needing to receive any signal. The robots that start to move after collecting a variety of information from the environment through sensors and then interpreting in their microcontroller are called "autonomous robots". Autonomous robots are designed in a way to respond to factors such as sound, light, image and temperature thanks to the software on them. Therefore, a robot has to fulfill 3 basic functions to gain the feature of autonomous robot: To see, think and start to move (Özışık, 2017). Nowadays, new generation robots that are used in many production environments and are much more flexible and cheap can be trained by the front staff to perform tasks that were previously thought to be very difficult for the machine. It is a fact that new technologies have opened a new era for manufacturers in which people and machines in automation will increasingly work together (Chui, George, Manyika and Miremadi, 2017). According to the data of the International Robotics Federation (2017), it is predicted that the number of industrial robots used in automation systems around the world will reach 3 million, with an annual average increase of 14 % between the years 2017 and 2020.

Autonomous robots are the key technology for flexible production systems, which are one of the critical points of Industry 4.0. They are also one of the most important components of "smart factories". In smart factories, people, autonomous robots, machines controlling each other and other factors of production are in deep interaction with each other. Furthermore, in these factories, the machines work within the framework of the cyber security by communicating with each other, and they have the privilege to automatically stop production and correct the problem when a problem is faced (Davutoğlu, Akgül and Yıldız, 2017). In a smart factory, a cyber physical system performs the tasks of supporting the factory, people and machines that it communicates through IoT. When autonomous robot applications are evaluated in terms of the present technology level and prevalence, it is seen that not only in terms of Industry 4.0 and smart factories but all processes from production to logistics will be possible with autonomous robot technologies (Yazıcı, 2016).

2.7 Augmented Reality and Simulation

Virtual Reality (VR) is a whole of concepts and tools which enable to feel as if you were in a virtual world. Augmented Reality (AR) brings together the real world and the computer generated virtual world and enables to interact with the digital (virtual) world without separating from the real world (Ürey and Akşit, 2018). It is the live, direct or indirect physical appearance generated by enriching the environment and its contents in the real world with computer-generated voice, video and graphic data.

With augmented reality, the objects in the physical world are modified and detailed by the computer. The user brings together the real world around him/her and the pre-prepared knowledge and items of this world and controls them interactively thanks to the devices with augmented reality technology or wearable technologies. For instance, how the parts of an automobile engine should be dismantled can be easily understood with a pair of glasses with augmented reality by the fact that the glasses describes the part viewed from the virtual images integrated on it when the user looks at the engine. This technology also shows that the qualified staff will have a transformation to have equipment that can use these technologies.

The virtual models of products, materials and production processes prepared by using real-time data are called simulation. In other words, it is the virtual creation of the physical world together with the machines, products and people, by imitating a real process or system (Davutoğlu, Akgül and Yıldız, 2017). With simulation, companies can model the processes such as design, production, and marketing and can predict the steps to be taken to improve quality while reducing costs before the process. The measurements performed using objects and sensors while establishing simulation models enable to obtain real-like result. For instance, with watches or wristbands that employees will wear and that are monitored via a device, they can be used to optimize the locations of the most sold items by measuring and analyzing the operator actions in the process between the placement of an item on the shelf and receiving and packing it. With these simulations prepared, it is possible to create environments where the machines can be turned off automatically when the employees are in danger (MÜSİAD [Independent Industrialists' and Businessmen's Association], 2017, pp. 105).

2.8 Data Mining, Artificial Intelligence (AI) and Machine Learning

It is possible to convert huge amount of data such as social media, emails, sensor data, geographical indications, location data, photos or videos that are collected from a wide variety of sources into an added-value by processing these data and obtaining analysis results. The businesses that implement it can make predictions and have knowledge about their customers, followers, supporters, competitors, enemies or partners. Data mining techniques include a number of methods used to obtain meaningful information from the data. They are the methods preferred for huge amount of data since the methods that are not based on preliminary assumptions, as well as statistical methods, are also used.

The artificial intelligence studies that aim to artificially produce the intelligent behaviors of beings in the nature (Charniak and McDermot, 1985; as cited in Nabiyev, 2012: 25) and also take model the living systems that function excellently and the human brain are also used for purposes such as prediction, classification and clustering, besides giving products in different areas of daily life. The expert systems, genetic algorithms, fuzzy logic, artificial neural networks, and the techniques such as machine learning are generally called artificial intelligence technologies. Apart from these techniques, the algorithms such as ant colony, particle swarm and artificial bee by studying living things are used as artificial intelligence optimization techniques. In the general sense, the transfer of human intelligence to machines (computers and software) by modeling physiological and neurological structure such as nervous system and gene structure, and natural events is implied by artificial intelligence. In brief, artificial intelligence is the computer systems that "think and behave like people and think and behave rationally" (Balaban and Kartal, 2015: 16) and that have the behaviors of living things which are accepted to be clever. The artificial learning (machine learning) and deep learning methods using artificial intelligence and especially artificial neural networks are used in smart factories and for the programming of robots with the applications developed for image recognition, natural language processing, translation, and automatic voice recognition (Atalay and Çelik, 2017).

2.9 Additive Manufacturing and 3D Printers

3D printer is used in additive manufacturing performed with computer, CAD software, machine equipments and layered material. 3 Dimensional or 3D printer is a machine that converts digital 3D computer data (three-dimensional CAD drawing) into real objects that can be held by hand, and can print almost all mechanical parts. Some costs like stock will be removed since production data can be provided at the desired time and in a shorter time to produce the product loaded in the computer environment with 3D printers. Along with 3D printers used in many fields such as genetics, information technologies, medicine, industry, clothing and jewelry, artificial veins, organs and human tissues are also produced from bio-organic materials. As a result of studies carried out for the products produced to have the ability to automatically change shape according to the environmental conditions they are in, besides being three dimensional, 4D printers that make this kind of production have begun to be used (EBSO, 2015).

3 Pioneers of Industry 4.0 Transformation

Industry 4.0 projects a transformation in which information and network technologies are intensive. For this reason, it is essential that businesses should first complement their technological infrastructure and equipment. However, furthermore, this revolution projects a system that integrates all business processes with all stakeholders and customers and is constantly updated through data transfer. For this reason, Industry 4.0 transformation needs to be planned altogether on the basis of society, state, industry and businesses. In this section, the changes that have taken place in the business since the first time it was put forward and the possible developments to be experienced in the continuation of the process will be discussed through the examples pioneering this revolution.

The Fourth Industrial Revolution, which has begun to take place in the world under the leadership of Germany, has become important in all countries and economies on a global basis in a short period of time along with the effects of their studies carried out by pioneering countries and companies. Due to the rapid spread of information and the aspects of other revolutions mentioned in the introduction section, it can be said that Industry 4.0 has a potential to enable the world's developed and developing countries to be in a different position in a while in the economy. Nowadays, although the countries such as Germany, Japan and the USA are pioneering this transformation, the countries such as China, South Korea and India are rapidly rising to the position of leading countries with the serious step they have taken.

According to the report prepared in 2013 by the Federal Government of Germany's working group established in 2012 (Kagermann, Wahlster and Helbig, 2013), 8 steps need to be completed for the Fourth Industrial Revolution to be successful. These steps are the determination and standardization of reference hardware architecture, capacity to manage complex systems, providing industry with comprehensive and high-speed telecommunication infrastructure, safety and security, working organization and design, continuous education and professional development, harmonization of laws and legislation, and efficient use of resources. In the recommendations of the Industry 4.0 Platform, which was established based on this vision, on how to implement the vision, Industry 4.0 is defined as "a new value chain organization and management throughout the life cycle of products" (Herman, Pentek and Otto, 2015). Germany is still pioneering with the changes and strategies applied in the production and marketing by the giants of the sector like BMW, Bosch, Siemens, along with the importance they have attached to industry for a long time and their pioneering structure on engineering issues. It is seen that the transformation experienced in all areas from giant corporations to fast-growing start-up initiatives has been realized step by step. For instance, Siemens takes its power in the world market from automation technologies and has developed autonomous production systems with self-regulation and follow-up capability. Powerful integrated software in which product life cycle is managed which is called Digital Enterprise can be shown as an example for the investments of Siemens, which envisages that each component in the production flow, the virtual and real world are interconnected and that the data generated by these processes are analyzed with big data. In the Bosch Rexroth factory in Hamburg, Bosch is building a system in which the product itself, the machine that produces it and the human factor following it speak the same communication language and operation is performed by deciding on the incoming product type in the smart production line supported by RFID technology. The data generated by this communication network is simultaneously provided to the monitoring screens, and the production is controlled and optimized through a common network. With the Internet of Things (IoT), transformation into smart production and then smart factories is realized by ensuring that they keep the properties of the products in mind. As a pilot project for the city of Monaco, Bosch carries out the Smart City project based on the transport network created with the help of data generated by monitoring and optimization of road works and parking areas. In the automotive sector, the companies like Mercedes Benz, BMW, Audi and Wolkswagen are moving rapidly regarding the manufacturing of automobiles compatible with the IoT concept (Aydın, 2018).

The concept of "Industrial Internet" is preferred in the United States, which is in the leading position in the world in industrial and information technologies with Germany. "Manufacturing USA" founded in 2012 in the country where two national institutions were established in this area (Coşkunoğlu, 2016) focuses on the development of manufacturing technologies. The Industrial Internet Consortium, founded by Cisco, General Electric, AT&T, IBM and Intel in 2014, with 218 members by 2018, prioritizes to accelerate the developments in the fields of inter-machine communication network and intelligent analytical and to determine the technological priorities.

With the "Made in China 2025" Strategy Paper published in 2015, the Chinese Government aims to bring the industrial infrastructure to a completely higher level and to change the manufacturing industry in the form of "large but not strong". Four transformations including transition to innovation, low-cost competitive advantage with quality benefit competitive advantage, increasing the scope of green manufacturing, and transition from production manufacturing to service-oriented manufacturing are planned in the paper. It is stated that the following eight policies determined will be followed for strong competition: production connected to intelligent digital network, development of product design ability, development of production technology innovation system, improved production base, improvement of product quality, green manufacturing, creation of global competitive entrepreneurial groups and development of superiority industry, and development of modern manufacturing services (Çetin, 2018).

Japan, which is aware of the importance of fully utilizing the innovations such as IoT, big data, AI and robotics through the fourth industrial revolution but additionally emphasizes that the presentation of these innovations in various sectors and in all areas of daily life will increase productivity and create new demand, has called this development "Society 5.0" by including the entire society (The Japan Government, 2018). The areas and targets that this strategy paper initially includes are as the following: (1) To initiate a mechanism to carry out experiments for new businesses for a certain period of time, apart from the existing regulations. (2) The introduction of open data policy by the government to promote innovative products and services in eight areas, especially in health services, agriculture and transportation. (3) To provide spaces for people with an entrepreneurial spirit by creating an agile environment where entrepreneurial ideas can create and sustain innovation. (4) To establish a business system to accept private investments in universities and to create an incentive system for universities to collaborate with the sector. (5) The integration and storage of personal medical information (records such as medical control, treatment, nursing care, etc.) using large data analysis until 2020 to provide personalized medical care, and the use of AI and robots in long-term care facilities. (6) To introduce drone delivery services until 2020 by starting from mountainous regions in transportation and logistics, and to initiate driverless transport services for commercial purposes until 2020. (7) The realization of FinTech innovation with Blockchain technology, and the creation of a fast, functional and secure banking system that allows online transactions. The creation of software platform including more than 80 banks in this system until 2020, and the fact that non-cash payment reaches 40 % until 2027. Apart from these, the Japanese Government projects to overcome the labor shortages in the areas such as distribution, construction, agriculture, production and nursing by using the Industry 4.0 technologies and the data collected through these technologies. Furthermore, until 2019, it is stated that they will promote a structure approach that will be connected through information and communication technology in every aspect from research to design and supervision (The Japan Government, 2018).

The amounts of industrial robot production are also important in terms of showing the acceleration in the Industry 4.0 process. According to the latest report of International Federation of Robotics (IFR, 2017), Asian countries, especially China, South Korea and Japan constitute the locomotive power of robot production. According to the same report, approximately industrial robots were established for 10.000 employees in the manufacturing industry in 2016. According to these data that we can call the average global robot density, the most automated countries of the world are the Republic of Korea, Singapore, Germany and Japan. In evaluating the number of industrial robots operating per employee, it has been determined that the automotive industry has a significantly higher automation ratio than all other sectors. The robot density in general industry (all industries except for automotive) is still relatively low. However, the countries with an electronics industry have a higher ratio. While South Korea is on the top with 475 robots installed per 10,000 employees, it is followed by Japan with 214 robots, Germany with 181 robots and Sweden with 164 robots. However, although Germany and Sweden do not have a significant production area for the electronics industry, it can be said that they have closed the gap with other sectors. Finally, it is estimated that the total number of industrial robots produced in the world, which was 294.312 in 2016, will be 520.900 in 2020.

4 Conclusion

The Fourth Industrial Revolution transforms the countries, societies and economies more differently and quickly than other industrial revolutions due to the developments in information technology and software and the accumulation of knowledge that increase exponentially. This transformation, which is commonly referred to as Industry 4.0, will become one of the most important milestones of human history. It is important to understand Industry 4.0 along with aspects that touch not only on production but also on many areas of life and the economy, and to examine the components it has and features and their implementation in different countries. The countries and companies intending to get the developments experienced in the global world and to gain a share in global markets should internalize and begin to use these concepts. On the other hand, it will be a time-saving move to take part in this competition regardless of the stage by carefully examining the relevant examples.

References

Ashton, K. (2009). That 'Internet of Things' Thing. http://www.rfidjournal.com/articles/view?4986 (10.08.2018).

Atalay, M. and Çelik, E. (2017). Artificial Intelligence and Machine Learning Applications in Big Data Analysis. The Journal of Mehmet Akif Ersoy University Institute of Social Sciences, 9 (22), 155–172. DOI: 10.20875/makusobed.309727.

Aydın, N. (2018). Germany's Industry 4.0 Vision. http://www.endustri40.com/almanyanin-endustri-4-0-vizyonu/ (07.08.2018).

Balaban, M. E. and Kartal, E. (2015). Data Mining and Machine Learning (Turkish). İstanbul: Çağlayan Publishing.

Charniak, E. and McDermott, D. (1985). Introduction to Artificial Intelligence. Boston, MA, USA: Addison-Wesley Series in Computer Science.

Chui, M., George, K., Manyika, J. and Miremadi, M. (2017). Human + Machine: A New Era of Automation in Manufacturing. https://www.mckinsey.com/business-functions/operations/our-insights/human-plus-machine-a-new-era-of-automation-in-manufacturing (07.08.2018).

Coşkunoğlu, O. (2016). Industry 4.0: A Techno-Political Assessment, EMO The Journal of Electrical Engineering (459), 8–13, 2016 December.

Çetin, C. (2018). A Comparison Report: Industry 4.0 and Made in China 2025. https://cenkercetin.com/endustri-4-0-made-in-china-2025-karsilastirma-raporu/ (07.08.2018).

Davutoğlu, N.A., Akgül, B. and Yıldız, E. (2017). Economic Effects of Restructurıng on Busınesses and Sectors in Accordance with National Industry 4.0, The Journal of Academic Social Science, 5 (52), 544–567.

EBSO-Aegean Region Chamber of Industry. (2015). Industry 4.0: Conformıty Wıll Be Lost! Izmir: Oct. 2015.

Firican, G. (2017). The 10 Vs of Big Data. https://tdwi.org/articles/2017/02/08/10-vs-of-big-data.aspx (24.10.2017).

Giusto, D., Ieira, A., Morabito, G., and Atzori, L. eds. (2010) The Internet of Things 20th Tyrrhenian Workshop on Digital Communications. New York: Springer.

Hermann, M., Pentek, T. and Otto, B. (2015). Design Principles for Industrie 4.0 Scenarios: A Literature Review, Working Paper, Technische Universität Dortmund.

Holtkamp, B. and Iyer, A. (2017). Industry 4.0 The Future of Indo-German Industrial Collaboration. Gütersloh: Bertelsmann Stiftung.

Industrial Internet Consortium (2013). Fact Sheet. http://www.iiconsortium.org/docs/IIC_FACT_SHEET.pdf (09.08.2018).

Industrial Internet Consortium (2018). Current Members. https://www.iiconsortium.org/members.htm (11.08.2018).

International Federation of Robotic – IFR (2017). Executive Summary World Robotics 2017 Industrial Robots. https://ifr.org/downloads/press/Executive_Summary_WR_2017_Industrial_Robots.pdf (07.08.2018).Kagermann, H., Lukas, W. and Wahlster, W. (2011). Industrie 4.0: Mit dem Internet der Dinge auf dem Weg zur 4. industriellen Revolution. VDI nachrichten, 13.1 April 2011, 13, Berlin.

Kagermann, H., Wahlster, W. and Helbig, J. eds. (2013). Recommendations for Implementing the Strategic Initiative Industrie 4.0: Final Report of the Industrie 4.0 Working Group. Ed. Hellinger, A. and Stumpf, V., Acatech – National Academy of Science and Engineering, Forschungsunion Wirtschaft und Wissenschaft.

Kesayak, B. (2017). Endüstri 4.0, Anatolian Science Days, 17.12.2017 Activity Presentation. http://burakkesayak.com/wp-content/uploads/2017/12/End%C3 %BCstri-40-Burak-Kesayak.pdf (07.08.2018).

Khan, M. A., Uddin, M. F. ve Gupta, N. (2014). Seven V's of Big Data understanding Big Data to extract value. Conference of the American Society for Engineering Education, IEEE, DOI: 10.1109/ASEEZone1.2014.6820689, Bridgeport, CT, USA.

Kutup, N. (2011). Internet of Things; 4E Everywhere, Everyone, Every time, Every object link, İzmir XVI. Internet Conference Proceedings in Turkey 2 Dec. 2011.

MÜSİAD – Independent Industrialists' and Businessmen's Association. (2017). Industry 4.0 and Logistic of Future, 2017 Logistic Sector Report, Istanbul, Nov. 2017.

Nabiyev, V. V. (2012). Artificial Intelligence (Turkish). Ankara: Seçkin Publishing.

National Science Foundation (2018). Cyber-Physical Systems (CPS). https://www.nsf.gov/pubs/2018/nsf18538/nsf18538.pdf (10.08.2018).

Ohlhorst, F. (2013). Big Data Analytics: Turning Big Data into Big Money. New Jersey: Wiley Publicity.

Özışık, S. U. (2017). Introduction to Autonomous Robots, http://yapbenzet.kocaeli.edu.tr/otonom-robotlar-giris/ (11.08.2018).

Plattform Industrie 4.0. (2014). Was Industrie 4.0 (für uns) ist. http://www.plattform-i40.de/was-industrie-40-f%C3 %BCr-uns-ist (09.08.2018).

Republique Française. (2016). Nouvelle France Industrielle (NFI) – The New Face of Industry in France. https://www.economie.gouv.fr/files/nouvelle_france_industrielle_english.pdf (10.08.2018).

The Japan Government (2018). Abenomics, Boost Productivity. https://www.japan.go.jp/abenomics/productivity/#anc_b-1 (07.08.2018).

Ürey, H. and Akşit, K. (2018). What Is Virtual Reality and Augmented Reality? https://sarkac.org/2018/03/sanal-gerceklik-artirilmis-gerceklik-nedir/ (11.08.2018).

Yazıcı, A. (2016). Industry 4.0 ve Autonomous Robots, EMO The Journal of Electrical Engineering (459), 39, December.